MW01199813

Gothic Renaissance

MANCHESTER
1824

Manchester University Press

Gothic Renaissance

A reassessment

Edited by
ELISABETH BRONFEN
and BEATE NEUMEIER

Manchester University Press
Manchester and New York

distributed exclusively in the USA by Palgrave Macmillan

Published by Manchester University Press
Oxford Road, Manchester M13 9NR, UK
and Room 400, 175 Fifth Avenue, New York, NY 10010, USA
www.manchesteruniversitypress.co.uk

Distributed exclusively in the USA by
Palgrave Macmillan, 175 Fifth Avenue, New York,
NY 10010, USA

Distributed exclusively in Canada by
UBC Press, University of British Columbia, 2029 West Mall,
Vancouver, BC, Canada V6T 1Z2

British Library Cataloguing-in-Publication Data
A catalogue record for this book is available from the British Library

Library of Congress Cataloging-in-Publication Data applied for

ISBN 978 0 7190 8863 6 *hardback*

First published 2014

Typeset in Sabon by
Koinonia, Manchester
Printed and bound in Great Britain by
TJ International Ltd, Padstow

Contents

Contents

Part IV Persistence of the Gothic

Acknowledgements

As editors of this volume we would like to thank all contributors for participating in the conference we organized at the University of Cologne to advance the dialogue between scholarship on the English Renaissance and on Gothic literature. We would also like to thank all of them not only for their prompt submission of manuscripts but also for their patience in regard to the long editorial and publication process.

We would like to thank the Cologne team, Friederike Danebrock, Victoria Herche, Konstanze Kutzbach, Natascha Rohde, Dirk Schulz, Bettina Seidel and in particular Leonhard Kreuzer and Tobias Schmidt for their extraordinary organizational skills, diligence and untiring work before, during and after the conference.

The time-consuming preparation of the manuscripts for print was carried out by Laura von Czarnowsky, Friederike Danebrock, Esther Dolas, Victoria Herche, Meral Karrasch, Johanna Schorn and Sarah Youssef. We would like to thank all of them for their impressive skills in the editing process, corresponding with contributors, proof-reading and checking sources. Our particular thanks go to Friederike Danebrock whose skills as co-ordinator, mediator and careful reader were invaluable for the finalization of the manuscript.

We would also like to thank the German Research Foundation (DFG), the KölnAlumni, and the University of Cologne for their generous material and non-material support.

Last but not least we would like to express our gratitude to Manchester University Press for accepting this volume for publication. Our particular thanks go to Matthew Frost for his invaluable guidance and support.

Zürich/Cologne
Summer 2013

Notes on contributors

Catherine Belsey is Research Professor in English at Swansea University. Her books include *The Subject of Tragedy: Identity and Difference in Renaissance Drama*, *Shakespeare and the Loss of Eden*, *Why Shakespeare?* and *Shakespeare in Theory and Practice*. Her latest book is *A Future for Criticism*.

Andrea Brady is Senior Lecturer at Queen Mary University of London, where she teaches both early modern and contemporary writing. She has published articles on ritual and anthropological approaches to literature, embodiment, affect, subjectivity and prosody. Her publications include *English Funerary Elegy in the Seventeenth Century* as well as five books of poetry. She is director of Archive of the Now and runs Barque Press.

Elisabeth Bronfen is Professor of English and American Studies at the English department, University of Zürich. She is the author of *Over Her Dead Body: Death, Femininity and the Aesthetic*; *The Knotted Subject: Hysteria and Its Discontent*; *Home in Hollywood: The Imaginary Geography of Cinema*; *Specters of War: Hollywood's Engagement with Military Conflict* and, most recently, *Night Passages: Philosophy, Literature, and Film*. She is currenctly co-writing a book with Barbara Straumann on Elizabeth I as the first political diva.

John Drakakis is Emeritus Professor of English Studies at the University of Stirling, and he holds visiting professorships at the University of Lincoln and Glyndŵr University, Wrexham. He has recently published the Arden 3 Series edition of Shakespeare's *The Merchant of Venice* (2012), and has jointly edited and contributed to *Gothic Shakespeares* and to the *Arden Early Modern Drama Guides* volume on *Macbeth* (2013). He has edited various collections of essays, including *Alternative Shakespeares*, *Shakespearean Tragedy*, *Tragedy* (jointly), and has contributed articles and reviews to various learned journals, and book chapters to a number of published essay collections. He was the general editor of the Routledge English Texts series, and he is currently the general editor of the Routledge New Critical Idiom Series. He is also the general editor in charge of the projected revision of Geoffrey Bullough's *Narrative and Dramatic Sources of Shakespeare* and he is the editor of the *Major Tragedies* volume in this series. He is a Fellow of the English Association and an elected member of the Academia Europaea.

Andreas Höfele is Professor of English at Munich University. He is author of *Stage, Stake, and Scaffold: Humans and Animals in Shakespeare's Theatre*, which won the 2012 Roland H. Bainton Prize for Literature. His publications in German include books on Shakespeare's stagecraft, on late nineteenth-century parody and on Malcolm Lowry, as well as six novels. He served as President of the German Shakespeare Society 2002–11.

Lynn S. Meskill is Lecturer in English Literature and Translation at Université Paris-Diderot, Paris 7. She holds a BA in Classics from Princeton University and MA and PhD degrees in English from the University of Virginia. She is author of *Ben Jonson and Envy*. She has published articles on Jonson, Shakespeare and Milton in *Cahiers Elisabéthains*, *ELH*, *HLQ* and *The Swiss Papers in Early Modern Language and Literature*, among others. She is currently preparing 'Ben Jonson's Masques, 1605–1616' for *The Oxford Handbook of Jonson Studies*.

Beate Neumeier is Professor of English at the University of Cologne. Her research areas are gender, performance, and postcolonial studies. She has published on Renaissance and contemporary Anglophone drama, on contemporary Jewish writing, on postmodern women's writing, on gender and music in contemporary cultures, and with Kay Schaffer on indigenous literature and performance cultures in Australia. She is also the editor of the e-journal GenderForum and the database GenderInn. Currently she is writing a book on *Gothic Renaissance Monstrosities: Madness – Gender – Genre in English Renaissance Theater*.

Duncan Salkeld is Reader in Shakespeare Studies at the University of Chichester. He is author of *Madness and Drama in the Age of Shakespeare, Shakespeare Among the Courtesans: Prostitution, Literature and Drama 1500–1650*, and numerous articles on Shakespeare and Renaissance drama. He is currently writing a book on *Shakespeare and London* for the Oxford Shakespeare Topics series.

Per Sivefors is Senior Lecturer in English Literature at Linnaeus University, Sweden. He has published on Thomas Nashe, John Lyly and Christopher Marlowe, the last of whom was also at the focus of his PhD dissertation, *The Delegitimised Vernacular: Language Politics, Poetics* *and the Plays of Christopher Marlowe*. His research focuses on, among other things, early modern dream narratives, masculinity and urban culture. He is the editor of *Urban Preoccupations: Mental and Material Landscapes*.

Garrett Sullivan is Professor of English at Penn State University. He is the author of *The Drama of Landscape: Land, Property and Social Relations on the Early Modern Stage*, *Memory and Forgetting in English Renaissance Drama: Shakespeare, Marlowe, Webster* and *Sleep, Romance and Human Embodiment: Vitality from Spenser to Milton*.

Dale Townshend is Senior Lecturer in Gothic and Romantic Literature at the University of Stirling, Scotland. His publications include *The Orders of Gothic: Foucault, Lacan, and the Subject of Gothic Writing, 1764–1820*; four volumes in the Gothic: Critical Concepts in Literary and Cultural Studies series (with Fred Botting); *Gothic Shakespeares* (with John Drakakis); *Macbeth: A Critical Guide* (with John Drakakis); *The Gothic World* (with Glennis Byron); and *Ann Radcliffe, Romanticism and the Gothic* (with Angela Wright). He is currently at work on a monograph entitled *Gothic Antiquity: History, Romance and the Architectural Imagination, 1760–1840*.

Richard Wilson is the Sir Peter Hall Professor of Shakespeare Studies at Kingston University, and the author or editor of numerous books on Shakespeare and theory, including *Will Power: Studies in Shakespearean Authority*, *Secret Shakespeare: Essays on Theatre, Religion and Resistance*, *Shakespeare in French Theory: King of Shadows*, and *Free Will: Art and Power on Shakespeare's Stage*. His forthcoming book is a study of Shakespeare and democratic pluralism: *Our Good Will: Shakespeare's Wordly Theatre*.

Ulrike Zimmermann teaches British Literary and Cultural Studies at the University of Freiburg. She is the author of *Comic Elements in Women's Novels of Development from the 1960s to the 1980s*. Her research interests include seventeenth-century poetry, intersections of literature and science, and the contemporary British novel. She is currently working on her post-doctoral project on popularizations of the eighteenth century.

Introduction

Elisabeth Bronfen and Beate Neumeier

Since the emergence of the Gothic novel in the second half of the eighteenth century, authors have self-consciously acknowledged a cultural debt to Shakespeare's work, by virtue of either intertextual citation or explicit homage. As Horace Walpole wrote in his preface to *The Castle of Otranto*, 'Shakespeare, was the model I copied' (44). Having recourse to this national poet was constitutive, legitimizing, as it does, above all the mixture of genres so typical of the Gothic novel. Within the field of Gothic studies, much has been written about the manner in which 'Gothic writers' came to appropriate Shakespeare, along with Marlowe and Milton. At the same time, the reconfiguration of the term 'Gothic' from a historical genre ranging from Walpole to Mary Shelley's *Frankenstein*, to a mode of writing, traceable in different genres and media from the nineteenth century into contemporary culture, has necessarily reopened questions about the implicit historical onset of Gothic sensibility, aesthetics and textuality. This new conception of the Gothic has inspired a nascent dialogue between scholars from the field of Gothic studies and those of Shakespeare and the Renaissance. Among the first volumes to explore this vibrant interface are the collections of essays *Gothic Shakespeares* (Drakakis and Townshend), and *Shakespearean Gothic* (Desmet and Williams). While both collections address questions of Shakespeare's 'Gothic potential', the majority of essays focuses on the Bard's Gothic afterlife.

Our volume *Gothic Renaissance* represents an intervention into this developing critical debate. Our aim is to expand the existing discussion by focusing on the lines of connection between a Gothic sensibility and the Renaissance period, exploring Shakespeare's texts alongside and in relation to those by other playwrights, as well as to other textual genres, from poetry and epic narratives to ghost stories, prose dialogues and political pamphlets. It is precisely this widening of the focus that enables a careful historical investigation which avoids a dehistoricized and inflationary use of the term Gothic. What then does it mean to postulate a

Gothic Renaissance, to attribute a Gothic sensibility to both dramatic and non-dramatic texts written in early modern England? If the term 'Gothic' was first introduced in the field of art history as a synonym for the barbaric, conceived in contrast to the harmonious symmetry of the classical, its most prominent themes involve tales of the supernatural, of spectral appearances, witchcraft and the seduction by demonic forces. The complex emotional responses Gothic sensibility speaks to are the fear, surprise and awe called forth by a foregrounding of the fragility of human existence, of the presence of death in the midst of life and the delimination of human freedom which the laws of mortality dictate.

To speak of a Gothic sensibility, however, also draws attention to the fact that at issue are both an intellectual and an affective approach towards the world. The attitude assumed in relation to power structures, psychic dispositions and aesthetic representations of these is, further-more, based on an acute sense of boundary blurrings. First and foremost is the awareness of a sustained presence of magical thinking within a conception of the world increasingly ruled by the law of scientific ratio-nality. Gothic sensibility thus speaks to the incursion of the irrational into the rational, the extraordinary into the ordinary everyday, the monstrous into the human, bringing into focus the nocturnal side of diurnal social and psychic activities. It addresses subversive fantasies of transgression, whether in regard to gender (troubling stable notions of masculinity and femininity), in regard to social orders (challenging hegemonic patriarchal or sovereign power), or in regard to disciplinary discourses (dictating what is deemed licit and what illicit and deviant). The disruption may also, however, pertain to the boundaries of an individual's identity, opening up to the truth to be found in visions, hallucinations, and madness, or to the desires released when the cultured subject no longer represses her or his allegedly barbaric instincts.

What the Gothic puts on display is, then, a shift from the strictly codified public life to an inner world at once liberating and imprisoning in its privileging of subjective fantasies and anxieties. To conceive of Macbeth's and Hamlet's ghost-seeing, Ophelia's madness or the reanima-tion of Hermione's statue as early modern articulations of Gothic sensi-bility means foregrounding how violent eruptions of radical subjectivity (whether ambition, melancholia, hysteria or jealousy) render visible the presence of forbidden desires within a normative order of the world. Dramatically embodied, these psychic energies give voice to the toxic underbelly of symbolic laws, which can be suppressed but never fully obliterated. And yet, while the transgressions we attribute to Gothic sensibility serve to trouble identity categories, dominant knowledge systems and hegemonic power structures, they never fully shatter these.

Their revolutionary impulse is always again contained. As the power-hungry soldier, the death-driven prince, the sexually distraught daughter all find their predestined death, their challenge to the order of things is once more stabilized.

Equally seminal for the line of connection between the Gothic culture that was to intervene in the Enlightenment project around 1800 and the cultural shift from the medieval to the early modern around 1530 is the fact that both draw attention to the sustained presence of archaic cultural energies. With its interest in ruins, crypts, graveyards and hidden spaces that serve as sites of secret and hidden knowledge, Gothic imagination emerges as an articulation of cultural nostalgia. It evokes a past which the present looks to either as a source of inspiration and comfort or as the embodiment of a barbarism that must, once more, be overcome. Indeed, ghost stories, blurring the distinction between life and death, as well as tales of vampires, returning from their graves to find nourishment among the living, speak to the way the past returns to feed on the present. In a similar vein, prophetic dream visions and hallucinations (as these abound in both early modern and Gothic culture) speak to the idea of a prior knowledge of the supernatural either yearned for as a correction to the dominant mode of thinking or invoked as a seminal threat to the laws of rationality.

Gothic sensibility is thus both revolutionary in its challenge to the hegemonic ordering of the world and conservative in its recourse to archaic cultural energies. Precisely by drawing attention to cultural anxieties regarding a destabilization of identity categories, it helps to redraw these. While any discussion of the familiar ascriptions of the Gothic as a 'hybrid genre', 'literature of subversion' and 'transgressive mode of writing' must be situated historically, it is our aim to relate these issues back to the early modern period as a poignant moment of transition, in which categories of individual, gendered, racial and national identity began to emerge, and to relate the religious and the pictorial turn within early modern textual production to a reassessment of Gothic culture. It is precisely the notion of subjectivity and its transgressions as developed during the Renaissance which once again become prevalent under the auspices of the revolutionary moments that emerge from the world of the late eighteenth century, and which are reformulated again in contemporary culture.

It can be argued that the attempt to locate texts asserting the existence of a Gothic sensibility *avant la lettre* (rereading Shakespeare and the Renaissance period in terms of a pre- or proto-Gothic potential) is inevitably engaging in what Mieke Bal has called a 'preposterous' historical endeavour. While the word 'preposterous' literally means contrary to nature, reason, or common sense, Bal offers an ingenious spin on the term. To look preposterously at the literature of the past through later refigurations that have coloured our conception of it means drawing attention to what remains hidden when one limits oneself to more conventional intertextual influences. Such a revisitation of past texts does not collapse past and present 'in an ill-conceived presentism', nor does it 'objectify the past and bring it within our grasp, as in the problematic positivist historicism'. Instead, this 'reversal, which puts what comes chronologically first ("pre") as an after-effect behind ("post") its later recyclings', for Bal entails a way of doing history, of dealing with the past today (6–7). With this collection of essays, we propose looking back at dramatic and non-dramatic texts of the English Renaissance through the lens of the Gothic culture that emerged in the late eighteenth century, precisely because, as moments of cultural transition, both define themselves by looking back at the prior historical moment from which they developed. At issue is, thus, a double backward gaze. While the early modern imagination struggles with and against the barbarism of supernatural thinking it seeks to supersede, the Enlightenment project is predicated on bringing light to the remaining dark areas on the map of knowledge by (again) suppressing a more archaic magical thinking. The line of connection which the shared Gothic sensibility brings to the fore is, thus, the manner in which both the mid-sixteenth and the late eighteenth century are constitutively troubled by previous cultural energies, either erupting again or refusing to be suppressed, so as to give voice to the strange within the familiar.

In other words, we propose looking back at the early modern cultural imaginary through the lens of its subsequent recycling in Gothic culture so as to foreground how the Renaissance itself was looking back to the archaic knowledge of the supernatural, recycling prior cultural energies so as to contain them. By exploring the line of connection between these distinct but interrelated historical moments, two questions arise. What archaic knowledge has persisted, and in so doing has achieved a cultural afterlife in the form of remnants that call upon and resuscitate a prior mode of conceiving and making sense of the world? And what cultural energies, having already been overcome or repressed, have resiliently returned to be taken notice of again? The haunting so prevalently thematized by Gothic sensibility calls upon us to address how the past we look back at through its subsequent aesthetic refiguration splices together the notion of cultural survival with that of a return of the repressed. Our current critical interest in the Gothic asks us to interrogate where this rich and strange legacy begins. We do so because we are equally concerned with discovering what the haunting celebrated around 1800 says about its early modern predecessor. It is precisely through a careful historicization of the earlier texts that their Gothic resonances in later periods can be productively addressed. These resonances were felt by Gothic novelists from the late eighteenth century onwards and they are felt again – differently – in contemporary culture by writers as well as theatre and film directors of the late twentieth and early twenty-first centuries who return to Shakespeare and his contemporaries in the context of the current proliferation of the Gothic. To re-map Gothic literature onto the literary production of the Renaissance thus does not entail undoing the historical distinction between the two by collapsing two historical moments. Rather, it allows us to explore the consequences of this relation for a conjoined reading of both sets of cultural texts, with their similarities *and* differences in mind.

The scholarly interest in these resonances surfaces in psychoanalytic, feminist and post-structural readings of both the Renaissance and the Gothic, which, each onto their own, have persistently foregrounded issues of madness, monstrosity, trauma, desire and death, relating these to questions of genre, gender and national self-definition. Despite these shared theoretical approaches, it was curiously Freud's discussion of the uncanny, a ubiquitous term in scholarly work on Gothic fiction, which for a long time effectively barred the exploration of a Gothic Renaissance, in its explicit exclusion of the ghostly apparitions in Shakespeare's plays from the realm of the uncanny. However, the increasing focus on Kristeva's conception of the abject as a critical tool in Gothic and in Renaissance studies allows for an exploration and re-evaluation of possible links between both areas of research. In this context the notion of the monstrous as historically situated articulation of anxieties about processes of cultural transformation can highlight similarities as well as differences. The definitions of the monstrous as liminal, transgressive and transformative (Shildrick) draw attention to the negotiation of boundaries between supernatural/natural, human/animal, masculine/feminine, self/other, madness/sanity, spirit/matter which are decisive in Gothic as well as Renaissance studies. The monstrous refers to the moment of cultural transformation and its result, to transgression as well as affirmation of boundaries, foregrounding the constitution of as well as resistance against norms. Thus the monstrous is situated between tendencies of exteriorization (as external threat to be eliminated) and interiorization (as mere psychological projection).

In this context the English Renaissance period with its emerging emphasis on individual subjectivity and national identity seems indeed an apt starting point for a historically specific investigation into connections with the Gothic. The early modern obsession with monstrous creatures and horrifying phenomena can be accounted for only on the grounds of a complex web of historical discourses, as studies such as Stuart Clark's cultural history of early modern vision (2007) have shown, exploring the religious and philosophical, medical and political ideas and interests connected to the evaluation of phenomena like witchcraft and magic, madness and demonology (Clark). The 'preposterous' critical gaze this book proposes is that we revisit the manner in which early modern discourses of scientific rationality could only contain but never obliterate such magical thinking, by recalling a similar gesture of exteriorization on the part of the Enlightenment project. Any cultural valorization of unveiling requires dark uncharted areas on the map of knowledge to which the light of reason can be brought. The Gothic responds to this equation of truth with disclosure by making obscure once more the knowledge it insists we cannot have direct access to, or which we prefer not to know in any unmitigated manner (see Bronfen). Looking back at the early modern period through the lens of the Gothic brings a seminal distinction to light. While the Renaissance is haunted by the very magical thinking it is in the process of displacing, Gothic culture emerges in the late eighteenth century at a time when the rational discourse has reached its acme. What was initially a gesture of abjection returns as a gesture of reverting back to a conception of the world that privileges the nocturnal, the transgressive, the spectral and the extraordinary.

Tracking the lines of connection between Gothic sensibilities and the discursive network of the Renaissance, the chapters in this book facilitate a re-evaluation of both. Indeed, they draw our attention to a discussion of what cultural forces produced the development between different historical moments. Thus the Gothic English Renaissance seems to foreground transformational moments and processes, negotiating and reformulating the boundary between the natural and the supernatural, the human and the non-human, the norm and the monstrous in the context of the religious, philosophical and scientific turn of the time. The monstrous creatures of late eighteenth and nineteenth century Gothic novels, on the other hand, point towards the return of a repressed disruption, while contemporary versions of the Gothic seem to be obsessed with the dissolution of boundaries. Our hope is that by making a claim for a culturally persistent 'boundary-work', this volume will produce a critical discussion aimed at filling in the gap we can merely gesture towards.

The chapters of this volume address a wide variety of Renaissance writers and literary genres, from Shakespeare and Webster to Middleton and Jonson, from Spenser to Donne, from drama to epic to poetry, to folk tales to political pamphlets, linked to an investigation into the later impact of a Gothicized Renaissance. The manifold resonances between the chapters in terms of primary textual references to Renaissance texts as well as in terms of theoretical approaches and questions raised testify to the many connections opening up a rich field of further research into Renaissance Gothic. The chapters have been arranged in four parts, beginning with readings that pick up and expand on treating Shakespeare's dramas in the light of Gothic concerns. The second part extends the conversation to other Renaissance dramatists. The third part focuses on non-dramatic genres of writing in the Renaissance, while the final section rethinks the persistence of Gothic sensibility as this links modern texts to Shakespeare in light of the inaugural moment we claim the Renaissance to be. Although the opening section of this volume is dedicated to Shakespeare, the contributors venture out in their chapters to establish connections to other writers and genres. Shakespeare's *Hamlet* is the point of departure for John Drakakis's investigation of notions of death and decay as well as for Catherine Belsey's exploration of early modern stage ghosts. Drakakis takes the use of a real skull in Gregory Doran's RSC production of the play (2008) as the starting-point for a discussion of the implications of rereading the Renaissance through the history of the Gothic in terms of the current obsession with notions of death, material and virtual reality. Drawing on a wide variety of Renaissance writers including Donne, Webster and Middleton as well as on Gothic novelists such as Horace Walpole, Ann Radcliffe and Isabella Kelly, he discusses possible connections and their legitimacy in connection to theoretical approaches from Freud to Bataille and Derrida.

Catherine Belsey uses a historical approach to explore Shakespeare's introduction of 'mystery, uncertainty, equivocation (the components of the uncanny)' to the Renaissance stage through an integration of 'the popular tradition of fireside ghost stories' in the intertextual web of his plays. Taking up key terms of the Gothic such as the macabre, terror, equivocation and the uncanny, Belsey explores Shakespeare's use of ghostly apparitions for a 'blending of existing conventions to change the parameters for fiction', addressing uncertainties about the relation between spirit and matter, about the reliability of the senses. Belsey locates the difference of Shakespearean ghosts from earlier stage ghosts rooted in the classical tradition in their direct interaction with the world of the living, in the evocation of terror shared by the onstage characters, and in the persistence of uncertainty and equivocation. Accordingly 'Shakespeare's alteration of paradigm might be most evident' in plays like *The Changeling*, *The Lady's Tragedy/Second Maiden's Tragedy*, *The Duchess of Malfi* or *The Atheist's Tragedy*, even if this is where 'his direct influence is least apparent'. Belsey thus identifies Shakespeare's own *Macbeth* as 'the main beneficiary of *Hamlet*'s bequest to posterity' in terms of an undecidability which 'enlightenment science longed to dispel', and which 'later Gothic continued to permit in fiction'.

Per Sivefors uses a different approach to historicize Shakespearean Gothic by investigating Renaissance dream theories in relation to notions of conscience, arguing that it is an increasingly 'ambiguous status of conscience [which] pushes dreams in direction of a psychologizing approach – dreams as revealing truths about the human self' after the Reformation. Thus the Reformation shift towards linking individualized interiority, conscience and guilt is seen as prefiguration of the 'internalized conscience' of the Gothic (Sage). In this context the (proto-)Gothicism of the nightmares in Shakespeare's *Richard III* is connected to their 'function of a guilty conscience'. The 'staged vision of the ghosts becomes an image of Richard's divided interior' as 'the level of introspection is more important than the level of divine retribution'. In this sense the Shakespearean nightmares anticipate 'an irresolution between supernatural and psychological causes' in Gothic fiction (Hogle 213).

In her chapter on the Gothic elements in Shakespeare's dramatic historical re-imagination of the Wars of the Roses, Elisabeth Bronfen introduces the issue of gender into her discussion of the political and aesthetic deployment of spectral apparitions. Focusing on Queen Margaret's uncanniness as 'woman and ruler', who 'embod[ies] the political unconscious of her world', her reading of Shakespeare's history plays 'through the lens of contemporary popular culture' allows her to locate the plays' 'Gothic sensibility' in the 'ambivalence about feminine political power read through subsequent recycling, resurfacing in contemporary cultural imagination' such as Tony Gilroy's film *Michael Clayton* (2007). At issue in her reading is the Gothic legacy of the monstrous female body as this gives voice both then and now to 'dark positions in political power games'. At the same time, linking current films attesting to a cultural anxiety about female politicians and Shakespeare's Gothic warrior queen in his early history plays, she also locates 'the spectral power on which the mutual implication of dramatic violence on stage and political violence off stage thrives', as another part of the cultural legacy of Gothic sensibility.

In the chapters in the second section, presenting other Renaissance dramatists, the definitions of the Gothic foreground notions of uncertainty and equivocation and/or notions of fear in terms of the uncanny or the abject, often in connection to notions of hybridity, of mixing (as in the grotesque, the bizarre). Drawing on Todorov's concept of the fantastic and Kristeva's abject, Beate Neumeier focuses on the nexus between cognitive and affective uncertainties in conjunction with a historical analysis of the impact of notions of vision, death and desire for the negotiation of early modern boundaries between spirit and matter, the human and the non-human and its gendered implications through ghostly apparitions as well as monstrous creatures like witches or devil-dogs and hybrid genres such as tragicomedy.

Questions of genre are equally central to Lynn Meskill's exploration of the 'proto-Gothic obsessions' of Ben Jonson, who is probably one of the least likely Renaissance authors to be associated with such an endeavour. However, as Meskill persuasively argues, the 'labyrinthine poetics' of Jonson's comedies and his masques in particular testify to a 'seventeenth century Gothic as combination of Jacobean charnel house and the Grotesque'. Meskill reads *The Masque of Queenes* in terms of the grotesque and hybrid with regard to characters, genres, registers and references. In this context Jonson's excessive notes on the margins turn into an 'account of authorial creation of a kind of monster out of fragments and pieces'. Thus his marginal references to witchcraft (drawn from 'a variety of sources … from antiquity, folktales, modern authorities, personal memories of stories and rumours') serve both to rationalize and to heighten the effect of terror, which culminates in Jonson's 'monstrous mixing of the living and the dead' in his 'vision of Queen Anne', 'crowned by the dead' queens of past ages.

The third section, aimed at taking stock of a Gothic textuality of non-dramatic genres of writing in the early modern period, begins with a chapter by Duncan Salkeld, who recognizes 'the fusion of death and desire' on the early modern English stage as origin 'of the kind of aesthetic now recognisable as the Gothic'. Identifying the courtesan as the embodiment of this fusion, he reads the Zoppino dialogue as a paradigmatic text signalling the shift from a dialectic relation to a fusion of fascination and revulsion with a 'contaminating female body' through a scopophobic experience. Salkeld traces this obsessive desire for the dead female body to the English Renaissance stage, and to plays like *The Revenger's Tragedy* and *The Second Maiden's Tragedy*. The link between death and desire (in religious and sexual terms) is also recognized as one of the key features of 'Gothic affinities in metaphysical poetry' by Ulrike Zimmermann. Her reading of Donne's poetry foregrounds the proto-Gothic mode as a way to deal critically with historical and cultural heritage, particularly with Petrarchan love poetry via assimilation, parody, and distortion through notions of excess and literalization, as in 'The Dampe', where the speaker's deadly female lover is scrutinized with medical expertize.

Garrett Sullivan turns to another variant of monstrous femininity in his analysis of Spenser's *Fairie Queene* and of Gothic readings of Acrasia as vampire. According to his argument, 'readings of Spenser's text that centre on psychic processes such as projection, or denial, or abjection find substantiation in the tripartite soul', as 'the tripartite soul introduces into the conception of human vitality a vocabulary for depicting and exploring the nature of self-division'. At the same time Sullivan emphatically emphasizes historical difference, clarifying that 'the tripartite soul enables the Gothic to recognize itself in Spenser'. The importance of historical difference is equally central to Andrea Brady, whose chapter explores the political implications of Renaissance Gothic from different historical and cultural angles. Andrea Brady analyses the complex implications of the return of supernatural phenomena in mid-seventeenth century pamphlet accounts of ghostly hauntings (about 'real sightings as well as rhetorical ghosts in political satire') against a growing 'widespread scepticism'. She traces this return not only to the persistence of folk tradition but also to a conscious attempt by the Cambridge Platonists Henry More and Joseph Glanville to restore a 'consensus which was eroding – in divine retribution, in immortal soul, in providence of history, in vision as access to truth'. The defence of ghostly apparitions is identified by Brady as a 'conservative' project to ward off 'the threat [they believed] scepticism posed to church and state'. Brady's analysis shows how the uncertainty and equivocation conjured in early modern plays is counteracted not only by a turn towards the uncanny in terms of psychological interiorization but also by an insistence on the supernatural as complementary movements towards closure.

The final section addresses the issue of a cultural legacy of the Gothic which links eighteenth and nineteenth century narratives back to the early modern period, and particularly the manner in which Shakespeare's plays blur boundaries between the living and the dead, English national identity and its Scottish other, as well as the human and the inhuman. A gendered aspect of the Gothic stands at the centre of Richard Wilson's analysis of cryptomimesis in *The Winter's Tale*, 'an unhomely Gothic horror hidden beneath the homely dwelling of a romance'. Drawing on Kristeva's notion of the abject, and linking Freud's mourning and melancholia to Bataille and Derrida, Wilson explores the play's monstrous liminality, tracing its ambivalences about the boundary between life and death, in terms of notions of resurrection and of being buried alive. 'Retelling the play as a proto-Gothic text' thus 'through a "perversion" of Shakespeare brings the play's own "perversities" to light'. In a truly Gothic twist Wilson ends his exploration of the 'subterranean affinity between Shakespeare and Gothic narrative' with a fascinating rendering of the haunting history of Shakespeare's house in Stratford visited by E. A. Poe. The political dimension of the construction of a Gothic Shakespeare in the eighteenth century is explored on a national scale in Dale Townshend's historical analysis of the 'complex relationship' between the terms Scottish and Gothic. Distinguishing between a political and an aesthetic Gothicism, Townshend reads the construction of Scottish Gothic through a 'phantasmatic projection' of Shakespeare 'as our British rather than English Gothic Bard' in response to the 'threat of Scottish nationalism' embodied in Ossian as Scottish Bard. In this sense the rise of the Gothic novel is aptly linked to the 'othering of Scotland' in the latter part of the eighteenth century.

Our volume ends with a final 'monstrous legacy of a Renaissance construe[d] as irrepressibly Gothic and ominously modern', taken up in Andreas Höfele's reading of Shakespeare's *The Tempest* through Oscar Wilde's late nineteenth century Gothic novel *The Picture of Dorian Gray*. Höfele takes Wilde's reference to Caliban in the preface of the novel as a starting-point for a comparative investigation into the human/animal boundary within early modern and post-Darwinian discourses revealing 'the grounds of the late nineteenth century Gothicization of the Renaissance' in the striking affinities between unstable early modern boundaries and the 'metamorphic', 'abhuman' Gothic body of the *fin de siècle* (see Hurley 3–4). Foregrounding a fascinating 'swap of epistemic affiliations', Höfele shows how 'Dorian Gray roots himself in Renaissance Knowledge culture', while 'Caliban is adopted into the image store of popular science' turning into the 'Shakespearean icon of Darwinism'.

The collection of essays thus helps us to isolate three distinct but interrelated links between the early modern cultural imaginary and Gothic sensibility. The first involves a troubling of hegemonic order, pitting the irrational against the rational, femininity against patriarchal authority, bestiality against the human, insurgency against authoritative rulership, and ghostly visitation against the world of the living. The contester to dominant power is often shaped into a composite figure, equating the feminine with magical thinking and subversive transgression or the ethnic other with barbarous instincts. By giving voice to the remains or returns of repressed knowledge, Gothic sensibility draws attention to the earlier cultural energies that will never fully be overcome. The second link pertains to the fact that this scene of instruction – 'monstrous' in that by recalling a past it offers a prophetic warning – self-consciously uses fiction as the site of the possible. Here disturbances of the hegemonic norm (the ordinary, the plausible) can be played through with impunity, identity boundaries can be broken down, bodies reshaped. The conceptual experiments these aesthetic texts afford, render visible the very process of repression and return. The point of the Gothic mode is to affect the audience or readers not only intellectually, but above all viscerally; to perform on the level of emotional response the destabilization of categories thematically at issue. They draw the spectator and reader into the magical thinking they unfold, calling upon their imaginary capacity to partake in a world that takes but the form and shape of airy nothing. By self-consciously addressing the spectral quality of any engagement with fictional texts, they call upon us to suspend our disbelief, regardless of whether the supernatural is ultimately explained, simply accepted, or once more repressed.

The third link between Gothic sensibility and the early modern cultural imaginary resides in this period's ambivalence regarding the incursion of the supernatural into the ordinary. It could, as Theseus in *A Midsummer Night's Dream* might maintain, simply be a trick of an overly heated imagination, or it could be the result of actual witchcraft. If, in turn, it was deemed to be a reliable expression of magic, it could be either malign or benign, producing either horror or delight, and as such sharing with the audience a nightmare vision or that of a brave new world. As Jonathan Bate and Dora Thornton argue in the exhibition *Shakespeare: Staging the World*, there is the political witchcraft embodied by the three sisters in *Macbeth*, which troubled James's accession to the throne and whose ungovernable, barbarous power he alludes to in his tract *Daemonologie* (1597). But there is also the enchantment of Prospero in *The Tempest*, bringing justice to usurpers and opening our awareness not just to a new world beyond the British Isles but also to the sustained imaginary power of the theatre stage (and the printed page), where the ghosts of the past take shape over and over again. And there is the restorative magic of Paulina, bringing with it the resurrection of a cruelly maligned wife in *Winter's Tale*, and with it the restitution of a royal marriage. As site of the possible par excellence, fiction proves to remain the arena where the antagonism between these two intertwined notions of magical thinking, politically subversive and emotionally uplifted, can be sustained.

Works cited

Bal, Mieke. *Quoting Caravaggio: Contemporary Art, Preposterous History*. Chicago: University of Chicago Press, 1999.

Bate, Jonathan and Dora Thornton. *Shakespeare: Staging the World*. London: The British Museum Press, 2012.

Bronfen, Elisabeth. *Night Passages: Philosophy, Literature and Film*. New York: Columbia University Press, 2013.

Clark, Stuart. *Vanities of the Eye: Vision in Early Modern European Culture.* Oxford: Oxford University Press, 2007.

Desmet, Christy and Anne Williams, eds. *Shakespearean Gothic.* Cardiff: University of Wales Press, 2009.

Drakakis, John and Dale Townshend, eds. *Gothic Shakespeare.* Abingdon: Routledge, 2008.

Hogle, Jerrold E. 'Afterword: The "Grounds" of the Shakespeare–Gothic Relationship.' *Gothic Shakespeares.* Eds John Drakakis and Dale Townshend. Abingdon: Routledge, 2008. 201–20.

Hurley, Kelly. *The Gothic Body: Sexuality, Materialism, and Degeneration at the Fin de Siècle.* Cambridge: Cambridge University Press, 1996.

Sage, Victor. *Horror Fiction in the Protestant Tradition.* Basingstoke: Macmillan, 1988.

Shildrick, Margrit. *Embodying the Monster: Encounters with the Vulnerable Self.* London: Sage Publications, 2002.

Walpole, Horace. *The Castle of Otranto. Three Gothic Novels.* Ed. Peter Fairclough. Harmondsworth: Penguin, 1986. 37–148.

Part I
Shakespearean hauntings

1

Yorick's skull

John Drakakis

Whose skull?

The summer season of 2008 at the RSC aroused a little more excitement than usual, because the actor who was then currently playing Doctor Who on television, David Tennant, was to play Hamlet in a new Greg Doran production at the Courtyard Theatre. Tickets were hard to come by, and the average age of audiences dropped significantly. The glossy programme produced for the occasion detailed the history of the company's rehearsal programme, and Doran's entry for 'week 7' included a photograph of a reclining Tennant, his left hand across a raised left knee, gazing pensively at a skull placed on the floor against a bag in front of him. Evidently Hamlet had returned to Elsinore and the first thing that he encountered was a skull. This photograph is one of a collage of three, one consisting of Gertrude (Penny Downie) clutching a bunch of red roses and looking down into an imaginary grave, and the other of a perturbed Osric (Ryan Gage), suspended between his two interlocutors, looking away from the gesticulating finger of Hamlet (David Tennant), and towards a disdainful Horatio (Peter de Jersey). Nowhere in the programme narrative is specific mention made of the skull that occupies pride of place in the first of these three inset photographs. Instead, Doran offers a brief account of the company's collective journey to an understanding of the play's central themes:

> We have explored the historicist perspective (is Polonius a portrait of Lord Burleigh, Queen Elizabeth's chief minister? Is Hamlet an autobiographical portrait of the Earl of Oxford?) We've argued about the play's politics. It's an intensely dangerous world of hyper-surveillance, in which Hamlet himself seems largely politically disinterested. We've delved into the psychoanalysis of poisoners, and rejected Freudian analysis of the oedipal nature of the closet scene. But to bring the play home to each of us, to allow it to touch our own lives, and to get even closer to the iconic questions touching our own mortality that the play poses, we have more work to do. (RSC *Hamlet* A Rehearsal Scrapbook)

The skull, foregrounded in the top left corner of the page, functions to underscore 'the iconic questions touching our own mortality' that Doran, speaking for the company as a whole, identifies as the central theme of the play. Audiences who saw the play at Stratford-upon-Avon *saw* a skull at the beginning of Act 5, and assumed that it was merely a 'theatrical' prop, a representation of a 'real' skull.

However, at the end of the season at Stratford-upon-Avon Doran announced that Yorick's skull was, in fact, a real human skull belonging to a pianist, André Tchaikowsky, who had died in June 1982, but who had, according to Anthony Hopkins in a quotation from *The Daily Telegraph* for 14 August of that year, nurtured 'a life-long ambition to go on the stage'. In what must be one of the most bizarre of bequests, Tchaikowsky had left his body to medical science, and his skull to the RSC in the hope that it might be used in a future performance of *Hamlet*. In *The Guardian* for 23 November 2008, David Smith wrote of an 'extra cast member … André Tchaikowsky, a Polish concert pianist and composer' and of a 'posthumous performance, which it is safe to assume makes up in consistency what it lacks in expressiveness'. *The Times* observed that 'Tchaikowsky starred in 22 performances of the "Alas, poor Yorick" scene in which Hamlet holds aloft the skull of the court jester unearthed by a gravedigger' (de Bruxelles). Apparently, in 1989 the actor Mark Rylance had rehearsed with the skull, but found the prospect of performing with it onstage uncomfortable, and so it was returned to the 'props department, where it resided in a tissue-lined box for twenty years' (BBC News). Doran is reported to have told *The Telegraph* that 'It was sort of a little shock tactic. Though of course, to some extent that wears off and it's just André in his box' (Reid). According to the curator of the RSC Archives, David Howell, Doran 'wanted to make the performance as real as possible' (*Daily Mail* reporter). The *Mail Online* website contains a photograph of David Tennant with the skull, along with photographs of 'Holocaust survivor André Tchaikowsky', and Derek Jacobi performing in a 1979 production of *Hamlet* using a plastic skull (apparently the stimulus for Tchaikowsky's bequest). It was also revealed that the company had to seek formal permission from the Human Tissue Authority in order to use the skull because it was less than a hundred years old. Doran himself explained (disingenuously) that he did not want the news of Tchaikowsky's skull to get out *before* the performance run had been completed because 'I thought it would topple the play and it would be about David acting with a real skull' (Waite).

The claim that the use of a real skull was designed to make the play more 'real', and was intended as a 'shock tactic', and the fear that if the news leaked out it would destroy the impact of the play by reducing it to a question of 'David acting with a real skull', is almost as bizarre as Tchaikowsky's original bequest. The effect of this effect depends entirely upon the audience knowing that Yorick's skull was not a representation but a real skull, and, in any case, many of the younger members of the audience had come to see, not a real actor (David Tennant), but Doctor Who as Hamlet. Nor should we overlook the musical history that resonates in the surname 'Tchaikowsky' and, in particular, its wider associations with musical interpretations of Shakespeare. Given the cultural resonance of names in this narrative, it would be difficult to speak unequivocally of an 'extra-fictional and extra-theatrical identity', notwithstanding the attempts of André Tchaikowsky's biographer, David A. Ferré, to append a facsimile copy of his death certificate and his will, to the final chapter of the book as part of a process of authentication. The role that Tchaikowsky's skull plays in the drama of *Hamlet* is to proliferate a series of 'voices', and voice, as Derrida tells us, is that which '*marks* the name or takes its place' ('*Hamlet:* That skull had a tongue in it, and could sing once') (Derrida 10). To this extent, Tchaikowsky *takes the place of* Yorick as an iconic representative of 'art' and 'history': concert pianist and 'holocaust survivor'. The boundary between the authentic and the fictional, between 'nature' and the mirror that drama holds up to it, has been crossed in this gesture of replacing the fictional and the representational with the 'real'; and what was evidently food for comedy in *The Daily Telegraph* headline, 'Alas poor André, I knew him Horatio' (Hopkins), turns out to encapsulate exactly one of the problems that the *revenant* André Tchaikowsky poses to the etiquette of theatrical performance, and that is in some ways indicative of the problem that Derrida faces in his conflation of the 'spectre' of Marx with the fictional spectre of the Ghost of Old Hamlet.

Skulls in context

The deployment of a real skull invokes the desire for authentication. Published along with the various responses that this theatrical ploy attracted were photographs of the real André Tchaikowsky, and viewers were directed to the *André Tchaikowsky Website* that provided a photographic history along with a full account of the bequest of the skull to the RSC. Queasy spectators might be disturbed to learn that instead of the imaginary Yorick's skull, whose presence might allow them the opportunity to 'get even closer to the iconic questions touching our own mortality that the play poses', they were looking at a real skull, the remains of a 'person', and a 'holocaust survivor'. For a moment, an inanimate object is endowed with a life and an afterlife, which almost takes the form of a resurrection, a gesture of 'taking André out of his box', as Doran casually observed. Or, again to invoke Derrida, of a 'being-with spectres' that 'would also be, not only but also, a *politics* of memory, of inheritance, and of generations' (Derrida xix).

In Shakespeare's play the 'Gravediggers' scene' is an occasion for dark comedy, and for recollection, although the use of the real skull of a 'person' whose identity has been concealed adds another dimension to this complex dynamic. In fictional terms the skull 'represents' the jester Yorick, but it also functions as the 'double' of an actual person, Tchaikowsky, whose own desire is realized in the moment of performance *beyond* death. What was Rylance's discomfort in 1989 – if it was not a manifestation of the actor's ego projecting on to Tchaikowsky's skull an untimely reminder of the fact of his own death – of creating a 'double' in which an earlier, more 'friendly aspect', the person of the accomplished concert pianist, reduced to a skull, is now transformed into an object of terror. The reasoning here is, of course, that of Freud's essay 'The Uncanny', although for the actor playing Hamlet death is a recurrent feature of performance. Indeed, in his 'Thoughts for the Times on War and Death' (1915) Freud distinguishes clearly between events such as 'war' in which 'People really die; and no longer one by one, but many, often tens of thousands, in a single day. And death is no longer a chance event' (Freud 79–80) and the compensatory worlds of fiction and theatre where 'we find the plurality of lives which we need' and where 'we die with the hero' but yet also 'we survive him, and are ready to die again just as safely with another hero' (79). Bringing the skull of Tchaikowsky on to the stage brings 'real' death into the fictional world of the play, thereby blurring the boundaries between reality and fiction. In a way that Doran could not have imagined when he planned his theatrical 'shock', the presence of Tchaikowsky's skull *acting the role* of Yorick, thereby fulfilling a 'lifelong desire', effectively assents 'to life even in death', and is part of Bataille's provocative definition of the erotic (Bataille 11). For Bataille, eroticism has its roots in the violent 'transition from discontinuity' (the realm of the individual) 'to continuity':

> It is a state of communication revealing a quest for a possible continuance of being beyond the confines of the self. Bodies open out to a state of continuity through secret channels that give us a feeling of obscenity. Obscenity is our name for the uneasiness which upsets the physical state associated with self-possession, with the possession of a recognized and stable individuality. (17–18)

At this early stage of his argument Bataille has in mind the 'petit mort' of orgasm, but a little later, in his discussion of how 'we perceive the transition from the living state to the corpse', he suggests that 'For each man who regards it with awe, the corpse is the image of his own destiny' (44). Indeed, in an anthropological discussion of the taboos surrounding the dead body, and the rituals that it elicits, he observes:

> According to this way of thinking, the violence which by striking at the dead man dislocates the ordered course of things does not cease to be dangerous once the victim is dead. It constitutes a supernatural peril which can be 'caught' from the dead body. Death is a danger for those left behind. If they have to bury the corpse it is less in order to keep it safe than to keep themselves safe from its contagion. Often the idea of contagion is connected with the body's decomposition where formidable aggressive forces are seen at work. The corpse will rot; this biological disorder, like the newly dead body a symbol of destiny, is threatening in itself. We no longer believe in contagious magic, but which of us could be sure of not quailing at the sight of a dead body crawling with maggots? (46–7)

It is the body in the state of decay that fascinates Bataille, and in particular the carnivalesque violence that is unleashed when the sacred figure of the king dies. Quoting Roger Caillois, Bataille observes that disorder occurs only during the time that the king's body is in the process of decomposing, and that it ends 'when all the rotting flesh has finally disappeared from the royal corpse, when nothing is left of the remains but a hard, clean, incorruptible skeleton' (67). André Tchaikowsky does not quite occupy the position of 'the sacred person of a king', although the emphasis upon his plight as 'a holocaust survivor', and the fact that he died prematurely of cancer, gives him an unusual iconic status. However, the case of Tchaikowsky's skull, while fascinating in its own right, points towards an engagement with Shakespeare's *Hamlet* that opens up for us an avenue into what we might call, provisionally, Renaissance 'Gothic', where all the ingredients that come together in a scene in which the grave, the vermicular body, the nature of death, its levelling effects and its terror, and living memory are all present.

Shakespeare's Yorick

The use of André Tchaikowsky's skull represents a form of transgression in that it violates what Georges Bataille identifies as 'the profane world [that] is the world of taboos' (67), in which the act of transgression offers a glimpse of 'the sacred'. Bataille goes on to describe the dialectic between 'the sacred' and the 'profane' that produces the following reaction:

Men are swayed by two simultaneous emotions: they are driven away by terror and drawn by an awed fascination. Taboo and transgression reflect these two contradictory urges. The taboo would forbid the transgression, but the fascination compels it. Taboos and the divine are opposed to each other in one sense only, for the sacred aspect of the taboo is what draws men towards it and transfigures the original interdiction. (68)

Bataille is concerned to identify what he calls 'the often intertwined themes of mythology', and to elucidate a fundamentally economic opposition between the world of 'work' and the transgressive excesses of the carnivalesque. But if we transport this dialectic into the Renaissance, and to a text such as John Donne's own funeral sermon, 'Death's Duel or A Consolation to the Soule Against the Dying Life and Living Death of the Body' delivered on 25 February 1631, then we are offered a graphic account of precisely what vermiculation and decomposition of the human body represent, and that the 'disorder' extends well beyond 'the hard, clean, incorruptible skeleton' that Bataille's articulation of Roger Caillois's anthropological account of ritual practices pinpoints. If Donne's account is not 'Gothic' in itself, it certainly lays the foundations for a number of recurrent Gothic themes:

> But for us that dye now and sleepe in the state of the dead, we must al passe this *posthume* death, this *death* after *death*, nay this death after buriall, this *dissolution* after *dissolution*, this *death* of *corruption* and *putrifaction*, of *vermiculation* and *incineration*, of *dissolution* and *dispersion* in and *from* the grave. When those bodies that have beene the *children* of *royall parents*, and the *parents* of *royall children*, must say with *Job, to corruption thou art my father,* and *to the Worme thou art my mother and my sister.* Miserable *riddle*, when the *same worme* must bee *my mother,* and *my sister,* and bee both *father* and *mother* to my *owne mother* and my *sister,* and bee both *father* and *mother* to my owne *mother* and *sister, beget,* and *beare* that *worme* which is all that miserable *penury*; when my *mouth* shall be *filled* with *dust,* and the *worme* shall *feed,* and *feed sweetly* upon me, when the *ambitious* man shall have no *satisfaction,* if the *poorest alive* tread upon him, nor the *poorest* receive any *contentment* in being made *equall* to *Princes,* for they *shall bee equall* but *in dust.* (Donne 317–18)

Here death may be the great leveller, but the tomb also becomes the site of incest and the means whereby the most basic categories that sustain the social order are violated. Andrew Marvell's overtures 'To His Coy Mistress' do not go quite this far, although they share some aspects of this topography:

> Thy beauty shall no more be found;
> Nor, in thy marble vault, shall sound

My echoing song: then worms shall try
That long preserved virginity:
And your quaint honour turned to dust;
And into ashes all my lust.

(Marvell 249)

This is also much more suggestively graphic than Hamlet's mock quizzing of Yorick's skull: 'Now get you to my lady's table and tell her, let her paint an inch thick, to this favour she must come. Make her laugh at that', and the rhetorical question that follows: 'Why may not imagination trace the noble dust of Alexander till 'a find it stopping a bung-hole?' (*Hamlet* 5.1.182–4 and 193–4). We might compare Hamlet's ventriloquizing of Yorick's skull with the routine of the English comedian the late Tommy Cooper, to the extent that both laugh at the horrors of death. But such confrontations are transformed in a 'Gothic' text such as *The Abbey of St. Asaph* (1795) by Isabella Kelly where, forced 'to breathe the vapid air of corruption' in the tomb of Sir Eldred Trevallion, the heiress, Jennet Aprieu, receives something of a birthday shock:

> A strange noise interrupting her prayer, she looked wildly round, and beheld a human skeleton on the earth before her: Not a fibre remained – yet the bare ribs shook – the ghastly skull rose slow, yet visible, to view: and disconsolately bowing, seemed to implore commiseration. Something glistened within the hollow sockets, which once enclosed the orbs of sight, and a faint shriek issues from the yawning jaws.
>
> Trembling, she gazed a moment, till horror seized her heart, and with loud convulsed gasps, she cried, 'It is – oh – great God above – it is the murdered Sir Eldred! Oh perturbed spirit, that hath forsook the realms of peace, to hover round this low un-honoured spot, and with a silent yet prevailing voice, crieth, "Earth, oh cover not my guiltless blood" – Receive my vow. That if delivered from these caves of death, thy funeral rites shall be performed, – and that thy much injured shade may rest in peace!' (Kelly)[1]

This is high melodrama that elicits its effects by embedding more than one *Hamlet* allusion in this passage. The 'perturbed spirit' of Old Hamlet's ghost is brought into alignment with the now terrifyingly animated skull of Yorick that, apparently, emits 'a deep sigh [that] penetrated her ear', followed by 'piteous moans' and then 'an anthem, softly melancholy', that allowed her to hear 'the soothing accents with pleasing wonder', after which, 'the skull, parting from the neck, with shrill shrieks, rolled to her foot' (Kelly). Sir Eldred's shrieking skull is the last straw, forcing Jennet, who could 'endure no longer; but perfectly enfrenzied, rushed from the baleful scene, and falling motionless at the entrance of another apartment, lost remembrance in total insensibility' (Kelly). Later in the novel it transpires that this entire scene is a fabrication, effected with the aid of 'a chemical preparation of phosphorus' (Kelly), and the ambient skull turns out to be the home of a rat.

I have commented elsewhere on some of the ways in which Shakespearean texts function as a resource for Gothic writing (cf. Drakakis and Townshend 1ff), and indeed, the initiator of the genre, Horace Walpole, in his preface to the second edition of *The Castle of Otranto* confessed that 'That great master of nature, Shakespeare, was the model I copied' (Walpole 44). Dale Townshend has recently observed that the connection between Walpole and *Hamlet* was that of writer to an *alter ego* (Townshend, *The Orders of Gothic* 62ff) and that his obsession was with the play's 'paternal mythology long established as the sacred object of Horace Walpole's own identifications' (62). Indeed, when, in a letter of 13 January 1780 to Sir Horace Mann, Walpole *does* refer specifically to Yorick's skull it is in the context of reflecting on 'the ruin of England' and of seeking to defend his father's political reputation against 'an impotent cabal of mock-patriots'. He says:

> I soon forgot an impotent cabal of mock-patriots; but the scene they vainly sought to disturb, rushed on my mind, and like Hamlet on the sight of Yorick's skull, I recollected the prosperity of Denmark when my father ruled, and compared it with the present moment! I looked about for a Sir Robert Walpole – but where is he to be found? (Walpole, *Horace Walpole's Correspondence with Sir Horace Mann* 7)

A 'phantasmatic' and 'retrospective grafting of *Hamlet* on to the terms of his own experience is', as Townshend rightly points out, 'striking' (65). But the emphasis here is not, as it is in Shakespeare's play, or, indeed, as it might have been in *The Castle of Otranto*, upon the fact of human decay, or even upon the implication of the spectral in a dilemma in the material present, or indeed upon the process of haunting itself. It is, rather, upon a remembrance of times past, of an idyllic, perhaps even idealized, political existence in which the son Walpole adopts the persona both of Hamlet but also, perhaps, of Shakespeare's John of Gaunt (cf. *The Tragedy of Richard II* 2.1.40–66).

The example of Isabella Kelly, however, and of later writers in the Gothic tradition, suggests that it is more than simply a matter of either identification or resource that is at issue. Clearly in the case of Walpole it is a question of Shakespearean texts performing a mediating function that authorizes a particular reality as perceived by the son of a politically maligned father. But in the case of Isabella Kelly, Shakespeare stands in, as it were, for a larger narrative that functions to sustain the authority of what I have suggested is a 'minority' literature. Indeed, what we have been content to label 'quotation' – and what perhaps might more accurately be labelled different forms of appropriation – raises a further question concerning the extent to which Shakespearean texts (and we might extend this to encompass 'Renaissance' texts) are themselves embedded in an ethos that we might label 'Gothic'. Clearly, it is only by thinking of Walpole's appropriation of the *Hamlet* narrative as a 'phantasmatic' story, which might act in such a way as to mask its function as a heuristic device that would help to make sense of a portion of his own autobiography, that his reference both to the play and to Yorick's skull might be labelled 'Gothic', although there is a sense in which his use of this quotation in his letter to Mann is of a different order from his appropriation of elements of the play in *The Castle of Otranto*. Of course, there is nothing to prevent us from reading symptomatically a connection between the two, although the frames of reference are noticeably different. In fact, the usage is of a different order from that of other commentators on the 'Gothic' components of Shakespeare's texts. For example, Nathan Drake's essays on 'Gothic Superstition' and 'On Terror' (1798), speak of 'the apparitions of Shakespeare' that 'are to this day highly pleasing, striking, and sublime features in these delightful compositions ... And although this kind of superstition is able to arrest every faculty of the human mind, and to shake, as it were, all nature with horror, yet does it also delight in the most sportive and elegant imagery' (Drake 155–6). Similarly, in the example from Kelly's novel, the immediacy of the shock of confronting an animated skeleton or a 'living' skull, whatever subsequent explanation may be involved to demystify its immediate effects, does not detract from the shock of pleasure with which the phenomena are first encountered both by the fictional character and vicariously by the reader. Furthermore, in her comments on the 'sublime' and the supernatural, Ann Radcliffe identifies particular features of Shakespeare, and her exemplary text is, again, *Hamlet*. She debates whether the witches in *Macbeth* should look like old women, and she argues that 'The wild attire, the look *not of this earth*, are essential traits of supernatural agents, working evil in the darkness of mystery' and that 'Whenever the poet's witch condescends, according to the vulgar notion, to mingle mere ordinary mischief with her malignity, and to become familiar, she is ludicrous and loses her power over the imagination; the illusion vanishes' (Radcliffe 165). Thus, she identifies the 'awe' in Shakespeare as emanating from the careful avoidance of 'every thing that is familiar and common', and she continues:

> In nothing has Shakespeare been more successful than in this; and in
> another case somewhat more difficult – that of selecting circumstances of
> manners and appearance for his supernatural beings, which, though wild
> and remote, in the highest degree, from common apprehension, never shock
> the understanding by incompatibility with themselves – never compel us,
> for an instant, to recollect that he has a license for extravagance. Above
> every ideal being is the ghost of Hamlet, with all its attendant incidents
> of time and place. The dark watch upon the remote platform, the dreary
> aspect of the night, the very expression of the office on guard, ... the recol-
> lection of a star, an unknown world, are all circumstances which excite
> forlorn, melancholy, and solemn feelings, and dispose us to welcome,
> with trembling curiosity, the awful being that draws near; and to indulge
> in the strange mixture of horror, pity, and indignation, produced by the
> tale it reveals. (166)

This is perhaps as concise a definition of what we might pejoratively
call the 'Gothic Shakespeare' as we might find. And it is different from
the Shakespeare that provides a key to Horace Walpole's autobiography
where a distinctly Renaissance sense of *repetition* and analogy are uppermost, alongside a feeling of nostalgia for the past rather than a feeling
for its superstitions and its profound 'mystery'.

The question is: how might the strange case of André Tchaikowsky's
skull, and his wish that it should be used in modern performances of
Hamlet, help to illuminate a 'Gothic' strain in Shakespeare's *Hamlet*
that we might even wish to extend to Renaissance writing generally?
Of course, the use of a real skull elicits a certain horrified queasiness in
the theatre spectator that, while not quite so melodramatic as that of
Isabella Kelly's heiress, invokes a momentary sense of alarm that representation and 'reality', the fictionalization of 'death' and death itself,
suddenly become confused with each other. Or to put it another way,
with the appearance of Tchaikowsky's skull in the role of Yorick, death
is, as it were, 'brought to life' on the modern stage, and a death that
carries with it, not a nostalgia for the past, but a genuine horror in the
face of historical events: death by cancer, and even more powerfully,
the Holocaust. In a culture where death itself, despite its spectacular
representations in modern film, is either transformed into simulacra or
discreetly sidelined and made the subject of various euphemisms and
elaborate rituals augmented with accompanying rhetorics, it is perhaps
difficult to reconstruct the impact that representations of the figure of
Death on the medieval and Renaissance stage, and in the visual art
of the period, must have had upon spectators. Difficult because in the
sixteenth century Death was a real and persistent presence, when to
'pluck out the heart of my mystery' (*Hamlet* 3.3.357), to use Hamlet's
words, was something that an audience could watch in real life as it was

being carried out. What is even more remarkable is that this preoccupation with Death in its physical manifestations – the skeleton, and the putrifying vermicular corpse – should be the object of fascination whose intensity was not diminished by religious belief. Indeed, this was not a 'primitive' phenomenon at all, but part of a very sophisticated discourse. But can we say that this evident obsession with the various forms of phantasmatic life,[2] of 'life after death' and the world of ghosts, spirits, and the entire paraphernalia of the numinous, amounts to a Gothic sensibility? Or does Shakespeare as the exemplary Renaissance writer, stand in as some kind of bard of 'Nature', exemplar of the Romantic 'sublime', whose plays resurrect, and give meaning to, a particular historical conjuncture when the 'irrational', the superstitious and the fantastic were still active in shaping experience, even as dominant and emergent forces were beginning to offer alternative explanations. The 'explanation' of the appearance of Shakespeare's Ghost of Hamlet's father is *not* to be found in the ingenious use of phosphorus, but rather in the residual existence of the catholic Purgatory, a busy location that could accommodate murdered fathers, and casualties of the battlefield such as Kyd's Don Andrea, the 'eternal substance' of whose 'soule' released from imprisonment in his 'wanton flesh' now awaits final judgement (Kyd 4), or even in attenuated form the 'spirit' of Webster's *Duchess of Malfi*. Don Andrea's 'wanton flesh' is transformed in Shakespeare's *Hamlet* into the protagonist's lurid description of Gertrude's living 'In the rank sweat of an enseamed bed' (*Hamlet* 3.4.90), and from there into the bizarre perversions of the Italianate ducal palace in Middleton's *The Revenger's Tragedy*. In this last example, the skull of Vindice's dead beloved, a stage property that was becoming ubiquitous becomes the focal point of every activity that characterizes the excesses of the Duke's corrupt court:

> Thou sallow picture of my poison'd love,
> My study's ornament, thou shell of death,
> Once the bright face of my betrothed lady,
> When life and beauty naturally fill'd out
> These ragged imperfections,
> When two heaven-pointed diamonds were set
> In those unsightly rings – then 'twas a face
> So far beyond the artificial shine
> Of any woman's bought complexion,
> That the uprightest man (if such there be
> That sin but seven times a day) broke custom.
>
> (1.1.14–24)

Vindice's memorialising of his 'betrothed lady' recalls a life, *and a death*, in much the same way that Yorick's skull prompts Hamlet's memory of the past – the latter feature missing in Walpole's letter. This vision of a specific feature of a post-lapsarian, mutable world steeped in corruption, there in Marlowe, Spenser, Shakespeare, Jonson, Marston, Middleton, and Ford, and throughout the corpus of Jacobean drama, is expanded in John Webster's *The Duchess of Malfi* through the observations of the malcontent Bosola:

> Man stands amaz'd to see his deformity
> In any other creature but himself.
> But in our own flesh, though we bear diseases
> Which have their true name only ta'en from beasts,
> As the most ulcerous wolf, and swinish measle;
> Though we are eaten up of lice and worms,
> And though continually we bear about us
> A rotten and dead body, we delight
> To hide it in rich tissue: all our fear –
> Nay, all our terror – is lest our physician
> Should put us in the ground, to be made sweet.
>
> (2.1.50–60)

T. S. Eliot's claim that 'Webster was much possessed by death / And saw the skull beneath the skin', and that Donne 'knew the anguish of the marrow / The ague of the skeleton' (49–50) captures exactly that combination of vermicular description and accompanying anxiety that was transformed into 'entertainment' in Gothic fiction. For Webster's Bosola not only are the emotions of 'fear' and the 'terror' that accompany the fact of death endowed with an authenticity but the disturbance they generate is also psychological. What disturbs the Duchess's brother Ferdinand is a 'mystery' – beyond explanation in the play – but it is *expressed* in his pathological desire to murder her, Antonio and their children. In the figure of Bosola the act of assassination itself prompts an unexpected *volte face* as he contemplates his motive for joining Antonio in revenge:

> The weakest arm is strong enough, that strikes
> With the sword of justice: – still methinks the duchess
> Haunts me: there, there! –
> 'Tis nothing but my melancholy.
>
> (5.3.344–47)

Where in Shakespeare the motive for the appearance of a revenant from the past is made explicit, as in the case of the appearance of Old Hamlet's ghost, or the ghost of Julius Caesar in the earlier play, in

Webster such 'historical' explanations are never clear and the 'haunting' Duchess might simply be Bosola's 'melancholy' – a debilitating state of mind that extends well beyond the event, and an attendant psychological 'effect' that provokes its recognition.

In an account of 'Perceptions of late Gothic Art in England', Alexandrina Buchanan distinguishes between a period prior to the eighteenth century when 'the use of Gothic forms seems to have derived from their importance in signifying function', and later when 'Gothic acquired its own aesthetic associations', chief amongst which were its inspiration of 'emotions too deep for rational description: the awe of nature, the love of one's country, the melancholy of history' (131). In his Introduction to *The Oxford Book of Gothic Tales* (1993) Chris Baldick raises the question of what he calls 'The anti-Gothicism of the Gothic' or 'the distrust of medieval civilization and its representation of the past primarily in terms of tyranny and superstition' that, he argues, 'has taken several forms, from the vigilant Protestant xenophobia so strongly evident in the first half-century of Gothic writing, to the rationalist feminism of Angela Carter's fiction' (xiii). In his justification of the convergence of Gothic and psychoanalysis, Dale Townshend has argued that both circulate 'within the same epistemic space' (10), which suggests that the Gothic must be perceived as a specific kind of engagement with 'history' that distinguishes it from other kinds of engagement. It is the question whether we can consider Shakespeare and his contemporaries as 'Gothic' writers in *their* culturally specific engagements with 'history' that intertextual events such as the re-animation of André Tchaikowsky's skull as the dead jester Yorick, bring into focus for us. Viewed in this way – and we could ask the question of whether what Spenser is doing in *The Faerie Queene* (1590) is any different from what Tennyson accomplished in his *Idylls of The King* (1856–85) – *Hamlet* may be perceived as a 'Gothic' revival of a narrative from the distant past. Except that in separating out the *formal* aspects of Gothic, thereby obscuring the actual political and cultural conditions of its production, may we not be neutralizing the term? Indeed, if *everything* is 'Gothic' – in just the same way that 'everything' is 'postcolonial', then nothing is. Or is it a case of what Tchaikowsky's skull *adds* to the performance of *Hamlet* that provides a text already part of a culture steeped in what Michael Neill has called 'issues of death', and that deals with 'the almost inconceivable horror of death's undifferentiated blankness' (14), a surplus that invests it with specifically 'Gothic' meanings? If the 'Gothic' engages with 'history', to what extent is that engagement one with the irreducible *fact* of historical difference?

Notes

1 I am grateful to Norbert Besch for providing me with the typescript of his forthcoming edition of Isabella Kelly, *The Abbey of St. Asaph* (1795), in advance of publication. The typescript is unpaginated.

2 The preoccupation with the life of 'dreams' is important during the period; for example, see Thomas Hill, *An Interpretation of Dreams* (London, 1576), or Thomas Nashe's *The Terrors of The Night* (1594), or, of course, Shakespeare's *Macbeth* (1605).

Works cited

Baldick, Chris, ed. *The Oxford Book of Gothic Tales*. Oxford: Oxford University Press, 1993.

Bataille, Georges. *Erotism: Death and Sensuality*. Trans. Mary Dalwood. San Francisco: City Lights Books, 1986.

BBC. 'Bequeathed Skull Stars in Hamlet.' BBC News 26 November 2008. http://news.bbc.co.uk/go/pr/fr/-/2/hi/entertainment/arts_and_culture/7749962stm.

Bruxelles, Simon de. 'Getting Ahead in the Theatre.' *The Times* 26 November 2008.

Buchanan, Alexandrina. 'Perspectives of the Past: Perceptions of Late Gothic Art in England.' *Gothic Art for England 1400–1547*. Eds Richard Marks and Paul Williamson. London: Victoria and Albert Museum, 2003. 128–39.

Daily Mail Reporter. 'David Tennant Realises Pianist's Dying Wish by Using the Skull He Left in His Will to Play 'Alas, poor Yorick' Scene in Hamlet.' *Mail Online* 25 November 2008.

Derrida, Jacques. *Specters of Marx: The State of the Debt, The Work of Mourning, & The New International*. Trans. Peggy Kamuf. New York and London: Routledge, 1994.

Donne, John. 'Death's Duel or, A Consolation to the Soule, Against the Dying Life, and Living Death of the Body.' *Selected Prose*. Ed. Neil Rhodes. Harmondsworth: Penguin Books, 1987. 310–26.

Drakakis, John and Dale Townshend, eds. *Gothic Shakespeares*. London: Routledge, 2008.

Drake, Nathan. 'On Gothic Superstition and On Terror (1798).' *Gothic Documents: A Sourcebook 1700–1820*. Eds E. J. Clery and Robert Miles. Manchester: Manchester University Press, 2000. 155–63.

Eliot, T. S. 'Whispers of Immortality.' *Selected Poems*. London: Faber and Faber, 1961. 49–50.

Freud, Sigmund. 'Thoughts for the Times on War and Death.' Trans. James Strachey. *The Pelican Freud*. Eds James Strachey and Alan Tyson. Vol. 12. Harmondsworth: Penguin Books, 1985. 57–89.

Hopkins, Anthony. 'Hamlet Gets a Skull in Bequest.' *The Daily Telegraph* 14 August 1982.

Kelly, Isabella. *The Abbey of St. Asaph* (1795). Ed. Tenille Nowak. N.p.: Udolpho Press, n.d.

Kyd, Thomas. *The Spanish Tragedy*. Ed. Philip Edwards. Manchester: Manchester University Press, 1974.

Marvell, Andrew. 'To His Coy Mistress.' *The Metaphysical Poets*. Ed. Helen Gardner. Harmondsworth: Penguin Books, 1957. 249–50.

Middleton, Thomas (Cyril Tourneur). *The Revenger's Tragedy*. Ed. Reginald A. Foakes. London: Methuen, 1966.

Neill, Michael. *Issues of Death: Mortality and Identity in English Renaissance Tragedy*. Oxford: Clarendon, 1997.

Radcliffe, Ann. 'On the Supernatural in Poetry' (1826). *Gothic Documents: A Sourcebook 1700–1820*. Eds E. J. Clery and Robert Miles. Manchester: Manchester University Press, 2000. 163–72.

Reid, Vicki. 'David Tennant: From Doctor Who to Hamlet.' *The Telegraph* 22 November 2008.

RSC *Hamlet* A Rehearsal Scrapbook. 2008. Royal Shakespeare Company. N. pag. 30 April 2013. http://www.rsc.org.uk/downloads/hamlet_2008_scrapbook.pdf.

Shakespeare, William. *The Tragedy of Richard II*. Ed. Charles Forker. London: Arden Shakespeare, 2002.

—. *Hamlet*. Ed. Harold Jenkins. London: Methuen, 1982. Arden series.

Smith, David. 'Pianist's Skull Plays the Jester.' *The Guardian* 23 November 2008.

Townshend, Dale. *The Orders of Gothic: Foucault, Lacan and the Subject of Gothic Writing, 1764–1820*. New York: AMS Press, 2007.

Waite, Debbie. 'Skull Gets Starring Role.' *Oxford Mail* 26 November 2008.

Walpole, Horace. The Castle of Otranto. Three Gothic Novels. Ed. Peter Fairclough. Harmondsworth: Penguin Books, 1986. 37–148.

—. *Horace Walpole's correspondence with Sir Horace Mann and Sir Horace Mann the Younger*. New Haven: Yale University Press, 1971. Vol. 9 of *The Yale Edition of Horace Walpole's Correspondence*. Gen. ed. William S. Lewis. 48 vols. 1937–83.

Webster, John. *The Duchess of Malfi*. Ed. John Russell Brown. Manchester: Manchester University Press, 1974.

2

Beyond reason: *Hamlet* and early modern stage ghosts

Catherine Belsey

The novelty of *Hamlet*

Gothic novelists, we know, regularly claimed descent from *Hamlet*, appropriating Shakespeare's authority, even when they transformed what they borrowed.[1] Were they simply cashing in on the stature of the writer who in the eighteenth century was fast becoming Britain's national poet, or were there deeper grounds for finding in the play a Gothic quality that our preference for psychological realism has tended to obscure? If we shift our focus from the sensitive prince to his spectral namesake, *Hamlet* dwells on the mysterious and the unaccountable. At the moment when early modern culture might be seen as gathering strength for the affirmation of science's power to map the world, while also preparing to specify the capacity for rational thought as the condition of human existence, Shakespeare's apparition defies the logic that guarantees both knowledge and the reasoning subject. To that degree, *Hamlet* explicitly refuses what would in due course become Enlightenment belief, pointing, if only in fiction, to the limitations of that orthodoxy. The imagination, it seemed, recognized more things in heaven and earth than were dreamt of in official philosophy (*Hamlet* 1.5.174–5).[2]

Although the Gothic novelists were not likely to have known it, as far as we can tell from the surviving evidence, Shakespeare's uncanny apparition represents a new departure in early modern drama, and the fascination of what exceeds mortal understanding was eagerly taken up by some of the dramatist's own contemporaries. Perhaps they, too, detected in *Hamlet* a direction in which fiction might extend its reach. If so, no wonder later Gothic novelists, exploring, behind the back of the Enlightenment, anxieties that reason preferred to ignore, saw in Shakespeare's play concerns that vindicated their own.

The novelty of *Hamlet* shows up by comparison with Thomas Kyd's *Spanish Tragedy*, initially performed in the 1580s, just over a decade earlier. The ghost of Andrea performs a prologue to Kyd's play, in the company of Revenge. This personified abstraction may represent

Andrea's deepest wish, as well as the promise of dark deeds to come when the action develops, but it is the ghost who holds the attention of the audience while he tells his story. A courtier and a lover, Don Andrea was killed, he recounts, fighting for his country. As soon as his friend Horatio had interred his body with all due rites, Charon ferried the dead Andrea to a Virgilian underworld. But the infernal judges, at odds over where to place him, directed him to Pluto's tower for a decision. On the way, he tells us, he glimpsed the deepest pit of hell, where classical imagery joined forces with medieval Christian iconography to show the Furies wielding their whips and Ixion turning his wheel, while usurers were forced to swallow molten gold, lecherous couples were wound about by serpents and perjurers were scalded in boiling lead. But hell was not to be Andrea's destiny. Instead, Proserpina returned him to the upper world in the company of Revenge, who now announces that there is earthly vengeance to come for Andrea's death. The two will sit and watch, Kyd's Revenge declares, 'And serve for Chorus in this tragedy' (*The Spanish Tragedy* 1.1.91). As the play goes on, the odd couple will witness the action from their choric space, without intervening directly in the story. If Andrea is gratified by the eventual outcome, he remains a spectator, not its motivating force.

We do not know how Andrea's ghost was presented. Did he wear the clothes of the courtier he once was, or the armour he died in? Alternatively, perhaps he appeared in a white shroud, flecked with mud from the grave. Was his face whitened with flour to convey the pallor of death? All these options are suggested by hints in other plays of the period (Dessen and Thomson 100),[3] but the text we have of *The Spanish Tragedy* gives no indication of the likely choices. In all other particulars Andrea might as well be a living being. Although he does not interact with the participants in the plot, he is clearly identified from the start by a name and a history. The ghost's utterances are gruesome; his exchanges with Revenge generate fearful expectations concerning what is to follow; but he is not uncanny.

How different, then, is the introduction of the Ghost in *Hamlet*. Our own anachronistic expectations have tended to obscure the mystery that surrounds his appearance. We prefer our wraiths ethereal and flickering, so that this solid apparition, clothed from head to foot in steel, seems altogether too substantial to be truly frightening to modern audiences. But if we set that thought aside for a moment, the role of the former King of Denmark is unlike Andrea's in almost every way. First, the Ghost plays a major part in the action of *Hamlet*. Without him there would presumably be no story: nothing, indeed, but a mourning prince forbidden the outlet of suicide by divine law. And second, Shakespeare invests this occult figure with mounting suspense. The Ghost appears to the guards at one o'clock in the morning, 'In the dead waste and middle of the night' (1.2.198), just as Marcellus begins the unnerving tale of their previous encounter at the same hour. Who or what is 'it', or 'he' ('a')? Their pronouns vary uncertainly. It *looks like* the dead king ... The figure offers no response to their fearful questions but vanishes as unaccountably as it came. Is it an omen, they wonder. At its second appearance, the phantom seems about to speak, when the cock crows to herald the dawn that dispels such creatures of the dark. In the event, the Ghost declares his identity only at a third manifestation, and then only to Hamlet, who risks his life and sanity to follow, as the spectre silently beckons him to a more solitary place.

Unlike Andrea, Old Hamlet is forbidden to tell the secrets of the world beyond the grave, though the little he does reveal about that purgatorial place is probably more terrifying than any detailed description might prove. Clearly, this revenant exists among the living as objectively as fiction permits: he first appears to bystanders whose minds, if not clear, are surely free of any obsession with Old Hamlet's death. And yet, when the prince becomes aware of the Ghost again in Gertrude's closet, the queen can see nothing. Could the spectral father that now returns be no more, after all, than a projection of the prince's distressed imagination? *Hamlet* raises the question but offers no conclusive answer.

The pre-Shakespearean Gothic that invests stage ghosts with terror is above all literary and classical. Putting on display the education provided by the grammar schools, dramatists drew lavishly on Seneca's plays and Virgil's *Aeneid* to create a range of variously tormented and vengeful spectres, whose appearance does much to deepen the horror of the plays but makes very little impact on their plots. Such ghosts inhabit a parallel plane that may never act directly on the world of the living characters. Seneca's own dead Thyestes and Tantalus appear only as prologues, and much English Seneca follows this pattern. Like Andrea, the ghost of Gorlois performs a purely choric role, delivering the prologue and conclusion to *The Misfortunes of Arthur* (1588) from an undefined space. Gorlois has come up from a classical underworld, to which, his vengeful mission duly accomplished, he descends again at the end of the play. *The Battle of Alcazar* (1588–89) confines its three ghosts to the dumb shows that precede Acts 2 and 3, where their companions are Nemesis and three Furies. Other Senecan phantoms appear in dreams, as they do in Shakespeare's *Richard III*.[4] In the early 1590s, Thomas of Woodstock is warned in a dream by the ghosts of the Black Prince and Edward III.

Time and place are a matter of indifference. Revenants who appear in the course of the action materialize wherever the context requires.

Thomas Heywood's Doctor Shaw, who has villainously misinterpreted Friar Anselm's prophecy, is reproached by the dead mendicant in his study, as he is 'pensively reading on his book' (*2 Edward IV* (1599), scene 19.0 SD). But more commonly their realm barely connects with the world of the living. In *Octavia*, ascribed to Seneca, the ghost of Agrippina speaks on the morning of the day Nero is to marry Poppaea, but she does not interact with the other characters: instead, she offers what is in effect a prologue to the wedding (lines 593–645). The ghosts in *Locrine* (1585–94) similarly preface the battles. After prophesying vengeance, Corineus stands aside (5.5.30 SD) to witness the martial encounter.[5]

Hamlet, however, was to introduce new options. There, without abandoning Seneca, Shakespeare also invoked, I have argued, the popular tradition of fireside ghost stories,[6] and in the process not only integrated the supernatural more firmly into the action, and gave it a specific setting, but also introduced features from vernacular narrative: mystery, uncertainty, equivocation — the components, in other words, of the uncanny. The enigma that now entered into their representation centred on the nature of the walking dead. 'What art thou?', asks the harrowed Horatio (*Hamlet* 1.1.49), echoing the question Brutus had addressed to the ghost of Caesar only slightly earlier: 'Art thou some god, some angel, or some devil / That mak'st my blood cold, and my hair to stare? / Speak to me what thou art' (*Julius Caesar* 4.3.276–8).[7] How were they to be understood, these figures who deconstructed the opposition between life and death? Were they bodies back from the grave, or spirits now divorced from the materiality of the flesh? Alternatively, were these apparitions better regarded as illusory, a creation of the mind, prompted by the sorrow or guilt of those who saw them? The uncertainties *Hamlet* foregrounded would in due course make their way into later Gothic fiction, but some of Shakespeare's own fellow-dramatists, too, were ready to profit from his invocation of the textual strategies that might have characterized a spine-tingling story recounted by an old woman on a winter's night.

The macabre

Like the former king of Denmark, the ghosts of the fireside tales were generally more material than our own. *Hamlet* must have been written between 1599 and 1601. At about the same time, John Marston was at work on *Antonio's Revenge*, which overlaps with the plot of *Hamlet*. We are not sure whether Marston borrowed from Shakespeare, or Shakespeare from Marston. Alternatively, perhaps they were both working, either independently or in collusion, from a common source, probably Kyd's lost *Hamlet*. Scholarly debate leaves unresolved the question of priority[8] but, for that very reason, *Antonio's Revenge* throws into relief both the difference of *Hamlet* and the distinct innovations that characterized Marston's own play.

The stories are close enough to justify comparison. Marston's villain murders Antonio's father, Andrugio, for love of his mother; he also has designs on Antonio, who masquerades as a fool. At one point the protagonist comes on 'with a book' and 'in black' (*Antonio's Revenge* 2.3.0 SD). Andrugio's ghost appears at dead of night to urge his son to revenge but, when he speaks, the classical tradition is strongly in evidence. He has not yet touched the 'banks of rest' on the other side of the Styx; he invokes Nemesis; and he ends with a Latin tag from Seneca's *Thyestes*: '*Scelera non ulcisceris, nisi vincis*' ('You do not avenge crimes unless you surpass them', *Thyestes*, lines 195–6; *Antonio's Revenge* 3.1.42–51).

If, however, the plot of *Antonio's Revenge* resembles *Hamlet* and the ghost invokes Roman drama, the setting of Marston's grisly apparition is different from either. No suspense attends his appearance: instead, it is as if Antonio conjures him inadvertently from the grave. The hero visits his father's sepulchre in St Mark's Church at midnight and the text dwells on the gloom of that dismal place, lit in the 'swart night' (3.1.1) only by tapers. The physicality of death is uppermost, as Antonio apologizes for his intrusion to those interred there:

> Graves, vaults, and tombs, groan not to bear my weight,
> Cold flesh, bleak trunks, wrapped in your half-rot shrouds,
> I press you softly with a tender foot.
>
> (3.1.9–11)

Indeed, Antonio continues, he too will soon be dead and buried, kissing his 'cold' father 'with bloodless lips': 'I pray thee, grave, / Provide soft mould to wrap my carcass in' 3.1.14–16).

This emphasis on the fate of the body in the earth, transferred in *Hamlet* mainly to the churchyard scene (5.1), owes nothing to Seneca or to Virgil. Instead, it stems from a medieval preoccupation with decomposition in the grave. The fifteenth century witnessed a fashion for *transi* tombs that depicted in life-size stone the emaciated corpse in its shroud. Meanwhile, a good many English parish churches included still older wall paintings of the legend of the Three Living and the Three Dead, where the revenants are distinguished by their tattered grave clothes and the worms that devour their entrails.[9] In the play, as Antonio addresses his father's 'mighty spirit' (3.1.27), a voice unexpectedly replies. There is no original stage direction, but the ghost's words make clear that a spectral figure rises from the sepulchre itself, tearing his wrappings as he does so:

> Thy pangs of anguish rip my cerecloth up;
> And lo, the ghost of old Andrugio
> Forsakes his coffin!

(3.1.32–4)

Such a *coup de théâtre* has no precedent among extant Elizabethan plays.[10] It is startling, gruesome, macabre, rather than uncanny.[11]

While Senecan shades return from a classical underworld, stage ghosts with a debt to the vernacular tradition come direct from their burial places. The *Woodstock* phantoms both announce that they have left their tombs (*Thomas of Woodstock* 5.1.58, 80). In Robert Greene's *Alphonsus King of Aragon* (1599) the reluctant ghost of Calchas is summoned from his rest by the witch Medea. 'What meanst thou thus to call me from my grave?' he asks querulously (line 955). When Marston so sensationally dramatizes what these earlier plays only name, placing his phantom among the tombs at the dead of night, he takes over for the stage a long-standing convention of popular ghost stories. A fifteenth century monk of Byland Abbey, who recorded what sound very like the fireside tales of his locality, tells that Robert of Boltby took to leaving his grave in the night and frightening the villagers of Kilburn. When the young men of the community assembled in the churchyard to intercept him, Robert Foxton was able to catch him on the way out. He placed this thoroughly corporeal revenant on the church stile and ran for the priest, calling out to his companion to hold on to the ghost until he got back. The same monk also noted down the tale of James Tankerlay, buried in the grounds of the Byland Abbey itself. Tankerlay made a habit of walking by night back to his home in Kirby, where he violently assaulted his former mistress. The monks put a stop to these nocturnal adventures by having Tankerlay's body dug up and tipped into Gormire Lake (James, 'Twelve Medieval Ghost Stories' 418).[12]

Unlike Andrugio and the Byland ghosts, classical phantoms are disembodied shades.[13] Kyd's Andrea makes Christian dualism confirm the classical tradition. Andrea is now a spirit, transformed by death from the time 'When this eternal substance of my soul / Did live imprison'd in my wanton flesh, / Each in their function serving other's need' (*The Spanish Tragedy* 1.1.1–3). The alternative understanding of ghosts as bodies back from the tomb has its roots in another pre-Christian customary belief. This appears in its purest form in the Icelandic sagas, where the dead all too often returned to harm the living, but the belief was widespread all over Europe (see Lecouteux). And despite the superimposition of Christianity on pagan ghost lore, if Reginald Scot,

Thomas Lodge and Samuel Harsnett are to be believed, early modern England continued to perceive churchyards as all too likely to 'yawn', yielding up their dead in the hours of darkness (*Hamlet* 3.2.391, cf. *Julius Caesar* 2.2.18). Places of burial still terrified the superstitious, they complained.[14]

Terror

What makes *Hamlet* special is its refusal to disentangle the strands of the intertextual heritage that goes to compose early modern ghost stories. Revenge is the Ghost's mission, in accordance with English Seneca. And purgatory is there, updating the Virgilian underworld described so graphically by Andrea (*Hamlet* 1.5.11–13). But is the apparition a 'spirit', as it claims (1.5.9), or a figurative 'mole' that belongs in the earth (1.5.170)? Should Marcellus strike it with his spear, or is Old Hamlet 'as the air, invulnerable', like Virgil's shades (1.1.50)? Has he burst his grave clothes, like Andrugio, and been cast up by the sepulchre as a 'dead corse' to walk the living world (1.4.47–52)? Above all, is he dangerous, in accordance with the pagan European tradition? The guards certainly think so and do their best to keep Hamlet from following his beckoning hand. 'What art thou?' The repeated probing, and the impossibility of resolving the questions posed, invest this ghost with an eeriness that, as far as the extant evidence goes, the stage had not witnessed before, conferring on the apparition a power 'to shake our disposition / With thoughts beyond the reaches of our souls' (1.4.55–6). Old Hamlet, in other words, threatens the stability of what culture gave the audience to know.

The strangeness of Shakespeare's visitant from another world is compounded by the terror of the characters in the story. Kyd's Andrea and the other stage ghosts I have named may have frightened playgoers but, even when they participate in the action of the play, there is little evidence that they had the same effect on the fictional characters they haunted. We may suppose that Marston's Antonio reacts with horror to the spectacle of the resurrected Andrugio, but the text gives this assumption no support until the later Antonio, now a bloody revenger, claims he no longer fears the revenant (*Antonio's Revenge* 3.5.14–16). The dead Andrugio also shocks his wife, when she draws the curtains to reveal him sitting on her bed: 'Amazing terror, what portent is this?' (3.4.64). But she says no more and her tears, it seems, are the effect of shame, not fear. By contrast, anxiety pervades the first act of *Hamlet*. As the play opens, the guards are already jumpy: 'Who's there?' 'Nay, answer me' (*Hamlet* 1.1.1–2). Francisco, who has completed his watch, is 'sick at heart' (1.1.9). 'What, has this thing appear'd again tonight?' asks the sceptic, Horatio (1.1.24). His perturbation, when he can no longer doubt the apparition, is the more pronounced: 'It harrows me with fear and wonder' (1.1.47).[15] 'Angels and ministers of grace defend us!' Hamlet exclaims, when at last he faces the spectre (1.4.39).

Terror is also a key experience in the popular narrative tradition. John Audelay's Three Living kings shake with fright as they confront their Dead similitudes. In the Byland tales, a ploughman flees in mid-conversation when he sees a spirit tearing at his companion's clothes (James, 'Twelve Medieval Ghost Stories' 419). Although the young men of the village agree to catch Robert of Boltby in the churchyard, all but two of them run away the moment he comes out of his grave. The fear was variously rationalized: revenants did physical damage; they spread pestilence; their interlocutors might die. But in practice this was no ordinary anxiety: animals, knowing nothing of reasons, confirmed the human awareness of a confrontation with the unaccountable. The oxen practically drowned for fear as they tipped James Tankerlay into Gormire Lake; in another fifteenth century tale, when William of Bradford saw a pale horse on the dark road before him, his little dog whimpered and cowered between its master's legs (James, 'Twelve Medieval Ghost Stories' 419). Audelay's verse narrative of 'The Three Living and the Three Dead' records that the first king's horse stands stock still at the sight of the ghosts, while his falcon drops to his fist in panic (lines 55–6). By such means the tales convey to their hearers the quality of a more than mortal terror, pointing to fears beyond the range of rationality.

It has become fashionable to explain Old Hamlet and his vernacular predecessors as remnants of the Catholic purgatory. But European ghost lore was well established long before the twelfth century, when the Church first thought of providing a phase of purgation for the deceased that would permit their returning spirits to solicit funds for the institution. And the surviving fireside tales often invest the walking dead with purposes quite incompatible with Christian orthodoxy. They may be substantial and threatening; they are also unpredictable and perplexing. Indifferent to the laws of nature and logic, which draw a fast line between the living and the dead, ghost stories remain to puzzle the intellect, at least in fiction. *Hamlet* may or may not tell us about Shakespeare's religious allegiances. More adventurously, the play testifies, on the eve of the Cartesian and scientific Enlightenment, to the continued imaginative power of a realm of experience unaccountable to the *Cogito*.

Repercussions

If *Hamlet* changed the conventions, this was not instantly evident: the stage in the new century was not immediately taken over by a parade of uncanny ghosts. Predictably, Ben Jonson resolutely maintains the classical tradition: the ghost of Sylla appears as the prologue to *Catiline* (1611), quotes Seneca's *Thyestes* and then leaves the action to unfold. Marston meanwhile, continues to combine sensation with Seneca in *Sophonisba* (1604–6), where Syphax conjures a ghost 'Out of the altar' as he kneels there. 'What damned air is formed / Into that shape?' asks this villain, choosing not to be mystified by anything more than the revenant's name. He also refuses to be afraid: 'Our flesh knows not ignoble tremblings' (*The Tragedy of Sophonisba* 5.1.38 SD, 39–41). The classical allegiance of George Chapman's *The Revenge of Bussy D'Ambois* (1607–12), too, is made clear by the stage direction defining the appearance of the ghost at the beginning of Act 5: '*Ascendit* Umbra Bussy'. The shade speaks in Senecan manner of his rise from 'the chaos of eternal night' (5.1.1). He has come back, he says, for justice. When Umbra reappears to whet the hero's purpose, the woman who loved him steps forward, but this revenant, like Virgil's ghosts, prohibits close contact: 'Forbear! The air, in which / My figure's likeness is impress'd, will blast' (5.3.48–9).

However, this play adds a new twist to the familiar pattern. Once the arrangements are duly made for the revenge he requires, Umbra promises a triumphal dance of the dead in celebration. And indeed, when Clermont kills Montsurry, '*Music, and the Ghost of* Bussy *enters, leading the Ghosts of the* Guise, Monsieur, Cardinal Guise, *and* Chatillon; *they dance about the dead body and exeunt*' (5.5.119 SD). But the play is determined to dispel any mystery. Clermont, as a reasonable man, doggedly explains the apparition:

> That spirits should rise in these times yet are fables,
> Though learned'st men hold that our sensive spirits
> A little time abide about the graves
> Of their deceased bodies, and can take
> In cold condens'd air the same forms they had
> When they were shut up in this body's shade.
>
> (5.5.133–8)

This determination to rationalize the uncanny differs from the tradition of fireside tales by as much as it anticipates the scientific aspirations of the Enlightenment.

Nevertheless, Shakespeare's tragedy was influential. *The First Part of Hieronimo*, a forepiece to *The Spanish Tragedy*, may just possibly offer an example. This play, probably Kyd's work in the first instance, seems to have been revised in 1603–4 and printed in 1605, long after his death. *1 Hieronimo* tells the story of Andrea up to the moment of his passage to the underworld. The presentation of the dead Andrea here differs radically from that of his ghost in the sequel. This grateful revenant mingles with the other characters, longing to thank his friend Horatio for according him due funeral rites. But Revenge prevents the wraith from speaking: the secrets of the dead, so copiously reported in *The Spanish Tragedy*, must not be revealed, Revenge here declares, to ears of flesh and blood (*1 Hieronimo* xii.11–14; cf. *Hamlet* 1.5.21–2). Moreover, like Old Hamlet in his mother's closet, the 'pale' Andrea (xii.5) remains invisible to all but his addressee. 'Look you how pale he glares', says the prince (*Hamlet* 3.4.125), but Gertrude can see nothing: 'This is the very coinage of your brain' (3.4.139). 'See', urges Horatio in *Hieronimo*, while Lorenzo replies, 'It is your love that shapes this apprehension'. 'Do you not see him plainly, lords?' insists Horatio (xii.2–4). But they do not: the ghost is perceptible only to Horatio and the audience.

Is it possible that *1 Hieronimo* owes these details to *Hamlet*? Perhaps the reshaping of Kyd's original paid tribute to Shakespeare's success. This must remain conjectural,[16] but we are on surer ground with Thomas Heywood's *The Second Part of the Iron Age* (?1612). Heywood's play covers some of the same terrain as the Player's speech in *Hamlet*. The story of the fall of Troy was well known from Virgil as 'Aeneas' tale to Dido' (*Hamlet* 2.2.447) and was much rehearsed in early modern England. Even so, textual echoes of Shakespeare's tragedy indicate that *Hamlet* played a part in the composition of this work.[17] Shakespeare is also detectable in the presentation of the revenants. At the end of Act 2, Heywood's Aeneas sees Hector's ghost:

> What art thou that with such a grim aspect,
> In this black night so darke and turbulent,
> Haunts me in every corner of my house?
>
> (*2 Iron Age* 384)[18]

'What art thou?' As if to confirm its relation to *Hamlet*, Act 5 of *2 Iron Age* turns its attention to the parallel story of Orestes, whose mother Clytemnestra joined with her lover to kill his father. This far less reluctant revenger appeals to heaven and hell for a sign, thus conjuring the ghost of his father, Agamemnon. The spectre rehearses his wrongs in dumb show, '*poynting unto his wounds: and then to* Egistus *and the* Queene, *who were his murderers, which done, hee vanisheth.*' Orestes calls him 'Godlike shape' (*2 Iron Age* 423; cf. *Hamlet* 3.4.56–61), while Clytemnestra sees nothing.

The uncanny

And yet, for all Shakespeare's likely influence in matters of detail, none of these ghosts is truly eerie, calculated to make the blood cold or the hair stand on end. Perhaps they are too perfunctory; some are not bearers of terror but broadly benign; above all, no suspense attends their appearance, no horrified fascination anticipates their utterances. They owe more to the classical heritage than to the popular tradition of fireside ghost stories. Andrea in *1 Hieronimo* is ferried off by Charon; Heywood's Hector quotes Virgil in Latin; his Agamemnon has left the Elysian fields to bear witness to the crime against him. Shakespeare's modification of the early modern Gothic has not penetrated deeply here.

Instead, my paradoxical proposition is that *Hamlet*'s alteration of the paradigm is most evident where the direct influence of Shakespeare's tragedy on text or plot may be least apparent, in those plays where, without losing their power to shock, ghosts also disturb the coherence of the world they invade. The possibilities Shakespeare opens up are most fully developed where mystery is sustained, good sense is troubled, or equivocation evades rational resolution. The ghost of Alonzo in *The Changeling* (1622), for example, owes nothing obvious to Old Hamlet, but the apparition is peculiarly disconcerting in a way that English Seneca is not. At the beginning of Act 4 a dumb show summarizes the marriage of Beatrice-Joanna to her chosen Alsemero in the absence of her father's choice, Alonzo. De Flores, bringing up the rear of the wedding procession, is smiling in celebration of his own prior sexual possession of the bride, when '*Alonzo's ghost appears to De Flores in the midst of his smile, startles him, showing him the hand whose finger he had cut off*' (*The Changeling*).

The most unsettling feature of this episode must be what is *not* there, the missing finger, which has taken on a posthumous life of its own in the course of the play. First, De Flores cuts it off his murdered victim's body in his effort to remove a diamond ring as proof that Alonzo is dead. But the ring will not come off the finger ('Not part in death?', exclaims De Flores (3.2.25)). This ring, it turns out, had been the first keepsake Beatrice sent her suitor. The dead finger, then, represents more than evidence of the crime: it is also an emblem of Alonzo's reluctance to relinquish his promised wife. De Flores passes on the amputated member as his own 'token' to Beatrice, with a macabre joke, reaffirming the point, in case we had missed it the first time, that the offering 'was sent somewhat unwillingly: / I could not get the ring without the finger' (3.4.27–9).

The phallic threat implied by this gift is obvious to a post-Freudian generation and was probably not lost on early modern playgoers.[19] In addition, it is worth noting that Freud's own exploration of the uncanny in fiction begins with the story of the Sandman, who so frightens Nathaniel because he is able to make children's eyes jump out of their heads (Freud 348–9). Severed organs, whether or not they symbolize castration, are capable of exciting a special frisson. Such detached body parts were not uncommon in early modern drama, among them the hand of Titus Andronicus, Hieronimo's tongue and the dead man's hand that Ferdinand gives the Duchess of Malfi. But in *The Changeling* this miniature corporeal revenant seems in addition to 'walk', as it circulates among Beatrice and her suitors.

The solution must be to return it to the grave. When Beatrice-Joanna recoils, De Flores makes light of the matter: a greedy hand thrust into a dish might as easily, he assures her, lose a finger to another's knife (3.4.33–4). Beatrice comes to terms with the event, as she will with the rape that follows. 'I pray', she impels him, 'bury the finger' (3.4.43). It is surely not illegitimate to imagine for an instant a miniature sepulchre, complete with little cerecloth, for the errant member. When, in the following scene, Alonzo's ghost shows De Flores and the audience his hand, all this accumulated imagery of possessive sexuality, gluttony and interment is invoked by the absent finger.

But the ghost is not appeased by the return of the missing part. At the moment when De Flores plots his final triumph, the fire designed to give him absolute possession of Beatrice, Alonzo appears again. 'What art thou?' exclaims De Flores (5.1.58). This time the spectre comes between his interlocutor and the starlight but, hardened in crime, the villain dismisses it as no more than 'a mist of conscience'. Beatrice, however, senses its eerie presence too:

> Who's that, De Flores? Bless me! It slides by.
> Some ill thing haunts the house; 't'as left behind it
> A shivering sweat upon me: I'm afraid now.
>
> (5.1.61–3)

'Who ...? It': Some unspecified incarnation of anxiety leaves Beatrice chilled as it slips past them without friction. By now, the play has earned the right to invoke the uncanny with no more detailed preparation.

The Changeling was the work of Middleton and Rowley. Ten or twelve years earlier, if *The Lady's Tragedy* is also his, Middleton had experimented in a different key with the macabre and the spectral. This play, also known as *The Second Maiden's Tragedy*, manages to have it both ways: a corpse *and* a ghost. When the two appear on stage identically dressed, the unease that attaches to all doubles is deepened by the fact that in this instance the revenants are one and the same person. The

Lady of the play has killed herself rather than submit to the desires of
the usurping Tyrant, who violates her tomb to put her dead body on
display as his mistress. Meanwhile, her spirit appears to her virtuous
lover, the rightful ruler, imploring him to restore the rest she cannot
enjoy while her body remains unburied.

Middleton's play is evidently concerned with the visual effects of its
uncanny invention: the sanctified spirit that materializes from the tomb
wears white, while the exhumed body is to be dressed '*in black velvet
which sets out the paleness of the hands and face*' (*The Lady's Tragedy*
A/B 5.2.13 SD).[20] As the Tyrant succumbs to poison, however, the spirit
reappears in identical black velvet. The original stage direction reads:
'*Enter the Ghost in the same form as the Lady is dressed in the chair*'
(A 5.2.153/B 5.2.128 SD). At this replication of images, even the necrophile Tyrant is perturbed: 'I called not thee, thou enemy to firmness, /
Mortality's earthquake!' (A 5.2.154–5/B 5.2.129–30). The ghost attends
the body as it is carried out for burial.

In one sense, the play only dramatizes orthodox Christian dualism:
flesh and spirit, interdependent in life, as Andrea explained in *The
Spanish Tragedy*, are separated irreversibly in death. The flesh is inert;
animation now belongs to the spirit alone. But we might suppose that
the soul, free of its earthly ties, would have no further concern with
the materiality of the discarded remains. Indeed, St Augustine, whose
doctrinal authority was paramount in the period, insisted that the
deceased are indifferent to the world they have left behind. Moreover,
remaining unburied was no impediment to Christian salvation. And yet
the fate of her body so disturbs the Lady's spirit that she comes back
to reclaim it. Augustine's point was that the dead did not return,[21] and
the Reformed clergy accordingly did their best to eliminate belief in
ghosts. They insisted that so-called spectres must be demons impersonating the dead, a likelihood the melancholy prince also considers
(*Hamlet* 1.4.40–2; 2.2.594–9). But the belief that the body would rise at
the Last Day, reaffirmed weekly in the recitation of the Anglican Creed,
seemed to license concessions to a less rigorous popular lore that refused
to surrender belief in ghosts, and ascribed to them varying degrees of
corporeality. It accords with classical tradition, too, that the Lady's
shade is unable to be at peace while her body is unburied. The question
this play's strange visual doubling leaves undecided is the nature of the
relationship between them. Does the interdependence of body and soul
survive death after all? If so, what exactly is it that either rests in the
grave or walks the earth?

Although the play makes proper reference to religious belief ('Thy
body shall return [to the grave] to rise again', confirms the reinstated

ruler (A 5.2.162/B 5.2.137)), *The Lady's Tragedy* is not a theological treatise but a play.[22] Where divinity in this period, while conceding that certain mysteries of the faith remained inaccessible to earthly reason, predominantly sought answers, early modern drama evidently relished the inexplicable and the undecided. When fiction privileges what exercises the imagination over what solicits conviction, when, in other words, it exceeds the bounds imposed by realism, it throws into relief the fears orthodoxy cannot accommodate. It was above all on the stage, the place, by definition, of illusion and magic, that the unknowable continued to exercise its uncanny compulsion, without insisting on the finality of resolution.

Indeed, fiction might precisely offer improbability as its own form of knowledge. Doesn't John Webster's *Duchess of Malfi* (1614) incite us to adopt the very possibility that common sense denies? In some respects this is the play that most sharply anticipates the strategies of the later novel, when it specifies a ruined abbey as the site of its supernatural encounter. Gothic prose fiction would go on to exploit the ominous possibilities of place, as well as time. In *The Monk*, for instance, as Raymond waits at one in the morning for his beloved Agnes, he reflects on the ancient building before him, 'Its ponderous walls ... its old and partly ruined towers ... its lofty battlements, overgrown with ivy' (Lewis 135). Contemporary writers also favoured castles and convents by night, in a state of decay and covered with creeper. Ruins, they knew, evoked death and decomposition, as well as a bygone and more superstitious age.

Ann Radcliffe credited *Hamlet* with creating on the battlements at Elsinore a context where each detail contributed to the awed expectation that awaits the apparition (Radcliffe 166). She is right to do so, but the tradition of haunted places goes further back in popular convention. The Three Dead appear in the forest, in mist and fog; the Byland tales name their own settings: a crossroads at night, the remote Lake Gormire, Kilburn churchyard, the grounds of the abbey. These are all liminal locations, likely contexts for the unexpected or the hitherto unseen. *Antonio's Revenge* situates its ghost in a church at midnight. But it was Webster who was to construct in the greatest detail a Gothic background for the Echo from the Duchess of Malfi's grave. Anticipating later novels, this text dwells on the 'the ruins of an ancient abbey' (5.3.2), where Antonio walks by night with Delio, fearful for his wife's safety. Part of a cloister yields an echo, 'So hollow, and so dismal', but so clear, 'That many have supposed it is a spirit / That answers' (5.3.6, 8–9). 'I do love these ancient ruins', Antonio reiterates. To be sure, in this space now open to 'stormy weather' (5.3.14) lie some who counted on shelter for their monuments until Doomsday. 'But all things have their end', Antonio reflects (5.3.17).

The decay of the buildings prompts him to recognize that churches too must have 'like death that we have' – and the Echo repeats his phrase (5.3.19). By analogy with the double, an echo is unsettlingly at once the same and different. In this instance, the repetition invests Antonio's utterance with new and sinister meanings. It is impossible, he continues, to fly your fate. 'O *fly your fate!*', reiterates the echo from the grave (5.3.35). He will not talk with a mere echo: 'Thou art a dead thing'. But '*Thou art a dead thing*', intones the voice (5.3.39). Delio takes the sound we have heard as a trick of the stonework (5.3.36) and the corresponding glimpse of his wife that it presents to Antonio's imagination as 'Your fancy, merely' (5.3.46). But dramatic irony confirms the implications of the setting. Knowing already that the Duchess is dead, playgoers are encouraged to share Antonio's apprehension that these exchanges are more than illusions, just as in due course the scene-painting in *The Monk* will incite readers to fear that the figure who emerges from the ivy-clad ruin will not be the living Agnes.

Projection

From the moment that *Hamlet* dwells on the Ghost's visibility to the prince but not to his mother, it comes within the bounds of possibility that revenants are no more than projections of the living mind. Melancholy could generate illusions, it was widely believed, and Hamlet concedes the possibility that the devil may be exploiting his condition (2.2.602–5). In other instances, guilt is identified as the cause of selective visibility. When the ghost of Friar Anselm reproaches Doctor Shaw in Heywood's *2 Edward IV*, the Messenger cannot see him, but in this instance the difference is immediately rendered intelligible: 'No, thy untainted soul / Cannot discern the horrors that I do', explains Shaw (19.58–9). The implication here is that such sights are objectively there, to be recognized by the guilty. If anyone is guilty in the closet scene, however, it is Gertrude, and she assures her son, 'This is the very coinage of your brain'.

Perhaps it is: the play leaves the question unresolved. On the one hand, the stage direction makes clear that the audience sees the Ghost; on the other, how else, we might reasonably ask, can drama present the content of a fantasy? When Horatio urges Old Hamlet, 'Stay, illusion' (1.1.130), he knows that it is no mirage: something, whether spirit of health or goblin damned (1.4.40), assumes the King of Denmark's person (1.2.244). Its existence is confirmed by the innocent guards.

But in Gertrude's closet, by contrast, the only available witness sees nothing. If, in the first place, ghosts raise the possibility that there are phenomena mortal thought cannot readily accommodate, they also pose the question, in the second, whether we can trust our minds not to deceive us.

Only decades before the *Cogito*, fiction faces consciousness with two distinct but related problems. Is the world amenable to reason? Can we be sure it exists independent of our own minds? René Descartes, born in 1596, would soon confront very similar questions. He would go on, however, to ground the reliability of cognition on the certainty of thinking itself. But what if thinking in turn were subject to imperatives it could not command? Cyril Tourneur's *The Atheist's Tragedy* (1611) comes close to embracing that option. This play rewrites (and reverses) *Hamlet*, adding more plot and more sensationalism, while clearing away the ethical ambiguities that face the reflective prince. In Tourneur's drama the retributive impulse, however natural, is declared contrary to the will of God. The ghost is firm with his son on this point: 'Attend with patience the success of things, / But leave revenge unto the King of kings' (2.6.21–2). Charlemont is a soldier, not a student, and his readiness to avenge his father's death is not in question. But Montferrers, murdered by his brother, returns a second time, not to reinvigorate his son's violent purpose but, instead, to remind him of the divine law against personal vengeance.

This play's debt to the presentation of Old Hamlet is readily apparent. Three soldiers are on guard, this time including the hero, although now it is Charlemont who wears armour. The time is one o'clock on a foul and stormy night. Oddly enough, however, Charlemont finds he cannot keep his eyes open and, as he falls asleep, his dead father appears in order to announce his own demise. The waking Charlemont is appalled and puzzled. Dream lore does not account for the apparition: he has not been anxious about his father; he is not given to fearful fantasies. Is it a message from his Genius? Heaven forbid! The Sergeant has gone on his round; the Musketeer has seen nothing. It must surely have been a nightmare. And Charlemont reflects on the strange powers of the mind to falsify perceptions and conflate impressions. In his dream he must have confused some violent event of the present war with the memory of his father (2.6.23–61).

This detailed exploration of the psychological processes involved in nightmares is unusual at this time. Medieval dreams, as we know from *The Nun's Priest's Tale*, may be the effect of an imbalance in the humours, but equally, it might be wise not to dismiss them too easily: the gods – and demons – speak in dreams. The ghosts who appear in their sleep to

Woodstock, Shakespeare's Richard III and Richmond, and Posthumus in *Cymbeline* are to be taken seriously. On the other hand, early modern sceptics derided the many surviving attempts at supernatural interpretation: 'A dream', Thomas Nashe stoutly maintained, 'is nothing else but the echo of our conceits in the day'; 'a bubbling scum or froth of the fancy' (154, 153).[23] While Charlemont allows that his dream might be supernaturally authorized, he also shares some of Nashe's incredulity, but he is readier still to suppose the experience motivated by his own deeper concerns, a response to 'th' imaginary presence of / Some bloody accident upon my mind' (2.6.51–2) in conjunction with the remembrance of his father (2.6.54). Freud would go on to share the view that the material of dreams comes from recent impressions combined with old memories. Charlemont anticipates Freud in proposing that the subject is the origin of its own nocturnal reveries; at the same time, like Freud himself, he concedes that the sleeping mind does not control their content. At this moment Charlemont trembles on the brink of discovering the waywardness of the unconscious mind, in conflict with rational thought.[24]

Ghosts have, in other words, more than one way to shake our disposition with thoughts beyond the reaches of our souls. But, for all its sophistication, Charlemont's interpretation of his dream proves wrong. At the very moment when he dismisses the apparition as no more than fantasy, the ghost reappears to confute him. And this time it is the Musketeer who sees the revenant first, mistaking it for an intruder. He calls on the newcomer to halt but the ghost pays no attention. As the figure advances through the mist, he threatens it with his musket, but still the apparition comes on. The Musketeer fires and, eerily, the shot passes straight through the ghost. Recognizing that he is up against a spirit invulnerable as the air, the soldier takes to his heels, leaving Charlemont to repudiate his former disbelief. Although Montferrers walks with the most moral of purposes, resembling a *memento mori* rather than a demon (5.1.27–31), and although Charlemont's courage is not in question, this ghost is a source of terror. Compelled to acknowledge that the figure bearing down on him is unearthly, Charlemont 'fearfully avoids it', the stage direction indicates (2.6.66 SD).[25] In the event, then, the play exchanges one uncertainty for another: in place of the unconscious, it opts for the uncanny. It is unlikely that Descartes would have settled for either.

Equivocation

Unlike medieval corporeal revenants, Tourneur's ghosts are close to the ethereal phantoms of modernity, 'for their essence is / Above the nature and the order of / Those elements whereof our senses are / Created' (*The Atheist's Tragedy* 3.1.84–7). Such spirits are emanations of a realm inaccessible not only to living bodies but also to mortal comprehension. Revenants remain inexplicable, despite the best efforts of human understanding. The two possibilities this play confronts, the ghost as unconscious projection and the ghost as unearthly visitant from a different plane, will both be taken up in later Gothic fiction. Neither is firmly rooted in the stage tradition prior to *Hamlet*. Senecan ghosts are not fantasms generated by the subject, nor are they uncanny. In the classical tradition, phantoms are disembodied shades; according to popular narrative, by contrast, revenants may well be material enough to inflict substantial violence on their interlocutors; theology held them to be demons that assumed human shape; sceptics treated them as delusions. But Shakespeare blends existing conventions to change the parameters for fiction. *Hamlet* equivocates.

Ironically, perhaps the main beneficiary of *Hamlet*'s bequest to posterity was Shakespeare's own *Macbeth*, where the revenant is only one ambiguous element in a play of equivocations, visual as well as verbal. Banquo's ghost sits in Macbeth's place at the feast: the original stage direction makes this clear (*Macbeth* 3.4.40 SD); Simon Forman saw the spectre; later plays allude to the event. And yet none of the other guests perceives anything odd. Lady Macbeth recognizes only an effect of her husband's fear, nothing more palpable than the 'air-drawn dagger' we had taken to be imaginary (3.4.61). What Macbeth himself sees is not, it seems, a Senecan shade but a figure characteristic, as his wife so astutely observes, of 'A woman's story at a winter's fire, / Authoris'd by her grandam' (3.4.64–5),[26] the animated corpse of vernacular convention, back from the grave:

> let the earth hide thee!
> Thy bones are marrowless, thy blood is cold;
> Thou hast no speculation in those eyes,
> Which thou dost glare with.
>
> (3.4.92–5)

Is the protagonist deluded? The play does not stay for an answer. It dwells, instead, on a terror beyond the reaches of his soul. Macbeth is quite 'unmann'd' by the encounter (3.4.72):

> What man dare, I dare:
> Approach thou like the rugged Russian bear,

> The arm'd rhinoceros, or th'Hyrcan tiger;
> Take any shape but that, and my firm nerves
> Shall never tremble: or, be alive again,
> And dare me to the desert with thy sword;
> If trembling I inhabit then, protest me
> The baby of a girl. Hence, horrible shadow!
> Unreal mock'ry, hence! – [*Ghost disappears*]
>   Why, so; – being gone
> I am a man again.

                                          (3.4.98–107)

What exactly is the source of his fear? That the ghost is not, after all, corporeal like the tiger, but a shadow, and thus impervious to Macbeth's skill in battle? That it defies the laws of nature in walking after death? Or that it demonically projects as substance Macbeth's own culpability for the murder ('take any shape but that')? And what is it that unmans the hero? The idea of a supernatural world inaccessible to his physical prowess? The confrontation with a realm of experience beyond human knowledge? Or the recognition that his own mind generates an unreal mockery, a horrifying fantasm it cannot subjugate?

    Such questions, unresolved in the play, as they are in *Hamlet*, would go on to haunt the later Gothic novel, as it continued to permit in fiction the return of an undecidability Enlightenment science longed to dispel, naming, if only *as* fictions, the anxieties reason repudiates. Perhaps all equivocations culminate in that most uncanny of ghost stories, *The Turn of the Screw* (1898). Is it, then, a coincidence that Henry James's novella pays oblique tribute to *Hamlet*, when Peter Quint makes his first appearance to the governess on the battlements at Bly? As the text makes clear, these crenellated towers are not architecturally motivated. Incompatible stylistically with the rest of the house, they are 'incongruous', romantic 'absurdities'. What, then, prompts their inclusion in the tale as the first setting for the revenant, who moves from one corner of the 'platform' to the other (James, *Turn of the Screw* 15, 16), unless an intertextual invocation of an earlier 'platform', where two sentinels witnessed an apparition as they patrolled the battlements at Elsinore (*Hamlet* 1.2.213), and, with the allusion, an acknowledgement of *Hamlet*'s unsurpassed influence on the later development of the genre?

Notes

This chapter is for Thea Reifler, who put the question that prompted it.

  1 Discussion of *Hamlet*'s influence is pervasive in studies of the Gothic, but see in particular Townshend, Williams, Purinton and Desens, Charnes.

  2 Except where otherwise indicated, Shakespeare references are to *The Arden*

Shakespeare Complete Works.

3 See also Induction, *A Warning for Fair Women*, lines 54–5.

4 In Seneca's *Troades* Andromache recounts how the shade of Hector urged her in a dream to hide their son (*Tragedies*, lines 443–60). For an early modern version, see *Seneca His Tenne Tragedies*.

5 The spectral Albanact is visible at his second appearance to his enemy, who seems more resentful than afraid, as his dead foe's return exacerbates the pain of defeat (3.7.36–7).

6 Belsey, 'Shakespeare's Sad Tale for Winter'.

7 At this time, 'what art thou?' might properly be addressed to a person, inviting an answer in terms of name, position, calling. But it could also embrace the wider issue (Adamson).

8 For a summary of the arguments, see Shakespeare, *Hamlet*, ed. Thompson and Taylor, 51–2.

9 Images of the legend survive in a number of English parish churches. For a sophisticated version of the story, see the fourteenth-century Arundel Psalter, beautifully reproduced with commentary in Binksi (plate 8 and pp. 134–8).

10 We have no way of knowing whether the *ur-Hamlet* offered a parallel. Seneca's Agrippina bursts through the ground; his *Troades* includes an account of the ghost of Achilles tearing his way through a chasm in the earth and heaving up the tomb (180) but the time is dawn and the setting is wild nature, not a cemetery.

11 Not that earlier stage ghosts lacked shock value. Thunder and lightning accompanies the apparitions in *Woodstock* and the ghost of Corineus in *Locrine*. It seems that the effects were created by fireworks. According to the satirical Induction to *A Warning for Fair Women* (before 1599), whenever a spectre cries out for revenge, 'a little Rosen flasheth forth, / Like smoke out of a Tabacco pipe, or a boyes squib' (lines 59–60).

12 I have discussed the implications of the Byland tales in more detail in 'Shakespeare's Sad Tale for Winter' (14–22).

13 Virgil's Sibyl reminds Aeneas that he cannot fight the inhabitants of the underworld with his sword: They are *'tenuis sine corpore vitas'* (thin, bodiless lives) (*Aeneid* VI.292).

14 Scot 153, Nashe 148, Harsnett 134.

15 Nor, as Hamlet waits for the revenant in the cold night, is the audience deprived of the conventional sound effects, though here they are naturalized as cannon shot (1.4.6 SD).

16 Lukas Erne argues persuasively that the revisions for performance by the Children of the Chapel are mainly burlesque in manner but he allows that this distinction is not absolute (14–46). It is conceivable, however, that the influence worked the other way round and that *Hamlet* pays tribute to Kyd. In addition to the uncertainties concerning the derivation of *1 Hieronimo* as we have it, there remains the further possibility that Kyd's *Hamlet* formed a bridge between the Andrea of the original *1 Hieronimo* and Old Hamlet.

17 For instance, Shakespeare's Pyrrhus is covered in blood, *'total gules'*, *'Bak'd and impasted'* with the dust of the parched streets (*Hamlet* 2.2.458–60).

Heywood's Sinon wants to see the Trojan entrails 'bak'd in blood and dust' (*2 Iron Age* 357); he promises 'tragicke slaughter, clad in gules and sables' (379).

18 It is not so much Old Hamlet, however, as Banquo who features in the ghost's reply: 'I shooke these lockes, now knotted all, / As bak'd in blood' (*2 Iron Age* 384). Cf. *Macbeth* 3.4.49–50.

19 The play has already sexualized fingers (1.1.236–8).

20 The two versions of Middleton's *The Lady's Tragedy* are printed in parallel as A and B.

21 See *Saint Austins Care for the Dead*, esp. 33–53.

22 For an account of the theological and philosophical debates concerning apparitions, see Clark 204–65.

23 *Woodstock* mistakenly dismisses the Duchess of Gloucester's prophetic dream as no more than the day's residues (4.2.28–39). An interest in psychologizing dreams evidently co-exists with the view that they are supernaturally authorized. See also Holland; Clark 300–28.

24 Cf. Chapman, *The Revenge of Bussy*. The Guise has heard a disembodied voice (not a ghost) and Clermont argues, ''Twas but your fancy, then, a waking dream'. His case is that in sleep common sense is 'bound', releasing 'th' imagining power / (Stirr'd up by forms hid in the memory's store, / Or by the vapors of o'erflowing humors)', with the effect of feigning many strange images (5.1.42–7). What distinguishes Charlemont's reflections is the conjunction of the day's traumatic residues with memory, and the specificity of the account.

25 As does Snuffe when he later takes Charlemont himself for a ghost (3.2.19 SD).

26 Webster's Francisco is sure that Isabella's ghost, also visible to the audience, is imaginary. Dismissing the apparition, he compares it to 'an old wives' story' (*The White Devil* 4.1.116).

Works cited

A Warning for Fair Women: A Critical Edition. Ed. Charles Dale Cannon. The Hague: Mouton, 1975.

Adamson, Sylvia. 'Questions of Identity in Renaissance Drama: New Historicism meets Old Philology.' *Shakespeare Quarterly* 61 (2010): 56–77.

Audelay, John. *De tribus regibus mortuis. The Poems of John Audelay*. Ed. Ella Keats Whiting, Early English Text Society o.s. 184. London: Oxford University Press, 1931. 217–23.

Belsey, Catherine. 'Shakespeare's Sad Tale for Winter: *Hamlet* and the Tradition of Fireside Ghost Stories.' *Shakespeare Quarterly* 61 (2010): 1–27.

Binski, Paul. *Medieval Death: Ritual and Representation*. London: British Museum Press, 1996.

Chapman, George. *The Revenge of Bussy D'Ambois*. Ed. Robert J. Lordi. Salzburg: Institut für Englische Sprache und Literatur, Universität Salzburg, 1977.

Charnes, Linda. 'Shakespeare and the Gothic Strain.' *Shakespeare Studies* 38 (2010): 185–206.

Clark, Stuart. *Vanities of the Eye: Vision in Early Modern European Culture.* Oxford: Oxford University Press, 2007.

Dessen, Alan C., and Leslie Thomson. *A Dictionary of Stage Directions in English Drama, 1580–1642.* Cambridge: Cambridge University Press, 1999.

Erne, Lukas. *Beyond 'The Spanish Tragedy': A Study of the Works of Thomas Kyd.* Manchester: Manchester University Press, 2001.

Freud, Sigmund. 'The "Uncanny"'. *Art and Literature.* Ed. Albert Dickson. London: Penguin, 1985. 335–76.

Greene, Robert. *Alphonsus King of Aragon 1599.* Ed. W. W. Greg. Oxford: Malone Society, 1926.

Harsnett, Samuel. *A Declaration of Egregious Popish Impostures.* London, 1603.

Heywood, Thomas. *The First and Second Parts of King Edward IV.* Ed. Richard Rowland. Manchester: Manchester University Press, 2005.

—. *The Second Part of the Iron Age. The Dramatic Works of Thomas Heywood.* Vol. 3. London: Pearson, 1874. 347–431.

Holland, Peter. '"The Interpretation of Dreams" in the Renaissance.' *Reading Dreams: The Interpretation of Dreams from Chaucer to Shakespeare.* Ed. Peter Brown. Oxford: Oxford University Press, 1999. 125–46.

James, Henry. *The Turn of the Screw.* Ed. Deborah Esche and Jonathan Warren. New York: W. W. Norton, 1999.

James, M. R. 'Twelve Medieval Ghost Stories.' *English Historical Review* 37 (1922): 413–22.

Kyd, Thomas. '"The First Part of Hieronimo" and '"The Spanish Tragedy"'. Ed. Andrew S. Cairncross. London: Edward Arnold, 1967.

—. *The Spanish Tragedy.* Ed. Philip Edwards. London: Methuen, 1959.

Lecouteux, Claude. *Fantômes et revenants au moyen âge.* Paris: Imago, 1986.

Lewis, Matthew. *The Monk: A Romance.* Ed. Christopher MacLachlan. London: Penguin, 1998.

Marston, John. *The Tragedy of Sophonisba. Three Jacobean Witchcraft Plays.* Eds Peter Corbin and Douglas Sedge. Manchester: Manchester University Press, 1986.

—. *Antonio's Revenge.* Ed. Reavley Gair. Manchester: Manchester University Press, 1978.

Middleton, Thomas. *The Changeling.* Ed. Douglas Bruster. *Thomas Middleton: The Collected Works.* Eds Gary Taylor and John Lavagnino. Oxford: Clarendon Press, 2007. 1632–78.

—. *The Lady's Tragedy.* Ed. Julia Briggs. *Thomas Middleton: The Collected Works.* Eds Gary Taylor and John Lavagnino. Oxford: Clarendon Press, 2007. 833–906.

Nashe, Thomas. *The Terrors of the Night. Thomas Nashe.* Ed. Stanley Wells. London: Edward Arnold, 1964. 141–75.

Purinton, Marjean D. and Marliss C. Desens. 'Shakespearean Shadows' Parodic Haunting of Thomas Love Peacock's *Nightmare Abbey* and Jane Austen's

Northanger Abbey.' Shakespearean Gothic. Eds Christy Desmet and Anne Williams. Cardiff: University of Wales Press, 2009. 87–110.

Radcliffe, Ann. 'On the Supernatural in Poetry' (1826). *Gothic Documents: A Sourcebook 1700–1820*. Eds E. J. Clery and Robert Miles. Manchester: Manchester University Press, 2000. 163–72.

Saint Austins Care for the Dead, or His Bouke Intit'led De cura pro mortuis. English Secret Press, 1636.

Scot, Reginald. *The Discoverie of Witchcraft*. London, 1584.

Seneca. *Tragedies*. 2 vols. Ed. and trans. John G. Fitch. Cambridge, MA: Harvard University Press, 2002, 2004.

—. *Seneca His Tenne Tragedies, Translated into Englysh*. London, 1581.

Shakespeare, William. *The Arden Shakespeare Complete Works*. Eds Richard Proudfoot, Ann Thompson and David Scott Kastan. London: Bloomsbury, 2011.

—. *Hamlet*. Eds Ann Thompson and Neil Taylor. London: Thomson Learning, 2006.

—. *Macbeth*. Ed. Kenneth Muir. London: Methuen, 1951.

The Lamentable Tragedy of Locrine: A Critical Edition. Ed. Jane Lytton Gooch. New York: Garland, 1981.

Thomas of Woodstock or Richard the Second, Part One. Eds Peter Corbin and Douglas Sedge. Manchester: Manchester University Press, 2002.

Tourneur, Cyril. *The Atheist's Tragedy*. Eds Brian Morris and Roma Gill. London: Ernest Benn, 1976.

Townshend, Dale. 'Gothic and the Ghost of *Hamlet.' Gothic Shakespeares*. Eds John Drakakis and Dale Townshend. Abingdon: Routledge, 2008. 60–97.

Webster, John. *The Duchess of Malfi*. Ed. John Russell Brown. London: Methuen, 1964.

—. *The White Devil*. Ed. John Russell Brown. London: Methuen: 1960.

Williams, Anne. 'Reading Walpole Reading Shakespeare.' *Shakespearean Gothic*. Eds Christy Desmet and Anne Williams. Cardiff: University of Wales Press, 2009. 13–36.

3

'What do I fear? Myself?': nightmares, conscience and the 'Gothic' self in *Richard III*

Per Sivefors

For anyone investigating Shakespeare as an anticipation of or link to the Gothic, *Richard III* would provide a good case in point.[1] Generally, Shakespeare and the Gothic exemplify what Chris Baldick identifies as 'a common repertoire of shared anxieties', that is, 'fear of death, of decay, and of confinement' (xx).[2] But the case for *Richard III* could be made on a more specific level, not only because of the play's insistent dealing with the horror elements of dreams and nightmares but because this focus anticipates the kind of 'internalized conscience' that Victor Sage has argued is a prerequisite of Gothic fiction (Sage 70–126). It is of course no news that after the Reformation, and the confessional conflicts that it entailed, an immense importance came to be attached to conscience as a faculty that could help the individual through moral and religious dilemmas.[3] However, the two most extended dream sequences of Shakespeare's play, Clarence's dream of his death in 1.4 and Richard's vision of his past victims in 5.4 – both of which deal extensively with conscience – stage the characters' mindset in ways that can be seen as 'Gothic' in their concern with self-division, guilt and horror. Thus, analysing *Richard III* from a historicized understanding of nightmares and conscience can provide some insight into the links between the play and later representations of similar thematic and tropological concerns.

This chapter, then, suggests that the dream sequences of *Richard III* stage anxieties about inwardness and the human psyche that can be historicized in terms of early modern changes in the ideas of dreams and the function of conscience. Understanding both dreams and conscience primarily from the horizon of the Reformation process in the sixteenth century, it also establishes a theological perspective in discussing classical and early modern dream theories, particularly those of nightmares and what they were thought to 'reveal' about the human psyche. This set of contexts takes us to the connections that Gothic fiction establishes to *Richard III*, and part of the concluding discussion will consist in a juxtaposition of Richard's nightmare scene to the finale of Lewis's *The*

Monk – a text that offers a succinct parallel to the ambiguity concerning supernatural events and inwardness that we find in Shakespeare's play.

This approach, however, calls for a more detailed contextualization of both dream theory and the notion of conscience. I suggest basically that the ambiguous status of conscience in the play pushes the dreams of the play in the direction of a more 'psychologizing' approach that emphasizes the dreams as the revealers of truths about the human self. Such a perspective of course suggests a wider historical understanding, and, while there may have been no radical new ideas on dreams in the period under analysis (Holland 129), the heterogeneity of early modern opinion is striking.[4] In terms of dream theory, in the Renaissance there was a wide range of ideas of dreams and dreaming, and the notion of what constituted the dreaming human self was – as the scholarship of recent decades has often pointed out – quite different too.[5] Simply put, there were dreams and there were dreams; some dreams were thought to predict the future whereas some did not. 'All dreames from diuers causes grow, / And from th'interior, or th'exterior flow' (sig. E4r), as Thomas Lodge claimed in *A Fig for Momus* (1595). However, in literary representation especially it is sometimes hard to tell which category a given dream belongs to. Indeed, when Clarence, Richard III's soon-to-be-murdered brother, says that he has spent 'a miserable night, / So full of ugly sights, of ghastly dreams' (1.4.2–3), he suggests what in classical dream theory was called *insomnia*, nightmares which have no prophetic value. But, as anyone familiar with the play knows, Clarence's troubled dream does have 'meaning' as it foretells the future – the very next scene in fact sees him dead. Similarly, the various ghosts of family members and friends that appear in Richard's sleep seem to be more than just phantoms created by Richard's distress, as they actually do predict, correctly, his imminent downfall. One modern editor of the play, John Jowett, suggests that 'Shakespeare may not have been particularly mindful of classical and medieval dream theory, but part of the dream's potency lies in its transgression of dream categories' (193). As we have already seen, this appears true, but why would such a transgression happen in this particular way in *Richard III*? And why would these dreams be so insistently 'Gothic', or rather proto-Gothic, in their connection with horror, death and ghosts?

First of all, the liminal and uncertain status of the dreams themselves can be said to open up the 'irresolution between supernatural and psychological causes' that Jerrold Hogle sees as an important link between Shakespearean nightmares and those of classic Gothic texts such as *The Monk* (Hogle, 'Afterword' 213). According to Hogle, it is uncertain whether the supernatural in Lewis's novel 'is really independent of psychological projection or more the externalized product of it' (212). The roots of this uncertainty can arguably be found in the ways in which dreams and visions were theorized in Western cultural history. For example, Artemidorus' *Oneirocritica* (available in English translation in 1606) drew a sharp division line between 'oneiros' and 'enhypnion', the former predicting the future and the latter being caused by present states of affairs such as fear or hunger (14–16). Macrobius' *Commentary on the Dream of Scipio*, which was to become hugely influential in the Middle Ages and onwards, drew on Artemidorus in dividing dreams into five categories – enigmatic dreams, prophetic visions, oracular dreams, nightmares and apparitions – of which the last two 'have no prophetic significance' (88).[6] Nightmares, according to this scheme, 'may be caused by mental or physical distress, or anxiety about the future', the former being exemplified by 'the man who fears the plots or might of an enemy and is confronted with him in his dream or seems to be fleeing him' (88). Such dreams, the argument runs, 'are noteworthy only during their course and afterwards have no importance or meaning' (89). Taken at face value, though, Macrobius' dream theory would hardly account for the complex dream figurations that we find in *Richard III*. Clarence's dream is ostensibly a nightmare yet does foretell the future, as the audience quickly finds out.

It is necessary therefore to seek out a more immediate historical and ideological context for the dreams in addition to classical theory. For example, after the Reformation the belief in prophetic dreams, although still prevalent, became increasingly problematic. The Protestant view usually was that prophetic dreams, though having been possible in the past, were no longer so. In Hogle's words, by the eighteenth century for Protestants the notion of the supernatural 'has become linked ... to a Catholic iconography now presented nearly always as discredited and hollow' ('Afterword' 213). As numerous critics have pointed out, the Gothic predilection for various supernatural events (including dreams) can in itself be traced to a Protestant 'othering' of Catholicism.[7] It should be emphasized that this is a tendency with clear roots in the Reformation. To Protestants themselves, it was a truism that prophetic dreams largely, if not exclusively, belonged to the unreformed past. 'If we expect revelations in our dreames, now, when Christ is come, we shall deceive our selves: for in him are fulfilled all dreames and prophecies', wrote Reginald Scot in his *Discoverie of Witchcraft* (107). Lewis Lavater similarly gives voice to a Protestant 'professor of the Gospell', who claims that 'since the Gospell was preached vnto vs, very fewe spirits haue ben sene of any man' (183). At the same time, false prophecies of various kinds could have fatal consequences simply because they induce fear. John Foxe, in his account of Clarence's death in *Actes and Monuments*, says that there is a rumour 'whiche surmiseth the cause [of Clarence's death] to ryse vpon the vayne feare of a foolishe Prophecie, commyng no doubt (if it were true) by the crafty operation of Sathan' (849). The instigator of dreams and prophecies, Foxe says, is the devil,

> against whose deceatful delusions, Christen men must be wel instructed, neither to meruell greatly at them, though they seme straunge, nor yet to beleue them, though they happen true. For Satan beyng the prince of this world, in such thynges worldly can foresee what will followe, & can say truth for a mischeuous end, and yet for all that is but a Satan. (850)

Thus, as Carole Levin points out, Foxe can take dreams seriously, especially when they were the dreams of those he defended – the martyrs (Levin 64–6). On the whole, however, the inclination is to warn against dreams because they may be delusions induced by the devil – as in the case of Clarence.

However, if the idea of prophetic dreams was often thought to be problematic and theologically unsound, the suggestion that dreams revealed truths about the dreamer seems to have become increasingly common in the course of the seventeenth century. Sir Thomas Browne, though not at all denying the possibility of divine dreams, subtly changes the perspective when he writes that 'However dreames may bee fallacious concerning outward events, yet may they bee truly signifi-cant at home, & whereby wee may more sensibly understand ourselves' (477). Similarly, Owen Felltham's discussion of dreams in the second edition of *Resolves* (1628) opens with the statement that '*Dreames* are notable *meanes* of discouering our owne *inclinations*. The *wise man* learnes himselfe as well by the *nights blacke mantle*, as the *searching beames* of *day*' (52). Arguably, the consequence of this shift is that the hierarchy between prophetic and non-prophetic dreams is blurred: even the shadier parts of the soul reveal something about who you are. And if this development still places the emphasis on moral instruction, it also anticipates the early Gothic insistence on night as a revealer of the inward secrets of the self.[8]

However, even texts that reject the idea of moral significance tend to establish links between dreams and (shady) self. Indeed, in Thomas Nashe's *The Terrors of the Night* (1594), even the dismissal of the significance of dreams becomes a source of exuberance, as the restlessly associative narrative style of the work can be said to parallel the state of mind it sets out to describe. In a manner that can clearly be seen as 'proto-Gothic', Nashe claims that devils populate every corner of the world: 'there is not a roome in anie mans house, but is pestred and close packed with a campe royall of diuels ... Infinite millions of them wil hang swarming about a worm-eaten nose' (sig. B3v).[9] Yet both dreams and the writer's own text are dismissed as mere flights of fancy without any further moral significance: 'to say the troth, all this whole Tractate is but a dreame, for my wits are not halfe awaked in it' (sig. D3r). These parallel states anticipate a Gothic 'writing of excess' (Botting, *Gothic* 1), for, as Scott Brewster points out, 'Gothic does not merely transcribe disturbed, perverse or horrifying worlds: its narrative structures and voices are interwoven with and intensify the madness they represent' (281).

Needless to say, this analysis raises the much-discussed question of what constituted and structured the early modern self. Especially important is the sense in which the self can be said to be 'theatricalized'. For example, the already-mentioned Sir Thomas Browne, as Reid Barbour points out, 'applauds [his] dream as an elevated performance, somewhere between those mysterious yet "outward and sensible motions" produced by church ornament and ceremony at which he kneels, and the ordered and witty surprise served up by a good Fletcherian comedy played extempore for a private audience of one in the theatre of his bed' (116). As we shall see, Richard's dream – though hardly comical, especially not to himself – bears a strong imprint of a theatricalized notion of the human psyche. This conception is important to bear in mind when analysing the dreams of Shakespeare's play. Particularly, the idea of the psyche as a battleground of good and evil forces – not unlike the forces in a morality play – squares with both the theological context outlined above and the structure of the dreams themselves. While classical dream theory emphasizes either the future (predictive dreams) or the present (anxiety dreams), the dreams of *Richard III* are fundamentally concerned with *past* events and how to make up for or make moral sense of them.[10] Clarence sees a reminder of his past perjury in the extended vision of his father-in-law, whereas Richard is exposed to a gruesome parade of all his past victims, exclaiming 'O coward conscience, how dost thou afflict me!' (5.4.158). Their conscience therefore becomes a central aspect of the function of the dreams. In this sense, the dreams both embody the notion of conscience and reinforce the idea of the self-as-theatre; as a matter of fact theatricality is reinforced precisely through the emphasis on conscience. Described as a faculty partly located outside the human being, conscience was, in William Perkins's characterization, 'a thing placed of God in the middest between Him and man, as an arbitrator to give sentence and pronounce either with man or against man unto God' (qtd in Braun and Vallance xvi). This legal metaphor frequently appears in other accounts of conscience.[11] But it also helped to structure the conscience itself, as scholars have noted. For example, Garrett Sullivan usefully distinguishes between the witnessing and judging functions of conscience (120), and Alexandra Walsham similarly points out that conscience was seen as 'an invisible witness to give sentence against sin, as well as an instrument of divine vengeance and wrath' (33).[12] Thus, early modern accounts of conscience emphasize a sense of constant self-scrutiny that is fundamentally tied up with the Protestant emphasis on individuality over community. In fact, as Camille Wells Slights has observed, Protestant notions of conscience involve an individualized interiority that is 'generated thorough a deliberate process of analysis that involves detachment from, as well as focus on, the self' (236). The idea of conscience, then, contributes strongly to the peculiar individual self-examination that Clarence and Richard subject themselves to.

From the context of conscience, the dreams of *Richard III* are not so much about predicting the future as about coming to terms with the past, and doing so in the form of partly detached self-scrutiny. It is arguably this casuistic function of the dreams that contributes to their strong element of horror – a function that clearly presages Gothic fiction in its emphasis on the witnessing function, for as Sage points out, horror fiction itself is strongly 'legalistic' in its form (xx). From that perspective, conscience can be said to take on a nightmarish quality as it locks humans inside a universe of guilt. As John Wilks argues, 'even when the conscience is enlightened by a proper response to God's words, it seldom rises above its purely negative character as a register of man's chronic burden of guilt ... a "yoke", always in some degree evil' (42). As a consequence, although dreams in the end might have some sort of significance for the future as moral guides, the negative definition of conscience rather pushes the idea of dreams in the direction of revealers of past sins and the punishments for them. As historians suggest, conscience may have been seen by Protestant theologians as a faculty that operated 'as both the guide and the judge of moral actions' (Braun and Vallance xvi). Still, the understanding of conscience as a register of guilt comes to emphasize its function as judge rather than as guide.[13] It is suggesting a 'Gothic' nightmare world where conscience has little function but to remind the individual of his or her transgressions and imminent suffering for them.[14] While this reminding function can be said to be rational, it also jeopardizes the notion of conscience as a guide for the future. Neither conscience nor dreams, then, seem to help the individual to make rational choices.

A particularly complex problematization of the dreaming mind and its relation to conscience occurs in *Richard III* in Clarence's retelling of his dream in Act 1 scene 4. The account by Clarence, who is imprisoned and about to be murdered at the instigation of his brother Richard, ostensibly points to a 'pure' nightmare sequence, of anxiety and distress. The dream, Clarence says, has been full of horrors:

> O, I have past a miserable night,
> So full of ugly sights, of ghastly dreams,
> That, as I am a Christian-faithful man
> I would not spend another such a night
> Though 'twere to buy a world of happy days,
> So full of dismal terror was the time.
>
> (1.4.2–7)

But the audience, which knows more than Clarence of the plots against his life, soon suspects that his dream has a deeper significance. Some of the 'terror' Clarence describes arguably taps into deeply embedded paranoias about Catholic France, which is, Clarence says, his destination: 'Methought I was embarked for Burgundy' (1.4.9). The horror of Clarence the 'Christian-faithful man' on his way to Catholic France then can be said to foreshadow the deep anxieties about, and othering of, Catholicism that is a trademark of early Gothic fiction (Sage *passim*). However, Clarence's paranoia is characteristically expressed on the level of self-scrutiny and consideration of the individual's own possible guilt. Describing his own death by water, Clarence suggests that this is brought about – seemingly unintentionally – by his brother:

> Methought that Gloucester stumbled, and in stumbling
> Struck me, that sought to stay him, overboard
> Into the tumbling billows of the main.
>
> (1.4.17–19)

Previously, Clarence has said that the king 'harkens after prophecies and dreams' (1.1.54), and these prophecies have told that the letter G should disinherit the king's sons. Clarence, whose Christian name is George, believes it to concern him. At the same time, the audience is well prepared to get the irony behind this: only thirty lines earlier, Richard has said that he is wilfully misleading both Clarence and his father:

> Plots have I laid inductious, dangerous,
> By drunken prophecies, libels and dreams,
> To set my brother Clarence and the King
> In deadly hate the one against each other.
>
> (1.1.31–4)

Since Richard's title is Gloucester with a G, we already here have a hint that Clarence's dream is not just an empty nightmare vision. There is 'truth' in it, only not the truth that Clarence and the king expect. In his account of his dream, Clarence describes it all as an accident, though the image of drowning could of course be said to anticipate his subsequent demise in a 'malmsey butt' (1.4.244). The dream, then, clearly deals with premonition. But since the audience has been exposed to Richard's previous comment on false dreams as well as Margaret's elaborate curse including the 'tormenting dream', the interpretative moment as such becomes problematic. In other words, the audience is confronted not only with the predictive value of the dream but with the value of interpretation itself – a perspective that occurs elsewhere in Shakespeare's plays.[15] While the play therefore suggests that dreams can be interpreted, the question of *what* the interpretation embraces – past, future, exterior, interior – may be less clear.

In order to clarify this complex issue, we might look at how the monologue works on the level of trope and structure. Clarence's dream narrative abounds with images that expose the interior, the mind, as a site of conflict. When the watery landscape of the dream invades Clarence's body, it emphatically does so through his organs of perception:

> Lord, Lord, methought what pain it was to drown,
> What dreadful noise of waters in my ears,
> What ugly sights of death within my eyes!
>
> (1.4.21–2)

This process not only extends to Clarence himself but is suggested to be a universal condition of the dream-world, as is suggested by his description of the 'fearful wrecks' and 'ten thousand men that fishes gnawed upon' (1.4.23–4). Clarence sees innumerable riches at the bottom of the sea, but they consistently intrude on the parts of the body associated with the mind and with perception:

> Wedges of gold, great anchors, heaps of pearl,
> Inestimable stones, unvalued jewels.
> Some lay in dead men's skulls, and in those holes
> Where eyes did once inhabit there were crept,
> As 'twere in scorn of eyes, reflecting gems
> Which wooed the slimy bottom of the deep,
> And mocked the dead bones that lay scattered by.
>
> (1.4.25–31)

Here, it is into the eyes, or their sockets, that the gems, eerily, have 'crept'.[16] If the passage expresses the commonplace idea that worldly riches are but vanities in the face of death, it also suggests a confusion of hierarchies as regards the dreaming mind itself (what is inside and what is outside?). In this respect the scene reflects early modern beliefs about dreams as a locus of dissolved boundaries. As Nashe put it, 'no such figure of the first Chaos whereout the world was extraught, as our dreames in the night. In them all states, all sexes, all places are confounded and meete together' (sig. C4r). Indeed, Clarence's dream also confuses boundaries with respect to interior and exterior – the latter insistently invades the former and the invisible world of the interior is put on display.

As the dream then reveals, there is no doubt that this inversion is connected to the idea of conscience. At first, it may seem as if the emphasis is on the pure nightmare quality of the sequence. 'Awaked you not with this sore agony?' asks Brakenbury, to which Clarence replies:

> O no, my dream was lengthened after life.
> O then began the tempest to my soul,
> Who passed, methought, the melancholy flood
> With that grim ferryman which poets write of,
> Unto the kingdom of perpetual night.
>
> (1.4.39–44)

Arguably, this passage underlines the fact that nightmares and melancholy were routinely connected in early modern thought. For example, Robert Burton claimed that one cause of religious melancholy is dreams and visions in which the devil speaks with the soul (3.325).[17] In a different vein, Nashe dispenses with the religious framework in favour of a more mechanistic view that reverses the causal chain between nightmares and melancholy: 'euen as slime and durt in a standing puddle, engender toads and frogs and many other vnsightly creatures, so this slimie melancholy humor still still [*sic*] thickning as it stands still, engendreth many mishapen obiects in our imaginations' (sig. C2v). Like the 'slimy bottom' of Clarence's dream, then, the melancholy mind seems to generate its own set of horrors.

Yet the idea of conscience in the dream complicates the nightmare aspect, but it also – unlike much medical theory at the time – suggests that nightmares and conscience are indissolubly entwined.[18] The ghosts of Warwick and Edward Prince of Wales show up to remind Clarence of his crimes, assisted by 'a legion of foul fiends' that

> howlèd in my ears
> Such hideous cries that with the very noise
> I trembling waked[.]
>
> (1.4.55–7)

As in the preceding part of the dream, organs of perception are violated, in this case even with the result that Clarence awakens. As a consequence, both the witnessing and judging functions of conscience come into play as Clarence muses on the dream:

> O Brakenbury, I have done those things
> Which now bear evidence against my soul
> For Edward's sake, and see how he requites me.
> I pray thee, gentle keeper, stay by me.
> My soul is heavy, and I fain would sleep.
>
> (1.4.63–7)

What we – and Clarence – are brought to realize is that the figures he sees in his dream are in fact personifications of his own conscience (Wilks 88). It may seem, then, as if he is merely fulfilling a scheme of divine retribution, for as Perkins and other Protestant theologians would have argued, conscience, despite its evil aspects, is valuable as an instrument of justice (Wilks 89). But conscience itself seems to come under question in the play: for Clarence the anxiety about his guilty conscience is expressed in powerful images of interpenetrating interior and exterior, as if the exact nature and location of conscience were in fact unclear, or at least sources of considerable distress. If conscience is both the expression of one's own self and of God, then attempts at expelling it from oneself must result in horror.

In fact, in the play conscience is on the verge of becoming an itinerant entity, as in the ensuing scene featuring Clarence's murderers, who express pangs of guilt but remind each other of the financial reward awaiting them:

> FIRST EXECUTIONER. Where is thy conscience now?
> SECOND EXECUTIONER. In the Duke of Gloucester's purse.
> FIRST EXECUTIONER. So when he opens his purse to give us our reward, thy conscience flies out.
> SECOND EXECUTIONER. Let it go, there's few or none will entertain it.
>
> (1.4.116–21)

Conscience, then, is something that 'flies out' at the very sight of a money-bag, but it also becomes a dreaded 'other' that one has to be cleansed from – like a beggar, for example, as the second executioner points out: 'It beggars any man that keeps it. It is turned out of all towns and cities for a dangerous thing, and every man that means to live well endeavours to trust to himself and live without it' (1.4.129–31). The conventional character of the image – conscience as a beggar at the sinful person's door – is obvious, but a consequence of it is also that conscience is something to fear, something that invokes horror as much as any nightmare. From a Protestant context, the emphasis on individual over community can be embodied in the image of a solitary person trying to expel his or her guilty conscience. But this image also suggests that conscience can never be fully externalized: it is forever there as a beggar on your doorstep. In fact, the voice of conscience is described as something that even opens up your body, a wound, as Ned Lukacher aptly characterizes it: 'What is unique to Shakespeare is his disturbing synthesis or juxtaposition of the mouth and tongue of conscience with the gash or wound in the flesh, as though the pain of the call of conscience from within the mind were like nothing so much as a gaping wound that speaks' (204). In this image of pain and distress, conscience and nightmares are therefore ever close to each other, as Clarence's dream demonstrates.

This is of course no less true of the second extended dream sequence in the play, in which Richard's victims appear as ghosts on stage to confront him with his past misdeeds. To an even higher extent than Clarence's dream, the scene could be said to illustrate early modern notions of the self as theatre. Taken in a strictly realistic sense, the dream, with its formalized pattern of entrances, exits and rhetorically wrought speeches, may not seem very much like a dream at all. It certainly displays traits of the Macrobian nightmare in the sense that it 'may be caused by mental or physical distress, or anxiety about the future' (Macrobius 88). At the same time, conscience becomes a funda-mental structuring device in the scene, deepening the sense in which Richard's dream deals with far-reaching issues of guilt and repentance.[19] The words 'Despair and die' are repeated, mantra-like, reminding Richard of the fate that awaits him and compelling him to use the word himself ('I shall despair', 5.4.179). As a concept central to Calvinist theology, despair was connected to nightmares, but it also hinged on the idea of conscience and the individual's own relation to his or her past.[20] It also denoted a state in which the individual's link to God has been definitively broken. In this, Richard's state of mind is different from Clarence's or even the murderers'. If the scene with Clarence's dream and his subsequent murder reveals a far-reaching paranoia about the power of conscience to penetrate the human being, Richard's dream, on the other hand, displays a self that has finally broken down into a divided one rather than being under attack from the outside. Conscience, it seems, is 'afflicting' Richard purely from the inside – at least he insists that there is no one 'at his arm' except himself:

> Soft, I did but dream.
> O coward conscience, how dost thou afflict me!
> The lights burn blue. It is now dead midnight.
> Cold fearful drops stand on my trembling flesh.
> What do I fear? Myself? There's none else by.
> Richard loves Richard; that is, I am I.
> Is there a murderer here? No. – Yes, I am.
> Then fly. – What, from myself? – Great reason why:
> Lest I revenge. – What, myself upon myself?

> Alack, I love myself. – Wherefore? – For any good
> That I myself have done to myself. –
> O no, alas, I rather hate myself
> For hateful deeds committed by myself.
>
> (5.4.157–69)

The excessive repetition of the first person pronoun of course creates the impression of protesting too much: self-division, rather than a balanced subject, is what the insistent assertions of selfhood generate. As Wilks points out, 'for the first time, Richard is really alone' (97), and in waking up from his dream, Richard is unable to externalize the horrors that have beset him. Moreover, his conscience cannot be stopped from providing accounts of his crimes:

> My conscience hath a thousand several tongues,
> And every tongue brings in a several tale,
> And every tale condemns me for a villain.
>
> (5.4.170–2)

Again, as in Clarence's dream, there is the suggestion of intrusion, of inward movement ('brings *in*'), but the difference is that the intrusion entails an assertion of selfhood that is as unconvincing as it is repetitive. The relative positions of self and conscience are in fact less clear than ever in the play. Commenting on these lines, Jowett suggests that 'there could be a suggestion that Richard's conscience resides with the audience' (344), but the passage might more plausibly refer to the parade of ghosts he has been exposed to. Unusually for a Renaissance play, the dream is staged in front of the audience rather than retold by a character, and this visualization arguably contributes to the sense of a divided self that we get from Richard's subsequent monologue.[21] Thus, rather than suggesting that Richard's conscience is located outside himself, the staged vision of the ghosts becomes an image of his divided interior.

However, because of their very physical shape on the stage, the question arises whether the ghosts can actually be seen as mere projections of Richard's state of mind. We should perhaps be wary of writing off the ghosts as images without any 'supernatural value' to an early modern audience, given the various well-known anecdotes of actual supernatural beings suddenly appearing on stage together with the actors.[22] None the less, the play clearly emphasizes horror over terror in its accentuated image of a solitary self: it is Richard's grappling with his own conscience and subject position that is the dramatic culmination of the scene, not the accusations of the ghosts. Thus, the play can be said to veer towards a 'psychologizing' model precisely because the position of conscience is unclear. As Botting says of the Gothic era, 'psychological rather than supernatural forces became the prime movers in worlds where individuals could be sure neither of others nor of themselves' (*Gothic* 12). Thus, if nightmares have been tools that Richard has used to manipulate his brother and the king with, they now have become part of an internal conflict that cannot be expelled.

In this respect, then, *Richard III* anticipates the uncertain status of supernatural and psychological models in Gothic fiction. As Hogle reminds us, in linking Shakespeare to Lewis's *The Monk*, 'actual ghostliness in the Gothic Story is more or less inseparable from psychological projection' ('Afterword' 213). In fact, there are clear parallels between Richard's state of fear and Ambrosio's: 'He dreaded the approach of sleep: No sooner did his eyes close, wearied with tears and watching, than the dreadful visions seemed to be realized, on which his mind had dwelt during the day' (Lewis 426). Drakakis rightly points out ('Introduction' 8–9) that Lewis's account owes much to Marlowe's *Doctor Faustus* in its depiction of the guilty sinner and the infernal punishment he receives. However, the case could be made for *Richard III* as well, since it is in fact Ambrosio's *victims* as much as the devil who haunt him.[23] Finding himself among demons in 'sulphurous realms' (426), Ambrosio sees the ghosts of Elvira and her daughter, who 'reproached him with their deaths, recounted his crimes to the Dæmons, and urged them to inflict torments of cruelty. Such were the pictures, which floated before his eyes in sleep: They vanished not till his repose was disturbed by excess of agony' (427). Indeed, Ambrosio displays a physical reaction similar to Richard's in musing on his guilt:

> Then would He start from the ground on which he had stretched himself, his brows running down with cold sweat, his eyes wild and phrenzied ... He paced his dungeon with disordered steps; He gazed with terror upon the surrounding darkness, and often did He cry,
>   'Oh, fearful is the night to the Guilty!' (427)

As in the case of Shakespeare's play, it is not wholly clear whether the ghosts of Ambrosio's victims are supernatural apparitions or mere mental images. They may be characterized as 'pictures, which floated before his eyes in sleep', but the devil also later points out to Ambrosio that 'It was I who warned Elvira in dreams of your designs upon her daughter' (440), thus blurring the boundary between supernatural and psychological. Yet the very setting of the scene underlines the extent to which fear and guilty conscience have become individualized states (the dungeon being possible to read as a figure for Ambrosio's own mind). As already pointed out, Richard's expression of guilt after his dream also emphasizes, for the first time in the play, his essential loneliness. What *Richard III* and *The Monk* could be said to share is the staginess of their depiction of the supernatural: Shakespeare's play has the ghosts parade in front of the protagonist whereas Lewis's literary style has an essentially theatrical, visualizing dimension to it.[24] At the same time, the texts emphasize the dream-state of the respective characters and the fact that they are out of touch with the real world around them. Of course Richard, unlike Ambrosio, claims to have shaken off his bad conscience in stating later, 'Conscience is but a word that cowards use' (5.5.38). However, as Wilks perceptively argues, Richard's 'Machiavellian creed' in this line also condemns him to a 'solitary individualism' (90). In that sense, then, Shakespeare's play presents a 'Gothic' interior in which the conflicts of the mind are both put on display and withdrawn from the outside world.

If there is a 'Gothic' trait to be distilled from *Richard III*, then, it is precisely in its emphasis on dreams – especially nightmares – as a function of the guilty conscience. Arguably, this emphasis is also what generates the 'horror' effect of the play. However, it also sets the play squarely within its own historical and theological context, as questions of conscience are vital to the Reformation culture in which Elizabethan theatre emerged. *Richard III*, as a play, puts considerable stress on the notion of conscience as a source of paranoia and fear. Its main characters are of course all guilty in the sense that the play depicts them as deserving their punishment. But it arguably does so not so much on the level of divine retribution as on the level of introspection: especially in Richard's soliloquy, this introspective turn – heralded by an incessant repetition of the first person pronoun – becomes a source of distress that can only be temporarily overcome. Dreams are thus on the verge of becoming 'truly significant at home', to repeat Sir Thomas Browne's phrase, and this liminal status is, as this chapter has attempted to show, also what makes *Richard III* relevant from the point of view of Gothic writing.

Notes

1 This chapter is not concerned with *Richard III* in the 'Gothic period', i.e. the eighteenth and nineteenth centuries. However, it should be noted that although the play was staged in the eighteenth century only in Colley Cibber's heavily altered version, which in fact removes some of the more 'Gothic' features of the play (including Richard's dialogue with himself in 5.4), the performance of David Garrick in the latter part of the century could evoke praise in clearly Gothic terms such as Fanny Burney's 'sublimely horrible' (Jowett 87).

2 Drakakis, commenting on Baldick, lists a number of Shakespearean plays that would exemplify such anxieties, but omits *Richard III* (Drakakis,

'Introduction' 8). Generally speaking, Renaissance literature, Shakespeare in particular, provided a rich configuration of resources for Gothic writing of the late eighteenth and early nineteenth centuries; for discussion, see for example Botting, *Gothic* 35; Bronfen; Drakakis, 'Introduction'.

3 For discussions of early modern notions of conscience, see Braun and Vallance; Brown, *Donne and the Politics*; Gallagher; Lukacher; Slights; Sullivan 119–25; Thomas; Walsham.

4 Holland sees Freud's *Interpretation of Dreams* as a 'shock to the system' of a kind that has no correspondent in early modern culture. It may be argued, however, that the idea of a radical paradigmatic shift obscures the continuities that are there throughout Western history (continuities that Freud himself was of course well aware of). Particularly, the idea of interpretation as such is a constant that has been contested but hardly definitively dismissed; for a polemic on the topic, see Hobson, especially 15–31.

5 With few exceptions, the research on early modern dream theory is a fairly new field. Anthologies and other works on historical dream theories tend to skip lightly over the early modern period; for notable exceptions, see Brown, ed.; Hodgkin et al., eds; Levin. Shorter, more specialized studies can be found in Alwes; Masten; Sivefors. Among discussions of the dream sequences in *Richard III*, Garber 15–26 and Levin 99–105 offer comparatively detailed analysis but do not establish any links to the Gothic aspect.

6 For discussions of Macrobius in the Middle Ages, see for example Russell 75–8, 94–114.

7 See Baldick xii–xiv; Botting, 'Preface' 5; Sage.

8 As Fred Botting points out, in a discussion of Young's *Night Thoughts*, 'Darkness enables a person to perceive the soul within, it expands the mind by producing a consciousness of its own potential of divinity' (*Gothic* 34). On the other hand, as Elisabeth Bronfen suggests, such an insight comes at a price: the awareness of night is available only in reported form, as a story that can never be fully grasped (40–1).

9 Drakakis explicitly compares Coleridge's poem 'The Pains of Sleep' (1803) to 'the garish fantasies' of Nashe's work in arguing that the imagery of former is 'much closer to the ethos of "Gothic" fiction than to a more accurately historical sense of the Gothic' ('Introduction' 6).

10 As Artemidorus insists, '*oneiros* differs from *enhypnion* in that the first indicates a future state of affairs, while the other indicates a present state of affairs' (14).

11 One example is Richard West's poem *The Court of Conscience* (1607), which even personifies conscience as a hangman: '*Dicke Whipper* now (mans conscience 'tis I meane,) / Knowing the guiltie hearts of euery sort, / Hath summoned a meeting, where all men, / Are to repaire in person at that Court' (sig. A4r).

12 For more discussion of the theatrical/dialogical functions of conscience, see for example Gallagher, who points out that conscience can be seen as 'the embodiment of an internally dialogized structure, one that called into question, first, the identity of the speaking persona ... [C]*onscientia* defined

one's voice as a continually shifting response to the flux of one's social and psychological experience; it represented the intrinsic dialogism – and the intertextuality – of one's discourse' (265).

13 For further discussion of conscience as a 'register', see Sullivan 120–1.

14 As Botting points out, one central development of Gothic is precisely its increasing emphasis on individual guilt: in the Romantic era, 'Gothic became part of an internalized world of guilt, anxiety, despair, a world of individual transgression interrogating the uncertain bounds of imaginative freedom and human knowledge' (*Gothic* 10).

15 For example, in the account of Calpurnia's dream in *Julius Caesar*, which is given two markedly different kinds of significance: either that Caesar should go to the senate or that he should not. As Garber suggests, though, both interpretations are 'true': one says that Caesar will die – which he does – and the other that the republic will revive through his blood (which is also true, although not in the sense Caesar believes). See Garber 53–8.

16 In this, the implication of the jewellery is consistent with Artemidorus, who insists that when men dream of jewels it always portends bad luck: 'For a man, they signify deceit, treachery and serious complications in business affairs not because of the material, but because of its form and design' (86). Interestingly from the perspective of *Richard III* and its story of a usurper, a class aspect is also suggested in Artemidorus' scheme: gold in dreams is generally auspicious unless it is for example 'beyond a person's station in life (as, for example, in the case of poor men, crowns, lavish adornments, and many coins)' (87).

17 At the same time, melancholy could be associated with an iconographic and symbolic dream-world, as in Robert Greene's *A Quip for an Upstart Courtier* (1592), in which the narrator, 'damped with a melancholy humor, went into the fields to cleere my wittes with the fresh aire: where solitarie seeking to sollace my selfe I fell in a dreame, and in that drowsie slumber, I wandered into a vale all tapistred with sweet and choice flowers'. These events teach him, among other things, 'to thinke nature by hir weedes warnd men to be wary and by their secret properties to checke wanton and sensuall imperfections' (sig. B1r).

18 As Timothie Bright's *Treatise of Melancholy* (1586) made clear, there was an obvious difference between melancholy and conscience with respect to their anchoring in reality: 'Whatsoeuer molestation riseth directly as a proper obiect of the mind, that in that respect is not melancholicke, but hath a farther ground then fancie, and riseth from conscience, condemning the guiltie soule of those ingrauen lawes of nature, which no man is voide of' (sig. N1r).

19 In fact, Raphael Holinshed clearly separates nightmares from the idea of prophetic dreams as he says of Richard's vision that it was 'no dream but a punction and prick of his sinful conscience' (458). In that sense, dreams would by definition be prophetic ones, which Richard's is not. Guilt, on the other hand, clearly is another matter, which the scene in the play also emphasizes.

20 For the connection between despair and nightmares, see for example Philip Goodwin's *The mystery of dreames, historically discoursed* (1658), which relates the case of the Italian Protestant Francesco Spira, whose recantation made him fall 'into such a despairing condition, that he was filled with the horrors of *Hell*, not only in his wakefull times, but in his sleeping Dreames' (sigs. Q2r–v).

21 Of the few other examples in Renaissance drama, the dumb show representing the eponymous hero's dream in John Lyly's *Endymion* is thought to be a later interpolation inserted to conform – unsuccessfully – with the spoken account of the dream. (For discussion of this, see Pincombe 111.)

22 See for example Prynne's *Histriomastix*, with its account of 'the visible apparition of the Devil on stage at the Belsavage Play-house, in Queen Elizabeth's days' (Chambers 423), or an anecdote of a performance of *Doctor Faustus* at Exeter, where the actors 'were all dashed ... for they were all persuaded, there was one devil too many amongst them' (Chambers 424). Of course, many of these stories had an anti-theatrical agenda, though such an agenda could of course not have been effective without an actual uncertainty as to the existence of supernatural beings.

23 As Robert Miles points out, *The Monk* even sends up Marlowe's play in its gross depiction of Ambrosio's punishment: 'as a representation of divine justice it ought to have a ring of truth to it; instead, it has the ring of Marlowe's *Doctor Faustus*, which it parodies' (54).

24 As Punter puts it, 'we are not required to *believe* in the supernatural by Lewis – this is assumed: rather, we are required to *see* it before us, lurid and gory as a stage ghost' (*Literature of Terror* 1.61).

Works cited

Alwes, Derek. 'Elizabethan Dreaming: Fictional Dreaming from Gascoigne to Lodge.' *Framing Elizabethan Fictions: Contemporary Approaches to Early Modern Narrative Prose*. Ed. Constance C. Relihan. Kent: Kent State University Press, 1996. 153–67.

Artemidorus. *The Interpretation of Dreams*. Trans. Robert J. White. Park Ridge: Noyes, 1975.

Baldick, Chris. 'Introduction'. *The Oxford Book of Gothic Tales*. Ed. Chris Baldick. Oxford: Oxford University Press, 1992.

Barbour, Reid. *Religion and Literary Culture in Seventeenth-Century England*. Cambridge: Cambridge University Press, 2002.

Botting, Fred, ed. *The Gothic*. Cambridge: D. S. Brewer, 2001.

—. 'Preface: The Gothic'. *The Gothic*. Ed. Fred Botting. Cambridge: D. S. Brewer, 2001. 1–6.

—. *Gothic*. London: Routledge, 1996.

Braun, Harald and Edward Vallance, eds. *Contexts of Conscience in Early Modern Europe, 1500–1700*. Basingstoke: Palgrave Macmillan, 2004.

—. 'Introduction'. *Contexts of Conscience in Early Modern Europe, 1500–1700*.

Eds Harald Braun and Edward Vallance. Basingstoke: Palgrave Macmillan, 2004. x–xviii.

Brewster, Scott. 'Seeing Things: Gothic and the Madness of Interpretation.' *A Companion to the Gothic*. Ed. David Punter. Oxford: Blackwell, 2000. 281–92.

Bright, Timothie. *A Treatise of Melancholie*. London, 1586.

Bronfen, Elisabeth. 'Shakespeare's Nocturnal World.' *Gothic Shakespeares*. Eds John Drakakis and Dale Townshend. Abingdon: Routledge, 2008. 21–41.

Brown, Meg Lota. *Donne and the Politics of Conscience in early modern England*. Leiden: Brill, 1995.

Brown, Peter, ed. *Reading Dreams: The Interpretation of Dreams from Chaucer to Shakespeare*. Oxford: Oxford University Press, 1999.

Browne, Sir Thomas. *The Major Works*. Ed. C. A. Patrides. Harmondsworth: Penguin, 1977.

Burton, Robert. *The Anatomy of Melancholy*. 3 vols. London: Dent, 1932.

Chambers, E. K. *The Elizabethan Stage*. Vol. 3. Oxford: Clarendon, 1945.

Drakakis, John and Dale Townshend, eds. *Gothic Shakespeares*. Abingdon: Routledge, 2008.

—. 'Introduction'. *Gothic Shakespeares*. Eds John Drakakis and Dale Townshend. Abingdon: Routledge, 2008. 1–19.

Felltham, Owen. *Resolues: Diuine, morall, politicall*. London, 1628.

Foxe, John. *The first volume of the ecclesiasticall history contaynyng the actes and monumentes of thynges passed in euery kynges tyme in this realme*. London, 1570.

Gallagher, Lowell. *Medusa's Gaze: Casuistry and Conscience in the Renaissance*. Stanford: Stanford University Press, 1991.

Garber, Marjorie. *Dream in Shakespeare: From Metaphor to Metamorphosis*. New Haven: Yale University Press, 1974.

Goodwin, Philip. *The mystery of dreames, historically discoursed*. London, 1658.

Greene, Robert. *A Qvip for an Vpstart Courtier*. London, 1592.

Hobson, J. Allan. *Dreaming: A Very Short Introduction*. Oxford: Oxford University Press, 2002.

Hodgkin, Katharine, Michelle O'Callaghan, and S. J. Wiseman, eds. *Reading the Early Modern Dream: The Terrors of the Night*. London: Routledge, 2008.

Hogle, Jerrold E. 'Afterword: The "Grounds" of the Shakespeare–Gothic Relationship.' *Gothic Shakespeares*. Eds John Drakakis and Dale Townshend. Abingdon: Routledge, 2008. 201–20.

—. 'The Gothic Ghost of the Counterfeit and the Progress of Abjection.' *A Companion to the Gothic*. Ed. David Punter. Oxford: Blackwell, 2000. 293–304.

Holinshed, Raphael. *Chronicles of England, Scotland, and Ireland*. Vol. 3. London, 1808.

Holland, Peter. '"The Interpretation of Dreams" in the Renaissance.' *Reading Dreams: The Interpretation of Dreams from Chaucer to Shakespeare*. Ed. Peter Brown. Oxford: Oxford University Press, 1999. 125–46.

Jowett, John. 'Introduction' and footnotes. *Richard III*. By William Shakespeare. Oxford: Oxford University Press, 2000. The Oxford Shakespeare.

Lavater, Lewis. *Of Ghostes and Spirites Walking by Nyght*. Eds J. Dover Wilson and May Yardley. Oxford: Shakespeare Association, 1929.

Levin, Carole. *Dreaming the English Renaissance: Politics and Desire in Court and Culture*. Basingstoke: Palgrave Macmillan, 2008.

Lewis, Matthew. *The Monk*. Ed. Howard Anderson. Oxford: Oxford University Press, 1995.

Lodge, Thomas. *A fig for Momus containing pleasant varietie, included in satyres, eclogues, and epistles*. London, 1595.

Lukacher, Ned. *Daemonic Figures: Shakespeare and the Question of Conscience*. Ithaca: Cornell University Press, 1994.

Macrobius. *Commentary on the Dream of Scipio*. Trans. William Harris Stahl. New York: Columbia University Press, 1952. Records of Civilization, Sources and Studies 48.

Masten, Jeffrey. 'The Interpretation of Dreams, circa 1610.' *Historicism, Psychoanalysis, and Early Modern Culture*. Eds Carla Mazzio and Douglas Trevor. New York: Routledge, 2000. 157–85.

McLuskie, Kathleen. 'The "Candy-Colored Clown": Reading early modern Dreams.' *Reading Dreams: The Interpretation of Dreams from Chaucer to Shakespeare*. Ed. Peter Brown. Oxford: Oxford University Press, 1999. 147–67.

Miles, Robert. 'Ann Radcliffe and Matthew Lewis.' *A Companion to the Gothic*. Ed. David Punter. Oxford: Blackwell, 2000. 41–57.

Miyoshi, Masao. *The Divided Self: A Perspective on the Literature of the Victorians*. New York: New York University Press, 1969.

Montaigne, Michel de. *The Essays of Montaigne*. Trans. John Florio. London: Nutt, 1892.

Nashe, Thomas. *The Terrors of the Night*. London, 1594.

Pincombe, Michael. *The Plays of John Lyly: Eros and Eliza*. Manchester: Manchester University Press, 1996. The Revels Plays Companion Library.

Punter, David, and Elisabeth Bronfen. 'Gothic: Violence, Trauma and the Ethical.' *The Gothic*. Ed. Fred Botting. Cambridge: D. S. Brewer, 2001. 7–22.

Punter, David, ed. *A Companion to the Gothic*. Oxford: Blackwell, 2000.

—. *The Literature of Terror: A History of Gothic Fictions from 1765 to the Present Day*. 2 vols. Harlow: Longman, 1996.

Rhodes, Neil. *Elizabethan Grotesque*. London: Routledge and Kegan Paul, 1980.

Russell, J. Stephen. *The English Dream Vision: Anatomy of a Form*. Columbus: Ohio State University Press, 1988.

Sage, Victor. *Horror Fiction in the Protestant Tradition*. Basingstoke: Macmillan, 1988.

Scot, Reginald. *The Discoverie of Witchcraft*. Ed. Montague Summers. London: Rodker, 1930.

Shakespeare, William. *Richard III*. Ed. John Jowett. Oxford: Oxford University Press, 2000. Oxford's World Classics.

Sivefors, Per. "'All this tractate is but a dream'": The Ethics of Dream Narration in Thomas Nashe's *The Terrors of the Night.*' *Textual Ethos Studies, or Locating Ethics*. Eds Anna Fahraeus and Ann Katrin Jonsson. Amsterdam: Rodopi, 2005. 161–74.

Slights, Camille Wells. 'Notaries, Sponges, and Looking-glasses: Conscience in Early Modern England.' *English Literary Renaissance* 28.2 (1998): 231–46.

Sullivan, Garrett A. *Memory and Forgetting in English Renaissance Drama: Shakespeare, Marlowe, Webster*. Cambridge: Cambridge University Press, 2005.

Thomas, Keith. 'Cases of Conscience in Seventeenth-Century England.' *Public Duty and Private Conscience in Seventeenth-Century England: Essays Presented to G. E. Aylmer*. Eds John Morrill, Paul Slack and Daniel Woolf. Oxford: Clarendon, 1993. 29–56.

Walsham, Alexandra. 'Ordeals of Conscience: Casuistry, Conformity and Confessional Identity in Post-Reformation England.' *Contexts of Conscience in Early Modern Europe, 1500–1700*. Eds Harald Braun and Edward Vallance. Basingstoke: Palgrave Macmillan, 2004. 32–48.

West, Richard. *The Court of Conscience or Dick Whippers Sessions*. London, 1607.

Wilks, John S. *The Idea of Conscience in Renaissance Tragedy*. London: Routledge, 1990.

4

Queen Margaret's haunting revenge: the Gothic legacy of Shakespeare's Wars of the Roses

Elisabeth Bronfen

In one episode of *Political Animals*, Elaine Barrish (Sigourney Weaver), a divorced former First Lady, serving as Secretary of State, invokes a comparison to historical female politicians to explain her own will to power: 'I took this job as secretary of state because I feel I can make a difference. Eleanor Roosevelt, Cleopatra, Elizabeth the First. That's the kind of company I want to keep'.[1] I take this recent mini television series as my point of departure for a discussion of Shakespeare's historical re-imagination of the Wars of the Roses, because both texts cross political power struggles with a battle of the sexes, though they do so at different historical moments as well as in different media. The series's reference to the queen whom Shakespeare was never allowed to put on stage, as well as to the one to whom he gave his best tragic role, allows me to foreground the manner in which the cultural after-life of early modern theatre in contemporary cinema and television anticipates a Gothic sensibility. If Weaver's Secretary of State invokes powerful women of history in order to explain how she intends to make a difference, she does not only point to the fact that the enmeshment of femininity and political power she makes claims to has a tradition. Equally important, she suggests that the specific political power women have had in the past haunts the present cultural imaginary as well. For her to name Cleopatra and Elizabeth I in their association with Eleanor Roosevelt as her models speaks both to the way the reality of past female politicians inspires a desire for making a difference and the way the issue of women and politics remains historically unfinished business.

While each in her own way came to be known for the way she either gave public body to the political agenda of the powerful sovereign at her side, or, in the case of Elizabeth I, staunchly refused to share her political power with a man, the association between Cleopatra and Gloriana of early modern England foregrounds how the gender of a rule impinges on the way actual political struggles have recourse to theatrical means even while recasting these as mass entertainment. As Stephen Greenblatt has argued, Shakespeare's plays in general are concerned with both the production and the containment of subversion and disorder, regardless whether this pertains to a struggle between generations, genders or classes. The salient correspondence between these two discourses, he explains, consists in the fact that Elizabethan playing companies 'contrived to absorb, refashion, and exploit some of the fundamental energies of a political authority that was itself already committed to histrionic display and hence was ripe for appropriation'. These energies, he adds, were both released and organized by the political and the theatrical.[2] If, in Renaissance England, a poetics of political power was inseparable from a poetics of theatre, it was, however, also inseparably bound up, as he goes on to note, with the figure of Queen Elizabeth, a ruler whose power was not only constituted in 'theatrical celebrations of royal glory and theatrical violence visited upon the enemies of that glory' (Greenblatt 64) but also grounded on a radical ambivalence regarding a female sovereign.

The association between the last pharaoh of Egypt and Elizabeth I which continues to have a resilient cultural afterlife is based on the fact that both were renowned for their skill at public performances of their political agendas. As Jonathan Bate and Dora Thornton note, while Shakespeare's Cleopatra cannot be reduced to an allegorical representation of his Queen, 'audiences would have been provoked into seeing the parallels: a woman ruler in an overwhelmingly male world, the identification between the queen and her country' (140). Equally seminal is the way the ambivalent fascination for their audacious politics came to be tied up with their insistence on being present on actual battlefields. In her famous speech at Tilbury, Elizabeth I invokes her hybrid gender in relation to her will for war, proclaiming to her troops that she has come amongst them 'not for my recreation, and disport, but being resolved, in the midst, and heat of the battaile, to live, or die amongst you all ... I know I have the bodie but of a weak, feeble woman, but I have the heart and stomach of a King, and a King of England too.'[3] Shakespeare's Cleopatra, in turn, defends her insistence on taking part in the battle against Caesar Octavius, by explaining to Mark Antony's right hand, Enobarbus, 'A charge we bear i' th' war / And as the president of my kingdom, will / Appear there for a man. Speak not against it, / I will not stay behind' (*Antony and Cleopatra* 3.7.16–19).

By turning to Shakespeare's other warrior queen, Henry VI's wife Queen Margaret of France, this chapter offers another example of the ambivalence regarding feminine political power that continues to resurface in our contemporary cultural imagination. At issue is the way a will to battle survives in the political arena, even in periods of interstice between actual battles, because any woman making claims to public authority is the adversary of someone. The containment of subversion which the Elizabethan theatre offers, and which continues to be the template for mass entertainment today, proves to be a two-edged sword. By having recourse to dramatic form and poetic language, Shakespeare's history plays not only reflect and reflect *on* the theatricality of the politics in his own time but also speak to the radical doubt which female political power continues to provoke. Before offering a reading of Shakespeare's dramatic historical imagination of the Wars of the Roses, I want, therefore, to invoke a few more examples for our current engagement with this anxiety so as to underscore how our contemporary cultural imaginary is riddled with precisely the ambivalent containment of a feminine will to political power provoked and played through in Shakespeare's early histories. By reading the earlier plays through the lens of recent mainstream films and television, my premise is that this is *the* medium most comparable to the Shakespearean stage in its mass appeal. At the same time, I am picking up on what Mieke Bal calls doing a 'preposterous history', namely looking back at themes, figural constellations and rhetorical devices deployed by early modern plays through the lens of their subsequent recycling in contemporary cinema.[4]

In Tony Gilroy's *Michael Clayton* (2007) we first see Karen Crowder (Tilda Swinton) standing alone in front of a mirror, breathing heavily as she tries to wipe away the spot which the sweat under her armpits has left on her pristinely clean white blouse. Once she has managed to calm herself, she will return to her scene of combat and, with utter ruthlessness, fight for her personal power interests in a battle over a chemical company's use of pesticides. Although she does not shirk from ordering her opponents to be killed, one of them, the lawyer Michael Clayton (George Clooney), brought in to fix his firm's dealings with her company, manages to escape the attempt on his life and returns to challenge his adversary in public. He has brought the police with him, so that she can do nothing more than faint once her clandestine power game has been brought out into the open. The final image we have of this bold businesswoman is her frail body, fallen to the floor, a visual formula for the vicissitudes of fortune that befall women who ruthlessly strive for political power. In her ambition, Karen Crowder had embodied the unregulated capitalist greed that Tony Gilroy's film narrative seeks to critique by staging the struggle between the law firm and the pharmaceutical company as a situation of domestic war. Her downfall is dramaturgic proof that the dark forces she has been part of (a capitalist enterprise gone out of control) have successfully been vanquished. Over her fainted (albeit not dead) body, the film offers its imaginary resolution for the real contradictions current capitalism poses. By disclosing a woman, audacious in her lust for power, to be a rogue player, the system as such can be salvaged and the man who found her out turned into a public hero. The film thus recycles a narrative formula installed by Shakespeare's early history plays as well as his late tragedy *Antony and Cleopatra*, namely the way an unsavoury political battle comes to be contained once it can be presented as the derailed obsessions of a woman.

Gilroy's film, however, also marks a recent trend in Hollywood, where self-confident female politicians, having come into their own again, recall classic Hollywood's understanding of the female glamour star as queen. While Sarah Bernhardt recorded her version of Elizabeth I as early as 1912, performances of queenship in Hollywood had their heyday in the 1930s, with Greta Garbo as Queen Christina, Marlene Dietrich and Elisabeth Bergner as Catherine of Russia, Katherine Hepburn as Mary Stuart of Scotland, Claudette Colbert as Cleopatra, while Elizabeth I was brought to the silver screen by both Flora Robson and Bette Davis. As Hollywood returned to the royal epic genre in the 1950s and early 1960s, it brought back some of its previous stars, with Bette Davis once more impersonating the old Virgin Queen while Jean Simmons gave her face to the young Bess. The most iconic revival of queenship on the screen, Elizabeth Taylor's interpretation of the last Egyptian pharaoh, however, also marked the end of the classic Hollywood studio system, with female stars compelled to seek out different genres, most notably the romantic comedy and the family melodrama, to put the contradiction between public ambition and private happiness on display.[5]

In the 1990s, however, royalty re-emerged on screen with idiosyncratic twists. In *The Queen* (2006), Helen Mirren (who that year also performed Elizabeth I in an HBO series), portrays Elizabeth II as a woman who uses her political intelligence to counter British culture's fatal desire for celebrity news coverage. That same year Meryl Streep appeared as the queen of the fashion world in *The Devil Wears Prada* (2006), canny when it comes to securing her power yet also fairy godmother to the romantic luck of the young woman who had assisted her. As the CIA agent Corrine Whitman, Streep returned to the arena of public power in *Rendition* (2007), proving to be as ruthless as any man in her decision to have an Arab-American engineer arrested and tortured without certainty of his ties to a terrorist organization. While Gavin Hood's film is staunchly critical of this political policy, it does allow its star one moment of rhetorical glory. In a patriotic speech, Streep's CIA agent defends herself by claiming that, to protect the security of the USA, any politician must be willing to sacrifice lives. The actress's skilful presentation of a position that undercuts the film's explicit ideology plays to the double-voicing already present in Shakespeare's plays, when these bring on stage precisely those dangerous feminine forces which must ultimately be vanquished.

It is above all Cate Blanchett, however, who gave a new face to queenship at the end of the twentieth century. If, in *Elizabeth* (1998), Shekhar Kapur focuses on the transition from the natural body of a woman to the symbolic body of the queen, *Elizabeth: The Golden Age* (2007) foregrounds her status as victorious warrior. And while the first film nods towards George Sydney's *Young Bess* (1953) with its narrative about how successful queenship is predicated on the sacrifice of personal romance, the second recalls how, at the onset of the Second World War, Michael Curtiz had cast Elizabeth's successful battle against the Spanish Armada in contemporary political terms. If, in *Fire Over England* (1937), the adversary Spanish King resembles the fascist dictator Franco, in Shekhar Kapur's recycling he resembles Ahmadinejad of Iran.[6] The correspondence between these recent films (recycling as they do an earlier decade of cinematic royalty) and Shakespeare's early histories consists, as will be discussed in more detail below, in the way women, appropriating for themselves an active role in the political arena, are conceived. Even though the conflict between intimate individual and public persona is foregrounded, they are shown to be fully emplaced in the political sphere. In contrast to the female stars who fight their way through the Alien or Terminator films, these women politicians are no outsiders, seeking to disclose social and political corruption. Unlike the femme fatale in neo-noir they also do not stand for an enjoyment of lethal transgression. Rather, they stand for the law, even if (or precisely because) they play through its violent side. They are completely within the symbolic order, putting up their fight so as to preserve it. When they have recourse to violence and corruption they do so to assure the survival of a socio-political system they fully believe and trust in.

Why has Hollywood come to privilege female characters for an embodiment of this dark position in political power games, recalling the power machinations of Gothic fiction? Is there a hidden assumption that female rulers are more ruthless in their actions? Is this because, as Lady Macbeth in her desire to be unsexed so poignantly articulates, for them to move into the arena of politics they must break with attitudes of generosity, sympathy and kindness conventionally attributed to women? Does this say something about the current roles women play in their respective political parties? Because the Secretary of State in *Political Animals* could just as well have included Queen Margaret in her pantheon of role models, Shakespeare's dramatic conception of this warrior queen takes on new topicality. This audacious woman, as skilled in battle as she is in diplomacy, is the only character to appear in all four of Shakespeare's first histories and thus stands for a resilient will to survival. As Jean E. Howard suggests, in Shakespeare's historical re-imagination of the Wars of the Roses, Margaret 'embodies strengths that contradict the patriarchal view that women are inherently weaker than men and therefore less suited to have dominion either in the state or in the household' (Greenblatt et al. 293).[7] The demonization her ruthless audacity as mother and politician calls forth is part of this legacy.

Gothic sensibility, in turn, comes into play when we revisit the cultural anxieties surrounding women in public office on the Shakespearean stage through the lens of their re-emergence on the screen. In the histories Queen Margaret emerges as an uncanny figure, neither only a woman nor only a ruler but both, self-consciously using the allure of her physical appearance to sustain her symbolic role as mother of the future King of England. And she is an uncanny figure because while her appearance in England causes past civil discord to erupt, the curses she speaks before being once more banished to her homeland will reverberate in her absence. My wager is that, since Shakespeare couldn't bring Elizabeth I to the stage, it is the portrait of this other warrior queen that we can revisit to understand how our contemporary moment is possessed by the cultural survival of the conflicted fascination surrounding queenship in the past. The female force that Shakespeare's early histories are able to stage speaks to a re-evaluation of the still contested feminine political power today.

Let us, therefore, move to the texts themselves. The first of these early histories pits the kind-hearted Henry VI, unable to intervene in and resolve the strife between the embattled nobles of his court, against his ambitious French wife. As Jean E. Howard notes, presented as 'a sexualized figure of gender disorder, Queen Margaret fills the vacuum created by her husband's own weakness. In their relationship, traditional gender hierarchy is stood on its head' (Greenblatt et al. 203).[8] Her appearance in England immediately calls forth a front line inside the country, shifting the political tension from an external war with France to an internal war amongst aristocratic brothers. Far from being the actual cause of this crisis, however, at her body a civil dissention is called forth and negotiated that has been brewing for quite some time. As such, her function in this early history anticipates a Gothic sensibility. As contested foreigner turned domestic queen, she serves as the privileged site where internal tensions riddling the English court since Richard II was deposed come to haunt the present. She fits the part because she both exceeds and falls short of what is expected of the Queen of England. Although she is in possession of magnificent beauty, she brings no dowry into this marriage and is thus, as several courtiers point out, unfitting as a match for a king who has returned victorious from his battles.

At the end of *1 Henry VI*, Suffolk praises the foreign woman whom he had earlier gone to woo in the name of his king, predicting that her 'valiant courage and undaunted spirit, / More than in women commonly is seen, / Will answer our hope in issue of a king' (5.5.70–73).[9] His hope that she may give birth to a legitimate heir to the throne only barely covers his actual political interest in her queenship. Through her he hopes, as he confesses in the very last line of the play, to bolster his own political power, ruling 'both her, the King, and realm' (5.5.108). At the beginning of *2 Henry VI*, we then discover how her undaunted feminine decisiveness is received in England. Over the body of this newly installed queen, the strife between the house of Lancaster and that of York finally comes to be ignited. Richard Plantagenet, Duke of York, believes he recognizes a clandestine capitulation in relation to France in a marriage which he claims 'dims the honour of this warlike isle!' (1.1.124). In his mockery that Henry VI had to give up two dukedoms for his wife he recalls past history, resurrecting a spectral world against which the present cannot hold its own in stature: 'I never read but England's kings have had / Large sums of gold and dowries with their wives; / and our King Henry gives away his own, / To match with her that brings no vantages' (1.1.127–30). Given that he had himself hoped these lands would fall into his possession, at issue implicitly is also his own political disappointment.

Most salient about the political discontent surrounding Queen Margaret, however, is the fact that she is fighting on two fronts. She has quickly realized that in the arena of court intrigues she must not only defend herself against the malicious accusations of the Yorkists, who were always against her marriage, but also against the political authority of her husband's uncle, Humphrey, Duke of Gloucester. She will not allow the man, who has assumed the role of the King's Protector, to tell her what she is to do. At stake, after all, is the legitimacy of her claim to the title of Queen. 'What? Shall King Henry be a pupil still / Under the surly Gloucester's governance?' she asks the Duke of Suffolk in front of a group of petitioners, adding to the complaint, 'Am I a queen in title and in style, / And must be made a subject to a duke?' (1.3.46–9). So as to help bring about the execution of the man whose power over her husband she dreads, she briefly aligns herself with her earliest enemy, the Duke of York. After the death of Gloucester, however, this clandestine pact will prove to have dealt a decisive blow to the king's power. York will successfully turn his own betrayal against both his sovereign and the queen, his former ally. Not only does he rally his men to fight against Henry VI by openly accusing him: 'thou art not king; / Not fit to govern and rule multitudes' (5.1.93–4), but, more pointedly, his war furore is aimed at a queen he calls a 'blood-bespotted Neapolitan, / Outcast of Naples, England's bloody scourge!' (5.5.117–18).

In this political climate, where the aftereffects of past civil dissention haunt the present, Queen Margaret actually has no free choice. A stranger in England, she is utterly dependent on the approval of her husband, both for her symbolic and for her corporeal survival. The violence she either helps stimulate or clandestinely endorses keeps mounting to match the escalated attacks on her legitimacy as queen. Like the mythic Cleopatra, she finds she can respond to Henry VI's progressive helplessness only by increasing her willingness to use all weapons at her disposal: her beauty, her eloquence and ultimately her knowledge of the art of war. Since it is at her person that the violent fantasies of the rebellious courtiers come to be negotiated, she retaliates by taking this violence to its extreme. Part and parcel of the Gothic sensibility we can discern in her figure *avant la lettre* is the way she renders visible what up to this point had fed political discontent without being directly addressed; embodying the political unconscious of her world.[10] During the battle at the end of *2 Henry VI*, when it has become painfully clear that the king's forces will lose the day, she taunts her husband with the question of his legitimacy: 'What are you made of? You'll neither fight nor fly, / Now is it manhood, wisdom and defence, / To give the enemy way, and to secure us / By what we can' (5.2.74–7).

Although she is pursuing very different power interests from those of her opponents, she shares their assessment of this king. His lack of self-assertion as sovereign and man has prompted him to agree to putting his name to a document in which he shows himself prepared to disinherit his son and sign over the throne to Richard of York, on the condition that he be allowed to reign as king during his lifetime. Outraged at this foolish peace treaty, Margaret mobilizes her own troops. In contrast to her husband, she is not only willing to fight like a man for her son's royal rights. She also does not shy away from cruel mockery of her enemies. Staging her triumph after having captured her arch-enemy at the beginning of *3 Henry VI*, she forces York to place a paper crown on his head, only to demand back both: 'Off with the crown, and, with the crown, his head' (1.4.107). As mother to the future Lancaster king, she viciously fights against the dethronement of the current one so as to defend not only the legitimacy of her own title but also that of the line of kings still to emerge from her family. York, her equal in contempt, derides her by calling her an Amazonian trull and she-wolf of France, 'whose tongue more poisons than the adder's tooth!' (1.4.112). His denigration translates the battle among brothers over the throne of England into a gender battle. The Gothic inflection Shakespeare's tetralogy unfolds consists in the way it uses Margaret's personal transgression of classic feminine virtues to address the repetition loop of violence which comes to be replayed over and again when power-hungry men challenge the divine rights of their sovereigns. Along with the ghosts of Henry IV and Henry V implicitly invoked throughout these three early histories, the text also implicitly calls forth the spirit of transgressive femininity from the tragedies of antiquity. Women, Edward, the usurper of the throne proclaims, 'are soft, mild, pitiful and flexible; / Thou stern, indurate, flinty, rough, remorseless' (1.4.141–2).

In York's mouth, the queen's royal pride and ambition turn into signs of a monstrous inhumanity, rendering her as a gruesome Gothic figure. And yet, far from silencing her, his denigrating words having called forth the fatal thrust of her dagger open up a new scene of war. York's son Edward will also have recourse to the rhetoric of gender anxiety so as to screen out his own illegitimate appropriation of power and the clandestine executions that made his successful claim to the throne possible. If, by marrying Henry VI, Queen Margaret was meant to render less dangerous the border separating her native France from her new home, England, her enemies, who insist on her having brought the previous war's front line with her, declare her to be an uncanny political body that combines an external enemy with an internal one. After the death of Henry VI, his successor Edward, in turn, is compelled to split the symbolic body of the deceased sovereign from this allegedly monstrous queen. To legitimate his own rise to power he must find his uncle to be innocent of all the political machinations that led to his premature abdication. By producing a line of argument which put the blame for the complex intrigues that came to undermine the will of the recently deceased king elsewhere, he hopes to rehabilitate the symbolic name of Henry VI. In this he recalls Octavian's need to cleanse Antony from all shame his fatal romance with Cleopatra had cast on him, sustaining the Gothic repetition loop these early histories thematically feed on.

Because she is an outsider to Edward's domain of power in two senses (female and of French origin), the deposed queen proves to be the perfect target for his political ploy. He readily declares her responsible for the continuation of violence in England, taunting her with the accusation 'For what hath broach'd this tumult but thy pride?' (2.2.159). Invoking the same nomenclature of ideal femininity his father had, as though the dead York were speaking through him, he adds, 'Hadst thou been meek, our title still had slept; / And we, in pity of the gentle King, / Had slipp'd our claim until another age' (2.2.160–3). What is significant in Edward's re-appropriation of gender trouble for the sustaining of an illegitimate claim to the throne is not merely the resolve with which Margaret insists on fighting through her power interests at all costs. At issue also is the extremely fragile status of her position as ruler. She consistently rallies her troops to fight in her name so as to reaffirm the sovereignty the men around her relentlessly want to take away from her. At the same time it is precisely the fragility of her own political power which endows her with a clarity of vision regarding the limits to what she, as a foreigner and a woman, can do. The Gothic quality she can be seen to be endowed with thus takes on a further dimension. She neither recalls the spirit of previous warrior queens nor can she simply be targeted as a monstrous body in her enmeshment of alluring beauty and martial furore. She also possesses a gift of prophesy that conflates an accurate assessment of the present with an ability to imagine its catastrophic outcome. Her astute courage consists in an ability to soberly take into account the contingency of all political power struggles so as to calculate her particular battles with utmost precision.

Although she claims to be fighting to reinstall her son as the future king of England, her resistance to the usurper Edward is never sustained by the personal sentimentality of a mother. Instead, she is sustained in her valiant if destructive will to battle by her desire for symbolic legitimacy and as such functions as the pivot in the systemic violence Shakespeare's early history plays put on stage. By spurring on the tragic repetition compulsion of betrayal and revenge underwriting the Wars of the Roses, she renders visible the logic of a political culture drenched in violence. She not only enacts the ruthless thirst for power which her opponents have always claimed for her but also performs a political point made by Michel Foucault regarding the mutual implication of war and politics. 'War is the motor behind institutions and order', he explains, with the civil law of peace itself a coded war:

> We are therefore at war with one another; a battlefront runs through the whole of society, continuously and permanently, and it is this battlefront that puts us all on one side or the other. There is no such thing as a neutral subject. We are all inevitably someone's adversary. (Foucault 50–1)

By embodying the principle of a ubiquitous adversarial spirit underwriting politics, whether in peacetime or in a sustained civil war, Queen Margaret exceeds the misogynist allegations that the men, anxious about feminine political power, project on to her. Because her fate renders visible how fickle all political power games are, how quickly things can turn in unexpected and incalculable ways, she stands in for the uncontrollable pivot in this national history of violence.

Her prophetic sight is predicated on the fragility of her position within this system of power doubly foreign to her as a French woman. From the start she knows she could trust none of her political alliances, not even those allegedly gained through her marriage with Henry VI.[11] While her opponents detect in her unswerving ambition a sign for her inhuman monstrosity, her allies interpret it as a grandiose appropriation of masculine heroism. It is worth recalling that in the world of the Renaissance, marked as it was by ever shifting political forces, women conventionally assumed two roles. Either they brought money and land as dowries into a marriage and thus guaranteed the peace between embattled royal houses. Or the children they gave birth to rendered the royal succession secure. Explicitly conceived as stakes in political alliances, women were not, however, meant to display any independent power interests or political ambitions of their own, only to sustain those of their families. In her radical insistence on self-determination, Margaret thus emerges as a cipher for the suspicious fascination with which many actual female rulers were regarded in the early modern period. At the same time, her unencumbered will for battle also proves to be the logical consequence of her prescient calculation of her situation, speaking to the contradictory feelings regarding female political power that have survived until today. Reduced to her function as a mother, she not only fights for the white rose against the red, but also unleashes her own war in the name of her son. In fact, however, she stands apart from the very war amongst brothers she thus keeps alive, looking askance at this fraternal rivalry.

Her oblique gaze gages a political condition in which everyone is inevitably someone else's adversary in the decidedly unsentimental manner of *realpolitik* precisely because, as a woman, she can never forget her own dependency on the power contingencies that define her as a political subject in this sustained civil war. She is willing to risk everything because she knows that she can lose everything, even the fruits of her own motherhood: the son, who alone can make sure that her own political power will be sustained. After having lost her last battle, with all her allies dead and her husband killed, she turns to the only weapon still left to her. A culmination of her prescient vision, her terrible prophecies set in at precisely the moment she takes the corpse of her son Edward into her arms after he has been stabbed by the Earl of March. The Gothic repetition loop dramaturgically played through at her body is such that this awful and awe-inspiring insight will, in *Richard III*, lead to a rich and strange bond between embattled female rulers. In this last of the histories about Henry VI, however, the prediction she makes, marked as it is both by mourning and by her desire for revenge, serves to bring to the attention of those on stage and off the systemic repetition compulsion of violence that had been inscribed in the political strife between brothers all along. The last words she speaks, before she is forcibly removed from the stage in *3 Henry VI*, are: 'So come to you and yours as to this prince' (5.5.80). To silence this Gothic foreboding of his own demise and instead celebrate what he hopes is the beginning of his lasting joy, Edward, having usurped the throne to become King of England, exiles Margaret to France.

But these are not her last words in Shakespeare's early histories. Because she is able to judge her own complicity in the brutal intrigues that led to the usurpation of her power and thus shows herself to be unwilling to veil herself in false innocence, she is also the one who can correctly gauge the situation of her successor. In the first act of *Richard III*, she calls Elizabeth, who at the side of Edward IV is now the reigning queen, 'poor painted queen vain flourish of my fortune' (1.3.241).[12] Evoking a bleak future regarding the political ambitions of Richard, now Duke of Gloucester, she assures her 'the day will come that thou shalt wish for me / to help thee curse this poisonous bunch-back'd toad' (1.3.245–6). At first, Elizabeth still tries to shield herself from this Gothic foreboding by telling herself that, in so far as she never did Margaret any wrong, she is innocent of any sad lot that might befall her. Assuming the exact opposite attitude as the deposed queen, she foolishly believes that she can keep her distance to the political intrigues her husband is engaged in. She is soon forced, however, to recognize that after her husband's death this selfsame Richard, once he has become the new King of England, wishes to marry her daughter. For this reason, she bonds not only with his mother, who curses her own son because she declares his backhanded treachery to be a shame to her maternity. She will also find herself compelled to form an alliance with the rival, who, from the very beginning, had insisted that because no one can be an innocent player in a political arena shaped by betrayal and revenge, no one can walk away unharmed. The final Gothic twist Shakespeare's early histories attribute to his dramatic reconception of Queen Margaret is that, once they are forced to view their world with sober eyes because they can no longer overlook the terrible deeds Richard has committed, the women of the house of York come to be haunted by the cursing spirit of the foreign warrior queen of the house of Lancaster.

Initially, the old Queen Margaret, who has not yet embarked for her homeland, merely listens to the complaints of the other women from the safety of her hiding place. Having stepped into their field of vision, however, to forewarn them that they will call upon her to help them curse, she takes on the role of a mirror held up against their foolish desire not to see what they cannot afford not to acknowledge. Once more calling up her own sorrow, she offers by virtue of an analogy of names a telling correspondence between her sad fate and the woe of both the present queen and the current king's mother:

> If sorrow can admit society,
> Tell o'er your woes again by viewing mine.
> I had an Edward, till a Richard kill'd him;
> I had a husband, till a Richard kill'd him:
> Thou hadst an Edward, till a Richard kill'd him;
> Thou hadst a Richard, till a Richard kill'd him.
>
> (4.4.38–43)

Her invocation not only renders visible that the way of justice has taken a new path. Her story also serves to inspire a desire for revenge on the part of the woman who has appropriated her own title as queen. In the course of this play, Margaret will, indeed, teach Elizabeth how to curse. With a touch of malice, she also assures her new ally that her woe makes those in France smile. Watching over the last episodes of this civil war from the safe distance of her homeland, she can assume the Gothic spirit of an avenging angel. Her keen courage in the past, one might surmise, serves as a model of feminine power; it infects the imagination of the current Queen Elizabeth and inspires her to prevent the marriage between Richard III and her daughter.

In so far as Margaret's curses force both women of the house of York to suspend all fantasies of non-complicity, they articulate a poignant ethical insight. To rephrase Stanley Cavell's discussion of the conditions of tragedy: if political disasters occur because individual players keep repeating precisely those actions which brought about the tragic course of events in the first place, then real abdication consists in stopping and seeing what one is doing (Cavell 81). The insight that will avert future disaster is predicated on a refusal of blindness, insisting instead on a sober and unsentimental recognition of the tragic consequences which any power struggle between noble families entails. If Margaret is the one to draw attention to the fatal loop of cursing, revenge and a lust for a renewed cycle of retribution, she is also the one who implicitly helps bring about the peace treaty that her kind-hearted but politically inept husband had failed to reach. The logical consequence of a political culture of civil war, in which everyone is inevitably the adversary of someone else, however, is that peace can be found only once all the sons of the rebellious house of York have been destroyed. The lust for violence on the part of the embattled brothers must, thus, first culminate in one last spectacle of battle. Decisive for the importance Shakespeare ascribes to the female politician who is the only figure present in all four early histories is that this fatal necessity comes to be played out under the aegis of the voice that had foreseen the destruction of Richard III from the start.

In the final act of *Richard III*, the resolution to this civil war is anticipated in the spectral theatricalization of battle's violence, staged for the single-minded tyrant who is not willing to recognize that, by his refusing to stop and see, the fatal consequences of his actions will inevitably catch up with him. Or put another way, the Gothic staging of imminent disaster forces him to see what he had not wanted to hear. It is worth recalling that Richard had responded to Elizabeth's declaration of her sorrows and the curses of his own mother by exclaiming: 'Either be patient and entreat me fair, / Or with the clamorous report of war / Thus will I drown your exclamations' (4.4.153–5). The self-conscious, albeit implicit reflection on actual political violence in the England of his day on the part of the dramatized violence that Shakespeare's *Richard III* brings to the stage, thus thrives on the following analogy: As a result of his wilful blindness to the political consequences of his violent usurpation of power, the king will be forced to acknowledge the unavoidability of his tragic fate once it has been performed for him as a morality play. In this Gothic vision, the ghosts of his victims give body to the cursing voice of old Queen Margaret, who, though she has been exiled to France, remains a spectral presence throughout the final act of the play.

It belongs to the narrative formulas of representations of war that the night before an important battle is given special treatment on stage. One might recall the Chorus at the beginning of Act 4 in *Henry V* evoking a scene in which the moon presents to the English troops ghosts of their fellow soldiers, while the 'royal captain of this ruined band / Walking from watch to watch, from tent to tent' (4.1.29–30) eases their anticipation of danger with this 'little touch of Harry in the night' (4.1.47). In the final act of *Richard III*, both Richard and Richmond ask for paper and ink, so as to prepare themselves for the martial violence about to be unleashed in Bosworth Field. While Richmond soon falls into a deep, refreshing sleep, his opponent Richard finds himself confronted with all those whose untimely deaths he was responsible for. Among these the ghost of Lady Anne, his wife, calls upon him, 'tomorrow in the battle think on me, / And fall thy edgeless sword: despair and die' (5.3.163–4). One might imagine Queen Margaret, who foretold that she would follow this civil war to the end from her safe distance in France with cruel laughter on her lips, to be the hidden director of this spectral show. Indeed, one might take this speculation a step further and interpret her to be the master of Richard's personal unconscious, after having already helped articulate the political unconscious of an England torn in civil war. Once the terrible ghostly visions have left him, he admits, 'shadows tonight / Have struck more terror to the soul of Richard / Than can the substance of ten thousand soldiers, / Armed in proof, and led by shallow Richmond' (5.3.217–20).

If Margaret thus continues to be the Amazon her enemies declared her to be throughout the histories surrounding her husband Henry VI, the battle for Richard III's soul is one she wins. Taking their shape in the ghostly apparitions of all the victims of his terrible power play, her curses force her opponent to heed his conscience even if he preferred to repress the knowledge it has for him. Against this voice he cannot defend himself, even after dawn has set in. Before the actual battle begins, Richard admonishes himself, 'Let not our babbling dreams affright our souls; / conscience is but a word that cowards us' (5.3.309–10). Nevertheless, he succumbs to the curse old Queen Margaret brought into circulation. The spectral voices of the deceased can no longer be banished from the scene of battle. Instead, Bosworth Field transforms into the stage where the very power of those feminine woes and curses which he tried to occlude with his sounds of war return in the shape of the opponent army that will succeed in bringing about his demise as warrior and king.

In this last, gruesome spectacle, attesting to Shakespeare's anticipation of Gothic culture, we also, however, recognize the spectral power on which the mutual implication of dramatic violence on stage and political violence off stage thrives throughout these early histories. The fulminant theatrical enactment of war in which Shakespeare's historical re-imagination of the Wars of the Roses culminates, emerges from and vanishes back into the force of poetic language itself. It gives shape to a complex spectacle of ghosts – the dead, catching up with and changing the course of the present, as well as a repressed knowledge, catching up with and changing the fate of a flawed political figure, but also the voices of a set of dramatis personae, who come from the past to speak to us very much in the present. And at the centre of all these spectral apparitions stands Queen Margaret, a pivot between past and present, absence and present, a set of history plays and their cultural afterlife.

Notes

1 Created by Greg Berlanti, the series aired in 2012.
2 For a discussion of the political use to which Elizabeth I's pageants, processions and progresses were put, see also Louis Montrose.
3 See also Richardine Woodall 187–204.
4 See Mieke Bal's introduction to *Quoting Caravaggio* 7–44.
5 For an overview of royalty on screen see Elizabeth A. Ford and Deborah C.

Mitchell; for a discussion of the final era of costume epics in Hollywood, see Michael Wood.

6 For a discussion of Elizabeth I's afterlife on screen, see Elisabeth Bronfen and Barbara Straumann 252–70.

7 See Jean E. Howard's introduction to *3 Henry VI*.

8 See Jean E. Howard's introductions to *2 Henry VI*.

9 The edition of *1 Henry VI*, *2 Henry VI*, and *3 Henry VI* used is the one edited by Andrew S. Cairncross.

10 I take this concept from Fredric Jameson, especially his insistence that the Real of History can only be reconceived in the violent aftereffects it has had. Queen Margaret's war furore emerges as precisely such an affective trace of past dissent.

11 In this prescient attitude toward her own political power she anticipates the reality of Hillary Clinton's campaign for the US presidency as well as the depiction of women in positions of political power in current mainstream cinema.

12 The edition used is edited by Antony Hammond.

Works Cited

Bal, Mieke. *Quoting Caravaggio: Contemporary Art, Preposterous History*. Chicago: University of Chicago Press, 1999.

Bate, Jonathan and Dora Thornton. *Shakespeare: Staging the World*. London: The British Museum Press, 2012.

Bronfen, Elisabeth. *Crossmappings. Essays zur visuellen Kultur*. Zürich: Scheidegger & Spiess, 2009.

—, and Barbara Straumann. 'Political Visions: The Two Bodies of Elizabeth I.' *The Rituals and Rhetoric of Queenship. Medieval to early modern*. Eds Liz Oakley-Brown and Louise J. Wilkinson. Dublin: Four Courts Press, 2009.

Cavell, Stanley. 'The Avoidance of Love: A Reading of *King Lear*.' *Disowning Knowledge in Six Plays of Shakespeare*. Cambridge: Cambridge University Press, 1987.

Ford, Elizabeth A. and Deborah C. Mitchell. *Royal Portraits in Hollywood: Filming the Lives of Queens*. Lexington: The University Press of Kentucky, 2009.

Foucault, Michel. *'Society Must Be Defended': Lectures at the Collège de France, 1975–1976*. New York: Picador, 2003.

Greenblatt, Stephen. 'Invisible Bullets.' *Shakespearean Negotiations*. Berkeley: University of California Press, 1988.

Greenblatt, Stephen, Walter Cohen, Jean Howard and Katharine Eisaman Maus. *The Norton Shakespeare: Based on the Oxford Edition*. New York: W. W. Norton & Company, 1997.

Jameson, Fredric. *The Political Unconscious. Narrative as a Socially Symbolic Act*. London: Methuen, 1981.

Montrose, Louis. *The Subject of Elizabeth. Authority, Gender, and Representation*. Chicago: University of Chicago Press, 2006.

Political Animals. Created by Greg Berlanti. USA Network. 15 July–19 August 2012. Television series.

Shakespeare, William. *King Richard III*. Ed. Antony Hammond. 3rd edn. London: Arden Shakespeare, 1981.

—. *King Henry VI, Part 3*. Ed. Andrew S. Cairncross. 2nd edn. London: Arden Shakepeare, 1964.

—. *King Henry VI, Part 1*. Ed. Andrew S. Cairncross. 2nd edn. London: Arden Shakepeare, 1962.

—. *King Henry VI, Part 2*. Ed. Andrew S. Cairncross. 2nd edn. London: Arden Shakepeare, 1957.

Wood, Michael. *America in the Movies*. New York: Columbia University Press, 1975.

Woodall, Richardine. 'Shakespeare's Queen Cleopatra. An Act of Translation.' *Queens & Power in Medieval and early modern England*. Eds Carole Levin and Robert Bucholz. Lincoln: University of Nebraska Press, 2009.

Part II

Gothic Renaissance theatre

5

Vision and desire:
fantastic Renaissance spectacles

Beate Neumeier

'Begone! Relieve me from the sight of your detested form.'
(Mary Shelley, *Frankenstein* Chapter 10)

Gothic Renaissance

The proliferation of the Gothic across different media and the concomitant critical interest in the Gothic as a mode in the wake of psychoanalytic and post-structuralist analyses of marginalized monstrous others has finally led to a re-evaluation of the relationship between the Gothic and its Shakespearean 'model'. Moreover, the historically oriented exploration of the English Renaissance in terms of a pictorial and a religious turn and their interrelationship has contributed to a surfacing of affinities between early modern obsessions and the Gothic (see Introduction). Thus key terms of Gothic criticism such as the uncanny, the abject and the monstrous have been applied increasingly in recent Renaissance drama scholarship, particularly in conjunction with historical analyses of the religious, philosophical and medical discourses of the time, from Stephen Greenblatt's occasional use of the term uncanny in *Hamlet in Purgatory* (2001) to Mark Thornton Burnett's exploration of notions of monstrosity (2002), to Susan Zimmerman's analysis of the abject in conjunction with the religious shift of the Reformation (2005) and Maurizio Calbi's mapping of uncanny, abject and monstrous bodies in connection to early modern anatomical science (2004). Although none of these studies makes the connection to the Gothic explicit, it is in their linking of a psychoanalytically informed terminology to a careful historical exploration of the complex discursive network of the early modern period that its specific 'Gothic sensibilities' emerge.

The English Renaissance stage gave shape to ghosts, witches, and fairies, to devil-dogs, lycanthropes and ass-headed humans to foreground these processes, discussing, negotiating and reformulating boundaries between human and animal, female and male, natural and supernatural

powers and their cultural implications. Moreover, the impact of the
theatre itself is often cast in terms of these 'boundary disputes' (Greenblatt 244), particularly in Puritan pamphlets cautioning against the
monstrous transformations of spectators entering the theatre as devout
Christians, and coming forth 'possessed of the Diuell' (John Greene
1615), or 'transformed into dogges' (John Rainoldes 1600) through the
infernal art of players who 'metamorphose ... into Monsters' themselves (William Prynne 1633) (for further reference see Reynolds,
Transversal Subjects 35–7). Thus, it is not only notions of transgression of boundaries but particularly notions of transformation which
are foregrounded in a wide range of Renaissance discourses in political
and religious pamphlets, in medical and psychological treatises, as well
as in poetry and theatre, which obsessively thematize and enact foundational questions about notions of identity and reality.[1] It is through
the insistence on questions about transformational processes as cognitive and affective problem of radical uncertainty that the early modern
shaping of cultural boundaries takes place. In this context Renaissance
theatre not only functions as a complex discursive network and as a
space where these issues are being negotiated, but is itself being shaped
in the process. A re-evaluation of Renaissance drama in the light of the
Gothic thus necessitates a re-evaluation not only in terms of the staging
of transformational processes but also in terms of the emergence and
transformation of dramatic genres.

Rereading the Renaissance in terms of a 'Gothic transformation' inevitably draws attention to the applicability of the theoretical approaches
connected to the uncanny, the abject and the monstrous. Thus Freud's
definition of the uncanny resulting from a surfacing of repressed childhood complexes ('verdrängten infantilen Komplexen') and surmounted
primitive beliefs ('überwundene primitive Überzeugungen') about the
boundary between life and death seems of limited use, in so far as the
latter source of the uncanny is based upon a firmly established notion of
common reality ('Boden der gemeinen Realität') which in Freud's essay
explicitly excludes Shakespeare's ghostly apparitions (Freud 271–2).
Rather than signalling the surfacing of surmounted animistic beliefs,
Renaissance theatre stages and enacts the very *process* of 'surmounting'
through verbal and figural transformations and metamorphoses. In this
context Todorov's concept of the fantastic as a liminal category situated
between the uncanny and the marvellous, signalling a fundamental
cognitive uncertainty, seems more applicable, particularly in connection
to Kristeva's concept of the abject as *affective* horror of in-betweenness,
because both terms differently foreground the complex, preliminary and
inevitably incomplete processual character of movements towards affec-

tive and cognitive resolution (cf. Lee). I would like to borrow Todorov's term in this modified sense, without adhering to his distinct limitation of the literary fantastic along Freudian lines to the period between the rise of the Gothic novel in the late eighteenth and the advent of psychoanalysis in the early twentieth century. The theatre as the most visible visual medium of the early modern period uses the fantastic (*phantad-, phantázein*) 'to make visible' the cognitive and affective horrors of uncertainty about reality and identity, which are fundamentally linked to questions about the act of seeing, the nature of perception and its relation to knowledge. These uncertainties emerge in transformational processes foregrounding *themes of vision* and *themes of desire* and their intersections with shifting emphasis (to borrow Todorov's distinction without its theoretical underpinnings). The obsession with monstrous creatures and horrifying phenomena in early modern culture is part of an intricate discursive web, the complexities of which Stuart Clark has traced in his analysis of *Vanities of the Eye* (2007) in connection to 'the major historical developments ...: the vogue for visual artifice, the exploration of demonology, religious reformation, and philosophical scepticism' (Clark 5).[2]

This notion of a fantastic in-betweenness seems more inclusive and less historically charged than the related notion of the monstrous, which doesn't seem to apply to all the configurations in question, despite a shared theoretical conceptualization in terms of the liminal, the transgressive and the transformative (see also Shildrick; Cohen; Lykke and Braidotti; and Mittman and Dendle). Significantly, investigations into Renaissance teratology not only foreground the interrelatedness of rival discourses about 'prodigious, natural and distant monsters' (Davies 52) but also emphasize a 'close link between cognition and emotion in the case of monsters' (Davies 58). Thus the intersections of uncertainties about perception and desire discussed in connection to the fantastic seem closely connected to the emotions ascribed to readings of the monstrous, namely 'horror, pleasure, and repugnance – which overlapped and co-existed during much of the early modern period' (Daston and Park 180).

The fantastic as a term highlighting these connections seems like an apt starting-point for an analysis of a Gothic Renaissance exploring the cognitive and affective uncertainties in transformational processes, which cannot be resolved in terms of the internalized uncanny or of the externalized marvellous. The Gothic proper thus appears as the haunting link between early modern and postmodern obsessions with transformational processes (Neumeier, *Modern Gothic* 141–51). The fantastic in-between of early modern theatre allows for a specifically disturbing realization

of the transformational processes between animate/inanimate, super-
natural/natural, human/animal, male/female, enabling simultaneity
as well as oscillation between contradictory positions and conflicting
readings, which the plays enact in different ideologically dependent and
genre-related ways. In the following I would like to focus on configurations of transformation, which not only are central within the Gothic
mode but which have been particularly productive in the early modern
period, when the theatre enacted 'boundary disputes' through ghostly
apparitions and shape-shifters like witches, werewolves and devil-dogs,
foregrounding their transformations in and of the dramatic genres of
tragedy and tragicomedy.

Ghostly apparitions

While the ghostly resurrections of later Gothic fiction often appear either
as haunting spectral visions or as reanimations of dead materiality,
privileging the marvellous or the uncanny, early modern playwrights
seem obsessed with foregrounding them in terms of cognitive uncertainty and affective in-betweenness in the context of religious, medical
and philosophical debates about questions of perception and desire,
turning the crisis of 'European visual cultures' (Clark 2) into a theatrical spectacle. Shakespeare's plays in particular can be read as a
veritable anatomy of this process, unfolding its discursive network and
foregrounding its implicit cultural anxieties.

Thus the ghostly apparitions in *Hamlet* are at the centre of the play's
exploration of radical uncertainties about the relation of vision and
knowledge through 'a deliberate forcing together of radically incompatible accounts of almost everything that matters' (Greenblatt 240),
linking discussions about demonology and madness, art and idolatry,
memory and forgetting. From the opening debate about the nature of
the apparition onwards, the first act compulsively returns to this initial
scenario through successive verbal and visual variations culminating in
the ghostly encounter between father and son. The suggested readings
of the ghost in religious, political and psychological terms foreground
the act of perception and its link to ambivalent notions of fear and
desire from Horatio's acknowledgement of 'fear and wonder' (1.1.42)
to Hamlet's uncertainty about its origin from heaven or hell (1.4.21).
The incompatibility of the suggested readings testifies to the desire for
disambiguation and to its failure, as the eventual encounter between
Hamlet and the apparition evokes the father *and* the heavenly or hellish
supernatural power, the memory of the past *and* the vision of future
revenge, oscillating between de- and refamiliarizing transformations.

The ghostly admonition, 'remember me' (1.5.91) links Hamlet's subsequent decision to put on an 'antic disposition' (1.5.173) back to his 'nightly colour' (1.2.68), the 'cognitive nightmare' of melancholia which in early modern England was thought to be bound to 'visual fixations' on images of the past (Clark 54–5).

The first act thus sets the stage for an exploration of the intricate interrelationship between perception and desire and the concomitant difficulty of separating cognitive uncertainties and affective ambivalences. The closet scene between Hamlet and Gertrude returns to this scenario as repetition with a difference, shifting the emphasis more firmly from cognitive questions about perception towards questions about emotional response. The audience witnesses Hamlet's wilful resurrection of the past in front of the mother as a transformational process from presenting his visual picture to its verbal interpretation, to the embodied ghostly apparition. Hamlet's description of the fatherly image ('Look here upon this picture ... / A combination and a form indeed / Where every *god* did seem to set his seal' 3.4.52, 59–60) calls upon the religious discourses of idolatry and iconoclasm. Hamlet's insistence on the inseparability of the senses ('eyes without feeling, feeling without sight' 3.4.70.8) in contradistinction to Gertrude's choice to forget and to read his vision as madness appears as intervention in the debate about the magic transforming power of re-membering as intersection of desire, vision and language. Significantly, Hamlet's vision is shared by the audience, which witnesses a complex layering and interplay of ghostly readings, oscillating between notions of psychological projection, supernatural apparition and theatricality. The play thus enacts a fantastic shifting process of contradictory readings of the relationship between spirit and matter, image and corporeality. It insists on the undecidability between incompatible readings of the apparition on a *cognitive* and an *affective* level, even if it seems to signal a shift towards the uncanny by moving from the ghostly vision as a shared experience (centring on questions of vision) in the opening scenes to an individualized and interiorized experience (centring on questions of affect) in the closet scene, and from an exploration of emotions as effect of cognitive uncertainty to a primary interest in the workings of affective instabilities.

Webster's *Duchess of Malfi* addresses these issues with a difference and in reverse order in the torture scene and the echo scene, moving from a primary investigation into emotional ambivalences to an insistence on cognitive uncertainties. The torture scene stages a cruel parody of a ghostly resurrection for the duchess proceeding from the fragmented body part of the cut-off hand to the seemingly unified image of the

corpses of her loved ones, to (what could be read as) a grotesque animation through the performance of the madmen. However, this succession of disjointed aspects of spirit and matter cannot be integrated into
a coherent ghostly vision, but is rather designed to destroy the very
notion of coherence. However, Webster's ironic inclusion of the audience
in Ferdinand's artful deception of the duchess's vision foregrounds the
fundamental unreliability of perception, while the following revelation
of the truth of the lifelike wax work of Vincentio Lauriola (4.1.114) to
the audience before the advent of the madmen heightens the effect of
the predicament on the still unknowing duchess. The sadistic spectacle
of the torture scene functions as a cognitive and affective test case
about the mastery of vision. Ferdinand's success, however, is even more
limited than Hamlet's in the closet scene, as he may trick the duchess's
perception, but cannot master her response, whereas Gertrude does
not share Hamlet's ghostly vision, but eventually seems to be affected
by the torturing images conjured in his words. By contrast Webster
foregrounds the futility of Ferdinand's attempts to extricate himself from
the scene as unseen director of a spectacle, which ironically turns into an
exteriorization of his inner vision and emotional state. Thus, inevitably,
the madmen share his obsession with the mastery of vision through
references to optical instruments ('I'll draw it [doomsday] nearer by a
perspective, or make a glass that shall set all the world on fire' 4.2.73–5)
as well as his obsession with the human/animal boundary and its affective implications ('let us howl ... / Some deadly dogged howl' 4.2.61–2).

The play grounds Ferdinand's need for a mastery of vision in his
fear of the duchess's sight and his emotional proximity to her. Thus
the iconoclastic urge of the disenchanted idolater can be acted out only
under the cover of darkness or with the help of Bosola as his stand-in,
who in turn can only execute his final murderous task in the disguises
of the tomb maker and the bellman. Despite all attempts at reducing
the duchess to 'a box of worm-seed ... a little crudded milk, fantastical
puff-paste' (4.2.124–5) she remains 'Duchess of Malfi still' (4.2.142),
performing the art of dying ('I perceive death .... / Best gift is they can
give, or I can take' 4.2.224–5) against all artful designs ('plagued in
art' 4.1.111). Hauntingly, this power of the duchess does not end in
her death, after which Ferdinand alternates between orders to cover
and to uncover her face ('cover her face: mine eyes dazzle'; 'let me see
her face again' 4.2.264 and 272), while Bosola turns from executioner
to avenger. The ghostly presence of the duchess haunts the entire fifth
act, performing her resurrection with ambivalent implications about
the boundary between life and death, the dead rotting corpse and the
eternal spirit.

The ambivalences about actual ghostly apparitions, addressed in the first act of *Hamlet*, are taken up in the echo scene of the last act of *The Duchess of Malfi*, shifting the focus from the iconoclastic urge of Ferdinand, which has played itself out, to the idolizing love of Antonio. While Antonio's friend Delio insists on superstitious imagination as an explanatory pattern for the ghostly echo ('Your fancy, merely' 5.3.46), Antonio seems to oscillate between disbelief and belief, recognizing his duchess's voice and later her ghostly figure ('on the sudden, a clear light / Presented me a face folded in sorrow' 5.3.44–5). But even the claimers of disbelief are countered ironically by the way in which they are verbalized: 'Echo, I will not talk with thee, / For thou art a dead thing' (5.3.38–9). The ghostly stage presence of the duchess is evoked through the use of her voice and presumably her figure ironically appearing at the very moment when the echo claims that Antonio will 'never see her more' (5.3.42). What Antonio, who is ignorant of the duchess's death, may read as a premonition of the future is for the audience a hauntingly fateful truth. The play foregrounds the theatrical artificiality of ghostly images only to ironically insist on their power. Every demystifying reading of events is ironically followed by a stubborn return of the belief in their magic signifying nature. Despite the different successive scenarios evoking and staging notions of a ghostly resurrection in Shakespeare's *Hamlet* and Webster's *Duchess of Malfi*, the transformational processes presented in both plays through intersections of religious and scientific discourses insist on foundational uncertainties about vision and desire, opting for an unsettling, ineluctable fantastic in-betweenness, which resists all attempts at closure.

Witches, werewolves and changelings

English Renaissance theatre gave birth to a variety of metamorphic creatures, foregrounding their fantastic in-betweenness as expression of a radical uncertainty about boundaries of supernatural/natural, human/animal, male/female. Emphasizing intersections of perception and desire, these creatures specifically tend to express gender anxieties in the context of debates about demonology and madness, idolatry and iconoclasm. Most famously, the witches in *Macbeth* represent this fantastic in-betweenness in a play about 'the act of seeing' (Diehl 191), in which 'everything is on the border between fantasy and reality' (Greenblatt 193). The audience witnesses the initial transformation of Macbeth's reading of the witches as 'imperfect speakers' (1.3.68) who leave him with a 'suggestion whose horrid image doth unfix my hair', and 'thought, whose murder yet is but fantastical' (1.3.138), to his belief in their 'perfect'st report' (1.5.2) in the letter to his Lady. Shifting the emphasis from the question of the witches' 'nature' to questions of reading them, the play focuses on the attempt of a willed devilish transformation of Macbeth and the Lady, foregrounded in her famous calling upon the spirits ('Come you spirits / ..., unsex me here' 1.5.38–9) as well as in his threatening the witches with an 'eternal curse' (4.1.121).

On a psychological level the audience is invited to watch Macbeth's hysterical oscillation between obsessive desires to confirm his murderous vision of the prophecy ('I'll make assurance double sure' 4.1.99) and its inevitable falsifications ('Then comes my fit again; I had else been perfect ... / But now I am cabined, cribbed, confined, bound in / To saucy doubts and fears' 3.4.20, 23–4), complemented by Lady Macbeth's desperate wish to forget ('These deeds must not be thought / After these ways' 2.2.32–3) what she diagnoses in Macbeth as 'the very painting of your fear' (3.4.60), as being 'quite unmann'd in folly' (3.4.73), contrasted by her own consecutive descent into madness. Ironically, at the end of the play the fundamental uncertainty of vision, the inability to establish a stable connection between sign and meaning, foregrounded in the witches' appearance and prophecy as well as in the later ghostly apparitions and nightmarish imaginings, is countered – as feminist criticism has shown – by a reaffirmation of gender boundaries in the transformation of Lady Macbeth from witchlike heroine into madwoman and of Macbeth from demonic hero into despairing but unrelenting warrior (see also Adelman; Neely). Taking up current debates about witchcraft and demonology, madness and gender, the play participates in the cultural process, which will lead to a naturalization of gender boundaries, and a gradual separation of the spiritual from the material world. The focus, however, is still on the 'boundary disputes' and the ensuing uncertainties through a staging of literal and metaphorical configurations of fantastic in-betweenness.

In Webster's *Duchess of Malfi* all the main characters are associated with images of shape-shifting creatures questioning the human/animal/ supernatural boundaries. The duchess turns into a witch in Ferdinand's view ('For they whose faces do belie their hearts / Are witches ... and give the devil suck' 1.1.309–11), Bosola sees himself as a familiar of the monstrous hellish brothers ('It seems you would create me / One of your familiars' 1.1.258–9), who in turn are perceived as vultures by the duchess ('Go tell my brothers, when I am laid out, / They then may feed in quiet' 4.2.236–7). Although these images are not literalized in fantastic corporeal transformations, their effect depends on more than metaphorical significance. Thus Ferdinand's association of the duchess with the witch ('The witchcraft lies in her rank blood' 3.1.78) seems disconcertingly justified, when he later acts out her cursing image ('shall make you howl in hell for't' 4.1.40) through what the doctor insufficiently diagnoses as lycanthropy. In demonological discourse Satan was believed to be able to perform evil 'in the shape of a wolf, while placing the *experience* of having performed them in the imagination of someone else' (Clark 138). Moreover, as this deception of the imagination was thought to possibly extend to the witnesses 'of such transformations',[3] Ferdinand's state appears as an even more unsettling reminder of a highly ambivalent spectator position.

In a play which abounds in allusions to optical instruments, these shifts in perception evoke anamorphic pictures of early modern perspective art, combining mutually exclusive visions and thus drawing attention to the gap in-between, before the eye settles on one of the offered options. Most centrally, the play stages the attempts of the duchess to come alive against idolizing and demonizing gender images of 'a holy relic' (3.2.139), 'the figure cut in alabaster / Kneels at my husband's tomb' (1.1.453–4), and of the witchlike whore, insisting instead on the transformatory process of life, foregrounded in the visible signs of pregnancy and ageing. At the same time all attempts to resist fixation are inevitably cast in symbolic images, from the description of the duchess's intended wooing in terms of a masculine heroic quest to the final question about her image in view of death ('Who do I look like'), tellingly answered by Cariola: 'Like to your picture in the gallery ... ; / Or rather like some reverend monument / Whose ruins are even pitied' (4.2.30–4). The whole last act ironically stages the duchess's posthumous transformation into a saint-like martyr, re-establishing (with a difference and up to a point) the power of images.

Significantly it is Bosola, who most fantastically shifts shapes from malcontent to torturer, tomb maker, bellman and eventual avenger, who sums up the play's epistemological underpinnings in his speech about the human/animal boundary (2.1.45–60), in which he moves from the literal hybrid to the metaphorical bestial in human nature, to 'our terror' (2.1.59) of human decay, foregrounding the fear of shape-shifting as fear of life's metamorphic process towards death. The price of the duchess's desire for change is the acknowledgement of mortality and of the vanishing of all certainties on a cognitive as well as on an affective level. The play obsessively conjures up images of bodily decay, of 'unsettling, slippery images of the interstitial, the in-between: images of dung, poison and blood' (Zimmerman 143), foregrounding death as 'something rejected from which one does not part, from which one does not protect oneself as from an object ... it beckons to us and ends up engulfing us' (Kristeva 4). Webster's play participates in the described 'boundary disputes' through a complex discursive network drawing upon religious as well as scientific viewpoints, while at the same time evoking the horrifying in-betweenness of 'the corpse, seen without God and outside of science' as 'the utmost of abjection ... death infecting life' (Kristeva 4).[4]

In Middleton's and Rowley's *The Changeling* questions of affective in-betweenness are centralized in a series of radical emotional transformations unsettling the boundary between desire and disgust, attraction and repulsion. While these shifting emotions are still linked to cognitive questions about perception, the primary focus is on these emotions themselves, their uncertain origins and disturbing effects. While the play's opening presents the relation between perception and emotion, outside and inside, within the conventional framework of love at first sight, the dialogue between the love-struck couple, Alsemero and Beatrice-Joanna, almost immediately shifts the focus of attention from desire to disgust. At first this seems at least partly explicable, because the sudden arousal of a mutual desire between the newly found lovers changes Beatrice-Joanna's former love into loathing ('our eyes ... are rash sometimes' 1.1.72–4). More disturbingly, however, this is followed by a curious discussion of her inexplicable loathing of the servant DeFlores whose sight she abhors. The unaccountability of this aversion is presented as a secret in conjunction with the secret of her father's castle ('Our citadels / Are plac'd conspicuous to outward view / ... but within are secrets' 1.1.164–6), which will eventually reveal itself as the madhouse that the subplot is set in.

The pervasive gendered imagery of imprisonment correlates the castle and the madhouse with the heroine, mapping the desperate but futile attempts at securing the boundary between inside and outside on to the female body. By the end of the play Alsemero's desire has changed into disgust, the view of 'the temple where I first beheld her' (1.1.1) has turned into that of the charnel house ('The bed itself's a charnel, the sheets shrouds / For murdered carcasses' 5.3.83–4). But the play links the common notion of female changeability ('a beauty to deformity' 5.3.32) to a wider investigation into the foundation of affects. Accordingly Alsemero discusses Beatrice-Joanna's personal confession of an inexplicable excess of loathing towards DeFlores as an existential human dilemma, a 'frequent frailty in our nature' (1.1.116). The explanatory hints at demonic affiliations of DeFlores, morally justifying the heroine's initial loathing, remain as insufficient as the speculations about the aesthetic reasons of her aversion ('This ominous ill-fac'd fellow more disturbs me / Than all my other passions' 2.1.52–3). The play stages a disturbing collapse of the boundary between hate and love, desire and disgust, as Beatrice-Joanna's feelings for DeFlores turn him from a partner in crime and her 'lust's devil' (5.3.53) into 'a man worth loving' (5.1.76). Allusions to Beatrice-Joanna as fairies' child, safely turning her into a non-human other, are evoked but not seriously explored, as the horror of changeability seems to arise from human nature itself.

The madhouse of the comic subplot literalizes these inexplicable emotional transformations in the appearance of madmen dressed up as birds and beasts, 'that act their fantasies in any shapes ... / ... As their wild fancies prompt 'em' (3.3.193–8). The real madmen, however, inhabit the castle. Consequently, the promised dance of the madmen 'to make a frightful pleasure' (3.3.260) doesn't have to be staged at the end, as Beatrice-Joanna and DeFlores have danced it all along ('while I coupled with your mate / At barley-brake; now we are left in hell' 5.3.162–3). Middleton/Rowley's play foregrounds the 'giddy turning' (1.1.156), the 'bottomless' abyss (5.3.6 and 5.3.120), shifting the focus towards an exploration of affective uncertainties, producing unsettling suggestions about the inseparability of desire and disgust, and its gendered implications.

The configurations of shape-shifting in Shakespeare's *Macbeth*, Webster's *The Duchess of Malfi*, and Middleton/Rowley's *The Change-ling* address anxieties about female desire in terms of witchcraft and madness as a troublingly unresolved issue, insisting on a fantastic in-betweenness rather than on a reassuring closure. However, the increasing shift of emphasis from staging uncertainties about the *nature* of events to the *reaction* to those events, signals a gradual shift in emphasis from religious and moral discourses about cognitive uncertainties to medical and psychological discourses about affective uncertainties, and a correlative shift to the uncanny as explained supernatural, enabling the return of the supernatural in the safer realm of the marvellous.

Tragicomic transformations

As the increasing focus on individual interiority and psychopathology in tragedy marks a gradual turn to the uncanny, offering explanations that will secure the boundaries between matter/spirit, human/animal, male/female, tragicomedy emerges as a dis-eased fantastic genre of in-betweenness evoking contradictory emotional responses, in which the containment generated by the plot conclusion can be effectively unsettled by a destabilizing emphasis on theatrical self-reflexivity. The Gothic potential of this varied genre often consists in countering on an affective level the boundaries which are established on a cognitive level, allowing for an unsettling return of a fantastic in-betweenness. Tragicomedy can be read as a response to the described cultural crisis and the anxieties it produced, simultaneously offering solutions and doubts about their adequacy. Dryden's remark that 'our English tragicomedy must be confessed to be wholly Gothic' (Dryden 146) thus seems like an apt evaluation of a genre defined by contemporaries as a 'monstrous' conjunction of incompatible effects and affects ('grief and laughter are so very incompatible, that to join these two copies of nature together, would be monstrous … and yet … this is what our Shakespeare himself has frequently been guilty of' Sewell vii; see also Maguire 103–4).

Shakespeare's *Winter's Tale* and Rowley/Dekker/Ford's *The Witch of Edmonton* mark two ends of the spectrum of tragicomedy in their discussion of ghostly resurrections and monstrous creatures, pushing the form towards romance and domestic realism respectively. Shakespeare's *The Winter's Tale* uses the model of pastoral romance to transform the tragic movement towards Hermione's death into the wish-fulfilment of a happy reunion. At the same time the play foregrounds underlying ambivalences about ghostly returns and embodied resurrections addressing the topic in successive variations which foreground unsettling links between fear and desire.

The theme of a ghostly resurrection is introduced by Antigonus, whose story about his ambivalent nightmare vision of Hermione as a mourning saint turning into an avenging angel cursing him, aptly predicts his own death. The vision is particularly effective, because Antigonus explicitly disclaims any belief in the truth of dreams ('I have heard but not believed the spirits o' th' dead / May walk again' 3.3.15–16). Rational scepticism, however, does not diminish the frightening experiential effect of the dream ('Affrighted much, / I did in time collect myself, and thought / This was so, and no slumber. Dreams are toys, / Yet for this once, yea superstitiously, / I will be squared by this' 3.3.36–40). This scene ambivalently sets the stage for a series of references to metamorphoses of gods into animals, to hybrid plants ('nature's bastards' 4.4.83) and to the disguises of royals as shepherds, preparing for the final transformation, the resurrection of the stone statue into the breathing body of Hermione, through a series of successive discussions emphasizing its unsettling literal and metaphorical implications.

Thus the reminder of Hermione's female perfection in life ('a perfect woman … unparalleled' 5.1.15–16) evokes frightening images of her possible resurrection as an avenging possessive ghostly wife preventing the usurpation of her place by a potential successor (as this 'would make her sainted spirit / Again possess her corpse, and on this stage, / … appear soul-vexed' 5.1.57–9). This is contrasted with the report of the lifelike perfection of her statue as an artistic achievement ('a piece many years in doing, and now newly performed by that rare Italian master Giulio Romano' 5.2.86–8), and with the onlookers' experience of 'wonder' (5.3.22) and 'magic' (5.3.39), when the statue is uncovered. However, while Perdita kneels down in reverence, Leontes still is haunted by guilt ('my evils conjur'd to remembrance' 5.3.40). Paulina's warning that she might be accused of 'wicked powers' (5.3.91), when she will 'make the statue move indeed' (5.3.88), disturbingly aligns her with Ferdinand's masterminding of the duchess's being 'plagued in art'. But Paulina's benevolent intentions allow her to successfully play the magician/god, although the final plea for faith before the resurrection ('It is required / You do awake your faith' 5.3.94–5) seems to invite the scepticism, which is duly expressed in the Gentleman's report, Polixenes' and Leontes' questions and Hermione's own allusions. However, the confirmation of a rational explanation is deliberately withheld: 'There's time enough for that, Lest they desire upon this push to trouble / Your joys with like relation' (5.3.129–31).

The staged transformational process has evoked contradictory religious and psychological discourses about ghostly returns and bodily resurrections and their implications for the boundary between life and death, spirit and matter. But it ends with an insistence on the experiential quality of a fantastic in-betweenness, which resists unequivocal explanations and questions the gain of closure. Hermione's resurrection ambivalently attests to the uncanny power of memory and guilt about the ghostly return of the beloved wife as well as to the power of the belief in the miraculous return of the idolized embodiment of saintly perfection. To adapt Rosemary Jackson's description of the Gothic effect: Hermione 'slides away from the powerful eye / I which seeks to possess' her as a descending goddess or a clever trick (Jackson 46). Even if the machinery of the fairy tale is foregrounded, this does not lead to a sobering effect. The 'real' Hermione inevitably remains fantastically in-between the cultural and theatrical images created. If tragedy moves towards new boundaries, privileging medical-psychological over religious-moral explanations with the help of the new sciences, the self-conscious theatricality of tragicomedy insists on the process of transformation and celebrates art as privileged space to explore the persistent anxieties about the boundaries in question and the deficiencies of an either/or solution.

On the other end of the tragicomic spectrum Rowley/Dekker/Ford's play *The Witch of Edmonton* (1621) pushes the form to its limits towards domestic drama and the poetic justice of two executions and a wedding. While both plays explore the ambivalences of wish-fulfilment, *The Winter's Tale* focuses on affective uncertainties about the boundary between life and death, whereas *The Witch of Edmonton* foregrounds the social and moral implications of boundary issues about the human and the demonic.

The play by William Rowley, Thomas Dekker, and John Ford does not refute the existence of witchcraft, but rather tries to differentiate between superstitious popular beliefs and serious demonological considerations, focusing on the historical event of the trial and execution of Elizabeth Sawyer in the year of the play's composition and first performance. In *The Witch of Edmonton* the willed transformation of the title character Elizabeth Sawyer, presented as an old isolated mistreated woman, falsely accused of witchcraft, into a witch taking revenge on the community ('Cause I'm poor, deformed and ignorant ... Must I for that be made a common sink / For all the filth and rubbish of men's tongues / To fall and run into?' 2.1.3–8) is enacted with the devilish assistance of a dog-shaped blood-sucking 'thing called Familiar' (2.1.36), forcing her into the devil's pact. However, even after her transformation the play keeps the ambivalence between the perception of and sympathy for her as a scapegoat for every evil within the village, and as an abhorred threatening witch intent on evil doings. The play increases the tension between those conflicting perspectives to the very end, when Sawyer appears most helplessly human and most witch-like at the same time, desperately conjuring her devil-dog companion with whom she shares a devilish 'black lust' (5.1.4).

In this context the corporeal stage presence of the devil-dog is used for an insistence on contradictory perceptions and evaluations of him/it as a dog, a supernatural being, and a theatrical device evoking onstage reactions between terror and desire, repulsion and attraction, fear and – most disturbingly – pity, creating a multiplicity of images and readings which resist all attempts at closure. In the tragic plot about the bigamist Frank Thorney, who turns into a murderer, the devil-dog's supernatural agency is emphasized, while in the comic plot about the young villager Cuddy Banks, who needs a love charm in order to fulfil his desires, the doggish potential is foregrounded, whereas the witch-plot capitalizes on both readings.[5] However, at the same time these clear-cut distinctions are undermined as all narrative strands focus on ambivalent intersections between social coercion, psychological disposition and evil power in shaping notions of identity and reality. Thus the appearance of the devil-dog in the bigamy-plot just before the murder raises questions about whether the devil-dog is a materialization of Frank's evil thoughts, as the devil-dog's remark, 'the mind's about it now' (3.3.2), seems to suggest, or an embodiment of satanic power planting murder in his innocent mind, as Frank's utterance ''Tis done now, what I ne'er thought on' (3.3.16) seems to imply. However, all attempts to mark the boundaries between the psychological and the demonic only lead back to their inseparability. Yet, in contradistinction to the witch-plot, Frank's public repentance at least enables the forgiveness of all of those whom he had wronged before his execution takes place. It is the protagonist of the comic plot, Cuddy Banks, however, who despite his awareness and enjoyment of the devilish side of the devil-dog, treats the creature like a dog, whom he even pities at the end, suggesting alternative lives for him as 'an honest dog' (5.1.153) who might 'serve in some nobleman's, knight's, or gentleman's kitchen, ... Or ... translate [him]self into a lady's arming puppy' (5.1.167–72). This attitude seems to empower him to finally drive the devil-dog off stage, encouraging the creature's last transformation from threatening supernatural agency into a barking dogginess that can be chased away.

The Witch of Edmonton can thus be read as an exploration of the attempts to exorcise fantastic uncertainties about the intersections of the supernatural and the natural, the human and the demonic by incorporating the supernatural into a 'realistic' depiction of a world, which despite its social deficiencies is governed by providence. This is foregrounded by the transformation of the black devil-dog into the white dog of divine retribution towards the end, urging Elizabeth Sawyer to confess her crimes, putting her in mind of the 'winding sheet' (5.1.37). Her rejection of this 'puritan paleness' (5.1.53) and her insistent preference of his former 'black colour' serve to justify her execution ("'Tis the black colour / Or none, which I fight under' 5.1.51–2). Ironically, the satanic power of the devil-dog can thus be revealed as part of the providential plan, while the eroticized discourse of old Elizabeth Sawyer's 'black lust' for her 'sweet Tom-boy' (5.1.81) renders her radically other at the end ('O my best love! / I am on fire, even in the midst of ice, / Raking my blood up till my shrunk knees feel / Thy curled head leaning on them. Come then, my darling. / If in the air thou hover'st, fall upon me / In some dark cloud' 5.1.9–14). The reassuring closure of her removal from the play, however, is effectively counteracted by foregrounding the injustices and questioning the value judgements of the community till the very end.

The Witch of Edmonton participates in a cultural movement attempting 'to reconcile the new focus on the empirical world with traditional Christian cosmology' through what has been called an 'experimental' or 'empirical demonology' (Capoferro 105). The printed version of the play, dating from 1658, coincides with a remarkable return of the fascination with the supernatural in mid-seventeenth-century texts as part of a 'politically conservative' project to counter the threatening implications of an increasing erosion of belief in manifestations of the supernatural in the context of the rise of empiricism (cf. Andrea Brady, Chapter 10 below). Thus the 'empirical supernaturalism' (Capoferro 69) of apparition narratives and providential narratives written from the mid-seventeenth century onwards has been read as mediation, 'bridg[ing] the gap between the empirical and non-empirical within a recognizable aesthetic framework' (Capoferro 70). In this context the emergence of the fantastic as expression of ontological hesitation has been linked to the gradual rise of the novel in terms of a process of fictionalization ('the fictional works associated with the fantastic took over the mediatory task that in the early stages of modern empiricism was accomplished by purportedly factual texts') (Capoferro 61).[6] However, early modern drama, rather than just preceding the fantastic, appears as a major shaping factor of the fantastic as an aesthetic expression of epistemological uncertainty, providing the groundwork for the rise of the Gothic novel and its shifting focus between the uncanny and the marvellous.

In *The Witch of Edmonton* the demand for a fairytale suspension of disbelief of *The Winter's Tale* is replaced by a demand for the belief in the providential workings of poetic justice. But tragicomedy – while attesting to the desire for certainty – still insists on the fantastic tensions involved in this transformational process. The comic or serious resolution of this tension will eventually foster dramatic genres relying on smile or pity respectively, while the fantastic uncertainties about perception and desire will return with a difference in the genre of the Gothic novel, framed by the uncanny and the marvellous. In this sense Frankenstein's horror at his creation expresses the desire for closure: 'Begone! Relieve me from the sight of your detested form.' But Mary Shelley's text proves that the fantastic as a persistent reminder of an ineradicable in-betweenness will never be gone.

Notes

1 'The early modern English theatre was dangerous, ... because it demonstrated an understanding of identity as transformational' (Reynolds, *Performing Transversally* 159).

2 Cf. also 'between the fifteenth and seventeenth centuries European visual culture suffered some major and unprecedented shocks'; 'In one context after another, vision came to be be characterized by uncertainty and unreliability, such that access to visual reality could no longer be normally guaranteed' (Clark 2).

3 Cf. Clark's discussion of Claude Prieur (Clark 139).

4 For a detailed analysis of the abject in Webster's play see Maurizio Calbi and Susan Zimmerman.
5 For a detailed analysis cf. Nicol.
6 Capoferro reads Shakespeare's *Hamlet* and *Macbeth* as mere 'precedents of the fantastic' (58), as the ontological instability addressed is not yet grounded in 'a neat extra-literary distinction between what is empirical and what is not' (58).

Works cited

Adelman, Janet. *Suffocating Mothers: Fantasies of Maternal Origin in Shake-speare's Plays, 'Hamlet' to 'The Tempest'*. New York and London: Routledge, 1992.

Burnett, Mark Thornton. *Constructing 'Monsters' in Shakespearean Drama and early modern Culture*. Basingstoke and New York: Palgrave Macmillan, 2002.

Calbi, Maurizio. *Approximate Bodies: Gender and Power in early modern Drama and Anatomy*. London and New York: Routledge, 2004.

Capoferro, Ricardo. *Empirical Wonder: Historicising the Fantastic, 1660–1760*. Bern: Peter Lang, 2010.

Clark, Stuart. *Vanities of the Eye: Vision in early modern European Culture*. Oxford and New York: Oxford University Press, 2007.

Cohen, Jeffrey Jerome, ed. *Monster Theory: Reading Culture*. Minneapolis and London: University of Minnesota Press, 1996.

Daston, Lorraine and Katherine Park. *Wonders and the Order of Nature, 1150–1750*. New York: Zone Books, 1998.

Davies, Surekha. 'The Unlucky, the Bad and the Ugly: Categories of Monstrosity from the Renaissance to the Enlightenment.' *Monsters and the Monstrous*. Ed. Asa Simon Mittman and Peter J. Dendle. Farnham and Burlington, VT: Ashgate Publishing, 2012. 49–75.

Diehl, Huston. 'Horrid Image, Sorry Sight, Fatal Vision: The Visual Rhetoric of Macbeth.' *Shakespeare Studies* 16 (1983): 191–203.

Dryden, John. 'A Parallel of Painting and Poetry (1695).' *Essays of John Dryden*. Ed. W. P. Ker. Oxford: Clarendon, 1900. 115–53.

Freud, Sigmund. 'Das Unheimliche.' *Psychologische Schriften. Studienausgabe Band IV*. Frankfurt: Fischer Taschenbuch Verlag, 1982. Translated as *The Uncanny*. London: Penguin, 2003.

Greenblatt, Stephen. *Hamlet in Purgatory*. Princeton and Oxford: Princeton University Press, 2001.

Jackson, Rosemary. *Fantasy: The Literature of Subversion*. London: Methuen, 1981.

Kristeva, Julia. *Powers of Horror. An Essay on Abjection*. New York and Oxford: Columbia University Press, 1982.

Lee, Judith. 'Freed from Certainty: Toward a Feminist Theory of the Literary Fantastic.' *The Fantastic Other. An Interface of Perspectives*. Eds Brett

Cooke, George E. Slusser and Jaume Marti-Olivella. Amsterdam and Atlanta, GA: Rodopi, 1998. 257–76.

Lykke, Nina, and Rosi Braidotti, eds. *Between Monsters, Goddesses and Cyborgs: Feminist Confrontations with Science, Medicine and Cyberspace.* London and Atlantic Highlands, NJ: Zed Books, 1996.

Maguire, Nancy Klein, ed. *Tragicomedy: Explorations in Genre and Politics.* AMS Press: New York, 1987.

Middleton, Thomas and William Rowley. *The Changeling.* Ed. N. W. Bawcutt. Manchester: Manchester University Press, 1986.

Mittman, Asa Simon and Peter J. Dendle, eds. *The Ashgate Research Companion to Monsters and the Monstrous.* Farnham and Burlington, VT: Ashgate Publishing, 2012.

Neely, Carol. *Distracted Subjects: Madness and Gender in Shakespeare and early modern Culture.* Ithaca, NY: Cornell University Press, 2004.

Neumeier, Beate. 'Postmodern Gothic: Desire and Reality in Angela Carter's Writing.' *a/e: A Decade of Discontent: British Fiction of the Eighties.* Eds Wolfgang Riedel and Thomas M. Stein. 48 (1993): 89–97. Rpt *Modern Gothic: A Reader.* Eds Victor Sage and Allen Lloyd Smith. Manchester: Manchester University Press, 1996. 141–51.

Nicol, David. 'Interrogating the Devil: Social and Demonic Pressure in *The Witch of Edmonton.*' *Comparative Drama* 38.4 (2004–5): 425–45.

Reynolds, Bryan. *Transversal Subjects: From Montaigne to Deleuze After Derrida.* New York: Palgrave Macmillan, 2009.

—. *Performing Transversally: Reimagining Shakespeare and the Critical Future.* New York: Palgrave Macmillan, 2003.

Rowley, William, Thomas Dekker and John Ford. *The Witch of Edmonton. Three Jacobean Witchcraft Plays.* Eds Peter Corbin and Douglas Sedge. Manchester: Manchester University Press, 1986.

Sewell, George. 'An Essay on the Art, Rise and Progress of the Stage.' *The Works of William Shakespeare.* Eds Alexander Pope and George Sewell. Vol. 7. London, 1725.

Shakespeare, William. *The Norton Shakespeare.* Eds Stephen Greenblatt, Walter Cohen, Jean E. Howard and Katharine Eisaman Maus. New York: W. W. Norton & Company, 2008.

Richard Proudfood, Ann Thompson and David Scott Kastan. London: Bloomsbury, 2011.

Shildrick, Margrit. *Embodying the Monster: Encounters with the Vulnerable Self.* London, Thousand Oaks, New Delhi: Sage Publications, 2002.

Todorov, Tzvetan. *The Fantastic: A Structural Approach to a Literary Genre.* Trans. Richard Howard. Cleveland: Case Western Reserve University Press 1973.

Webster, John. *The Duchess of Malfi.* Ed. John Russell Brown. Manchester: Manchester University Press, 1974.

Zimmerman, Susan. *The early modern Corpse and Shakespeare's Theatre.* Edinburgh: Edinburgh University Press, 2005.

6

From grotesque to Gothic:
Ben Jonson's *Masque of Queenes*

Lynn S. Meskill

Shakespeare is a natural starting point for a 'preposterous history' of the Gothic mode (Bal). In the preface to *The Castle of Otranto: A Gothic Story* (1764), Horace Walpole describes him as 'the model I copied' (44), and Ann Radcliffe refers to *Julius Caesar*, *Hamlet* and *Macbeth* in her essay 'On the Supernatural in Poetry' to illustrate the difference between 'terror' and 'horror' (145ff.). In her three-volume series *The Girlhood of Shakespeare's Heroines* (1850–52) Mary Cowden Clark's invented childhood of Lady Macbeth in 'The Thane's Daughter' is a Gothic piece inspired directly from *Macbeth*. Yet, Shakespeare is not the only dramatist or poet to inspire writers of Gothic fiction. Christopher Marlowe's *Doctor Faustus* served as a prototype for at least one Gothic protagonist; Faustus and Frankenstein both share a desire to learn the 'secrets of heaven and earth', the mysteries of natural philosophy and the 'raising of ghosts and devils' (Shelley 296, 299). The works of John Ford ('*Tis Pity She's a Whore*), John Webster (*The Duchess of Malfi*, *The White Devil*), and Thomas Middleton (*The Revenger's Tragedy*) may well have been the remote sources of many of the macabre, gruesome, as well as melancholic effects found in Gothic writing a century later. *The Duchess of Malfi*, in particular, is reminiscent of the eighteenth century Gothic novel with a ruined abbey, haunted by the echoing voice of the ghost of the murdered duchess. The skulls, the graveyards, the tombs, the sepulchres, the bones, the worms – the charnel house, in other words – are an integral part of the pre-Gothic backcloth of these and many other Jacobean and Caroline plays. The *vanitas* and *memento mori* topoi find their most Baroque formulations in these authors' works. Michael Neill has argued that many of the grim effects in Jacobean tragic endings reflect the way 'tragedy absorbed the motifs from the Dance of Death. The effects of such cross-fertilization are most apparent in plays such as *Hamlet*, *The Atheist's Tragedy*, *The Revenger's Tragedy* and *Hoffman* which make extensive use of the macabre spectacle' (81). In the drama of the early modern period, these charnel house effects were used to horrify spectators and remind them of their own mortality. These dramas were, at the same time, strongly inspired by medieval Gothic elements such as the fifteenth-century *transi* or cadaver tombs in which the effigy of the dead person, as they would have looked in life, was doubled by the statue of a decomposing corpse underneath. If the loathsomeness of bodily extinction was exaggerated and enhanced, it is clear that the *frisson* of scopic pleasure that must surely have been both in the medieval period and in the Renaissance, as today, an intended part of their effect, was also very much accompanied by the real terror Death represented in Christian terms even in an age of scepticism and doubt.[1]

Of all the Elizabethan and Jacobean dramatists, Ben Jonson seems least part of a 'pre' or 'proto' history of the Gothic. In fact, a 'Gothic' Jonson would appear, at first glance, to run counter to a certain traditional view of Jonson as a poet following closely in the footsteps of Horace, preoccupied with decorum and virtue, and possessing none of the 'fancy' or fantasy of the Shakespearean imagination. All the elements which we find in other dramatists and which we associate with the pre-Gothic seem to be missing in Jonson's works. Yet, Jonson's grotesque characters coupled with the poet's permanent obsession with the 'mortality' of his own work, led to works that were grotesque in form and morbid and melancholy in atmosphere. To examine Jonson's work 'preposterously', it might be useful to historicize the seventeenth-century 'Gothic'. It could well be defined as a combination of the Jacobean 'charnel house' and the 'grotesque', a term originally used to describe a certain style of painting in which human and animal figures are mixed incongruously with foliage, flowers and fruits creating bizarre and fantastic shapes. Jonson's concern with the charnel house in conjunction with the grotesque is most visible in the court masques. In the post-performance publication of the texts and descriptions of the performance of the masques, the poet repeatedly confronts the spectre of the masque's death. In the preface to *The Masque of Blacknesse* (1605) for instance, he justifies the printing of the masque by claiming to 'redeeme' the 'spirits' from 'oblivion' even after the body was dead (169, lines 8–14).[2] 'So short-lived are the bodies of all things', writes Jonson in the preface to the masque *Hymenaei* (1606) 'in comparison of their soules' (209, lines 6–7). It is because the body is corruptible, the masque aims to 'lay hold on more remov'd mysteries' (209, lines 18–19).

I would suggest that these 'mysteries' to which Jonson refers in *Hymenaei* are particularly morbid and macabre in another masque, *The Masque of Queenes* (1609). What is specific to *The Masque of Queenes* is its emphasis on horror. Jonson's descriptions of the masque as performed, as well as his marginal commentary and scholarly annotations, are meant to achieve the spectral effects of the court masque without the aid of candlelight, eerie music, strange costumes and magically moving, gigantic stage sets, which would certainly have awed the spectators of the performance. Moreover, the dangerously heterodox spectacle of the figures of witches on stage chanting charms against the world order and, specifically, King James's kingdom cannot be underestimated. Terry Castle's description of nineteenth-century 'phantasmagorias', spectacles in which magic lanterns were used to produce 'fantômes artificiels', may perhaps give us a feeling for what *The Masque of Queenes* may also have tried to achieve (33).[3]

The effect of *The Masque of Queenes* on its contemporary audience was surely powerful. Stephen Orgel has commented upon how the perspective stage must have appeared to an early seventeenth-century English audience, unfamiliar with a visual perspective that had become common in Italy. Jonson testifies to the 'beauty', but also, implicitly, to the strangeness, of the artificial perspective of the stage set for *The Masque of Blacknesse*:

> The Scene behind [the performers on stage] seemed a vast sea (and united with this that flowed forth) from the termination, or horizon of which (being levell of the *State* [i.e. where the King sat], which was placed in the upper end of the hall) was drawne, by the lines of Prospective, the whole work shooting downewards, from the eye; which decorum made it more conspicuous, and caught the eye a farre off with a wandering beauty. To which was added an obscure and cloudy nightpiece. (*Masque of Blacknesse* 171, lines 82–90)

In addition to technically sophisticated perspective views, stage machines were able to perform wonders. The turning stage machinery in *The Masque of Queenes* was able to suddenly make the witches 'vanish' and within minutes put in their place a 'glorious and magnificent Building, figuring the House of Fame, in the upper part of which were discovered the twelve Masquers sitting upon a Throne triumphall' (*Masque of Queenes* 301–2, lines 357, 359–62). It may be very useful to keep in mind these stage wonders when considering the possible emotions felt by the audience, with regard not only to the anti-masque of witches in *Queenes* but also to the gigantic and monstrous figure of Fame and the House of Fame in the pediment of which all twelve masquers sat. In printing his description of the court masque, Jonson may well have had to find a means, like Mary Shelley with *Frankenstein*, to transcribe an already *lived* terror: 'Oh! If I could only contrive [a story] which would frighten my reader as I myself had been frightened that night!' (Shelley 264). Like Shelley's, Jonson's art is to 'describe' what has already taken place: 'I have found it! What terrified me will terrify others; and I need only describe the spectre which had haunted my midnight pillow ... making only a transcript of the grim terrors of my waking dream' (Shelley 264). In his effort to capture the horror of one night at court, Jonson offers us what is probably his most 'Gothic' text.

Jonson has often been portrayed by scholars as the epitome of the neoclassical and rational poet, whose aim is to teach and instruct, mixing 'pleasure and profit' in imitation of Horace. The early modern dramatist is closely associated with the Roman poet in the scholarly imagination for a number of reasons: first, Jonson translated Horace's *Ars Poetica* from Latin into English; second, he clearly identified with the character of Horace in his play *Poetaster* (1601) – a play about writers and their fame – and, finally, he translated a number of Horace's poems. Moreover, references to Horace in Jonson's plays, poems and masques are legion. This admiration and imitation of Horace would seem immediately to invalidate any kind of argument for a proto-Gothic Jonson. According to the authors of *Gothic Documents: A Sourcebook*, Horace's *Ars Poetica* was even a kind of *locus classicus* of the 'Anti-Gothic' in the eighteenth century:

> Critics of the eighteenth century tended to make a difference between useful literature, which illustrated moral truths and did so in a rational and plausible manner and illegitimate writing which failed to do either of these things ... Horace's *Ars Poetica* was by far the most frequent resort of opponents of Gothic fiction and drama ... probability, literary decorum, is the vital condition for the ethical usefulness of literature. (Clery and Miles 173)

Horace was one of the key models for the Enlightenment sensibility, and he epitomizes the anti-Gothic. In the *Ars Poetica*, Horace condemns improbable events and unbelievable creatures, whose shapes are 'like sick-men's dreams' (Horace, *His Art of Poetrie* 305, line 9). Rationality, proportion and harmony are the foundations of a Horatian poetics. In the *Ars*, Horace describes monsters and chimaeras as laughable. The horrors committed by Medea, who kills her own sons, or Atreus, who eats his nephews for dinner, are things which should not be 'seen' on the stage, but rather 'told', because if these stories were seen on stage they would be completely unbelievable. Horace writes: 'Quodcumque ostendis mihi sic, incredulus odi' and Jonson translates: 'What so is showne, I [do] not believe, and hate' (Horace, *Ars Poetica* 466, line 188; Horace, *His Art of Poetrie* 317, line 269). Jonson's own rule of thumb, briefly mentioned in his *Timber, or Discoveries*, is that an artist must always submit original, chaotic and wild imaginings to a shaping and forming judgement. The need to 'returne to our Judgement' in order to prune and cut that which is ridiculous and therefore necessarily *odious* owes much to the *Ars Poetica*.[4] Jonson's famous statement that Shake-speare should have 'blotted' more of his lines finds its source in this Horatian idea of decorum.[5]

Yet, while critics are keen to identify Jonson with the Roman author of the *Ars Poetica* and claim that he saw himself as an early modern Horace, Horace is *not* the only model or artist that inspired Jonson.[6] In his play *Poetaster*, Jonson identifies himself as a writer, not just with Horace but also with the youthful Ovid *and* the established Virgil, both of whom he also places sympathetically and symbolically on the stage.[7] Moreover, we must be wary of making too much of Jonson's Horatian pronouncements and connections; the Renaissance cited and utilized Horace as a matter of course. To quote or refer to the *Ars* was a kind of reflex action to show that you were a serious writer. Writers would cite Horace, if only in order to subsequently step away from the touch-stone, as a means of putting an aspect of their own individuality into some kind of relief, while, at the same time, assuring the reader of their literary *bona fides*.

An example of this strategy of citing Horace to simultaneously assert one's own place in a literary tradition and one's place *outside* of it can be seen in the first sentence of Montaigne's essay 'On Friendship' in his *Essais*. Montaigne compares his own 'art' in writing essays to that of the painter of grotesques (*crotesques*), an art which he describes as situating itself in the empty space surrounding and framing (*le vide tout au tour*) a beautiful and finished painting (*un tableau élabouré de tout sa suffisance*). Montaigne claims that his essays are like those fantastic (*fantasques*) paintings, characterized by variety and strangeness (*variété et éstrangeté*), monstrous bodies, with pieced-together (*rappiecez*) limbs, possessing neither clear form (*certaine figure*) nor order or proportion (183). Montaigne then cites the opening lines of Horace's *Ars*, lines that have gone down in history as the emblem of the Horatian disgust of a hybrid monster in the context of 'a poetics of the reasonable'.[8] Yet Montaigne valorizes the negative space of the grotesque painting. While claiming to be incapable of making a 'beautiful' painting, he makes a claim for an anti-Horatian art of the grotesque. In the *Trattato dell'arte de la pittura* (1584), Giovanni Paolo Lomazzo claimed that grotesques were a 'second language, a spirited but enigmatic gloss on the standard language of monumental figuration', the standard language of Vitruvian proportion and harmony. The quality needed by a painter of the grotesque, according to Lomazzo, is 'a certain frenzy and natural strangeness (*natural bizarria*) … for this, both natural inspiration and artifice (*furia naturale ed arte*) have to work together jointly' (qtd in Peacock 226). For both Montaigne and Lomazzo, the production of the grotesque represented another 'language', in clear contradistinction to that of a certain standard and monumental imagination. According to Gisèle Mathieu-Castellani, Montaigne's claim to prefer the margin to the painting (or the 'enigmatic gloss' to 'monumental figuration') was an 'anti-Horatian project' (71). Montaigne's is an aesthetic of the hybrid, the fantastic, the fragmentary and the capricious. Within this aesthetic the essayist claims and defends a discontinuous, meandering style that follows the hazardous and accidental train of his own thoughts rather than creating a structure to direct and channel thought. The humanist writer finds the liberty of self-expression in this *grotesque* method of writing. His is a poetics that is labyrinthine, secretive, cryptic, enigmatic and even hieroglyphic.[9] As such, it is a poetics that is highly personal and a reflection of the artist. Yet, paradoxically, this 'anti-Horatian' opening to 'On Friendship' does not prevent Montaigne from citing Horace as an authority on his theme throughout the essay. In the end, Montaigne never calls Horace into question. Instead, his authority, paradoxically, enables Montaigne to claim novelty.

Montaigne's description of his 'grotesque' method in the *Essais* can shed light on Jonson's own 'anti-Horatian' project. In Jonson's masques (and in *Volpone*, *The Alchemist*, *Bartholomew Fair*, for that matter), the 'monsters', which serve as 'anti-masque' characters, are indeed 'grotesques', strange and hybrid creatures. These characters are placed on the stage to set into relief an ideal or virtue. Like the twisting and turnings of animals and plants in the margins surrounding a 'beautiful painting', the anti-masque grotesques are in direct contrast and opposition to that rational, classical and illuminated principle which is its opposite, namely the idealized figures of the court masque and their Platonic dances. The anti-masques were composed of characters and creatures from a variety of different genres and kinds which included: pastorals (satyrs, nymphs, shepherds), Greek and Roman mythology (Charon, Mercury, Hercules, Atlas, Pallas Athena, Cupid, the Sphinx), the streets of London (heralds, printers, cooks, alchemists), other countries (Irishmen, Welshmen, gypsies, pygmies), personifications from emblem books (Reason, Virtue, Love, Truth, Opinion), literary genres (Epithalamion), natural elements (Moon, Night, Niger River, Ocean) and so on. What is astonishing is not only the range of possible elements but the odd mixture of elements from different 'kinds' that are yoked together under some pretence or other in each masque, some pretences more flimsy than others. Genres and registers (from serious and solemn to silly and ridiculous) undergo changes as suddenly as changes of scenery.

A late masque such as *Chloridia* (1630) takes this grotesque variety to a kind of extreme, but the changes of scene and characters (a direct result of the invention of the anti-masque) are elements of the Jonsonian masque from very early on.[10] In a rewriting of the abduction of Proserpine by Hades from Ovid's *Metamorphoses*, the masque opens with a duet between Zephyrus and Spring followed by a duet between Spring and 'Fountaynes' (752–3). At this point, an anti-masque consisting of a 'Dwarfe-Post from Hell' and two 'Lacqueys' interrupts this pastoral scene. After their little jig, the Dwarf explains who he is: '*Postilion* of Hell! Yet no *Mercury*. But a meere Cacodaemon, sent hither with a packet of newes!' (754, lines 129–30). The sub-devil then goes on to recount the 'news' from hell in the manner and tone of a chatty pamphlet sold in London, providing Londoners with curiosities and news from all over the world. The Dwarf's news from hell is all of this anecdotal and gossipy type. The denizens have been given a holiday and so the mythological world is turned upside-down as Tantalus finally eats the fruit which had been dangling perpetually at his lips, Ixion frees himself from his wheel and cuts capers, 'fetch friskals, and leades Lavaltos, with the *Lamiae*!' and Sisyphus bowls with his stone instead of pushing it up the hill. Once the news from hell is delivered, a warning is given to the court that 'other Goblins' are to come to 'trouble the *Gods*' with 'Tempests, Windes, Lightnings, Thunder, Rain, and Snow, for some new exploit they have against the Earth' and the Spring (754–5). These elements enter and the '*Scene* changeth, into a horrid storme' before being driven away by Spring (755, line 176). And this is not all. The changing of the scenery continues and suddenly the classicized figure of Fame appears beside the personified abstractions, 'Poesie, History, Architecture, and Sculpture', who join 'the Nymphs, Floods, and Fountaines' in a final series of songs and dances (760–1). *Chloridia* may well be considered an extreme example of the variety and profusion that could characterize a court masque. Yet, it may also bear witness to the need for novelty and variety to please and satisfy the curiosity of the royal patron and the court, at least once if not twice a year.

In *The Vision of Delight* (1617), Jonson indirectly provides us with an insight into the nature and source of the anti-masque grotesque, namely 'Night', the goddess of dreams and visions, and 'Phant'sy', the principle of imagination. In the opening of this masque, the character of 'Delight' enters the stage and calls upon Night saying that the 'sports' of Delight 'are of the humorous night' and that Night will not bring sleep but will keep the members of the court awake with '*Phantomes*', the spectral productions of 'Phant'sie':

By this time the Night, and Moone being both risen; Night hovering over the place, sung.

> Breake, Phant'sie, from thy cave of cloud,
> And spread thy purple wings;
> Now all thy figures are allow'd,
> And various shapes of thing;

(464, 42–7)

At night, the 'figures' of Phant'sy are 'allow'd'. The word 'figures' gives Night's speech a meta-theatrical effect, for the *figures* of the masque were the dances of the various anti-masques and masques. So, as Night broods over the court, Phant'sy is invoked to create any kind of figure or shape that she sees fit, to please and delight the spectators. She comes on to the stage and enumerates all the various 'dreames' she can create: 'If a Dreame should come in now, to make you afeard, / With a Windmill on his head, and bells at his beard; / Would you straight weare your spectacles, here, at your toes, / And your boots o' your brows, and your spurs o' your nose?' (466, lines 79–82). The anti-Horatian grotesque of Montaigne and Jonson finds its source in the Night giving leave to Fantasy to create any shape it would like, no matter how strange, ridiculous or wonderful. The policing agency of the day, and the Horatian model of decorum and imitation of nature, is turned inside-out and upside-down at night when the fantastic and bizarre in the tradition of Bosch hold sway. This is why the figure of 'Night' is ubiquitous in the court masques. She is the distant source of the revels themselves, offering the cover and secrecy necessary for Phant'sy to create the fantastic and the grotesque without being judged by their own author.

However, the presence of these hybrid and monstrous figures on stage is only one element of the grotesque in Jonson's masques. *The Masque of Queenes* may also be seen as a grotesque version of the humanist text and its scholarly gloss. Authorial commentary in the form of humanist marginalia and prose descriptions, explanations and comments, insinuates itself into the text in raised letters and weaves alongside and under the 'main' texts. Like the grotesques framing a painting, these marginal notes can be seen as a kind of grotesque border of *characters* or typographical signs. Here we have Lomazzo's 'engimatic gloss'. Yet, these marginalia are, at the same time, the mark of the 'serious' writer and allude specifically to Renaissance editions of classical authors. The lush marginalia, bordering and framing the marginal text, are testimony to the authorial obsession to turn the collaborative court spectacle into his own personal, erudite creation, publishing it as if it were the text by a classical author glossed by commentators. What is peculiar and strange, however, is that the annotator is the author himself, the exegete or glosser of his own work, of both the performance and the text. This excess, as well as hybrid mixture of description, explanation, citation and autobiographical references, renders Jonson's version of a post-performance description by the author of the performed masque in *The Masque of Queenes* unique in literary history.[11] The handwritten version dedicated to Prince Henry and the quarto and folio texts of Jonson's *Masque of Queenes* demonstrate how Jonson takes a piece of ephemera intended for the glory of the queen and her ladies, as well as the king, an astonishing spectacle produced by many hands and artists, and turns it into a semi-autobiographical memoir of the author at work. This memoir is, like Mary Shelley's *Frankenstein*, the true account of the authorial creation of a kind of monster out of fragments and pieces, out of the charnel house of bits and pieces of text. The end result is a strange narrative and a glimpse into some of the 'proto-Gothic' obsessions of an author whose humour in this masque is that of a melancholic, meditating on the 'phantasms' of the night, bringing dead queens to life on stage and wondering at his own monstrous mixing of the living and the dead.

The Masque of Queenes (1609) was created by Ben Jonson and Inigo Jones for Queen Anne of Denmark and her ladies and performed before the court of King James I. In the main show, the ladies were dressed to represent eleven famous queens from ancient history, including Penthesilea, Artemesia and Camilla from the *Aeneid*. Queen Anne, however, did not play one of the dead queens from history, she played herself and this, as we shall see, would create a certain uneasiness in the author of the masque. It is in the preface to *Queenes* that Jonson first introduces the concept of an 'anti-masque' to the masque. He writes that he 'devis'd that twelve Women, in the habite of Haggs, or Witches ... opposites to good Fame, should fill that part; not as a Masque, but a spectacle of strangenesse, producing mutliplicity of gesture' (282, lines 16–21). For this masque of 'Queenes', the anti-masque is conceived as a 'spectacle of strangenesse' and is composed of 'Hagges' and 'Witches' whose 'Queen', Hecate, possesses immense supernatural powers. The anti-masque was intended to act as a 'foil' to the masque to set it off, not unlike the setting of a jewel or the grotesque frame around a beautiful painting. The anti-masque set off and served as a contrast to the masque exactly as the grotesque beasts and foliage set off the painting they surrounded.

The two paragraphs that serve to open *The Masque of Queenes* can be read as the equivalent of Montaigne's opening lines in the essay 'On Friendship'. Like Montaigne, Jonson makes reference to Horace's

Ars Poetica in the opening paragraph of his introduction. He justifies his 'Argument' for the Masque, '*A Celebration of honourable, & true Fame, bred out of Vertue*' by claiming that it mixes 'delight' with 'profit, & example' as Horace suggests all art should do (lines 6–9). A cryptic marginal note catches the reader's eye immediately as it is the first typographical mark in the left margin of the page: 'a. *Hor. in Art. Poetic*' (line 8). Jonson will then turn to justifying the idea of an anti-masque of witches. He claims that it was the queen who insisted that some dance should precede her own. As a result, he claims, he created a 'spectacle of strangenesse' in which witches and hags (embodying a number of vices) opposed the queen and her ladies who represented 'true Fame'. While the anti-masque appears to be subordinate to the main masque, the succeeding three-hundred-odd lines of prose and poetry concern the witches (their aims, their language, their habits, their lore, their antiquity, their modernity), giving the lie to the perfect harmony, symmetry and order between the two 'halves' of the masque. The speeches, 'charmes' and doggerel verses of the witches work in tandem with the heavily annotated marginal notes of the author, which weave in and out of the text, as if the grotesque witches of the anti-masque were themselves surrounded by the grotesque, cryptic, strange and fantastical perorations of the author on a subject that clearly fascinated him. In other words, the spectacle of strangeness, the witches with their preposterous dances and dark charms, are accompanied by another *étrangeté*, that of the author's marginalia, rationalizing and testifying to a intimate and personal phantasmagoria of the author.

In *Pale Hecate's Team*, K. M. Briggs showed an appreciation for the very basic dark and frightening aspects of the witches in Jonson's *Queenes* rather than focusing on the hags as pseudo-medieval allegories of vices. She notes that Jonson's Hecate, 'out-Hecates Hecate', and many of the details in the witches' charms are 'designed to add to the robust macabre effects' or are simply 'straightforward gruesomeness' (87, 89, 91). 'Macabre' and 'gruesome' effects are perhaps also an important part of the printed masque. While Jonson, as we have seen, reasons that, as representatives of vices, the witches are perfectly appropriate to set off the virtuous queens, only a small part of the anti-masque is actually dedicated to this conceit. The lion's share of the anti-masque comes under the heading of 'straightforward gruesomeness'. So too, in the dedication of *The Masque of Queenes* to Prince Henry, Jonson is careful to show his work as adhering to certain didactic and wholesome purposes: 'it hath proved a worke of some difficulty to me to retrieve the particular authorities (according to your gracious command, and a desire borne out of judgement) to those things, which I writ out of fullnesse, and memory of my former readings' (281, lines 32–6). The author's justification for the lush and labyrinthine marginalia of the masque is to present 'authorities' for the prince's desire, 'borne of judgement'. Yet a close look at the actual 'authorities' and specific passages cited, as well as the writer's personal additions and commentaries, reveals not only the ancient and contemporary sources for Jonson's macabre effects but also the writer's clear *passion* not only for these texts, replete with references to magic, the raising of the dead, and ghastly rituals and rites, but also for popular witchcraft practices.

For instance, the first 'Charme' of the witches presents us with a desolate landscape (lines 52–60). The 'places' (line 55, note *f*) the witches inhabit in the English countryside are suffused with melancholy. They come from 'the fennes', the 'rocks', 'the dennes', the 'woods' and the 'caves' (lines 55–7). These watery, marshy bogs were commonly associated with stagnation and corruption, like the 'filthy air' of the witches of *Macbeth*. In the midst of this dark, gloomy and obscure landscape, Jonson adds the ghostly image of criminals dying on the gallows 'tree': 'From the Church-yards, from the graves, / From the dungeon, from the tree, / That they die on, here are wee' (lines 58–60). The marginal note which accompanies this first 'Charme' reveals a writer both keen to create a certain type of atmosphere and, at the same time, interested in creating a certain learned veneer: 'These places, in their own nature dire, & dismal, are reckoned up, as the fittest, from whence such persons should come; and were notably observed by that excellent *Lucan* in the description of his *Erictho. Lib. vi.* To which we may add this corollary, out of *Agrippa. De Occult philosop. Lib. i. cap. xlviii* (note *f*)'. The language of the note is that of a learned treatise: 'fittest', 'notably observed' and 'corollary'. The author makes it clear, as well, that his choice of 'dire, & dismal' places is a considered one: 'reckoned up', or weighed, not simply fantastical. But, hidden in the reference to Lucan's famous witch Erictho in Book VI of *The Civil War* and in the longish (untranslated) Latin quotation from Agrippa's *Occulta philosophia* lies the medieval, proto-Gothic sensibility of the author of *The Masque of Queenes*. From Lucan, Jonson takes the description of Erictho's habitation: 'To her it was a crime to shelter her ill-omened head in a city or under a roof: dear to the deities of Erebus, she inhabited deserted tombs, and haunted graves from which the ghosts had been driven' (Lucan Book VI, lines 510–13). Jonson's citation of Agrippa is from Chapter 48 of Book I of *Occult Philosophy*. The section quoted by Jonson describes the 'places' appropriate to the star 'Saturn', the planet of melancholy: 'all stinking places, dark, underground, religious, and mounrnfull places, as Church-yards, tombes, and houses not inhabited by men, and old, tottering, obscure, dreadfull houses, and solitary dens, caves, and pits, also fish-ponds, standing pools, fennes, and such like are appropriated to *Saturne*' (Agrippa 96). Jonson's note also cites the title of Book III, Chapter 42: 'By what wayes the Magicians and Necromancers do think they can call forth the souls of the dead' (488). According to Jonson's incomplete citation of Agrippa from Book IV, the 'best places' (*aptissima loca*) are those places where nocturnal visions and similar phantasms were known to meet, such as cemeteries and places of execution, where the bodies of the executed were left still unburied without any of the religious rites attending them.

The citations from Lucan and Agrippa in this pseudo-humanist document serve to show the antiquity and the 'authorities' that lie behind a rather simple witch's charm. Nevertheless, they can, conversely, be understood as very much serving to heighten certain macabre and melancholy effects. The text and the notes work in a relationship that cannot be seen as moving, so to speak, in one direction. The notes do not simply justify, explain and explicate the text. They add, they colour and, even more, they enhance the mood. Jonson's initial 'Charme' and the notes surrounding it all work to create a powerful atmosphere of melancholy and gloom even if there exists a constant tension between the need to rationalize through reference to authorities and the desire simply to add more and more ingredients to the descriptive pot.

The basic structure of the first 'Charme', an oscillation between the speech of the witches and authorial marginalia, remains basically the same throughout the anti-masque. What the reader of the masque and the notes becomes increasingly aware of is the growing *variety* of the author's sources and the hybrid mixture of authorities from antiquity and modern authorities from the sixteenth century as well as folktales and the writer's personal memories of stories, old wives' tales and even rumours from the previous reign of Elizabeth I. The grotesque in Jonson is partly this mixture of scholarly and unscholarly, high and low, the classical author and the village gossip. For instance, the second 'Charme' of eight lines is footnoted by no fewer than three rather lengthy notes all of which are filled with what can almost be called authorial *free association* rather than learned commentary:

> The Weather if fayre, the wind is good,
> Up, Dame, on your[g] Horse of wood:
> Or else, tuck up your gray frock,
> And sadle your[h] Goate, or your greene [i] Cock,
> And make his bridle a bottome of thrid,
> To roule up how many miles you have rid.

(lines 64–9)

This piece of doggerel is complemented by notes which give substance to the obscure, even hermetic, material presented in the 'Charme'. In note 'g', Jonson sends the reader to 'Delrio. *Disq. Magic.*' for a story about the 'Horse of Wood', but adds that for 'our Witches' this appellation refers to 'a broome staffe … a reed … a distaffe' citing both Remigius' *Daemonology* and Jean Bodin. In note '*h*', the 'Goate' is explained as 'the Devil himself … as appeares by their confessions', with citations from the same authorities as previous. Jonson adds, however, a more recent 'sighting' of the goat-Devil from the highest authority of all: 'His Majesty also remembers the story of the Divells appearance to those of Calicut, in that forme. *Daemonol. Lib. ii. Cap. iii.*'. The final note, '*i*', however, represents an interesting swerve, away from a certain dry discourse (though livened up a bit by the more recent 'story of the Devills appearance' in our midst, so to speak) of authority to a story of a 'greene Cock' that Jonson had heard when he was a boy. The story had clearly left a deep impression on the poet's imagination:

> Of the greene Cock we have no other ground (to confesse ingenuously) than a vulgar fable of a Witch, that with a Cock of that colour, and a bottome of blewe thred, would transport her selfe through the ayre; and so escaped (at the time of her being brought to execution) from the hand of Justice. It was a tale when I went to Schoole. (284, note *i*)

This moment of personal memoir stands out, although it is by no means unique in the text of *The Masque of Queenes*. The phrase 'a tale when I went to Schoole' is key. All of the elements – the cock, the thread, execution and school – are homely, if somewhat bizarrely mixed aspects of daily life. Jonson's own cocky escape from the 'hand of Justice', in other words his narrow escape from being hanged for killing a fellow actor, Gabriel Spencer, in a duel, must have seemed to him, in retrospect, like a kind of magic spool of blue thread that transported him through the air. In the case of Jonson, the escape was made by pleading benefit of clergy (in the ecclesiastical court in which he was luckily tried) showing that he could read Latin and therefore was learned and not, by law, fit for hanging.

In the notes to the third 'Charme', the reader is yet again struck by the motley tangle of ancient authorities, authorial commentary and personal reminiscence. Yet the main text and the notes are of an even more macabre and dismal nature than in the two previous poems. The 'Charme' opens with a description or what Jonson explains in his note is 'a *Periphrasis* of the night', beginning with a list of the animals that inhabit the nightworld:

The Owle is abroad, the Bat, and the Toade,
And so is the Cat-à-Mountain;
...
The Moone it is red, and the starres are fled,
But all the Skye is à burning:
The¹ Ditch is made, and our nails the spade,
With pictures full, of waxe, and of wooll;
Their livers I stick, with needles quick
There lackes but the blood, to make up the flood

(lines 75–6; 81–6).

In the dead of night, the witches dig into the ground to bury 'pictures' of 'waxe, and of wool'. In the extensive marginalia about this ritual burying of images, Jonson notes that stories of 'waxen Images' can be found in antiquity with 'that mischeife also of the needles', a reference to a kind of voodoo.

> This *rite* also of making a ditch with their nails, is frequent with our witches; Whereof see *Bodin; Remigius, Delrio, Malleus. Malefic. Godelman, lib. ii de Lamiis.* As also the antiquity of it most vively exprest by *Hora. Satir. Viii. Lib. i* where he mentions the pictures, and the blood of a black lambe, all which are yet in use with our modern witchcraft. (285, note *l*)

Jonson shows a keen interest in 'modern witchcraft' and the rituals of 'our witches' as well as a desire to show the continuity of witchcraft practice from antiquity to contemporary practices. The effect is both to rationalize superstition by citing all the main treatises of demonology and, at the same time, to exploit the macabre in ancient authors to enhance the terror of present-day witchcraft. In the last line of this note Jonson describes a particularly subversive piece of witchcraft. He writes about: 'certayne pictures of waxe found in a dunghill, near Islington, of our late Queenes; which rumours I myself (being then very young) can yet remember to have been current' (note *l*). Unlike the dream vision about the 'greene Cocke' in note '*i*', this reference to a kind of black magic being practised on images of Queen Elizabeth could be seen as dangerous gossip, a sign of a secret conspiracy to dismantle the body politic and, at some level, a taste of the dangers threatening the king himself. For, while King James's *Demonology* is a kind of scientific compendium of witchcraft, there is no doubt that after having been threatened by witches upon his ascension to the throne, the king was highly suspicious of them and believed to a certain extent in their powers to harm. Jonson's reference to the 'late Queene', Elizabeth I, as a possible victim of voodoo, in a masque that serves as a panegyric to eleven dead queens, cannot help but reflect eerily on the only living queen in the masque, Anne of Denmark, and the dangers that surround her. This reference to the 'pictures' of the dead monarch shows the extent to which Elizabeth I may have been the uninvited guest to Anne's masque and returns (like the repressed) throughout Jonson's text.

While it is difficult to reconstruct the performance from the masque text Jonson has left us, there can be no doubt that *The Masque of Queenes* was most probably intended to strike the spectator with awe and terror, rather than with amusement or delight. The sensational narrative is a heady mixture of gossip, rumour, treason and politics in manuscript, quarto and finally folio. Yet, on stage, the exploits of Jonson's witches must surely have amazed the spectators, simply by revealing what was most shocking. The witches swear (in a kind of conspiratorial oath) to throw the universe into chaos and attempt, on stage, in the view of the audience, to deliver out of the earth a rival claimant to the throne. The anti-masque in performance was surely a *tour-de-force* of 'horror', with the set including an 'ugly Hell, which flaming beneath, smoaked unto the top of the Roofe', the 'hollow and infernal music' accompanying the witches upon their entrance, their grotesque costumes 'some, with rats on their heads', carrying 'veneficall instruments' and using 'strange gestures' (lines 24–36). The curse of the 'Dame' must surely have been terrifying to the contemporary audience: 'Darken all this roofe / With present fogges. Exhale Earth's rottenest vapors; / And strike a blindnesse, through these blazing tapers' (lines 241–3). The actor playing the powerful witch was clearly placing a (real) curse upon the court itself, filled with 'blazing tapers' for the masque performance. Even more telling is that, in Charme 9, Jonson's witches may be said to finally burn the pictures of Elizabeth I made 'of waxe, and of wooll' (line 84) that had been buried in a ditch:

> About, about, and about,
> Till the mist arise, and the lights fly out,
> The Images neyther, be seene, nor felt;
> The woollen burne, and the waxen melt
>
> (lines 332–5).

The witches are, it may come as no surprise given the particularly treasonous nature of their efforts, driven from the stage after this Charme. *The Masque of Queenes*, in performance, took each member of the audience on a fairly frightening and awe-inspiring journey through the wild incantations and invocations of the witches, followed by the technically magnificent stage set of The House of Fame in which the twelve aristocratic Masquers sat. The dance and sudden disappearance of the witches from the stage is described at length by Jonson:

with a strange and sudden Musique, they fell into a magicall Daunce, full
of praeposterous change, and gesticulation, but most applying to their
property: who, at their meetings, do all things contrary to the custome of
Men, dauncing, back to back, hip to hip, their hands joined, and making
their circles backward, to the left hand, with strange phantasticque motions
of their heads, and bodies. All which were excellently imitated by the
Maker of the Daunce, Mr. Hierome Herne ... In the heate of their Daunce,
on the sudden, was heard a sound of loud Musique, as if many Instruments had given one blast. With which, not only the Hagges themselves,
but their Hell, into which they ranne, quite vanished; and the whole face
of the Scene altered; scarse suffering the memory of such thing: But, in the
place of it appear'd a glorious and magnificent Building. (lines 344–60)

While it is difficult to judge the degree of fear that such a staging would
have evoked in the audience, it seems that Jonson's description leaves
room to imagine an event of a certain terrifying quality. What are the
implications of staging the supernatural and a group of witches whose
main aim is to bring chaos to the Earth and specifically imagined as a
challenge to King James's 'soft peace'? The Dame urges her coven of
witches, not only to bring '*Chaös* ... once more' (lines 312–13), but to
conspire to overthrow the kingdom:

> I hate to see these fruits of a soft peace
> And curse the piety gives it such increase.
> Let us disturbe it, then; and blast the light;
> Mixe Hell, with Heaven; and make Nature fight
> Within herself; loose the whole henge of Things;
> And cause the Endes to runne back into their Spring.
>
> (lines 144–9)

At this rather climactic moment of dark and treasonous conspiracy,
Jonson has the witches 'relate' what they have brought to their coven.
This section, in which the witches stop loosing chaos on the world and
tell their Dame and the audience the ingredients they have brought to
the magic 'pot', does not serve, directly, to move forward the action of
the anti-masque which consists of the witches' attempts to force Nature
and Chaos to yield up a 'blue Drake', a new power or force, in a kind
of Hesiodic theogony. This act of telling each other what plants, liquids
and flesh each one has brought to their great work, to their 'Labor'
(line 285), constitutes a digression, and a rather long one at that. The
authorial justification for this digression is: 'This is also solemne in their
witchcraft, to be examin'd, either by the *Devill*, or their *Dame*, at their
meetings, of what Mischiefe they have done; and what they can confer
to a future hurt' (289, note *r*). Then (after a long Latin citation from
Remigius) Jonson adds that he will 'take occasion, not alone to expresse

the Things, (as vapors, liquours, herbes, bones, flesh, blood, fat, & such like, which are called *Media Magica*) but the rites of gathering them and from what places, reconciling (as neare as we can) the practice of Antiquity to the Neoterick, and making it familiar with our popular witchcraft'. The author, in other words, will use the occasion to list magical materials, the 'rites' of 'gathering' them as well as the 'places' these things were gathered. Moreover, the aim of the author, in annotating the witch doggerel with learned and abstruse citations, will be to 'reconcile' the old and the new, the past and the present.

How are we to interpret the ensuing four-line snippets of poetry, surrounded by learned annotation and, as in the previous 'Charmes', personal remarks and narrations by the author? They clearly serve to create a mood and atmosphere of deep gloom and superstitious fear. Yet in these verses what is most striking is the emphasis, in each witch's account, on the fragmentary quality of the item they have brought. This reminds us of *Macbeth* and, for instance, 'the Pilot's thumb'. The first Hag describes her addition to the witches' brew:

> I have been, all day, looking after
> A Raven, feeding upon a Quarter;
> And, soone as she turn'd her beake to the *South*,
> I snatch'd this morsell out of her Mouth.
>
> (lines 155–8)

Nothing is whole, all is in pieces. The witches in *Queenes* gather 'Wolves hayres' (line 159), 'mad Doggs foame', 'Adders ears' (line 160), 'the spurging of dead mans eyes' (line 161). Not only are these items fragmentary pieces of the body, but also bodily liquids. One of the witches 'Kill'd an infant, to have his fat' (line 176), another seeks 'The blood of the Frog, and the bone in his back' (line 184) and another: 'I scratch'd out the eyes of the Owle', 'I tore the Batts wing' (lines 197–8).

It is not the whole but the *part* that has talismanic power for the witch and, as we shall see, for the writer. What is unique in *Queenes* is the author's own account of how he wrote the verses and his desire to create something 'full of horror' (290, note 1). For instance, the witch's decision to 'snatch' the morsel out of the Raven's mouth 'at her turning toward the South' implies the 'prediction of a Storme' (note 1). So, he suggests that this 'ceremony' 'being observed make the act more darke, and full of horror'. The desire to add details that make the scene 'darke, and full of horror' is the author telling his reader of his own aims. His writing, like the witches' ceremony, is a ritual aimed at creating a certain macabre atmosphere. He mentions the fact that the witch doesn't 'cut her selfe', an interesting way of saying that the witch doesn't cut the piece off by herself, but rather takes the morsel from the Raven: 'as if that piece were sweeter which the Wolfe had bitten, or the Raven had pick'd, and more effectuous' (note 1). The ingredient has more power if it is second-hand and 'snatched' or stolen. This idea that the thing belonging to another is more precious, more powerful and 'sweeter' is the basis not only for Jonson's envious witches but also for his own creation. His need and desire to cite others, whether because they are authorities or simply 'sweet' and pleasurable, or, because he enviously prefers their work to his own, clearly participates in his witch's logic. For, just a few lines below this the word 'piece' will reappear: 'I have touched at this before ... of the use of gathering flesh, bones, & skulls: to which I now bring a piece of Apuleius, lib. iii. *de Asino aureo ...*' (291, note 4). By bringing a piece of Apuleius to the reader in the form of a note, a piece of dead flesh in other words, Jonson closes the gap between himself as author and the witches bringing fragments to the brew. The gathering of dead flesh, in the anti-masque, takes place in 'Charnell-houses' (line 168) and one of the witches clips 'a sinew' from a dead man swinging from the gallows: 'The wind had shrunke his veins' (lines 180–1). The witches gather plants such as 'Hemlock' (line 188) and 'Night-shade' (line 189) and Jonson explains in the adjoining note: 'I have her [the witch] gather them ... about a Castle, Church, or some such vast building (kept by Dogs) among ruines, and wild heapes' (293, note 9). The objects and the places all remind us of the Gothic. Yet, even more, the author's personal implication in the way the witches both destroy and attempt to create makes us think again of the hybrid nature of Frankenstein's creation: 'I collected bones from charnel-houses and disturbed, with profane fingers, the tremendous secrets of the human frame'. Like Frankenstein, Jonson also 'kept [his] workshop of filthy creation' (Shelley 315).

Yet, finally, the most stunning instance of what might be called Jonson's 'charnel-house style' is the monstrous vision he creates of Queen Anne herself. The poet is clearly at a loss as to how to describe the living queen. He cannot apply an epithet to her in the same way he does to the other queens. She cannot be 'chaste', like Artemisia, or 'brave', like Penthesilea. All the other queens have single epithets because they are dead and have come to be remembered in a particular way and for a particular virtue. They are frozen monuments to separate virtues and have become the models for emulation of these virtues. Anne of Denmark, as a living queen, is problematically unclassable in the same manner. She cannot be identified as an epitome in only one sphere, like a dead queen is remembered by posterity. The poet therefore makes her possess *all* the virtues: '[S]he, alone, / Possest all vertues, for which,

One by One, / They [The other eleven, dead Queens] were so fam'd'
(lines 416–18). At the same time that she encompasses all virtues in
herself, she is, paradoxically, also just 'a head' (line 418) at the top of
the pyramid. In terms of ordinary court flattery, such a positioning of
the queen at the apex of a pyramid seems like a pretty banal conceit.
Yet, the same drive that pushed him to self-comment in the marginalia
pushes the writer to explicate the relative position of the living queen;
in the lines which follow he plays with a strange etiological conceit
to justify Anne's position at the top of a pyramid composed of dead
queens: the ancient queens realized that they had formed a pyramid
without someone to fill the 'soveraigne Place', so they generously gave
this place to the sovereign, Anne: 'And, [they] wanting then a head, /
To form the sweet, and gracious *Pyramede*, / Wherein they sit, it being
the soveraigne Place / of all that Palace, and reserved to grace / he
worthiest Queene' (lines 418–20). At the same time, the poet feels the
need to explain further the source of this altruism on the part of the
dead queens: 'These [ancient dead queens], without envy, on her / In
life desired that honor to confer, / Which, with their death, no other
should enjoy' (lines 422–4). The convoluted syntax is very Jonsonian,
but, given the twisted idea being promulgated, it may be no accident
that the grammar is difficult to untangle. Free of the ordinary envy the
dead usually feel for the living (a commonplace in antiquity and, later, in
the Renaissance) the dead queens of the masque yield to a living queen
an honour usually 'enjoyed' in death. In other words, by pushing the
etiology, the explication for why Anne held the top place, far beyond
the requirements of pure flattery, Jonson creates a macabre image of a
living queen being crowned by the dead with the honours of one who
is dead and participating, at some level, in the world of the dead. And
yet, it may be that this grotesque etiology is not completely gratuitous.
Anne indeed needed to be invested with the honors enjoyed, still in the
popular imagination, with the recently dead, or 'late Queen' Elizabeth
I. Furthermore, the idea that the pyramid 'is wanting' or 'lacks' a head,
which Anne provides, gives us a clue as to what, in the masque writer's
imagination (and in the imagination of his contemporaries) may indeed
have been the very real specificity of Queen Anne: as the queen of James
VI of Scotland, later James I, she is the female successor of Queen Elizabeth I, but this only thanks to the fact James I's mother, Mary Stuart,
was beheaded and so prevented from all claims to the throne herself.
Anne's is the head that replaces the one lost by Mary Stuart.

Later in the masque, when, at the end of the long list of queens, as
well as an inventory of each of their individual deeds and history, Jonson
arrives, again, at Queen Anne, he is once again at a loss, preferring

simply to say that she needs no ceremony or praise as she is '*safe* in her princely virtue' (lines 661–2, my emphasis). Safety may be of the essence given the fates of Mary Stuart and the dangers that constantly haunted Queen Elizabeth. Both these queens were victims of violence, whether in the form of execution, treason, conspiracy, or, as we saw from Jonson's reference to wax images in 'Islington', magical curses. Jonson's description of Queen Anne in these lines is an exercise in empty praise: she is 'safe', she is 'above the neede of such Ceremony' (line 661), he has named her in his poems 'BEL-ANNA' (*Masque of Queenes*, line 663) a kind of bland, Spenserian type, and offers her the attribute of '*Fayre*' (line 664). Unlike the other queens, all of whom possess strong, and, as critics have noted, decidedly masculine virtues, Anne is given a colourless epithet that could be given to any anonymous, Petrarchan lady. He has not really praised, for fear of eliciting princely displeasure, for fear of stepping in the wrong direction, of attributing too much or too little and so attributes to her either all or nothing. Yet, for all his care in tiptoeing through the dangerous minefield of royal accolade, Jonson represents himself as having unwittingly perpetrated an enormous crime, equivalent to that of one of the most infamous of criminals from antiquity. Those who accusingly point a finger at him ask: '*How I can bring Persons, of so different Ages, to appeare, properly, together, Or, Why (which is more unnaturall) with* Virgil's Mezentius, *I join the living, with the dead?*' (lines 671–4). By bringing Queen Anne together on the stage with eleven dead queens, Jonson sees himself as having committed a crime against both nature and art. He implies that it is improper, from the point of view of the classical unities, to bring together '*Persons, of so different Ages*' together on stage. Yet, what is even 'more unnaturall' is not the grotesque mixture of different epochs but the practically obscene mixing of the living with the dead in a court masque where a living queen can be found in a charnel house, among the bits of flesh and bones brought by the hags as well as the 'piece of Apuleius' brought by the writer.

The author's comparison of himself, in his handling of Queen Anne, to the monstrous Mezentius may, at first, appear perplexing. Yet, it soon becomes clear that the tyrant king of Virgil's epic can be considered at the avant-garde of a particularly ingenious form of live burial. Mezentius was a king from Book 8 of Virgil's *Aeneid* who, for his own pleasure, would tie a living body to a corpse and watch that person die: 'Hand to hand and face to face, he made them / suffer corruption, oozing gore and slime / in that wretched embrace, and a slow / death' (Virgil 246–7, lines 484–8). Jonson's admission that he has 'buried' Queen Anne alive is a striking confession. The pyramid of great women, enthroned in the echoing House of Fame, is intended to represent a certain epitome of the beautiful and the good. By displaying this monstrous figure (and himself with it) to the reader, Jonson shows the dark side of the harmonious and rational order that he has been engaged in creating for the court. Even while he engages in fantasizing about the macabre monstrosity of binding the dead and the living, the author cries: 'Besides, if I would fly to the all-daring Power of *Poetry*, Where could I not take Sanctuary?' (lines 677–8); even while he denies implicitly that he is a monster, Jonson is actively at work in the 'filthy workshop' of his own creation. He does not hesitate to raise the spectre of the gruesome Mezentius, as he raised the witches and their 'praeposterous' (line 345) rituals. In fact, the writer seems to savour the comparison of himself to a monster and goes on to boast that he is impervious to judgement, claiming to be accountable to nothing and no one but *Poetry*, in which he will always find safety.

In fact, the writer seems to throw off his disguise as a writer for the court, aiming to please and to instruct, and to claim the monstrosity that inevitably emerges in the act of writing itself. From the perspective of *The Masque of Queenes*, we might see the Gothic as the *flight* toward *sanctuary* in 'the all-daring Power of Poetry', a kind of oxymoron. By finding himself out-of-bounds with regard to his grotesque mixing of the living and the dead, by realizing that he has buried his own queen in a tomb with the bones of eleven other dead queens and the carcasses of ancient writers, the writer seeks sanctuary. The desire for sanctuary and safety, however, is coupled with the desire to continue 'daring' and transgressing. The writer does not seek a sanctuary to escape arrest at the hands of the authorities, but claims a sanctuary within which he may continue performing the dangerous experiments of his art. What makes Jonson's portrait of Queen Anne so troubling is that even while he paints her in the blandest and palest hues, the creator cannot help but imagine that he is engaged in a work comparable to those of the foulest deeds of the most despotic king from antiquity. He, like the author or hero of a Gothic novel or story, is painfully aware of the deeply desirable underside of everything that is beautiful and good.

Notes

1 Note our own era's appreciation of the sexual and horrifying elements of a play like *'Tis Pity She's a Whore* at the expense of the religious and moral implications of the characters' actions in Cheek by Jowl's 2011–12 staging of the play. Posters of the television series *True Blood* and *The Vampire Diaries* were dead centre in the play's modern décor.

2 All references to Jonson's masques will be from *Ben Jonson*, ed. C. H. Herford and Percy and Evelyn Simpson, Vol. VII. I have placed the date of the masque performance in parenthesis. *Blacknesse* was first printed in Quarto in 1608. *Hymenaei* was published in Quarto the same year as it was performed, as was often the case.

3 According to Castle, Etienne-Gaspard Robertson's invention of a 'fantas-magorie' in 1798 emerged 'out of an interest in magic, conjuring, and optical effects' (33). 'Everything was done, quite shamelessly to intensify the supernatural effect. Plunged in darkness and assailed by unearthly sounds, spectators were subjected to an eerie, estranging, and ultimately baffling spectral parade' (32). Castle notes as well that 'One should not underesti-mate, by any means, the powerful effect of magic-lantern illusionism on eyes untrained by photography and cinematography' (35).

4 Jonson, *Timber, or Discoveries* 616, lines 1721–2. 'For all that we invent doth please us in the conception, or birth; else we would never set it down. But the safest is to *return to our Judgement*, and handle over again those things, that easinesse of which might make them justly suspected' (my emphasis).

5 Jonson, *Timber, or Discoveries* 583. '*I remember*, the Players have often mentioned it as an honour to *Shakespeare*, that in his writing, (whatsoever he penn'd) he never blotted out line. My answer hath been, would he had blotted a thousand. Which they thought a malevolent speech. I had not told poster-ity this, but for their ignorance, who choose that circumstance to commend their friend by, wherein he most faulted' (lines 647–53). This Horatian idea of 'rule' to 'stop' the flow of '*Phantsie*' (lines 657–68) is one Jonson picks up again in his poem 'To the Memory of my Beloved, The Author, Mr. William Shakespeare', heading the 1623 Folio: 'Thy Art, / My gentle *Shakespeare*, must enjoy a part. For though the *Poets* matter, Nature be, / His Art doth give the fashion. And, that he, / who casts to write a living line, must sweat / … and strike a second heat / Upon the Muses anvil …' (Jonson, *Poems* 392, lines 55–61). The metaphors of a 'second heat', 'blotting', and stopping the unreined flow of the fantasy are all part of the Horatian injunction to avoid the ridiculous, the laughable and the unbelievable.

6 Victoria Moul has most recently argued for the primacy of Horace (at the expense of other models) in Jonson's work. See *Jonson, Horace and the Classical Tradition*.

7 I have made this argument at greater length in *Ben Jonson and Envy*. See 99–109 in particular.

8 'Desinat in piscem mulier formosa superne': 'To put a fish's tail on a woman's body', Jonson's translation in *Horace, His Art of Poetrie* (305, lines 4–5). See Mathieu-Castellani for the 'poetics of the reasonable'.

9 For the hieroglyphic nature of the grotesque see Morel.

10 I do not have the space in this chapter to go into the role played by Inigo Jones, court architect and Jonson's collaborator on the masque, in promot-ing the grotesque in the masques. It is clear that the masque grotesque emerged in part from the collaboration between Jones and Jonson and not

from Jonson alone. According to John Peacock, Jones 'studied Lomazzo's treatise [*Trattato dell'arte de la pittura* (1584)] with sustained attention; and clearly Lomazzo's discussion of grotesques had important implications for his own use of ornament, especially on the proscenium arches of his masques and plays' (Peacock 227).

11 Descriptions by an author of a masque written and performed before royalty go back to George Gascoigne and his masques for Elizabeth I. A comparison with other authors' productions in this 'genre', namely 'A Description of a Masque', shows both to what extent Jonson is not alone in his post-performance printing of these texts and, at the same time, the extent to which he pushes the limits of 'description'.

Works cited

Agrippa, Henry Cornelius. *Three Books of Occult Philosophy, written by Henry Cornelius Agrippa, of Nettesheim … Translated out of the Latin into the English Tongue by J. F.* London, 1651.

Bal, Mieke. *Quoting Caravaggio: Contemporary Art, Preposterous History.* Chicago: Chicago University Press, 2001.

Briggs, Katharine Mary. *Pale Hecate's Team.* London: Routledge, Kegan & Paul, 1962.

Castle, Terry. 'Phantasmagoria and the Metaphorics of Modern Reverie' (extract). *The Horror Reader.* Ed. Ken Gelder. London and New York: Routledge, 2000. 29–46. [Originally published in *Critical Inquiry* 15 (1988)].

Clark, Mary Cowden. 'The Thane's Daughter'. *The Girlhood of Shakespeare's Heroines.* Vol. I. London: J. M. Dent & Co.; New York, E. P. Dutton & Co. [1907]. 79–149.

Clery, E. J. and Robert Miles, eds. *Gothic Documents: A Sourcebook 1700–1820.* Manchester: Manchester University Press, 2000.

Horace. 'His Art of Poetrie, Made English by Ben Jo[h]nson.' *Ben Jonson.* Eds C. H. Herford and Percy and Evelyn Simpson. Vol. VIII. Oxford: Clarendon Press, 1952. 305–55.

—. *Ars Poetica. Horace: Satires, Epistles and Ars Poetica.* Trans. H. Rushton Fairclough. Cambridge, MA: Harvard University Press, 1926.

Jonson, Ben. *Chloridia. Ben Jonson.* Eds C. H. Herford and Percy and Evelyn Simpson. Vol. VII. Oxford: Clarendon Press, 1952. 749–61.

—. *Hymenaei. Ben Jonson.* Eds C. H. Herford and Percy and Evelyn Simpson. Vol. VII. Oxford: Clarendon Press, 1952. 209–41.

—. 'Poems'. *Ben Jonson.* Eds C. H. Herford and Percy and Evelyn Simpson. Vol. VIII. Oxford: Clarendon Press, 1952.

—. *The Masque of Blacknesse. Ben Jonson.* Eds C. H. Herford and Percy and Evelyn Simpson. Vol. VII. Oxford: Clarendon Press, 1952. 169–80.

—. *The Masque of Queenes. Ben Jonson.* Eds C. H. Herford and Percy and Evelyn Simpson. Vol. VII. Oxford: Clarendon Press, 1952. 279–317.

—. *The Vision of Delight. Ben Jonson.* Eds C. H. Herford and Percy and Evelyn Simpson. Vol. VII. Oxford: Clarendon Press, 1952. 461–71.

—. *Timber, or Discoveries. Ben Jonson.* Eds C. H. Herford and Percy and Evelyn Simpson. Vol. VIII. Oxford: Clarendon Press, 1952. 563–649.

Lucan. *The Civil War.* Trans. J. D. Duff. London: Heinemann, 1962. The Loeb Classical Library.

Mathieu-Castellani, Gisèle. *Montaigne ou la Vérité du Mensonge.* Geneva: Droz, 2000.

Meskill, Lynn S. *Ben Jonson and Envy.* Cambridge: Cambridge University Press, 2009.

Montaigne, Michel de. *Essais de Michel Seigneur de Montaigne.* Paris, 1588.

Morel, Philippe. *Les Grotesques: Les figures de l'imaginaire dans la peinture italienne à la fin de la Renaissance.* Paris: Flammarion, 1997.

Moul, Victoria. *Jonson, Horace and the Classical Tradition.* Cambridge: Cambridge University Press, 2010.

Neill, Michael. *Issues of Death: Morality and Identity in English Renaissance Tragedy.* Oxford: Clarendon Press, 1997.

Orgel, Stephen. *The Illusion of Power: Political Theater in the English Renaissance.* Berkeley: University of California Press, 1973.

Peacock, John. *The Stage Designs of Inigo Jones: The European Context.* Cambridge: Cambridge University Press, 1995.

Radcliffe, Ann. 'On the Supernatural in Poetry.' *The New Monthly Magazine* 16.1 (1826): 145–52.

Shelley, Mary. *Frankenstein; or, The Modern Prometheus. Three Gothic Novels.* Ed. Peter Fairclough. Introd. Mario Praz. Harmondsworth: Penguin Books, 1968. 257–498.

Virgil. *The Aeneid.* Trans. Robert Fitzgerald. New York: Vintage Books, 1984.

Walpole, Horace. 'Preface to the Second Edition of *The Castle of Otranto.*' *Three Gothic Novels.* Ed. Peter Fairclough. Introd. Mario Praz. Harmondsworth: Penguin Books, 1968. 43–8.

Part III

Gothic textuality in the early modern period

7

Exhumations:
scopophobia in Renaissance texts

Duncan Salkeld

On 16 July 1559, Joan Foster stood charged at Bridewell Hospital with having 'very naughtily and lewdly' sought to 'enchaunt and as it were to coine and bewitch Margaret Storer' in order to engage her in 'lewd and evil purposes' with Foster's brother (*BCB* 1.10v).[1] Regarded as a procuress whose arts of enticement included witchcraft, Foster was somewhat lucky that, in Bridewell, her punishment would only be a severe whipping. Joan Ellyse, wife of a Westminster brewer, was less fortunate. Accused of 'practising witchcraft' and casting spells on her neighbours' cattle so that they languished and died, she pleaded guilty and was sentenced to hanging at Tyburn (Jeaffreson 1: 84–5). Yet for others punishment could be even worse. Foster's offence of 'coining' was metaphorical. When Thomas Marshall and Roger Newton were found guilty of counterfeiting two coins in 1607, they were sentenced to 'be hung ... and be laid on the ground still living, and their entrails be taken from their bellies whilst they should still be living and their heads be cut off, and their bodies be each divided into four parts, and the same quarters be placed where the Lord the King may be pleased to appoint' (Jeaffreson 2: 7–8). Protracted torture and execution occurred at the king's pleasure: coining hearts and minds, especially for sexual purposes, merited less harsh measures. Sixteenth-century susceptibilities to desire and death were, it seems, never entirely separable, and early modern dramatists found increasingly sophisticated ways in which to blend them on the English stage and so produce the kind of aesthetic we now recognize as the Gothic.

Macabre fusions of death and desire have a continental literary history in texts that ironically belong to comedy. In 1525, Pietro Aretino penned his satirical play *La Cortigiana* in which he lampooned not only the pretentiousness of Baldassare Castiglione's *Book of the Courtier* but the entire church hierarchy associated with the papal court. His play involves a pimp named Zoppino who persuades a procuress, Aloigia, to trick Maco, a young gull, into bed with a mere baker's wife instead

of the renowned Italian courtesan Camilla Pisana. Zoppino arranges for
the credulous Maco to sit in a special mould that will, he believes, literally make him into a fine and appealing courtier. Once out of his mould,
Maco gets to the point: 'I want to be Pope and I want to screw Camilla.
Now! Now! Let's get moving. I'm in a hurry! ... Nonsense, I say. I want
to screw her, I tell you! ... Christ, but I want to screw her!' (123, 127).[2]
The play levels its jokes repeatedly against the hypocrisies and credulity that sustained central power in Rome. A fishmonger tricked into
losing a fine fish declares, 'Damn Rome, the court, the church, everyone
who lives here, and everyone who believes in it!' (72). Messer Andrea
declares, 'whenever you hear someone saying anything good about the
Roman court, tell him he's not telling the truth' (75). And an old court
attendant, Valerio, observes, 'You never see a face at court that's not a
sham' (126). Aloigia, the procuress, turns this drama into more than a
picaresque tale of thieves, bandits and foolish victims. She spices it up
with her own take on the arts of enticement and inveigling ways used
by Roman courtesans, mentioning well-known women of the era such
as Angela the Greek, 'Matrema non vuol' ('Mummy doesn't want me
to'), Lorenzina, Beatrice Paregia and Camilla Pisana. Aloigia knows the
secrets that lie behind their beauty. These women have

> alembics for distilling, washes to take away freckles and the scars from
> the French disease, a strap to lift sagging breasts, tweezers for plucking
> eye-lashes, a flask of lovers' tears, a glass of bats' blood, dead men's bones,
> for torments and betrayals, owls' claws, vultures' hearts, wolves' teeth,
> bears' fat, ropes from people who've been hanged by mistake ... I'm the
> one they call on to clean their teeth and get rid of stinking breath, and do
> a thousand other services. (83)

Get up close to these women, Aloigia implies, and you are in for a shock.
This attitude towards courtesans – figures in whom signs of desire and
decay comingle – becomes intensified in a dialogue attributed to Aretino
by his publisher and first printed in 1539. Aretino's prose dialogues,
published in the 1530s, were regarded as so scandalous that they ended up
on the Vatican index of prohibited books of 1557. The papal authorities
had suppressed almost every copy of Marcantonio Raimondi's sexually
explicit engravings which carried accompanying verses by Aretino (see
Talvacchia 4–5). The prose dialogues, having no images, were perhaps
deemed less immediately subversive. An edition of Aretino's dialogues
in the British Library has on its first page both the title, *I Ragionamenti*,
and the spurious claim that it was published by John Wolfe in London
in 1584. This edition, known as the 'Bengodi' text, was, according to
the British Library catalogue, more probably printed on the continent
in the early seventeenth century. Aretino's *I Ragionamenti* originally

comprised two infamous, sexually explicit dialogues, the first between Nanna and Antonia, and the second between Nanna and her daughter Pippa. But the 'Bengodi' edition (BL shelfmark C.107.aa.32) collects within its pages a third dialogue attributed – along with the first and second parts – to Aretino. The authorship of this piece has long been in question. Raymond Rosenthal, Aretino's English translator, omitted it from his version of *I Ragionamenti* published in 1971, perhaps because he doubted that Aretino was its author. The late authority on Aretino, Giovanni Aquilecchia, who had consulted the British Library 1539 edition, also doubted its Aretinian provenance.[3] There the matter might be left, except for a few key factors: The first person to make this attribution was Aretino's publisher, Marcolini, in the work's first edition of 1539, and Aretino had ample opportunity to deny it; the dialogue has very many incidental verbal parallels with Aretino's other dialogues; and the alternative author proposed can be ruled out. In 1941, the Italian historian Umberto Gnoli noted that

> Apollinaire, following Bonneau and then Lanfranchi, considers the Zoppino dialogue, which is frequently cited because it contains most of the names of the courtesans then fashionable in Rome, not to have been written by P. Aretino. But this does not seem to me demonstrable. (Gnoli 18, n. 1)

Both Alcide Bonneau and Guillaume Apollinaire, in their respective editions of 1882 and 1909, denied that Aretino could have been its author (see *Les Ragionamenti* and *Les Ragionamenti ou Dialogues*). Gino Lanfranchi, editor of the first single Italian edition of 1922, followed Apollinaire in arguing that this was a work from the quill of the Spanish *émigré* and picaresque writer Francisco Delicado. He based this claim on the circumstantial grounds that Delicado moved to Rome around the turn of the sixteenth century and then to Venice after its sack in 1527, and, more generally, upon what he termed its 'gloomy Spanish flavour' (Gnoli 99). Paolo Bertani, in *Pietro Aretino e le sue opere* (1901), refers in a footnote to a 1539 edition, stating that the Zoppino dialogue constitutes a 'third part' of the *Ragionamenti*, with the earlier two parts being the dialogues between Nanna and Antonia, and Nanna and Pippa respectively (Bertani 362; see also Aquilecchia). Unfortunately, the British Library copy of the 1539 edition seems now to be lost. The first and second parts of the *Ragionamenti* were written in 1534 and 1536, with the Zoppino dialogue added at some time between 1536 and 1539. Delicado died in 1534 or 1535, and, since the Zoppino author echoes numerous phrases and lines from the two earlier dialogues, he is very unlikely to have been responsible for verbal parallels with the second part. Aretino was on excellent terms with

Marcolini and promised him that he would not use any other publisher for his writings (Bull 91). We might add that, on stylistic grounds alone, the vocabulary and tone of the passage spoken by Aloigia in Aretino's *La Cortigiana* is exactly that of the third part.

The Zoppino dialogue is as much a social and historical document as a work of fiction. It presents an account of the histories of many of the courtesans and prostitutes in early sixteenth-century Rome, rather like a later version of Athenaeus of Naucritas's *Deipnosophistae*, the thirteenth book of which discusses a great many courtesans from the classical era (Athenaeus XIII). Zoppino is out to shock his interlocutor into turning from his admiration for such women altogether. While Athenaeus's text mixes talk of courtesans with convivial discourses about food and banqueting, Zoppino's author sets out to create an almost pathological disgust. The dialogue between Zoppino, a former pimp now turned friar and Ludovico, another pimp who has tempted him with a young woman named Lorenzina, focuses on courtesans they have known. These include women who lived in Rome at the time, from Gianna the baker's daughter who only took men between her 'arse cheeks' to twin sisters nicknamed the 'Piemontesian executioners' after their father's profession. These women have emerged from obscure origins to become the centre of local gossip. 'Matrema non vuol' was apparently a 'sunny and spirited' girl who could recite Petrarch and Boccaccio by heart, her eloquence a match for Cicero. Beatrice, of the Campo Marzo suburb near the Vatican, was a washerwoman's daughter, also known as Cicalina ('she who talks a lot and nicely') and favoured by priests. She allowed a quack doctor to dress her in boys' clothes and take her 'horsey-style'. Another, Angela Greca ('the Greek'), had been kidnapped by ruffians and dumped at an inn but became much admired by a Vatican steward. Beatrice of Ferrara, daughter to a 'poor Spanish woman', rose from 'filthy conditions' to become 'one of the most attractive and classiest women in Rome'. The famous Tullia d'Aragona fled Rome for Siena and there brought up her daughter as a courtesan, claiming that the cardinal of Aragona was her father. 'Personally,' remarks Zoppino, 'I think that, at most what happened was that the cardinal's mule used to have a shit at Tullia's house; however, it is in just such ways that courtesans achieve nobility' (Herraez and Salkeld 107–9). These are just a few of the many women Zoppino mentions, and it is of course difficult to verify any of the purported facts he gives about them. But he also mentions Imperia, Rome's most renowned courtesan, who poisoned herself one stormy night in 1512, and whose fame lived long after her death. For Imperia, whose real name was Lucretia Cognati, a good deal of documentary evidence has survived.[4]

Some of these women achieved status, celebrity and even influence, but most of them – so Zoppino argues – concealed not just grotesque and physically repulsive bodies but malevolent cunning. He begins by outlining their ruses, strategies and well-worked methods of deceit:

> Take the man who comes over time after time, hands full, and pounds on their door; or the one who whistles in the night and is let in quickly – she calls him hers, and says: 'My only one, oh my sweetheart, my hope, my protector, I don't know what you have done to me, I feel like dying, you've put a spell on me. I can't eat, drink, or sleep. I'm always thinking about you, my heart, my soul, my darling!'
>
> And so, they do it together. And these women swear that they'll never do it with any other but him, declaring: 'Such and such a man wants to give me a dress, a diamond, a ruby, but I really don't ever want to serve him.' And to make sure you've got the point, they say: 'My darling, don't you know that all I have is yours too? And if my arse isn't enough, take my eyes and my heart too, anything, just so you love me as I love you.' (Herraez and Salkeld 92)

But it is not long before Zoppino's imagination turns to the darker sentiments of Aloigia's speech in *La Cortigiana*. The courtesans' interest in cosmetics, baubles and little gifts reveals a more sinister taste for fetishes and tokens cut from the corpses of executed criminals. He claims to have seen them late at night, along the city boundary and byways, carrying items they have stolen from the dead, not only clothes, shoes and even teeth but chunks of decayed human flesh to serve up for the next day's meal. He has glimpsed them 'in the witching hour, wild and dishevelled – or even completely naked – gesticulating weirdly like witches and uttering words I shudder to recall' (Herraez and Salkeld 93).[5]

Meeting at midnight, they gather in cabals or covens to utter incantations, recast church rituals and embrace each other carnally, using exhumed hair, teeth, ribs, eyes and umbilici as diabolic tokens. Zoppino aims to have a wide-eyed Ludovico rapt.

> What's more, I've seen plenty of them, barefoot and alone, carrying a stolen knife, outlining shapes and measuring the ground with a thousand ropes. Then they lay their clothes on the ground and clasp tightly to one another for a few pleasures.
>
> What would you think if I told you that last night I saw one from La Pace, carrying a burning lamp which had earlier been removed from the Crucifix, along with some oil with which to boil your hair, strings stolen from men's trousers, and nail clippings.
>
> They anoint tiles, and lodestone, and, at dawn, they take nails and inscribe their spells with them. Casting figures in wax or bronze so weird they'd harrow hell, they form hearts on hot ashes and pierce them with such words as these:

> Before this fire is spent
> Till to my door he wends,
> May my love sting you
> As I to this heart do.

They utter a mumbo-jumbo of words that would take a month to re-tell. And what's more, some of them anoint themselves with holy oil. I know some who anoint their lips and, as they go, kiss one another, asking what each is up to. They keep yet more items in their cupboards: hairs, herbs, ribs, teeth and eyes from the exhumed, blank papers, children's umbilici and the soles of dead men's shoes. So I can warrant you that beauty and caresses are the least of what makes make you dote on them: what counts are cemeteries, graveyards, dark sepulchres, enchantments and charms. (Herraez and Salkeld 93–4)

On the one hand, the Zoppino dialogue purports to give the 'facts' about a number of historical women, many of whom would have passed into obscurity without any trace that they once had lived. For this reason, it constitutes a valuable record of some remarkable individuals. Yet, on the other hand, Zoppino comes to bury, not to praise, their reputations, and then exhume them and appal the imagination of his audience. Hence, he argues, even the finest of these women are in truth physically horrifying and morally corrupt. His aim is to destroy the erotic potential of the female body, detailing the devilish artistry with which they film over filthy and decayed bodies with cosmetics, powders, oils and essences, and stop up running sores or open wounds with shreds and patches. Zoppino knows their secrets:

> And what about all those pestilent, toxic creams they put on their faces, lips and teeth, so that, sometimes, you'd be better off kissing a sewer rather than their faces? And what about those rags with grey and red stains that always speckle and stain their blouses? What causes that? Moss? If you only knew about the powder and crushed glass they put inside their vaginas in order to absorb that moisture inside. And it rubs on thousands of poor young men, making them seriously damage their cocks. Usually, they have lice and crabs too; so, if you knew a thousandth of what I know, you'd never want to see their faces again. It'd be the same if you'd seen them as I have, in household after household. I've seen them taking a shit in the evening and making such a noise as if they were firing off all the artillery of the Castel Sant' Angelo, or else, setting off a Catherine wheel. It sounded like the great clamour of unborn souls issuing from their arses. (Herraez and Salkeld 99)

In this duologue, Ludovico would exploit such women for the pleasures they provide, while Zoppino exploits them for an unpleasure gained by exposing women's bodies to a fantasized male gaze. The female body is redescribed as demonic, putrified and mutilated, transforming the courtesan from 'bad mother' to cadaverous witch. Her seductive body is accursed, an object of social decay, scarred by self-harm, one that in so many hidden ways generates and incubates infection. Femininity, in Zoppino's paranoid world, is marked by secretions and secrecies:

> First, they remove the strands of skin which continuously hang off them; then they peel themselves off and have a bath, one of those known as 'skimming baths'. And they like to darken their foul smelling, hairy limbs. And what about those putrefying lotions they put on their lips? Don't they reek? And that lubrication they produce while doing it – what causes that? Take it from one who knows – something even worse. (Herraez and Salkeld 98)

There is no sixteenth-century text that quite equals the Zoppino dialogue for prurience, vituperation and a disturbing sense of sexual disgust. Yet in certain respects, Zoppino's tale of the arts, tricks and ruses of courtesans bears important similarities with works of the picaresque, from Fernando de Rojas's *La Celestina* (1499), in which the bawd also resorts to witchcraft in procuring Melibea for Calisto, to Francisco de Quevedo's *El Buscon* (The Swindler) (1626). Quevedo's hero, Pablos, grew up in a low-life family, his father a barber and thief, and his mother by implication a whore and witch. Pablos explains that rumours about his mother and a flying goat almost saw her tarred and feathered. Her room was lined with skulls 'to put spells on the living', her hammock-bed was hung by old hangman's ropes, and she kept a rosary threaded with dead men's teeth (Quevedo 66–7). The English writer most closely associated with this kind of picaresque literature was Robert Greene, the pamphleteer and friend of Nashe who set out to expose the tricks and deceits of professional con-artists and prostitutes. Greene's pamphlet *A disputation, betweene a hee conny-catcher, and a shee conny-catcher* (1592) is designed to give clear warning to readers of the duplicities of courtesans, their 'amorous glances' and 'smirking Ocyliades', all designed to 'inueagle' and 'intrap' their victims:

> Besides, I haue here layde open the wily wisedome of ouerwise Curtizens, that with their cunning, can drawe on, not only poore nouices, but such as hold themselues maisters of their occupation. What flatteries they vse to bewitch, what sweet words to inueagle, what simple holines to intrap, what amorous glaunces, what smirking Ocyliades, what cringing curtesies, what stretching Adios, following a man like a blood-hound, with theyr eyes white, laying out of haire, what frouncing of tresses, what paintings, what Ruffes, Cuffes, and braueries, and all to betraie the eyes of the innocent nouice, whom when they haue drawne on to the bent of their bow, they strip like the prodigall childe, and turne out of doores like an outcast of the world. (sig. A2v, Harrison 4–5)

Shakespeare calls these tricks of the eye 'aliads' (Q1608) or 'Eliads' (F1623) in *King Lear* (4.4.25) and 'illiads' in *The Merry Wives of Windsor* (F1623, 1.3.54).[6] But none of these examples from the picaresque genre come near the Zoppino text for the intensity of its aversion to women it identifies simultaneously with desire and death. The Zoppino text is an anti-feminist *grimoire*, insisting on the fantasized and contaminating female body. Its equation of female sexuality with physical decay sees women as furtive agents of social infection. The Zoppino author seems to relish the ghastliness of his diatribe, and the result is that revulsion has become an expression of desire. Voyeuristic and vicious, Zoppino's rhetoric voices a twin affect where disgust has itself become pleasure, and (in turn) loathing a version of priapism. Disgust and desire have fused to a single term: simultaneous, double-voiced, and propelled by folded unconscious motives, the Zoppino text has fascination and revulsion no longer contending in a dialectic but as elements in one and the same 'scopophobic' experience.

Desire for the dead was something English dramatists explored gradually, as tragedies became increasingly lurid and far-fetched. In October 1611, Sir George Buc, educated at Chichester and Cambridge, received and read an untitled, anonymously authored manuscript playbook. He was one year into his post as Master of the Revels, having succeeded the previous incumbent Edmund Tilney. He marked the play up for amendment and then wrote 'This second Maydens Tragedy (for it hath no name inscribed) may with the reformations bee acted publikely'. Stylistic tests have pointed towards Thomas Middleton as the work's author, an attribution now accepted in the Oxford *Thomas Middleton: The Collected Works* (2008).[7] The play was performed in 1611 at the indoor Blackfriars theatre, and, although it bears some similarities to other plays by Middleton – notably *The Revenger's Tragedy* and *The Bloody Banquet* – it remains unusual for being particularly gruesome. Middleton was not averse to offering his audience sensational tragedy. He began *The Revenger's Tragedy*, for example, with Vindice carrying the skull of his 'betrothed lady' Gloriana (1.1.16), lately poisoned by the duke because she would not yield to the tyrant's sexual demands. Vindice talks with the skull, dotes on its beauty, and contrives, with his brother Hippolito, a suitably ghastly revenge. Knowing the old duke cannot resist a pretty lady, Vindice laces the skull's teeth with poison. In Act 3 scene 5, the duke kisses what he believes is a woman's face (but is of course the skull) and writhes in agony as his flesh is burned away by the poison. The brothers then set about using his corpse to undo their remaining enemies. In *The Bloody Banquet*, a usurping Tyrant forces the young queen to eat her lover's remains at a table set with his bleeding flesh and skull. But Middleton could bring the house down with laughter too. *A Mad World, My Masters* (1608) has an over-protective and jealous husband Harebrain (derisively also called 'Shortrod') gulled into allowing his wife to visit the house of a courtesan, where she has sex with her lover. The fictional pretext for this visit is that the courtesan is unwell and the wife is visiting a sick help-mate. Harebrain waits in a separate room while his wife copulates offstage with her lover, and the courtesan, to cover their groans, pretends to be in agony. Echoing the lovers' gasps and moans, ('Huff, huff huff ... Hey, hy, hy hy ... suh, suh'), the courtesan even fakes a conversation between the two women – all, of course, for Harebrain's ears: 'Oh no, lay your hand here, Mistress Harebrain. Ay there; oh there, there lies my pain, good gentlewoman. Sore? Oh ay, I can scarce endure your hand upon't.' Entirely taken in, Harebrain sympathetically tells the audience, 'Poor soul, how she's tormented' (3.2.203–6), hears her climax ('Fall back, she's coming'), and when his wife eventually emerges, he joyfully exclaims, 'Never was hour spent better' (3.2.216, 235–6). Three years later, in the play Buc named as 'The Second Maiden's Tragedy', Middleton mixed these modes, producing a grotesque and excessive drama that would make his audience laugh in fascinated horror.

The story of *The Lady's Tragedy*, as the Oxford *Collected Works* titles this 'second Maydens Tragedy', centres (unsurprisingly) on an unnamed 'Lady', fiancée to the displaced ruler Govianus, who refuses to marry his usurper, a male designated in the manuscript as 'The Tyrant'. Placed under arrest with Govianus, she begs him to end her life. He runs at her with a sword, gets half-way but then swoons. Frustrated at his inability, she does it herself and her body is interred in the cathedral. This of course does not put the tyrant off, and he demands the cathedral keys so that he may snatch her body from its tomb. He kisses her 'grey-eyed monument', opens the tomb, clasps her body (a stage-dummy) in his arms and embraces it.[8] Weeping over her, he is determined to 'possess' her fully (4.3.116). The actor playing the lady then appears as her ghost to a revived Govianus who, learning of the tyrant's intentions, sets out for revenge. In the final scene, the lady's body is brought into court dressed in black velvet, a chain of pearls and a crucifix, and given obeisance. Feeling that his lady lacks a bit of colour, the tyrant hires a painter to trick her out with an impression of bodily warmth, enough to assist him in believing that his 'arms and lips shall labour life into her' (5.2.118–19). The painter is unsurprisingly Govianus in disguise: he daubs her face and lips with poison, the Tyrant kisses her fully, and so meets his grisly end.

Desiring the dead is a peculiarity we associate with Gothic literature. When Victor Frankenstein first sews his monster together, he declares, 'I had selected his features as beautiful. Beautiful! Great God! His yellow skin scarcely covered the work of muscles and arteries beneath.' A woman in Bram Stoker's *Dracula* says of the vampire-bitten Lucy Westenra, 'She makes a very beautiful corpse, sir', and Sheridan Le Fanu ends his vampire novella *Carmilla* with the line, 'to this hour the image of Carmilla returns to memory with ambiguous alternations – sometimes the playful, languid, beautiful girl; sometimes the writhing fiend I saw in the ruined church' (Shelley 56; Stoker 162; Wolf 342). It is this dual affect, disgust as a form of desire, that Middleton repeatedly evoked in his plays. For Freud, 'scopophilia', or the pleasure of looking, was a formative component in the development of infant sexuality. But in *Beyond the Pleasure Principle*, he argued further that the sexual instincts that sustain human generation and survival are constituted by processes of repression: the wish to live must exert itself against a wish to die.[9] We might term the literary affect arising from such a complex 'scopophobia'. The scopophobic imagination at work in these early modern texts does not exactly make them 'Gothic', in the manner that we associate with works by Mary Shelley, Matthew Lewis or Ann Radcliffe, but their conflation of desire with revulsion lies at the heart of the Renaissance macabre. The eroticism of decayed femininity combined with an urge to self-destruction are key Gothic motifs, made most familiar, perhaps, in the stories of Poe and Stevenson, but also notably in *Wuthering Heights* (1847) where Cathy's self-starvation eventually leads to Heathcliff's ghoulish pleasure in attempting to disinter the woman he loves. Desire in these texts sickens and decays, and in that process sickness itself becomes erotically charged. Heathcliff's longing for the moment when his heart is stopped as he lies in Cathy's grave, his dead cheek frozen next to hers, is the novel's final scopophobic emblem (Brontë 298–90). Desire for the dead was unusual in the Victorian era but not unknown: Auguste Comte worshipped his late beloved Clothilde de Vaux and built an entire religious cult from the letters they had exchanged during their 'incomparable year' of 1846, and Victoria mourned her genitally pierced husband Albert intensely for years (see Crompton, Jalland). The Gothic may have been a later invention but it was in Renaissance texts that scopophobic fusions of sexual desire and physical decay found their most intense and startlingly visual forms of representation. The crowd-pleasing entertainment of horrific public executions on Tower Hill, Smithfield, Newgate or at Tyburn had given familiar precedent. It is perhaps worth noting that although the coiners Thomas Marshall and Roger Newton were just two of hundreds of men judicially hacked to death in full public view, no woman was butchered in this way. It was Shakespeare who uniquely and sensationally chose to give us that chilling image, in *Titus Andronicus* (1594) where directly after being raped, Lavinia stands for a few seconds alone on stage, her hands sliced off and her tongue cut out, coughing blood.

Notes

1 *Bridewell Court Minute Book* (BCB). Bethlem Archives and Museum. Beckenham, Kent.
2 Quotations from Aretino's *La Cortigiana* are cited by page number from Campbell and Sbrocchi.
3 Private communication: letter dated 31 May 1999.
4 For evidence of Imperia, see Salkeld, *Shakespeare Among the Courtesans*, 100–4.
5 This passage echoes *La Cortigiana* (1525), see Campbell and Sbrocchi 84. Extravagant similes, pseudo-etymologies and experiments in dialect of the sort evident in the Zoppino dialogue are also characteristic of Aretino. Quotations from the Zoppino dialogue are taken from a translation by Ana Garcia Herraez and Duncan Salkeld that follows my 'History, Genre and Sexuality in the Sixteenth Century: The Zoppino Dialogue Attributed to Pietro Aretino' (Herraez and Salkeld 49–116, 92–3). I refer to this work elsewhere, following Gnoli, as 'the Zoppino dialogue'.
6 All citations of Shakespeare are from Wells and Taylor, *The Complete Works*.
7 All citations of Middleton's plays are from Taylor and Lavagnino, *Thomas Middleton: The Collected Works*. For Middleton's authorship of *The Second Maiden's Tragedy* see Julia Briggs's edition in Taylor and Lavagnino, esp. 833; for Buc's alterations, see Taylor and Lavagnino, *Thomas Middleton and early modern Textual Culture*, 619, 621.
8 The 'grey-eyed monument' is Middleton's pun on Shakespeare's 'grey-eyed morn' in *Romeo and Juliet* (2.2.1).
9 Freud, *On Sexuality* 69–70, 109–13. Reddick and Edmundson *Sigmund Freud, Beyond the Pleasure Principle and Other Writings*: 'The theory that there are drives directed at self-preservation, drives that we ascribe to all living beings, stands in striking opposition to the hypothesis that the entire life of the drives serves to procure death' (79).

Works cited

Apollinaire, Guillaume, intro. and notes *Les Ragionamenti. Sonnets luxurieux: traductions nouvelles et morceaux traduits pour la première fois du divin Aretin*. Paris: Bibliothèque des Curieux, 1909.

Aquilecchia, Giovanni. *Sei giornate: Ragionamento della Nanna e della Antonia (1534), Dialogo nel quale la Nanna insegna a la Pippa (1536) by Pietro*

Aretino. Bari: Laterza, 1969.

Athenaeus. *The Deipnosophists*. Trans. Charles Burton Gulick. Cambridge, MA: Harvard University Press, 1937.

Bertani, Paolo. *Pietro Aretino e le sue opera*. Sondrio: E. Quadrio, 1901.

Bonneau, Alcide, trans. *Les Ragionamenti ou Dialogues du divin Pietro Aretino. Texte italien et traduction complète par le traducteur des Dialogues de Luisa Sigea*. Paris, 1882.

Bridewell Court Minute Book (BCB). Bethlem Archives and Museum. Beckenham, Kent. 14 May 2013. http://www.bethlemheritage.org.uk/archive/web/BCB.htm#BCB-01.

Brontë, Emily. *Wuthering Heights*. Ed. Ian Jack. Oxford and New York: Oxford University Press, 1981.

Bull, George. *Aretino, Selected Letters*. Harmondsworth: Penguin Books, 1976.

Campbell, J. Douglas and Leonard G. Sbrocchi, eds. *Cortigiana*. Ottawa: Dovehouse Editions, 2003.

Crompton, Albert, ed. *Confessions and Testament of Auguste Comte: And His Correspondence with Clothilde de Vaux*. Liverpool: Henry Young and Sons, 1910.

Freud, Sigmund. *On Sexuality: Three Essays on the Theory of Sexuality and Other Works*. Ed. Angela Richards. Harmondsworth: Penguin, 1977. Penguin Freud Library.

Gnoli, Umberto. *Cortigiane Romane, Note e bibliografia*. Arezzo: Edizioni Della Rivista, 1941.

Harrison, G. B., ed. *Robert Greene, A disputation between a Hee Conny-catcher and a Shee Conny-catcher*. London: Bodley Head, 1923.

Herraez, Ana Garcia and Duncan Salkeld. 'History, Genre and Sexuality in the Sixteenth Century: The Zoppino Dialogue Attributed to Pietro Aretino.' *Mediterranean Studies* 10 (2001): 49–116.

Jalland, Pat. *Death in the Victorian Family*. Oxford University Press, 1996.

Jeaffreson, J. C., ed. *Middlesex County Records (Old Series). Volume 1: 1550–1603. Volume 2: 1603–1625*. Originally Middlesex County Records Society, 1886. London: Greater London Council, 1972.

Middleton, Thomas. *Thomas Middleton: The Complete Works*. Eds Gary Taylor and John Lavagnino. Oxford: Clarendon Press, 2007.

Quevedo, Francisco de. *Lazarillo de Tormes* and *The Swindler: Two Spanish Picaresque Novels*. Trans. Michael Alpert. Harmondsworth: Penguin Books, 2003.

Reddick, John, trans., and Mark Edmundson, introd. *Sigmund Freud, Beyond the Pleasure Principle and Other Writings*. Harmondsworth: Penguin, 2003.

Salkeld, Duncan. *Shakespeare Among the Courtesans: Prostitution, Literature, and Drama, 1500–1650*. Farnham and Burlington, VT: Ashgate, 2012.

Shakespeare, William, *William Shakespeare: The Complete Works*. Eds Stanley Wells, Gary Taylor, John Jowett and William Montgomery. Oxford: Clarendon Press, 1986.

Shelley, Mary. *Mary Shelley, Frankenstein: or the Modern Prometheus*. Ed. Maurice Hindle. Harmondsworth: Penguin, 1985.

Stoker, Bram. *Dracula.* Ed. Maud Ellmann. Oxford: Oxford University Press, 1996

Talvacchia, Bette. *Taking Positions: On the Erotic in Renaissance Culture.* Princeton: Princeton University Press, 1999.

Taylor, Gary and John Lavagnino. *Thomas Middleton and early modern Textual Culture, a Companion to the Collected Works.* Oxford: Clarendon Press, 2007.

Wolf, Leonard, ed. *Carmilla and 12 Other Classic Tales of Mystery.* Harmondsworth: Penguin, 1996.

8

Bright hair and brittle bones –
Gothic affinities in metaphysical poetry

Ulrike Zimmermann

The Gothic mode

Despite the fact of its being a handy literary catchphrase, the 'Gothic' and the ensuing literary trend, if we want to call it thus, did not emerge as a more or less ready-made genre in the fantasy of Horace Walpole after he supposedly dreamt of a castle, which he realized in Strawberry Hill in the mid-eighteenth century. Moreover, the term 'Gothic' has long since ceased to be inextricably linked with the genre of the novel.[1] The Gothic has come to be taken as a way of seeing, and hence, of representation.[2] In *Art of Darkness* Anne Williams argues in favour of a metaphorical use of the term in Lakoff and Johnson's sense.[3] Gothic then becomes a cognitive category and does not purely pertain to aesthetic concerns and questions of décor (cf. Williams 17).

The success of the Gothic and the richness of critical responses, which lasted throughout the centuries and branched out in contemporary criticism, imply that the Gothic is much more than a literary subgenre with its peak in the 1790s. From its beginnings, the Gothic was never to be contained spatially or temporally. It took Europe by storm and has arrived stronger than ever in the twenty-first century – in a variety of genres: longer and shorter prose fiction, films, computer games.[4] What has remained is no longer a specific literary form but an aesthetic principle and a means of dealing with a variety of issues, depending on the respective socio-historical and political backgrounds. This chapter proposes to consider relevant terminologies and intersections of the Gothic and metaphysical poetry. Brief readings of selected poems by John Donne will serve as examples, and their historical position will yield insights into the proto-Gothic and its functions in metaphysical poetry.

The history of the Gothic as a term is an eventful one. Originally, the Goths were a Germanic tribe and invaders of Rome. Owing to the lack of knowledge about them, and to the fact that they left no written records, in later centuries they came to be associated with the Dark Ages. By the eighteenth century 'Gothic' was linked to 'a barbaric medieval past' (Punter and Byron 4) in an opposition to classical and neoclassical cultural values. But gradually different meanings started to be associated with the name of Gothic. Since the Goths had come to represent all Germanic tribes, they were also connected with the origins of the British. Their system of community representation was taken as a very early forerunner of the British constitution.[5] As a result they became part of the British political heritage in a positive sense. 'Prior to the French Revolution, nationalist pressures pushed the various meanings of "Gothic" in opposite directions. In so far as the word meant pre-Reformation "medievalism", it was negatively tarred with the Catholic brush. But in so far as it meant the cultural cradle of modern Englishness, it was positive' (Miles 15). With these almost paradoxical attributions as a background, in the course of the eighteenth century the Gothic acquired a crucial position in cultural debate. Its medieval side came to be re-assessed as an important counterbalance within contemporary society.[6] Gothic as conceived in the Gothic revival in the mid-eighteenth century stood for the irregular, the old, the primitive, and was seen as a refreshing force.

Metaphysical poetry: chronologies

Historically, metaphysical poetry is situated between Shakespeare and the Shakespearean Gothic[7] and the eighteenth century with its inception of the Gothic novel and the conscious use of 'Gothic' as a critical term.

The origins of metaphysical poetry can be taken as (late) Elizabethan. Shakespeare and Walter Raleigh are often the first two poets to be included in anthologies of metaphysical poetry. Standard anthologies, for example Helen Gardner's *The Metaphysical Poets* of 1957, tend to close with poets like the Earl of Rochester and John Norris of Bemerton.[8] John Donne (1572–1631) and Andrew Marvell (1621–1678) are usually taken as the main exponents of the metaphysical style. Arguably, some of Marvell's poetry with its regular rhyming couplets gestures towards neoclassicism.

It is striking that, as a critical term, 'metaphysical poetry' is just as protean as 'Gothic'. As we know, the poets in question did not call themselves metaphysical and never consciously belonged to a specific movement. Their lives and works were geographically, temporally and often also artistically quite far apart from each other. Essentially, critical posterity labelled the poetry. The reputation of metaphysical poetry changed in the eye of the beholder quite as much as that of the Gothic.

In an undated letter, William Drummond of Hawthornden, a contemporary of John Donne, mentions poets who use 'Metaphysical ideas and

Scholastical Quiddities' in their poetry. In 1693, John Dryden famously complains about Donne, 'He affects the metaphysics, not only in his satires, but in his amorous verses, where nature only should reign; and perplexes the minds of the fair sex with nice speculations of philosophy' (qtd in Gardner 15). In both statements, 'metaphysical' primarily refers to the subject matter of the poetry and only indirectly to a specific style or method. Philosophical speculations and scientific metaphors, both Drummond and Dryden seem to imply, should not have a place in love poetry.

The scholar who finally cemented 'metaphysical' as a term of literary criticism was Samuel Johnson. In his *Life of Cowley*, he notes that '[a] bout the beginning of the seventeenth century, appeared a race of writers, that may be termed the metaphysical poets' (Johnson 23). Johnson, speaking from within the framework of neoclassicism, is highly critical of these poets. However, his description includes elements which are still considered essential in definitions of metaphysical poetry today. Addressing the poets' wit, he speaks about style and rhetoric. '[W]it ... may be ... considered as a kind of *discordia concors*; a combination of dissimilar images ... The most heterogeneous ideas are yoked by violence together' (Johnson 25–6). Here Johnson describes one of the most important features, which has interested most critics and yielded a variety of results – the imagery employed by metaphysical poets.

In all three historical moments, the term 'metaphysical poetry' was used pejoratively, which is particularly true for Johnson's assessment. Talking about metaphysical poetry in the present day certainly does not imply a negative value judgement. At the same time, however, metaphysical poetry has become increasingly hard to define since its positive reappraisal by T. S. Eliot in 1921. Its boundaries are fluent, not fixed. It would go beyond the scope of this chapter to discuss at length the issues which the term raises for literary criticism, so some working assumptions shall be put forward.[9] Texts subsumed under the term metaphysical poetry seem to share more or less distinctly pronounced features, for example a specific use of imagery: extended metaphors or conceits (*concetti*), connecting fields of cognition or experience which supposedly are extremely far apart from each other. Whether metaphysical poets have predilections for specific metres remains disputable; sometimes spoken language is imitated; many poems have short, compressed lines, and others tend towards simple stanza forms.[10]

Terminological and conceptual parallels between the two labels, the Gothic and metaphysical poetry, are striking. Both seem to have their origins in negative value judgements, and both have been characterized by a delight in the irregular, the rugged. Both have come to stand for aesthetic values which consciously go against the tenets of neoclassicism – metaphysical poetry *avant la lettre*,[11] the Gothic simultaneously and *après*. An essential difference would be that 'Gothic' as a description was used self-consciously by its practitioners at an early stage,[12] while metaphysical poets did not call themselves metaphysical. Both terms have come to be used as conceptual categories, and critical definitions oscillate between more literal and more metaphorical senses of the terms.

The proto-Gothic in John Donne

An attempt to rethink metaphysical poetry in terms of the Gothic can only be a tentative one. In the following, readings of poems by John Donne will be tried. With respect to proto-Gothic elements, as one could call them, Donne's poetry is conspicuous, although other metaphysical examples can be found. When selecting poems which may lend themselves to Gothic readings, the ubiquitous problem of categorization must be faced once again. Which kind of poem should reasonably be included, and for what reasons? Important criteria would have to be the content and the prevalent imagery. The basic procedure would be to look out for the use of Gothic motifs, and for larger issues which might hide behind these motifs. The question of why the texts include relevant elements is crucial here. Since the Gothic concerns itself with matters of religion, spirituality and belief, Donne's biography, situated between two denominations, will add to the potential of the connection.

It is not necessary here to look for obscure metaphysical poems. Gothic readings of metaphysical poems may well start with a classic, the frequently anthologized 'The Canonization'.[13] The poem has been claimed as typically metaphysical for its imagery, but also for its beginning *in medias res*, in the middle of a dialogue. The speaker is exasperated with his partner in conversation: 'For Godsake hold your tongue and let me love' (l. 1). The poem proceeds to explain how the speaker and his beloved woman have a perfect love relationship, with the second stanza mocking Petrarchan love poetry,[14] and making use of its hyperbolic rhetoric at the same time. The fourth stanza envisages the lovers' death, with the well-known Elizabethan pun on dying.

> Wee can dye by it, if not live by love,
> And if unfit for tombes or hearse
> Our legend bee, it will be fit for verse;
> And if no peece of Chronicle wee prove,
> We'll build in sonnets pretty roomes;
> As well a well wrought urne becomes

> The greatest ashes, as half-acre tombes,
> And by these hymnes, all shall approve
> Us *Canoniz'd* for Love.

(28–36)

The speaker imagines the couple's afterlife in great detail: Will they become part of the written tradition? Will they have an enormous tomb,[15] which will speak to posterity not of their social standing but of the exemplary greatness of their love? In case the two were considered as not quite important enough to get a 'half-acre tombe', a small 'well wrought urne' would do just as well. The last stanza is concerned with an as yet unknown future, which is firmly located *after* the death of the lovers. Future generations are supposed to 'invoke' the two and 'Beg from above / A patterne of your love!' (44–5). The lovers have not merely become a role model, they have become saints. With a conflation of the sacred and the erotic, the poem envisions the canonization of two exemplary lovers. Except for the first stanza, in which a (presumably meddlesome) third party, who is critical of the relationship, is firmly rebutted, the poem is not concerned with the lovers' present tense at all. Rather, the speaker enjoys fantasies of a shared grave, in analogy to the shared bed, and of a legend that will immortalize and sanctify the lovers. The poem's dramatic quality opens up discursive fields of sacred and profane love, Petrarchan conventions and canonical procedures, while it is, on the whole, defensive, always implying that there is a sceptical addressee who needs to be convinced of the greatness of a love beyond death.

Connected to the entombment images of 'The Canonization', 'The Funerall' focuses even more strongly on the time after death. The poem is set between the death and the funeral of the speaker. The setting is not a particularly pleasant situation. Directly after death, the speaker's body has to be prepared for burial, and there are rites to be performed on it. Somebody comes in to shroud the speaker's dead body, and the speaker asks him not to damage the 'subtile wreath of haire' (3) he (the speaker) still wears on his arm. 'The mystery, the signe you must not touch' (4) because it is supposed to preserve the body, the 'outward soule' (5). The second stanza becomes more explicit about the personal value accorded to the hair: If the 'sinewie thread my braine lets fall / Through every part' (9–10)[16] can tie the body together 'and make mee one of all' (11), then the hairs 'which upward grew, and strength and art / Have from a better braine' (12–13) can do this all the better. But the gift of hair, according to the speaker, was not meant to hold his body together but was supposed to function as a kind of fetter, so that the speaker would always be reminded of the pain his beloved gave him. It is to be assumed that the speaker talks of an unfulfilled love relationship. No matter what the lady in question wanted to achieve exactly with her dubious gift, the speaker wants to be buried with the hair: 'For since I am / Loves martyr, it might breed idolatrie, / If into others hands these Reliques came' (18–20). By burying the speaker with the souvenir of his beloved, the tense relationship between the two is wiped out. The speaker ironically pretends to protect posterity from falling into false beliefs and making idols of the hair, and presumably of the bones of his arm around which the hair is wound, giving their origins a false interpretation. However, the speaker concedes that hair and bone are in fact relics – only they preserve a negative part of his lifetime. Quite conventionally, the speaker starts out with the image of death from unrequited love. But he extends this image: if he is a martyr, posterity might take him for a saint and be keen on relics from him. The language of these lines strongly points to a Catholic posterity, with the typical veneration of saints and their physical remains branded as 'idolatry' by the speaker. The poem ends with a flourish and a dig at the lady who rejected the speaker's love. The dramatic monologue shifts from addressing the person preparing the dead body for funeral to the lady in question. 'So, 'tis some bravery, / That since you would have none of mee, I bury some of you' (23–4). Implicitly the woman is threatened with just the same kind of experience the speaker is about to make, if we take the burial of her hair as *pars pro toto*.

'The Relique' makes the themes of 'The Funerall' explicit. Here, the speaker's fantasy is more gruesome, since he imagines his grave being dug up long after his death so that another body can be buried there as well. The first addressee of this text is an imagined gravedigger. He comes upon the bones of the speaker: the decomposition of the flesh is apparently far progressed, probably complete. As if these details were not enough, the gravedigger discovers 'a bracelet of bright haire about the bone' (6). This is a particularly ugly combination, even if the hair is not actually on a skull that we imagine the gravedigger to unearth, too, but wound round the radius and ulna which have been left bare after lying in the earth for some time.

The speaker hopes that after making this find, the digger will assume two people in the grave, take them to be lovers, and will leave them alone – because the hair would signify that they hope to be reunited on the day of the Last Judgement. Even long after death, the remaining symbol of devoted love should, according to the speaker, induce respect. However, if the digging-up should happen in

> a time, or land,
> Where mis-devotion doth command,

> Then, he that digges us up, will bring
> Us, to the Bishop, and the King,
> To make us Reliques

                                                              (12–16)

The course of history with its political and religious developments cannot be controlled by the speaker; he can have no idea in what kind of country he will be dug up again. In the view of a clueless posterity, 'Thou shalt be a Mary Magdalen, and I / A something else thereby' (17–18).[17]

The text is mocking, post-Reformation style, the Catholic reverence for saints, relics and other manifestations of superstition. As the speaker argues in the last stanza, the perfect love between the two buried lovers is enough for a miracle in its own right. The poem can be identified as metaphysical because of the near-incompatible metaphors, and also because of the kind of wit in which the speaker indulges. However, the poem is also interested in things that would make a great Gothic novel: dead bodies, unending devotion, gruesome scenes over open graves and a mocking distrust of Catholicism as a hub of superstitions, 'mis-devotions' and uncontrolled religious fervour.

Indeed, one of Donne's poems seems to narrate an episode from a Gothic text: 'The Apparition'. The beginning is conventional: once again, the speaker expects to die of love, an echo of courtly love poetry with its frequent invocation of death by the scorn of the beloved. The poem moves away from this outcome of abject devotion very soon. By the speaker's logic, the beloved becomes a murderess since she killed the speaker with her cold behaviour.[18] The tense then switches from the present into the future to make a prediction. The speaker's ghost will appear to the former mistress when she is in bed (with another man, as it turns out). We get a graphic description of this ghostly scene. 'Then thy sicke taper will begin to winke' (6). The scene is set: a dark bedroom illuminated by just one candle, which is flickering and about to be extinguished by a sudden cold draught. The former mistress becomes a 'poore Aspen wretch' because she trembles uncontrollably like the tree of the same name, and she is bathed in 'a cold quicksilver sweat'.[19] Her emotions and physical reaction to the apparition are highlighted in concrete and drastic terms. The speaker (as ghost) likes to have a bit of fun with his victim, who becomes 'a veryer ghost than I' by her paleness and trembling. However, in the poem the ghost withholds what he will say to the woman because he does not want her to be impressed now and risk that she should give in to his wooing and thus evade later punishment. With malicious joy, he prefers looking forward to his revenge to actual fulfilment in the here and now.

> What I will say, I will not tell thee now,
> Lest that preserve thee'; and since my love is spent,
> I'had rather thou shouldst painfully repent,
> Then by my threatnings rest still innocent.

(14–17)

In fact, the poem is a diminutive but carefully structured narrative about a haunted woman, with lovingly added details.[20] The implied threat to the woman's virtue, including a threat to her life, is definitely Gothic. We could read the woman as an early prototype of a Gothic victim, which would make the speaker a traditional victimizer. In a striking synchrony, this relationship can be reversed: the man is also the victim of the woman's attractions. The persecution and paranoia that Punter and Byron (273–7) cite as a feature of the Gothic are present in both ways. The speaker intends to follow his former lady wherever she goes after his death; at the same time he is absolutely convinced that, when he finds her again, she will be in a sexual relationship with another man. Furthermore, the social (and actual) violence associated with the Gothic is present as well in all poems we have looked at so far. The lover tries to pressurize his lady into acceptance; gravediggers disturb the rest of dead bodies and threaten unwittingly to desecrate them. Simultaneously, Donne's poems are darkly comic. From an unspectacular situation, the speakers' fantasy leads them, the reader (and the respective mistress), into graves, shrines, saintly legends and ghost stories. Hyperbole and a sense of melodrama are part and parcel of this kind of poetry.

'The Dampe' describes a similar after-death scene. Again, we encounter a speaker with a fairly morbid imagination. His friends want an autopsy of him because the cause of his death seems to be unclear. To their surprise – and here the poem mixes convention with contemporary scientific imagery – the doctors performing the autopsy find a picture of his mistress in the speaker's heart. The text thus conflates the literal and the metaphorical: the heart as the seat of emotions would of course be imprinted with a picture. After that discovery, the imagined proceedings take a surprising and slightly absurd turn. The dead body, with the breast cut open, will emit 'a sodaine dampe of love' (5)[21] which will work on all people present in the room, as it had worked on the speaker, and kill them, 'and so preferre / Your murder, to the name of Massacre' (7–8). Once again, the address shifts to a lady, and it is implied that the speaker died of unrequited love. After his death the woman proceeds to kill even more people, by the simple means that they see her picture. The lady is a Petrarchan revenant.

Nonetheless, hers are 'Poore victories' (9), as the speaker insists. The second stanza therefore imagines a different outcome. If the woman is pleased by her conquest of the speaker and willing to accept him, she is instructed to enter into an allegorical struggle with 'th'enormous Gyant, your *Disdaine*' and 'th'enchantresse *Honor*' (11–12), and the story will end differently from the autopsy scene. The lady is urged to overcome her honour and disdain, the two main opponents to the relationship. This struggle is represented not as purely allegorical but also as historical:

> And like a Goth and Vandall rize,
> Deface Records, and Histories
> Of your owne arts and triumphs over men,
> And without such advantage kill me then.
>
> (13–16)

Here we encounter 'Gothic' in its original usage, with the Goths as barbarians who, in default of an official history, are supposed to have erased other people's histories as they raided Europe. The lady has a history of conquests behind her, which the speaker asks her to wipe out and start afresh with him. The allegorical battle is expanded further. The lover musters up his 'Gyants, and [his] Witches too' (Donne 18), which are 'vast *Contancy* [sic], and *Secretnesse*' (19). This poem is positioned intriguingly between Petrarchan love concepts, medieval allegory and the invocation of literally Gothic behaviour. Is this a medieval, a metaphysical or a Gothic battle of the sexes? The text makes use of wide allusive fields, linking the conventional, the erotic and the historiographic.

Functions of the Gothic (or 'proto-Gothic') in metaphysical poetry: some suggestions

In the examples of Donne's poetry cited so far, apparitions, ghosts, and spirits abound. Speakers fantasize about their ghostly returns after death to take revenge upon an unfaithful lover. Living and thriving lovers find satisfaction in imagining a shared tomb for themselves and the beloved woman. The specificities of graves and tombs one might be given after death excite particular interest. It seems that a sense of morbidity and delight in its physical particulars needs to be satisfied in this kind of poetry. With a rhetorical vengeance, speakers relish in gruesome details, which they to some extent use to persuade their ladies to reciprocate their love.[22] But it would not be sufficient to describe this as a mere effective use of *memento mori* or *carpe diem* motifs. The poetic elaboration of bodily dissolution is more than a stylistic means to an end. The trappings of terror with their emotional excesses make for good metaphysical poetry: the dramatic quality, the wild imagery and the sense of immediacy.

Furthermore, the poetry is not merely anti-Petrarchan but über-Petrarchan at the same time by consciously overdoing the courtly lyric and taking its assumptions quite literally. Donne's speakers seem to answer back to Petrarch in two different ways. On the one hand, they re-invent love poetry by taking the lady from the pedestal down to earth and by focusing on an interpersonal relationship.[23] On the other hand, Donne's poetry engages in a re-literalization of Petrarch: the latter's speakers say they will die of their unrequited love – Donne's speakers can gladly embrace this idea, but imagine very graphically how this will look and feel like. What exactly is going to happen to a grand courtier and his mistress after death? Nothing but gruesome bits and pieces will remain of them, and only if they are lucky they might be turned into a false legend by superstitious Catholics, which seems to be the only afterlife available.

The preoccupation with death and afterlife, particularly from the position of a love relationship, has a variety of functions. One of them – the rhetorical function – is to impress the lady with a sense of urgency and dread. At the same time, ideas of death, burial rites, decomposition and sanctification seem too elaborate for mere rhetoric. There are two aspects that need further enquiry at this point. First, with the necessary caution, it might be worthwhile in the case of Donne to look at his biography. Second, for a Gothic reading of these poems, their historical location is a crucial factor.

Donne, like many of the relevant writers of metaphysical poetry, had religious interests and a profound religious education. His texts engage in a struggle with doubt and despair. What happens after death? Bones are left over from interred bodies, and a lasting reputation is only to be got by exemplary love, which, however, is misunderstood by following generations and turned into a superstition: the belief in saints and miracle-working relics. Sideswipes at Catholicism are conspicuous in Donne's poetry, whose origins were notably Catholic. He received his first education from Catholics, and he took no degree from Oxford, which he attended first, and then Cambridge, because as a Catholic he would not have been able to take the Oath of Supremacy. Several members of his maternal family died for their Catholic beliefs; his brother Henry was arrested for giving shelter to a Catholic priest and died in Newgate.[24] Donne might have had his doubts about the Catholicism he was socialized into and finally, in 1615 and probably after some pressure from James I, was ordained into the Church of England.[25] Whether Donne's motives were mainly opportunist or whether he engaged in a serious struggle for personal belief is disputable, but it is clear that he was concerned with religion and spirituality, and it is equally clear that a successful career for him was possible only if he renounced Catholicism. 'The movement from full integration in a Catholic family to the deanship of St Paul's may have less to do with epiphanies than with a series of small shifts, compromises with circumstances which do not necessarily call integrity in doubt and which do not make Donne idiosyncratic' (Parfitt 12). 'Small shifts' seems a euphemistic expression with a background such as Donne's, but generally Donne's conversion can be seen pragmatically. He realized his social aspirations, while at the same time his engagement with the religious life seems too serious to be taken as a superficial career move. Molly Murray provides a thorough analysis of the influence of conversion on early modern English literature, its themes and styles. She, too, thinks Donne's conversion sincere.[26]

The 'Songs and Sonnets', from which my examples have been taken, are usually read as work from the younger Donne, before his conversion, although the dating is not uncontroversial. It is probably not incidental that Donne's poetic *personae* express disgust at the more superstitious, folklore forms of Catholicism and mock the exalted religiosity which turns normal people into saints after their deaths, and which takes physical fragments of dead bodies, bones and hair as precious commodities. The flamboyance of Catholicism shines through in the poems: it has a certain attraction but is discredited as somewhat absurd at the same time. James Cannon has pointed out that this kind of debate also took place *within* the Anglican Church and therefore cannot be taken as a mere sign of an outward demarcation against the older faith: 'after the Elizabethan settlement' the as yet new Anglican church struggled 'against a superstitious belief in the holiness of churches, shrines and relics' (Cannon 209). When Donne in later life delivered his sermons at St Paul's, he took part in this debate.[27]

Donne's personal, religious and professional life is representative of the struggle between Catholicism and Protestantism. England in his time is in the middle of religious upheavals and power shifts in the wake of the Reformation. Anne Williams has pointed out that the history of Tudor England and Henry VIII would make a perfect Gothic story, as far as family relations and religious turmoil are concerned. 'Both Catholics and Protestants executed "heretics", and what constituted "heresy" was determined by whoever had the power to name heresies' (Williams 29). In the last third of the sixteenth century, the pressure on Catholics in England increased once more. In 1570, the Papal Bull proclaimed Elizabeth a heretic. The Catholic community was in a precarious position, caught between the decree of the Bull and questions of its validity, and loyalty to the sovereign. Furthermore, Mary, Queen of Scots, was a potential Catholic successor to the throne and a symbol of Protestant

fears (cf. Parfitt 8–9). Metaphysical poetry is situated within these political and religious tensions.

While the Gothic shows dramatic and potentially poetic qualities, the
poems by Donne, conversely, show a narrative quality, if we allow the
narrative to be episodic. Gothic affinities in metaphysical poetry are
numerous. Like the Gothic, metaphysical poetry favours the irregular,
the disturbing and the dark, and can be read as countering (neo)classical
tenets. Both use, to speak with Williams (30), 'literary categories to frame
or order the chaos of perceptions that in fact constitute "history"'. The
making and interpretation of history and religion are at the forefront of
metaphysical poetry quite as much as the making of ghost stories and
the secular religion of love. Maggie Kilgour has argued that the Gothic
has always been used as a means to deal with anxieties; the main anxiety
of eighteenth-century Gothic being the terror of the French revolution,
which would then be displaced on to remote, dark, Catholic and prefer-
ably continental sites (cf. Kilgour 14–15). Metaphysical poetry has
earlier anxieties. The tug-of-war between Protestantism and Catholicism, for one thing, is not yet solved, and Catholic succession to the
English throne was effectively precluded only with the Glorious Revolution.[28] The anxieties exhibited in Gothic modes within metaphysical
poetry are manifold. 'Gothic is … pervasively organized around anxieties
about boundaries (and boundary transgressions)' (Williams 16). There
is the power struggle between the denominations, crucially influencing
biographies. Religious tensions are played out partly in mockery, partly
in deadly earnest and an invocation of the last things. Besides, there is
also the question of how to accommodate the heritage of courtly love
poetry. The attitude here oscillates between assimilation and parody.
The Gothic mode – a proto-Gothic mode in the case of metaphysical
poetry – is a way to deal critically with heritage, history and the anxieties and fears connected to both. Distortion, assimilation and parody
join forces with occult occurrences, gruesome deaths and burials.
Similar to the Gothic novel, a malicious sense of fun with horror and
terror trappings pervades Donne's poems. Gothic representations thus
move freely between literary forms and are very well able to take shape
in poetry. The Gothic in metaphysical poetry allows for insights into
crucial issues of the seventeenth century; a density of Gothic elements
will point to an intersection of particularly sensitive issues, surrounded
by fears, but also taking the focus of contemporary thought.

Notes

1 On the debate of terminology and the critical history of 'Gothic novel' and 'Gothic romance', see Williams 2–3.
2 See for instance the concise introduction of Punter and Byron.
3 See the classic Lakoff and Johnson, *Metaphors We Live By*.
4 For the latest developments and approaches to the contemporary Gothic, see for example Brabon and Botting.
5 See for example Punter and Byron 3–5 and Miles 10–13. Miles elaborates on the reappraisal and political use of the term by the Whigs in the events leading to the Glorious Revolution.
6 Punter and Byron offer a concise description of the re-evaluation of the Gothic in the mid-eighteenth century, see 7–12. Also see Wright's introduction.
7 For a reconceptualization of Shakespeare in terms of the Gothic, see Drakakis and Townshend. E. J. Clery notes that Shakespeare is 'touchstone and inspiration for the terror mode' (30).
8 Grierson's paradigmatic collection concludes with Samuel Butler, who died in 1680, cf. Grierson. Patricia Beer in her introduction sees the end of metaphysical poetry with Marvell and Abraham Cowley, cf. Beer 1.
9 For a very accessible report on the development and uses of the term 'metaphysical', see Beer 1–12.
10 See for instance Gardner's suggestions, 18–19. Gardner also discusses the term 'strong-lined' as a possible description of metaphysical poetry.
11 Anne Williams names texts that seem to be Gothic *avant la lettre* 'born "B.W." ("Before Walpole")', cf. Williams 13.
12 Horace Walpole called *The Castle of Otranto* 'Gothic' in his preface to the second edition, see Clery 21.
13 All poems are taken from C. A. Patrides. All further line and page references are to this edition. There is a plethora of criticism on 'The Canonization'. William J. Rooney's debate with Cleanth Brooks's paradigmatic reading might be mentioned here, reprinted in Roberts 271–8. A post-structuralist example is Tilottama Rajan's reading, '"Nothing sooner broke": Donne's *Songs and Sonnets* as Self-Consuming Artifact', reprinted in Mousley 45–62.
14 Opinions are divided on Donne's position with regard to Petrarchan models, from suggestions of total subversion to perpetuation of the tradition on Donne's part. My tendency would be to argue that Donne accepted and consciously used Petrarchism, not without a lot of subversive play, however. From the huge amount of critical work, two articles may serve to give insights into the ongoing debate. The older, 'Donne's Petrarchism', is by Donald L. Guss, a more recent and equally paradigmatic one is Barbara Estrin's 'Small Change: Defections from Petrarchan and Spenserian Poetics'.
15 On the importance of tombs and the increasing need for (religious and, more recently, worldly) commemoration, see Gittings 166–8.
16 For example the nervous system, cf. Patrides 56.
17 See the note in Gardner 80. As Mary Magdalene was his close follower, this would turn the speaker into a figure of Christ, which he implies, but teasingly refuses to say.

18 Guss (151–2) mentions that the murderess motif goes back to a Neapolitan poetic tradition of the fifteenth century. This would be a palpable link to Catholic Italy, which figures so large in eighteenth-century Gothic.

19 A quicksilver sweat bath was a contemporary treatment for syphilis (see Patrides 44). The sweat here does not just denote the woman's fear but also hints at her sexual promiscuity.

20 These details would fit quite well into an overview of Gothic themes and motifs as suggested by Punter and Byron (259–87).

21 A dampe could for instance refer to the dangerous gases which can occur in mines, see Patrides 61.

22 Here Andrew Marvell's poem of persuasion, 'To His Coy Mistress', comes to mind, in which the speaker makes excessive use of images of death and decay to lure the addressee towards consummation of their love. It would be hard, however, to frame the *memento mori* motif as Gothic.

23 This technique had of course by Donne's time become a tradition of its own, with the prime example of Shakespeare's Sonnet 130.

24 See Parfitt 7–12, and Carey 19–21.

25 See Colclough 4–6.

26 'But this resolution did not preclude an ongoing interest in confessional change as a subject of speculation, an object of representation and … a model for expression' (Murray 71–2).

27 Cannon lucidly describes the intermingling of anti-Catholic propaganda and controversial issues within the Anglican Church. He argues that Donne's interests were more in the dispute in the Church of England than in fighting Catholic doctrine. Using a semiotic approach, Elizabeth Mazzola argues in *The Pathology of the English Renaissance* that Protestant theology was informed by literal and metaphorical relics from pre-Reformation times.

28 Kilgour stresses the role of the Glorious Revolution in the development of the Gothic, see Kilgour 12–13.

Works cited

Beer, Patricia. *An Introduction to the Metaphysical Poets*. London: Macmillan, 1980.

Botting, Fred. *Gothic Romanced: Consumption, Gender and Technology in Contemporary Fictions*. London: Routledge, 2008.

Brabon, Benjamin A., ed. *Postfeminist Gothic. Critical Interventions in Contemporary Culture*. Basingstoke: Palgrave Macmillan, 2007.

Cannon, James. 'Reverent Donne: The Double Quickening of Lincoln's Inn Chapel.' *John Donne's Professional Lives*. Ed. David Colclough. Cambridge: D. S. Brewer, 2003. 207–14.

Carey, John. *John Donne: Life, Mind and Art*. London and Boston: Faber and Faber, 1981.

Clery, E. J. 'The Genesis of "Gothic" Fiction.' *The Cambridge Companion to Gothic Fiction*. Ed. Jerrold E. Hogle. Cambridge: Cambridge University Press, 2002. 21–39.

Colclough, David, ed. *John Donne's Professional Lives*. Cambridge: D. S. Brewer, 2003.

Drakakis, John and Dale Townshend, eds. *Gothic Shakespeares*. Oxford and New York: Routledge, 2008.

Estrin, Barbara. 'Small Change: Defections from Petrarchan and Spenserian Poetics.' *John Donne*. Ed. Andrew Mousley. Basingstoke: Macmillan. 1999. 81–103.

Gardner, Helen, ed. *The Metaphysical Poets*. London: Penguin, 1985.

Gittings, Clare. 'Sacred and Secular: 1558–1660', *Death in England: An Illustrated History*. Eds Clare Gittings and Peter C. Jupp. Manchester: Manchester University Press, 1999. 147–73.

Grierson, Herbert. *Metaphysical Lyrics and Poems of the Seventeenth Century: Donne to Butler*. Revised ed. Alastair Fowler. Oxford: Oxford University Press, 1995.

Guss, Donald L. 'Donne's Petrarchism.' *Essential Articles for the Study of the Poetry of John Donne*. Ed. John R. Roberts. Hassocks: Harvester Press, 1975. 150–8.

Johnson, Samuel. *The Lives of the Poets*. Ed. John H. Middendorf. Vol. 1. New Haven and London: Yale University Press, 2010.

Kilgour, Maggie. *The Rise of the Gothic Novel*. London: Routledge, 1995.

Lakoff, George and Mark Johnson. *Metaphors We Live By*. 11th ed. Chicago: Chicago University Press, 1996.

Mazzola, Elizabeth. *The Pathology of the English Renaissance. Sacred Remains and Holy Ghosts*. Leiden, Boston, Cologne: Brill, 1998.

Miles, Robert. 'Eighteenth-Century Gothic'. *The Routledge Companion to the Gothic*. Eds Catherine Spooner and Emma McEvoy. London and New York: Routledge, 2007. 10–18.

Murray, Molly. *The Poetics of Conversion in Early Modern English Literature. Verse and Change from Donne to Dryden*. Cambridge: Cambridge University Press, 2009.

Parfitt, George. *John Donne: A Literary Life*. Basingstoke and London: Macmillan, 1989.

Patrides, C. A. *The Complete English Poems of John Donne*. 2nd ed. London: Dent, 1994.

Punter, David and Glennis Byron, eds. *The Gothic*. Malden, MA: Blackwell, 2004.

Rajan, Tillotama. '"Nothing sooner broke": Donne's *Songs and Sonnets* as Self-Consuming Artifact.' *John Donne*. Ed. Andrew Mousley. Basingstoke: Macmillan, 1999. 45–62.

Rooney, William J. '"The Canonization" – The Language of Paradox Reconsidered.' *Essential Articles for the Study of the Poetry of John Donne*. Ed. John R. Roberts. Hassocks: Harvester Press, 1975. 271–8.

Williams, Anne. *Art of Darkness. A Poetics of Gothic*. Chicago and London: University of Chicago Press, 1995.

Wright, Angela. *Gothic Fiction. A Reader's Guide to Essential Criticism*. Basingstoke and New York: Palgrave Macmillan, 2007.

9

Vampirism in the Bower of Bliss[1]

Garrett Sullivan

Edmund Spenser's *Faerie Queene* has long been linked to the Gothic through that term's associations with medievalism, native Englishness and, especially, chivalric romance. For instance, in 1762 Richard Hurd defends the 'general plan and *conduct* of the Faery Queen' from the censure of neoclassicists by asserting that, 'as a Gothic poem, [it] derives its METHOD, as well as the other characters of its composition, from the established modes and ideas of chivalry' (61, 62).[2] Less discussed is the critical tradition relating Book 2 of *The Faerie Queene* to the Gothic through the comparison of Acrasia to a vampire. Integral to the comparison is the spright-sucking of this passage:

> And all that while, right ouer [Verdant Acrasia] hong,
>   With her false eyes fast fixed in his sight,
>   As seeking medicine, whence she was stong,
>   Or greedily depasturing delight:
>   And oft inclining down with kisses light,
>   For feare of waking him, his lips bedewd,
>   And through his humid eyes did sucke his spright,
>   Quite molten into lust and pleasure lewd;
> Wherewith she sighed soft, as if his case she rewd.
>
> (2.12.73)

At the turn of the twentieth century, John Clark dubs Acrasia 'a vulgar person compared to [Tasso's] Armida, a sort of wanton vampire' (247).[3] Some sixty years later, A. Bartlett Giamatti observes that 'the male seems dead and there is a vampirish quality about Acrasia' (279). More recently, Camille Paglia has asserted that 'Acrasia is a Circean sorceress and vampire: she "through [Verdant's] humid eyes did sucke his spright"' (187), while Carolyne Larrington claims that 'Acrasia is addicted to the new lover, Verdant, gazing at him as if "seeking medicine", but she also feeds off him like a vampire' (145).

As commonplace as the comparison of Acrasia to a vampire is, critics have tended neither to substantiate it nor to develop its implications;

they go no farther than the analogy between the sucking of blood and of spirit.[4] And yet, as Anne Williams has intimated, there is a stronger link between these two figures. Williams draws an intriguing connection between Spenser's Acrasia and Bram Stoker's Dracula. She observes that Acrasia's

> demeanor ... is subtly, unsettlingly maternal ... In a parody of the mother/ child relation, ... she is the one taking nourishment, a vampirelike sucking (through his eyes) of her lover's 'spright' ... This situation may also remind one of *Dracula*, when Van Helsing and his helpers open Mina's bedroom door to find her sucking Dracula's blood. (224)

For Williams, Acrasia and Dracula both evoke nurture, sexuality and predation, and, in doing so, they represent striking reworkings of the maternal.[5]

In this regard, Spenser's text offers an example of Julia Kristeva's concept of abjection, which has been important for theorizations of the Gothic. Acrasia represents that which is 'thrown off' in order to consolidate a 'coherent and independent' identity reappearing as a threat to identity; in this case, what is abjected is the infant's identification with and dependence upon its mother at the moment of birth.[6] The full horror of Acrasia is captured in her remarkable overdeterminedness; as the critics surveyed here suggest, Acrasia is not only vampire and predatory mother but also cannibal, addict, succubus, lover and enchantress. And her actions have led to Verdant's loss of identity, as is suggested both by the erasure of the 'gold moniments' from his 'braue shield' (2.12.80.3) and by his remaining unidentified until finally rescued by Guyon.[7] Only then, when Acrasia is captured and the Bower of Bliss is destroyed – when, that is, the threat of the vampiric maternal has been quelled, and clear relations between self and other are restored – only then is Verdant named.

What I would like to do is place next to this reading one that centres not on psychic processes such as abjection but on relations among human, vegetable and animal life. I will argue that Verdant's self-loss can be attributed to what Spenser sees as the contradiction at the heart of humanness. In order to show this, I will first take up Aristotle's conception of vitality. Then, I will discuss how this conception informs Spenser's understanding of temperance, the central virtue of Book 2 of *The Faerie Queene*. Finally, I will discuss how Aristotelian vitality resonates with the Gothic's emphasis on self-loss and the non-self-identicality of the subject. Put enigmatically, I will argue for Aristotelian vitality's 'undeadness' in relation to modernist Gothic fiction.[8]

Aristotle's theory of vitality is expressed in the doctrine of the tripartite soul, which defines life in terms of the vegetative, sensitive (or animal) and rational souls:

> The lowest, called the vegetative soul, included the functions basic to all living things: nutrition, growth and reproduction. The second, the sensitive soul, included all of the powers of the vegetative soul as well as the powers of movement and emotion and the ten internal and external senses. The intellective soul, finally, included not only the vegetative and sensitive powers – the organic faculties – but also the three rational powers of intellect, intellective memory (memory of concepts, as opposed of sense images) and will. (Park 467)

As this definition shows, each of these 'souls' is most precisely understood as a specific set of bodily processes or capacities, all of which are present only in humans. However, early modern writers routinely conflate these souls with specific forms of life – for instance, they see the powers of the sensitive *soul* as constitutive of animal *life*. An example is provided by Robert Burton: 'The common Diuision of the Soule, is into three principall faculties; *Vegetall, Sensitue,* & *Rationall*, which make three distinct kindes of liuing Creatures: *Vegetall* Plants, *Sensible* Beasts, *Rationall* Men' (B7v). The faculties make the creatures, says Burton; the tripartite soul provides a mechanism both for differentiating among forms of life and for identifying those traits dominant to each form (plants are vegetal, beasts sensible and men rational).

And yet, the vegetative faculties, which include 'the functions basic to all living things', are present in humans, their powers subsumed into the rational soul. The same is true of the sensitive faculties. The doctrine that differentiates among forms of life also provides the basis for a conception of the human as ontologically variegated. The paradoxical nature of human vitality – different from but also encompassing plant and animal life – is captured by the Italian philosopher Giorgio Agamben:

> It is possible to oppose man to other living things, and at the same time to organize the complex ... economy of relations between men and animals, only because something like an animal life has been separated within man, only because his distance and proximity to the animal have been measured and recognized first of all in the closest and most intimate place. (15–16)[9]

Or, put somewhat differently, 'What is man, if he is always the place – and, at the same time, the result – of ceaseless divisions and caesurae?' (Agamben 16). This paradox is expressed in Aristotelian terms by Philippe de Mornay:

> In man we haue both the [vegetative] and the Sensitue [souls], the former vttering it selfe in the nourishing and increasing of him, and the later in

the subtilitie of sence and imagination, *wherethrough he is both Plant and Beast together*. But yet moreouer wee see also a Mynd which considereth and beholdeth, whiche reapeth profite of the things that are brought in by the Sences, ... & finally which pulleth a man away both from the earth & from al sensible things, yea and (after a sorte) from himself too. This doe we call the [reasonable Soule, and it is the thing that maketh man to bee man, (*and not a Plant or a brute Beast as the other two doe,*) and also to bee the Image or rather a shadowe of the Godhead. (226–7, my emphasis)

Again, paradox: man is 'both Plant and Beast together'; man is 'not a Plant or a brute Beast.'

The tripartite soul, then, provides the basis both for differentiating the human from other forms of life (through the rational powers) and for collapsing distinctions between human and animal or plant (through the presence within man of the sensitive and vegetative powers). For Mornay, full humanness is something that needs to be achieved through reason's 'pull[ing] ... man away both from the earth & from al sensible things'; it is only by doing so that a man lives up to his status as a creature made in God's image.[10] At the same time, such an operation leads to self-division or self-loss: man is pulled away '(after a sorte) from himself too'. The tripartite soul introduces into the conception of human vitality not only a sense of ontological variegation but also a vocabulary for depicting, and imaginatively exploring the nature of, self-division.

Additionally, the tripartite soul undergirds period conceptions of 'beastly' or 'brutish' behaviour. Such behaviour does not entail humans performing the same actions as animals, or, werewolf-like, becoming animals. Instead, 'beastly' behaviour connotes humans moving *toward* instead of *away from* 'al sensible things'; in that regard, beastliness describes a relationship of body to environment that is marked by the immoderate indulgence of the senses and passions. As Burton puts it, 'that w[h]ich crucifies vs most, is our owne folly, want of gouernment, our facilitie and pronenesse in yeelding to our seueral lust, and giving way to euery passion and perturbation of the minde, by which meanes we metamorphize our selues, and degenerate into beasts' (A4r–A4v).

Burton makes clear the connection between intemperance and beastliness. He also shows how the doctrine of the tripartite soul informs the conceptualization of temperance. To be temperate is to be (a proper) human; to be intemperate, a beast. Or, interestingly, a plant. Mornay writes of 'earthly man', defined by the predominance of the vegetative faculties: '[L]ike the Plant, [earthly man] myndeth nothing but sleeping and feeding, making al his sences and al his reason to serue to that purpose' (229). Mornay diverges from Aristotle in associating sleep with the vegetative rather than sensitive powers (though he is not unique in this regard; Milton does the same in *Paradise Lost*). The key point, though, is that intemperate behaviour can mark one as either beastly or plant-like. Conversely, it is by being temperate that one consolidates one's humanness and avoids 'metamorphizing' into either beast or plant. As temperance entails the rational soul 'exercis[ing the] vegetatiue and sensitiue faculties' in ways that ensure their subordination, so does it also perform humanness (Charron C6r). From the perspective of period discussions of the tripartite soul, then, humanness is not a given, but something that needs to be achieved through rational regulation of the sensitive and vegetative powers – through, that is, temperance. It is this connection between temperance and the attainment of humanness that is at the heart of the Bower of Bliss episode that concludes Book 2 of *The Faerie Queene*.

We can begin to see this connection by thinking further about Acrasia. As critics have long noted, Acrasia is associated with intemperance and incontinence. (Strictly speaking, these are not synonymous terms, but Spenser treats them as such.) Her name derives from the medieval Latin, and combines two meanings: 'badly mixed quality' and 'incontinence', the latter of which terms 'is analysed in some detail in Aristotle['s] *Nicomachean Ethics*' (Hankins 6). Aristotle defines incontinent man as one who knows to regulate his actions, but who acts against that knowledge in the face of strong passions.[11] Spenser's Acrasia, then, is an enchantress who seduces men into acting against what they know. And yet, that does not go far enough. As Harry Berger, Jr, puts it, 'Book II represents temperance as fear of [the condition of] *akrasia*, a fear that creeps from the common noun toward the proper name, that is, ... from attributes of self toward the personification of the other, from incontinence and impotence toward their putative cause in [the character] Acrasia' ('Wring' 88). In other words, as an enchantress, Acrasia renders Verdant intemperate, but she is also a projection of Verdant's incontinence. Spenser's allegory allows both possibilities to be operable, as Verdant is seduced by both self and other.

Also important here is the partial derivation of the common noun 'acrasia' from the phrase 'badly mixed quality' or 'bad mixture'. (In contrast, temperance connotes not only moderation but also 'mingling or combining in due proportion' (*OED* II. 3. a.) This bad mixture is cognitive in nature; in the words of the *OED*, acrasia is 'The state of mind in which one acts against one's better judgement' (*acrasia*, n.). That is, while the term 'acrasia' references humoral imbalance and passionate excess, it also describes the self-division implied by acting against judgement. Such action can be represented in terms of Aristotelian vitality, as the sensitive powers operating in defiance of the rational ones. In this regard, the common noun 'acrasia' reminds us that '[man] is both [or also] Plant and Beast together'.

Canto 12 is given over both to Guyon and the Palmer's journey to the Bower of Bliss and to their experiences in the Bower itself. While the two are greeted en route by a series of temptations, perils and object lessons, the crucial moment of the canto comes when they encounter Acrasia with the sleeping Verdant. In the episode immediately preceding this one, Guyon has nearly succumbed to the voyeuristic temptation of 'two naked Damzelles' in the lake (63.6). In contrast, we witness the post-coital scene described at the beginning of this chapter, in which Verdant sleeps 'after long wanton ioyes' (72.6). How are we to understand Acrasia's spirit-sucking? The answer lies in her status as Circean enchantress; her spirit-sucking inaugurates the metamorphosis of man into beast. Near the very end of both canto and book, Guyon asks the Palmer, 'what meant those beastes, which there did ly [?]' (84.9). The Palmer responds,

> these seeming beasts are men indeed,
> Whom this Enchauntresse hath transformed thus,
> [Formerly] her louers, which her lusts did feed,
> Now turned into figures hideous,
> According to their mindes like monstruous.
>
> (85.1–5)[12]

The 'seeming beasts' the Palmer describes represent a possible future for Verdant. Of course, their monstrous minds emblematize the complete hegemony of the sensitive powers, especially the passions, in their beastly lives. And, importantly, immoderate sleep is routinely associated with the ascendance of the passions, in large part because it is of the sensitive soul. Like the passions, sleep is beastly, an activity outside of the control of reason (Sullivan, 'Romance'). With all this in mind, Acrasia's actions imply the knight's pending transformation into an animal, a process enabled through his spirit being 'molten into lust and pleasure lewd'.[13]

Verdant, at this point unnamed, is associated not only with beastliness but also with the vegetal. We have already seen both Acrasia's 'greedily _depasturing_ delight' and his 'bedewd' lips; in both cases, Verdant is metaphorized as grass.[14] This pattern of description continues a few stanzas later, when he is described as having 'on his tender lips ... downy heare / [That d]id now freshly spring, and silken blossomes beare' (79.8–9). Verdant's facial hair evokes flowers complete with 'silken blossomes', and Spenser's pun on 'spring' enhances the effect. It is significant that it is while 'the young man' sleeps that this growth occurs. Spenser follows Aristotle in assuming that 'the nutritive part does its own work better when the animal is asleep than when it is awake' (Aristotle 723). And yet, this is hardly the whole story. Vegetal life co-exists with the young man's nobility, grace, 'manly sternnesse' and 'well proportiond face' (79.6, 7). The human – or, more specifically, the masculine – is amply delineated in the description of the sleeping Verdant. However, Verdant has through his intemperance defaced his nobility – suggesting an insult both to rank and to humanity – and, while his sternness and grace are still apparent, the context is one of impending transformation. In sum, Spenser presents Verdant as the romance version of 'earthly man', human, plant and beast together, and all at once. Spenser modifies the trope of Circean transformation so as to develop intemperance's association with the embrace of 'the earth & ... al sensible things'.

In sum, Verdant at the moment of his moltenness attests to the co-presence within the human of animal, vegetable and man. By the very end of Book 2, however, fluidity has apparently given way to stability. Guyon and the Palmer restore the knight to his identity. Only at this point does Spenser give us his name. The immediate circumstance of his naming is significant: 'But *Verdant* (so he hight) he [the Palmer?] soon vntyde, / And counsell sage in steed thereof to him applyde' (82.8–9). 'Counsell sage' takes the place of the bands Guyon and the Palmer first placed upon Verdant. That is, the restraints are both supplanted by and internalized as wisdom – undoubtedly, the wisdom of temperance. The restoration of human identity – of a name – goes hand in hand with the inculcation of the virtue of temperance. Temperance returns Verdant to himself and to humanity, offering a counter-metamorphosis to the one he embarked upon through his affair with Acrasia.

While Acrasia presides over the dissolution of Verdant's humanness, her actions find their opposite in those of a character that secures the distinctiveness of human life. At the end of canto 7, Guyon swoons after spending three days in the Cave of Mammon, during which time 'the vitall powres gan wexe both weake and wan, / For want of food, and sleepe' (7.65.2–3). This swoon is described as 'all his senses [being] with deadly fit opprest' (66.9).[15] Significantly, it is greeted with an angelic response; a 'blessed Ange[l]' (8.1.8) appears to protect the unconscious Guyon. Three things are most important for our purposes: first, Guyon's swoon evokes Verdant's sleep, while Acrasia's maternal predation is mirrored in reverse by the action of the Angel, who hovers over and protects Guyon; second, Guyon's intemperate neglect of both food and sleep echoes Verdant's intemperate overindulgence; and, third, both Guyon's swoon and Verdant's sleep trouble human identity. Like Verdant, the unconscious Guyon resembles animal, and perhaps vegetal, life. It is the fact of this resemblance that prompts the appearance of the angel, who emerges as if in response to Spenser's famous question, 'And is there care in heauen?' (8.1.1). The answer: 'There is: else much more wretched were the cace / Of men, then beasts' (1.2–3). The presence of the angel neutralizes the implications of the resemblance between sleeping man and beast; rhetorically, the angel reestablishes the distinction between man and beast that the swoon has worked to blur.

Critics have long recognized Guyon's swoon to be a turning point in Book 2.[16] From the moment that he awakens, Guyon's efforts to achieve temperate humanness begin in earnest, most notably through the education he receives in the House of Alma. The destruction of the Bower marks the final stage in the making of a temperate hero – a point underscored by the words that open canto 12: 'Now gins this goodly frame of Temperance / Fairely to rise' (2.12.1.1–2). And yet, Guyon's destruction of the Bower has often been noted for its apparent intemperance: no part of the 'goodly workmanship' of the Bower is saved from 'the tempest of [Guyon's] wrathfulnesse' (83.3–4).[17] A reason for Guyon's intemperate action emerges out of the parallel between his earlier swoon and Verdant's sleep. Guyon nearly succumbs to sexual temptation earlier in canto 12, and he confronts in the sleeping Verdant an image of his own intemperance. In other words, Guyon's violent destruction of the Bower can be seen as his angry denial of the resemblance between Verdant and himself. By extension, Guyon's act of denial is also the refusal of the presence within himself of animal and vegetable life. Temperance entails the acknowledgement and management of ontological self-division, while Guyon's wrathful intemperance expresses his denial of it.

The difficulties of achieving and maintaining temperate humanness are also made apparent through the 'seeming beasts' of the final stanzas of Book 2. Most important of these is Grill, who is restored to humanity but longs for his hoggish state; Grill 'chooseth, with vile difference, / To be a beast' (87.4–5). Grill appears as the incarnation of irredeemable intemperance. In the very final lines of Book 2, Guyon and the Palmer literally leave Grill behind: 'The donghill kind / Delights in filth and foule incontinence: / Let *Grill* be *Grill*, and haue his hoggish mind, / But let vs hence depart, whilest wether serues and wind' (87.6–9). As Fred Botting has written, 'Figures of excess, of immorality and monstrosity, are strangely integral to the establishment and maintenance of symbolic and social structures, simultaneously included and expelled as the threats that underwrite the promise of identity and order' ('Candygothic' 135).

Such is the case with Grill, that figure of excess whose appearance stabilizes Guyon's identity as Knight of Temperance, an identity jeopardized by his resemblance to Verdant and his wrathful destruction of the Bower. Through Grill, intemperance is figured not as a possibility emerging out of the precarious ontological circumstances of human vitality but as a vile act of will: Grill '*chooseth* … [t]o be a beast'. To let Grill be Grill is for Guyon and the Palmer to project intemperance on to the swinish creature that 'delights in filth and foul incontinence'. At the same time, it is to acknowledge obliquely that, like the ontological contradiction at the heart of human vitality, intemperance abides.

I have been suggesting that readings of Spenser's text that centre on psychic processes such as projection or denial or abjection find substantiation in the tripartite soul. Aristotelian vitality gives us the man who is *also* beast and plant; and it provides a vocabulary for describing non-self-identicality. In these regards, it is congruent with the Gothic, especially as it has been construed by psychoanalytic criticism. And yet, Spenser's seeming beasts, figures of incontinence, are only distant cousins to the 'abhuman' creatures – 'wolfish, or simian, or tentacled, or fungoid' – that Kelly Hurley has shown to populate modernist Gothic texts ('British Gothic Fiction' 190).[18] Neither Spenser nor Aristotle is a strong source for Gothic figurations of the self. Instead, the tripartite soul enables the *Gothic* to recognize *itself* in Spenser, and not only as a vampire. In a strict historical sense, this is an act of misrecognition. However, if Spenser can be compellingly read in Gothic terms, this is because the vocabulary of Aristotelian vitality is amenable to the Darwinian and Freudian revolutions that fuel Gothic representations of the inwardly riven self. Spenser most closely anticipates the Gothic in his recognition of the grave difficulty of maintaining the model of the human that temperance underwrites. It is in failures of temperance that we encounter loose analogues to the 'abhuman': 'seeming beasts' with 'hoggish minds'.

In anticipating the Gothic, then, both Spenser and Aristotle are 'undead' in Eric Santner's definition of the term. 'Undeadness' describes the continued vitality of a symbolic form that outlasts its original conditions of legibility; 'the symbolic forms in and through which this life is structured can be hollowed out, lose their vitality, break up into a series of enigmatic signifiers, "hieroglyphs" that in some way continue to address us – get under our skin – though we no longer possess the key to their meaning' (17). The 'undeadness' of these forms resides in the fact that they 'in some way continue to address us'. They do so in part because they are amenable to recontextualization, much as Acrasia can be labelled a vampire. At the same time, that Acrasia is recontextualized in precisely *this* way speaks to felt continuities between Aristotelian ontology and the ontology of vampirism. At issue in vampirism are life, death and undeath; in Aristotle and Spenser, human, animal and plant life – the stakes are different, but in each case sharply delineated boundaries are blurred, and putatively stable states prove fluid. Moreover, Spenser's Acrasia answers to what Linda Charnes has described as the Gothic's 'own special brand of dread: of something or someone [that does not invade from outside, but is] already "in the house" ..., issuing audible but indecipherable demands' (186). In so far as Acrasia embodies 'badly mixed' relations among animal, vegetable and human life, she is the figure that Guyon would most hope to expel from the house of the human. But Spenser well recognizes that Acrasia has *always* lived there, and that she will *never* leave.

Notes

1 A significantly different argument that utilizes some of the material in this chapter appears in Sullivan, *Sleep, Romance and Human Embodiment* 29–46.

2 For a recent discussion of Spenser, chivalric romance and the Gothic, see Helgerson, esp. 21–62.

3 See also Fox 173–4.

4 Larrington compares Acrasia to the succubus: 'a female figure – sometimes a supernatural emanation, sometimes a witch in thrall to demonic powers – who drains the vital juices from men, damaging their masculinity by making them too enervated to fight or to resist temptation' (146). Much of this definition could be applied to the vampire; as Fred Botting has asserted, 'The threat of wanton and corrupt sexuality is horrifically displayed in vampiric shape' (*Gothic* 148).

5 '[I]n the scene where [Dracula] is interrupted in the act of pressing Mina's mouth to his bleeding breast he appears as an inversion of Christ as Pelican, nourishing his subjects with his blood in an unholy communion, and as a mother suckling Mina with the milk of his blood' (Botting, *Gothic* 150). On Acrasia's association with the maternal, see Parker; and Craig, esp. 18.

6 'What we "throw off," [Kristeva] suggests, is all that is "in-between ... ambiguous ... composite" in our beings, the fundamental inconsistencies that prevent us from declaring a coherent and independent identity to ourselves and others. The most primordial version of this "in-between" is the multiplicity we viscerally remember from the moment of birth, at which we were both inside and outside of the mother and thus both alive and not yet in existence (in that sense *dead*). It is this "immemorial violence" that lies at the base of our beings and is one basis of the primal chaos calling us back, yet it is that morass from which we always feel we must "become separated in order to be" a definable person' (Hogle, esp. 7; interpolated quotations

are drawn from Kristeva). In Kristeva's words, 'The abject confronts us ... with our earliest attempts to release the hold of *maternal* entity even before ex-isting outside of her ... It is a violent, clumsy breaking away, with the constant risk of falling back under the sway of a power as securing as it is stifling' (13, emphasis in original).

7 *OED* monument, n. 5. b. 'A thing that serves as identification'. Spenser's usage provides the earliest example.

8 The term 'modernist Gothic' is derived from Hurley, 'British Gothic Fiction'.

9 Agamben asserts that 'Aristotle's nutritive life [i.e., the vegetative soul] ... marks out the obscure background from which the life of the higher animals gets separated' (14).

10 Elizabeth D. Harvey states that 'if the vegetable and animal souls are not finally subsumed into the rational soul, but rather coexist with it, then the sovereignty over all living things that God supposedly conferred upon human beings is called into question' (55).

11 In contrast, Aristotle's 'temperate man' doesn't feel the strong pressure of particular passions. As should be obvious, Spenser does not represent temperance in this way, as Guyon, Verdant and others are swayed by the passions before achieving temperate moderation. Spenser conflates incontinence and intemperance in his depiction of Acrasia.

12 Mind here means not 'the mental faculty of a human being' (*OED* mind, IV.19.a) but a 'way of thinking, habit of thought' (*OED* mind, IV.19.e). For more on these 'seeming beasts', see 2.5.27.

13 Molten refers to a substance, such as metal or tallow, which 'has been dissolved (in a liquid)' (*OED* 2) and/or 'has been melted and allowed to solidify again' (*OED* 1). The first meaning is most relevant here, although the spirit's liquefaction also presupposes its future solidification into a new, animal form.

14 To depasture is a verb used of cattle: 'To consume the produce of (land) by grazing on it; to use for pasturage' (*OED* 1). One of the *OED*'s examples is derived from Spenser's *View of the Present State of Ireland*: 'To keepe theyr cattell ... pasturing upon the mountayn ... and removing still to fresh land, as they have depastured the former.'

15 Sleep is routinely defined in medical texts as a binding or impotency of the senses. See Cogan 231.

16 See especially Berger, *The Allegorical Temper*.

17 See especially Greenblatt: 'Temperance ... must be constituted paradoxically by a supreme act of destructive excess' (172).

18 See also Hurley, *The Gothic Body*. The atavism of Stevenson's *Dr. Jekyll and Mr. Hyde*, Machen's *The Great God Pan* or Kipling's *The Mark of the Beast* does not find an obvious analogue in Spenser.

Works cited

Agamben, Giorgio. *The Open: Man and Animal.* Trans. Kevin Attell. Stanford: Stanford University Press, 2004.

Aristotle. 'On Sleep.' Trans. J. I. Beare. *The Complete Works of Aristotle.* 2 vols. Ed. Jonathan Barnes. Princeton: Princeton University Press, 1984. 1: 721–8.

Berger, Harry, Jr. 'Wring Out the Old: Squeezing the Text, 1951–2001.' *Spenser Studies* 18 (2003): 81–121.

—. *The Allegorical Temper.* New Haven: Yale University Press, 1957.

Botting, Fred. 'Candygothic.' *Essays and Studies 2001: The Gothic.* Ed. Fred Botting. Cambridge: D. S. Brewer for the English Association, 2001. 133–51.

—. *Gothic.* London and New York: Routledge, 1996.

Burton, Robert. *The Anatomy of Melancholy.* Oxford: Iohn Lichfield and Iames Short for Henry Cripps, 1621.

Charnes, Linda. 'Shakespeare and the Gothic Strain.' *Shakespeare Studies* 38 (2010): 185–206.

Charron, Pierre. *Of Wisdome.* Trans. Samson Lennard. London: Edward Blount and Witt Aspley, 1612?.

Clark, John. *A History of Epic Poetry (post-Virgilian).* Edinburgh: Oliver and Boyd, 1900.

Cogan, Thomas. *The Haven of Health.* London: Melch. Bradwood for Iohn Norton, 1605.

Craig, Joanne. 'Monstrous Regiment: Spenser's Ireland and Spenser's Queen.' *Texas Studies in Literature and Language* 43 (2001): 1–28.

Fox, Alistair. *The English Renaissance: Identity and Representation in Elizabethan England.* Oxford: Blackwell, 1997.

Giamatti, A. Bartlett. *The Earthly Paradise and the Renaissance Epic.* Princeton: Princeton University Press, 1966.

Greenblatt, Stephen. *Renaissance Self-Fashioning.* Chicago: University of Chicago Press, 1980.

Hankins, John E. 'Acrasia.' *Spenser Encyclopedia.* Ed. A. C. Hamilton. Toronto: University of Toronto Press, 1997. 6.

Harvey, Elizabeth D. 'The Souls of Animals: John Donne's *Metempsychosis* and early modern Natural History.' *Environment and Embodiment in early modern England.* Eds Mary Floyd-Wilson and Garrett A. Sullivan, Jr. Basingstoke: Palgrave, 2007. 55–70.

Helgerson, Richard. *Forms of Nationhood.* Chicago: University of Chicago Press, 1992.

Hogle, Jerrold E. 'Introduction: The Gothic in Western Culture.' *The Cambridge Companion to Gothic Fiction.* Ed. Jerrold E. Hogle. Cambridge: Cambridge University Press, 2002. 1–20.

Hurd, Richard. *Letters on Chivalry and Romance* (1762). Facs. ed. London: Routledge, 2001.

Hurley, Kelly. 'British Gothic Fiction, 1885–1930.' *The Cambridge Companion to Gothic Fiction.* Ed. Jerrold E. Hogle. Cambridge: Cambridge University Press, 2002. 189–207.

—. *The Gothic Body: Sexuality, Materialism, and Degeneration at the Fin de Siècle*. Cambridge: Cambridge University Press, 1996.

Kristeva, Julia. *Powers of Horror: An Essay on Abjection*. Trans. Leon S. Roudiez. New York and Oxford: Columbia University Press, 1982.

Larrington, Carolyne. *King Arthur's Enchantresses: Morgan and Her Sisters in Arthurian Tradition*. London: I. B. Tauris, 2006.

Mornay, Philippe de. *A Woorke Concerning the Trewnesse of the Christian Religion*. London: Thomas Cadman, 1587.

Paglia, Camille. *Sexual Personae: Art and Decadence from Nefertiti to Emily Dickinson*. New York: Vintage Books, 1991.

Park, Katharine. 'The Organic Soul.' *The Cambridge History of Renaissance Philosophy*. Eds Charles B. Schmitt et al. Cambridge: Cambridge University Press, 1988. 464–84.

Parker, Patricia. *Literary Fat Ladies: Rhetoric, Gender, Property*. New York: Methuen, 1987.

Santner, Eric L. *On Creaturely Life: Rilke, Benjamin, Sebald*. Chicago: University of Chicago Press, 2006.

Spenser, Edmund. *The Faerie Queene*. Ed. Thomas P. Roche, Jr. Harmondsworth: Penguin, 1978.

Sullivan, Garrett A., Jr. *Sleep, Romance and Human Embodiment: Vitality from Spenser to Milton*. Cambridge: Cambridge University Press, 2012.

—. 'Romance, Sleep, and the Passions in Sir Philip Sidney's *The Old Arcadia*.' *ELH* 74.3 (2007): 735–57.

Williams, Anne. *Art of Darkness: A Poetics of Gothic*. Chicago: University of Chicago Press, 1995.

10

Ghostly authorities and the British popular press

Andrea Brady

In the Marquis de Sade's famous formulation, the Gothic excesses of fiction – 'new novels in which sorcery and phantasmagoria constitute practically the entire merit' – are 'the inevitable result of the revolutionary shocks which all of Europe has suffered'. The reality which followed the French Revolution exceeded in horror anything that could be found in eighteenth-century novels, which 'became as difficult to write as monotonous to read'. To interest readers anesthetized by the shocks of history, novelists had to 'call upon the aid of hell itself' (108–9). The critique of the Gothic was repeated in an anonymous 'Letter to the Editor' of *Monthly Magazine* in 1797, which claims that 'we have exactly and faithfully copied the SYSTEM OF TERROR, if not in our streets, and in our fields, at least in our circulating libraries, and in our closets'. Dripping with irony, the author describes the Gothic as 'the wonderful revolution that has taken place in the *art* of novel-writing'; just when the novel had become tediously realistic, 'arose Maximilian Robespierre, with his system of terror, and taught our novelists that *fear* is the only passion they ought to cultivate' ('A Jacobin Novelist' 300). Tales of ghosts, sorcery and monstrosity were merely fiction's belated echo of the horrors of revolutionary violence. A similar argument was made following the revolutions in England in the mid-seventeenth century. Ghosts proliferated in the writing of this period too. But these ghosts were largely used ironically, to lampoon or subvert authority. The consequence of the English revolution was, in the view of some conservative commentators, to produce a dangerous scepticism – not merely about spectres but also about religious faith and political sovereignty. Like the excesses of the Gothic, the ghosts of seventeenth-century popular literature were dangerous, scandalous and potentially blasphemous: not because they *produced* terror, as the Gothic did, but rather because they undermined it. Critics of the Gothic argued that its readers might become inured to shock, or passionately over-excited; by contrast, seventeenth-century ghosts produced scepticism and ironic, Epicurean laughter.

Gothic writers of the eighteenth century often refer to the appearance of ghosts in Shakespearean tragedy as evidence of the continuity in English literary history of their own innovations in the genres of horror (see for example Aikin 282). But ghosts were also a staple of the seventeenth-century popular press. These pamphlet ghosts owed more to folklore and to the admonitory spectres of the *Mirror for Magistrates* tradition than to the dramatic ghost of Senecan or Shakespearean tragedy.[1] Like the stage ghost, the pamphlet ghost demanded revenge, mollification or remembrance from the living. In exchange for these services, ghosts invested the living with their spectral mandate, offered an eternal perspective on politics, sanctified particular interpretations of history and absolutized the exercise of human justice. But libels also used ghosts to satirize famous public figures, inviting readers to reflect as sceptically on politics as they would on a supernatural story.

Ghost sightings were a favourite topic for pamphleteers, and accounts of supernatural sights, wonders and demons were published frequently in the seventeenth century. Supernatural activity seems to have increased during the civil wars, when a large number of pamphlets described both 'real' sightings—wonders and ghosts which the authors wished to persuade readers had actually occurred—and 'rhetorical' ghosts, fictive appearances which authors used for conspicuously literary, political or rhetorical effect. Several major philosophical works analysing the doctrinal and physical nature of ghosts, as well as their occurrences from classical antiquity through the present day, also appeared in this period. These developed the spectrological debate between the Zürich pastor Ludwig Lavater, whose Latin treatise was translated into English as *Of Ghostes and Spirites Walking by Nyght* in 1572, and two Catholics: Noel Taillepied, whose *Traité de l'Apparition des Esprits* was published in Rouen in 1600, and Pierre Le Loyer, whose French treatise was translated as *A Treatise of Specters or Straunge Sights, Visions and Apparitions Appearing Sensibly vnto Men* in 1605. The demonological interests of James VI and I resulted in the publication of investigations into witchcraft in the early years of the seventeenth century, but after that few new philosophical studies of ghosts were published until the mid-1650s, when the Cambridge Platonists Henry More and Joseph Glanville began publishing their defences of spirit. More's chief spiritological work is *An Antidote against Atheisme* (1653), while Glanville's include *A Philosophical Endeavour towards the Defense of the being of Witches and Apparitions* (1666; most copies destroyed by the Fire of London, and reissued as *Some Philosophical Considerations Touching the Being of Witches and Witchcraft*, 1667), *A Blow to Modern Sadducism* (1668) and *Sadducismus Triumphatus: or, Full and Plain Evidence*

Concerning Witches and Apparitions (1681). In the same period, Robert Boyle published his preface to Perreaud's *Devil of Mascon* (1658), and Thomas Bromhall's *A Treatise of Specters* (1658) revisited the arguments of Lavater and Le Loyer. These works attempted to defeat what the authors saw as widespread scepticism about ghosts.

In part, that scepticism was a child of the Reformation; as Lavater had argued, with the refutation of Purgatory and the restoration of the authority of Scripture against superstition, 'all appearings of Soules and Spirites have quite vanished away' (183). However, despite the reformed churches' efforts to stamp out superstition, ghosts continued to be seen and discussed as part of an active folkloric tradition. As Stuart Clark has shown, these debates gradually transformed supernatural visions from a theological into a physical or scientific conundrum (see chapter 6). Although scepticism about spirits had been recorded since the time of the Gospel, when the Sadducees (according to Acts 23:8) refuted the existence of 'resurrection, or angel, or spirit', radical scepticism—inspired by Epicureanism and materialism, Pyrrhonist critiques of the fallibility of the senses, and Cartesian mechanism—was apparently fashionable among the upper classes in the mid-seventeenth century. Glanville criticized 'most of the looser *Gentry*' for deriding witches and apparitions: it was not the 'meer vulgar' but those of 'a little higher rank of *understandings*' who were most prone to scepticism (*A Blow* sig. B1v). Glanville and More continued to insist on the possibility of spectres in the face of new theories of the mechanics of vision and optics, as well as Descartes' subversion of the belief that souls could affect material bodies.[2] More entertained his friend Anne Conway with reports on ghost sightings, while Glanville corresponded with another occultist, Richard Baxter, and promoted their findings to the Royal Society (Conway 341–2, 345). Their interest in spectres has been contextualized as part of their disillusionment with Cartesianism and growing spiritualism starting from the mid-1650s (see Hutton 86 and Hall). However, More's and Glanville's interests in the occult have another context, in the pamphlets of the 1640s and 1650s, and the threat which they believed scepticism posed to the church and state.[3]

Ghosts interested natural philosophers in part because of the questions they raised about the nature of vision and the psychic interaction between sight, fantasy and reason. But these questions also had political implications. As Clark explains, 'to problematize sight ... was to problematize the positive things with which sight was symbolically and metaphorically associated, including many of the values of orthodox politics and political morality' (256). This chapter suggests that defenders of ghosts had to reclaim them from the political satire of the 1640s and 1650s. After outlining the relation between superstition, scepticism, and political obedience in the mid-seventeenth century, it will examine the political ghosts which haunted the popular press.

No Bishop, No King; No Spirit, No God

Coleridge critiqued Lewis's Gothic tale *The Monk* as a 'pernicious' and 'irreverent' blending of 'all that is most awfully true in religion with all that is most ridiculously absurd in superstition'. The excesses of his narrative show Lewis's 'sovereign contempt' for superstition, but also his insufficient respect for religion (197–8). These criticisms continue a long tradition of viewing superstition as entangled with – and potentially undermining – true faith. Overindulging in wonder for ghosts and monstrosities, Coleridge implies, tips the Gothic over into parody which threatens Christian belief as well. Similarly, many seventeenth-century writers argued that excessive credulity or interest in ghosts might bring the true mysteries of faith into disrepute. Although Protestant reformers associated ghosts with superstition and Catholic greed, they also believed that ghosts fulfilled an important doctrinal function. If ghosts are merely fantasy then

> the comfort that Gods Children would feele, should be onely imaginary and phantasticall, not reall: so likewise all the torments and troubles of the soule would have no perpetuity, nor true being; ... hell torments should be onely bug-beares to affright children, & meer conceits; and so likewise those eternall joyes in heaven, and heaven it self should only live, & be in imagination onely. (*A True Relation* sig. C4)

According to many writers it was the Epicureans, commonly associated with dangerous atheism, who promoted the idea that ghosts were invented to frighten children, women and the feeble-minded. Epicureanism also suggested that people could be politically liberated from their fear of the state by treating ghosts sceptically. According to Henry Hammond, 'speaking of the eternity of Torments threatned in another world, [Lucretius] confesseth that, if that were true, there would be no way of *resisting the religions and threats of the Divines*' (6–7). Lucretius speaks for the hope that people who were relieved of their superstitious fear would be religiously and politically liberated.

Le Loyer makes clear the disciplinary function of devils, ghosts and spirits by analogy: just as 'in each Common-Wealth, well instituted, there bee executioners ordained, for the punishment of Malefactors, and such as trouble and disturbe the publicke peace, and good of the common-weale', by which the commonwealth 'receiveth much more profite and commoditie', so likewise, God deputes some devils on earth for the profit and defense of the godly (26r). Freed from terror of God's executioner, people would be less likely to fear the king's. More concluded his *Antidote against Atheism* by approving 'that saying [which] was not more true in Politicks, *No Bishop, No King*; then this is in Metaphysics, *No Spirit, no God*' (142). Drawing together these seemingly distinct political and theological debates, More claims that the attack on episcopacy undermined the sovereignty of the king just as the attack on ghosts destroyed faith in God. Equally for Glanville, those who deny the religious and secular traditions which maintained the validity of ghosts might also deny the traditional authorities of law, custom, mitre and crown. Glanville warned that those who can believe that 'all the *wiser* world have agreed together to *juggle* mankinde into a common belief of *ungrounded fables*; that the *sound senses* of *multitudes* together may deceive them' will also believe that the '*Laws* are built upon *Chymera*'s; that the *gravest* and *wisest Judges* have been *Murderers* and the *sagest* persons *Fools*, or *designing Impostors*' (*A Blow* 6).

Disbelief in ghosts was also associated with dangerous heterodoxy. For many writers, doubting the reality of spirits was the first step towards materialism and disbelief in the immortality of the soul. The consequences for human behaviour would be disastrous. Thomas Browne, for example, warns that the greatest trick Satan ever pulled, to quote *The Usual Suspects*, was to convince people that he doesn't exist. By making men 'beleeve that apparitions, and such as confirm his existence are either deceptions of sight, or melancholy depravements of phancy', Satan 'advanceth the opinion of totall death, and staggereth the immortality of the soul' (257). To follow Browne's argument, which he shared with Glanville, if spirits cannot take on material form, then neither can the souls of the dead suffer physically. Scepticism about ghosts would thus lead to the sanctioning of all sorts of licentious behaviour. As one pamphlet asks, 'how childish the feares of wicked men? and who would, or need fear the terror of that great Judge?' (*A True Relation* sig. C4r).

For More and Glanville, one of the most dangerous materialists in this respect was Thomas Hobbes. In his *Leviathan*, Hobbes admits that 'there is no doubt, but God can make unnaturall Apparitions', though he does so infrequently (1.2, 92–3). Hobbes ridicules occult beliefs in order to undermine the power of religious authorities. He mocks 'ecclesiastics' as a genre of ghosts: '*Ecclesiastiques* are *Spirituall* men, and *Ghostly* Fathers. The fairies are *Spirits*, and *Ghosts*. *Fairies* and *Ghosts* inhabit Darknesse, Solitudes, and Graves. The *Ecclesiastiques* walk in Obscurity of Doctrine, in Monasteries, Churches, and Churchyards' (2.29, 370). The analogy extended to punishment and sedition. 'When the *Fairies* are displeased with any body, they are said to send their Elves, to pinch them. The *Ecclesiastiques*, when they are displeased with any Civill State, make also their Elves, that is, Superstitious, Enchanted Subjects, to pinch their Princes, by preaching Sedition' (4.47, 713–14). Hobbes contends that the ecclesiastics use spectral stories, portents and superstitious practices to advance their 'Ghostly Authority' over the 'Civill'. His argument for secularization was, in many ways, a reassertion of the Protestant critique of the power which Catholic priests exercised through the rituals and fear of Purgatory. But Hobbes also argues that subjects relieved of their superstition would be more easily governed: 'if this superstitious fear of spirits were taken away, and with it prognostics from dreams, false prophecies, and many other things depending thereon, by which crafty ambitious persons abuse the simple people, men would be much more fitted than they are for civil obedience' (1.2, 93). However, the Cambridge Platonists read Hobbes as undermining the certainties of spirit, Scripture and state. Henry More challenged 'such course-grain'd Philosophers as those *Hobbians* and *Spinozians*, and the rest of that Rabble' who 'slight Religion and the Scriptures, because there is such express mention of Spirits and Angels in them' (*Sadducismus Triumphatus*, Letter to Joseph Glanville 9). Rather than believing in spirits because they were attested by Scripture, adherents of Hobbes and Spinoza had begun to doubt Scripture because it contained stories not conformable to science.

During the 1640s and 1650s, mass sightings of supernatural phenomena were not uncommon.[4] Paradoxically, however, this period also provoked intense *scepticism* about the supernatural. For some commentators, Purgatory had induced 'slavish fear ... whereof many have all their lives long been held in bondage' (Henry Jones, Bishop of Clogher, qtd in Greenblatt 71). The abolition of Purgatory thus effected the liberation of the faithful from the venality and greed of Catholic priests. But that Reformation was incomplete. Christopher Hill has shown that nonconformists asserted that not only Purgatory but hell itself had been used to prop up religious and political persecution, and seemed 'if not to justify, at least to put in perspective the cruelty of the law' (Hill, *World Turned Upside Down* 178).[5] As Glanville warned, on the satisfactory resolution of the question of whether there are witches 'depends the Authority and just Execution of some of our *Laws*; and which is more, our *Religion* in its main Doctrines is nearly concerned' (*Sadducismus Triumphatus* part II, 1).

The restoration of the traditional authorities of church and crown would therefore require a restoration of the connection between divine and temporal punishment. More, Glanville and others set about reconstructing a hierarchy of spirits based on human hierarchies, reversing the conventional justifications for earthly hierarchy as based on divine design. Glanville, for example, conjectures that 'there is a *Government* runs from *Highest* to *Lowest*, the *better* and more *perfect* orders of Being still ruling the *inferiour* and *less perfect*' (*A Blow* 51); and Richard Baxter presumes that 'We may gather that in Heaven it self, there will be an orderly Oeconomy and difference of degrees of Superiority and of Glory, when there is so great difference through all the World' (9). In these ways, debates about the existence of ghosts, witches and spirits were central to the understanding of the immortality of the soul, the relation between the living and the dead, and the stability of civil and religious authority.

The pamphlet ghosts of the interregnum

Ghosts in the political libels of the 1640s and 1650s were frequently revived for use in acts of literary ventriloquism. Margaret Doody has described ventriloquism as the pre-eminent mode of polemical writing during the British civil wars (45). Theatrical ventriloquism was itself regarded as an occult practice, effected through demonic possession. The 'ventriloqui' were able, according to Kenelm Digby, to 'persuade ignorant people that the Divell speaketh from within them deepe in their belly ... whence it followeth that their voice seemeth to come, not from them, but from somewhat else hidden within them' (251); and Le Loyer described ventriloquism as a kind of spiritual possession, such as that which possessed oracles (14r). Glanville asserted that 'Ventriloquy, or speaking from the bottom of the Belly' is 'a thing I think as strange and difficult to be conceived as any thing in Witchcraft' and requires 'such assistance of the Spirits' (*Sadducismus Triumphatus* part II, 64). The pamphlet ghost who appears at midnight, forcing the writer to record its laments from another world, uses the writer as its ventriloquist; but the writer also ventriloquizes his own opinions through the voice of the ghost which he writes.

One of the most famous ghosts to be ventriloquized in this way was Charles I. In a pamphlet published in March 1660, the ghost of King Charles appeared to the author

> Not with that look and Majestie Divine
> He once on Earth, and now in Heaven doth shine;
> But with an Aspect horrider then theirs
> Who were his bloody Executioners.
>
> (*The King Advancing* 3)

This ghost is at once familiar, showing the look he had 'once on Earth', and transmogrified into an emblematic spectacle of suffering. Although he asks for pity and pacification, the ghost asserts that 'wishes fail! my blood from Earth doth rise / In reeking vapours, and ascends the skies, / Filling the whole Heav'n with its hollow cryes' (5). Taking the form of the 'man of blood', Charles's ghost is simultaneously retired from earthly conflict, into the peace of heaven where his enemies cannot touch him, and very much still interested in earthly politics, urging his former subjects to continue the conflict under the leadership of his heir (compare Crawford). This pamphlet depicts a complex transaction between the living and the dead. The king demands revenge, showing a reliance on his people that contradicts the disdain he showed for them in life. Having made his appeal, 'straight a Majestick face / And divine form, his humane shape did grace' (5): this interaction with his earthly subject relieves the ghost of his suffering, and allows him to reclaim the immortal political body stripped from him by his execution. The king conveys his divine authority to the living writer, and the writer apotheosizes the king, in a gift exchange which binds together the living and the dead.

Although this pamphlet develops the pathos of Charles's ghostly form, most of the libels use ghosts for satirical purposes. Humour had been associated with the ghost narrative since the time of Epicurus: 'The Philosophers of *Epicurus* sect did jest and laugh' at reports of spirits, according to Lavater (9), while Le Loyer criticized Lucian's denial of spirits and his tendency to scoff at his more learned respondents (sig. 21v). An example of a satirical ghost is the exchange between the spectre of Oliver Cromwell and his shrewish wife Joan at Tower Hill. Oliver explains that he has been released from hell because of the 'decensions, which is always rising between the Devil and I' (*The Case is Altered* 6). The couple discuss the inadequacy of their son Richard, who hadn't enough brains to ruin the country, and Joan complains that as a result, 'we poor reprobates' were 'dasht out of countenance, scoft, scornd, and derided, and even stunck in the nostrils of all sober minded people, worse then your wretched corps, did at the imbalming'. The intensely polluting corpse—bathed in the stink and infamy of the hangman's touch—contaminates the politically inadequate heir. This comic dialogue concludes by Cromwell turning on his allies, revealing their 'true' nature and voicing a desire for their ruin.

These satires often invoked ghosts in order to punish the living or the dead. One regular victim of satirical haunting was the Archbishop of Canterbury, William Laud. Laud was subjected to an extensive pamphlet campaign, in which texts assailed his dignity, forced him into confessions of treason and revealed his fear of damnation.[6] Laud's diary reveals that he was aware of the libel campaign against him. On 11 May 1641, he noted that 'libels are continually set up in all places of note in the city' (Laud, *Works* vol. 3, 83).[7] After Strafford's execution, Laud notes that 'no sooner was he gone into his rest, but the libellers, which during that time reviled him, fell on me ... And libels and ballads against me were frequently spread through the city, and sung up and down the streets' (Laud, *Works* vol. 3, 445–6).[8] He was forced to receive these libels during his imprisonment: on 27 August 1641, 'a letter, subscribed to John Browne, was thrust under the door of my prison. When I opened it, I found it a most bitter libel' (Wharton vol. 4, 32). Laud's diary was also used against him, in an edition strategically edited by William Prynne and printed by order of Commons on 16 August 1644 (Laud, *Breviate of the Life of William Laud*). This document fuelled criticism of Laud's superstitious nature: both of an ecclesiastical kind (the innovations in worship and church architecture which he introduced) and a personal one (the credence he gave to dreams and omens).[9]

Capitalizing on these well-known weaknesses, pamphleteers frequently mocked Laud with supernatural visitations, including one demanding personal revenge. Thomas Bensted, a drum major whom Laud had sentenced to hanging, drawing and quartering, appears to Laud when he is too troubled by his sins, 'fancies and imaginarie conceits' to sleep. Though Laud knows that fear and shadows 'have no substance and are caused by dull and melancholy fancies' (*Canterburies Amazement* 2), he suddenly sees 'the formidable figure of a quartered man: my Resolution now playes the unconstant woman; my whole body is a perpetuall palsie, my sences never were benum'd till now, my rationall part of man begin to forsake my drooping soule'. The ghost emasculates Laud and reveals the weakness of his faith. Bensted tells Laud that he has returned from heaven with a warrant for Laud's life (5). Heaven has already cast judgement on Laud's ecclesiastical innovations. But Bensted also haunts Laud for the most traditional of reasons: because his body is unburied. Laud set 'my dismembred joints upon the gates of this stately Citie for every one to gaze on', an action which 'favour'd not of that Christianitie which you seem'd to professe, unlesse it were of that superstitious Religion, that practices onely blood, and builds them Altars with the bones of Martyrs' (7). Bensted's ghost begs for the restitution of his remains, complaining that when his friends approach London Bridge, 'then is their griefe renewed with anxietie of mind, ready to strike them dead when they see my head, as if I were set up on purpose to crosse and perplexe them, or to examine their private businesses, or wherefore they come' (7). The ghost terrorizes Laud, just as the friends are terrorized by the sight of Bensted's remains.

Another in the procession of ghosts who appeared to Laud during his confinement in the Tower was his friend Thomas Wentworth, the Earl of Strafford. The two were imprisoned together, though Strafford was executed nearly four years before Laud. In one pamphlet Strafford returns to reprove Laud and to dispel the false rumour 'that I doe love thee'. He asks why Laud fears him: 'What substance have I to make thee affraid', 'A voice, a shade, or fancy at the most?' (*The Deputies Ghost* n.p.). As in many of these pamphlets, Strafford alludes to debates about the nature of ghosts in order to imply that Laud's fear is the product not of the apparition itself but rather of his superstition, guilt and lack of faith. Like all the ghostly assaults on Laud, the pamphlet imagines penetrating the Archbishop's seclusion and informing him of the public hate. Strafford declares that 'In any place where men abroad doe walke, / When dyes the Bishop? thus they use to talke'. Passing 'unseene' through the streets, the ghost sees 'the multitudes of paper sheets, / Sent from the Presse, and thus they cry them still, / Come buy a booke concerning little Will'. In a dizzying twist, this ghost alerts a fictional representation of a real person about the existence of books such as the one in which the ghost himself has been created. If Laud could see these books, it 'were enough to make you run starke mad': but this book brings itself to his attention in order to madden him. Strafford concludes by informing Laud that he will not see Bensted's ghost when he is finally executed, for Bensted will be in heaven; one fictional ghost alludes to a visit by another.

Like the libel slipped under Laud's door, ghosts could penetrate his seclusion. Ghosts could go anywhere; in this regard they resemble the imaginative mobility of the author. The ghost of the famous satirist Tom Nashe could 'cut through th'Ayre', 'ferrit' in the earth, 'And in an Augure hole my selfe can hide, / And heare their knaveries and spie unspide' (*Tom Nash his Ghost* sig. A1v). Just as he had done when he was a living writer, Nashe's ghost can spy into private spaces, overhear conversations and publicize confessions to the world. Stephen Greenblatt has described 'spectral vagrancy' as central to the fear ghosts aroused (108). But such vagrancy was also typical of libels—and made ghosts incredibly useful rhetorical devices.[10] Their spectrality also made them both less and more trustworthy. Although they are invoked in a genre which is synonymous with deception for many readers, ghosts also proclaim that they speak with an eternal veracity. Standing outside the law, beyond the reach of earthly powers, ghosts are more credible than the living. Tom Nashe became even more truthful when he was dead. The ghost of Nashe is completely uninterested in pleasing an audience, and liberated (as the Epicureans promised) from fear of retribution by the law: 'I am a *Ghost*, and *Ghosts* doe feare no Lawes; / Nor doe they care for popular Applause' (*Tom Nash his Ghost* sig. A1v). Nashe's declaration of independence can also be read as a vindication of the satirical author more generally, including the author of this pamphlet.

Ghosts also transformed the psychic punishment of being pursued by shame or guilt into a spatial ubiquity. Like an avenging fury, the ghost could hound the guilty always and everywhere. For example, in one pamphlet a captain's ghost accuses a count of prevailing upon him to murder an innocent gentleman. Although the count has evaded justice in life, the ghost promises that

> I will Haunt and Torment you in all your intended Divertisements, in your Visits and your Feasts, your Closet and your Bed; I will imbitter all your injoyments; I'll make you uncapable of taking any pleasure in your great Relations, or your large Possessions, your full Coffers, or your Honourable Titles, your stately Buildings, or your curious Gardens. I will be continually sounding in your Ears, the dismal Horrors, and unexpressable Torments I suffer for your sake; and never hope that you shall be rid of my Company, for I will haunt you as long as you live on earth, and then to the Grave. (*The Captain's Ghost* 2)

The ghost threatens a terrible intimacy: it will be there in the same closet, the same bed with the guilty party, weaving through his legitimate pastimes and possessions, pursuing him even into the afterlife.

A similar spectral vagrancy allowed ghosts, and thereby writers and readers, to penetrate the sacred or reserved spaces of political power. In a dialogue between the ghosts of Charles and Cromwell, Cromwell begs the king's forgiveness for invading the privacy of his royal dwelling and for plotting 'to ruine you and yours, and to set my self in your sted' (*A Dialogue betwixt the Ghost of Charls* 5). Cromwell confesses that he was troubled in life by the 'sting of Conscience': 'to tell you the truth my Reign was (as all Usurpers must be) more like to a Hell then a Heaven, my Palace being a Prison to me; … and if I had had not Enemies, my own thoughts had been enough; for if I lookt one way me thought I see you without a Head bleeding afresh, as if there had been a Deluge, to drown'd me and all my Crew in blood' (8). The ghost provides an insight into Cromwell's private thoughts. Unlike Charles, Cromwell died in bed. This peaceful death prevented his opponents from examining his body or his rhetoric for signs of corruption on the scaffold, and suggests providential approval for his life and policies. This pamphlet uses the ghost in order to trespass both in domestic or architectural spaces and in the private spaces of Cromwell's body and mind.

Another pamphlet, published in 1659, describes how the ghost of the regicide John Bradshaw is tormented by bad conscience. 'Pacing up and downe the dismal shades of the more frightfull night', Bradshaw was 'at last encountered, to its owne terror, by the Apparition of the late K. *Charles*' (*Bradshaw's Ghost* 4). Charles confronts the ghost of the regicide majestically, demanding 'what art thou (bold fiend) that thus darest trouble these forbidden lodgings'. Bradshaw's ghost answers that he is 'condemn'd with unwearied walking, to trace this loathed place'. Like Cromwell, Bradshaw admits that while he was alive, he was plagued by 'ghastly visions' of Charles's headless corpse. As he recalls the king's 'calm though provok'd *Majesty* … disdaining the terrors of an enforced death', he is 'torn in pieces with amazement' and feels 'the everlasting torments of a reprobated soul'. These torments make him wish for 'controverted *Purgatory*', rather than the hell which was specially prepared for him. Pamphlets like these revenge themselves on the regicides, afflicting them with eternal suffering and enacting in literary form the symbolic destruction which was often meted out to enemies of the public. When Cromwell, Bradshaw and Ireton's remains were hanged, their heads set up on poles on Westminster Hall, and their trunks reburied under the gallows at Tyburn on 30 January 1661, they were subjected to a ritual of 'multiple death' which excluded them from the community of the just. Such rituals were not uncommon in this period (Edwards, Lenihan and Tait 21). These material practices can be compared to the exhumation, desecration and punishment of their rhetorical remains in satires and libels.

While custom maintained that executed criminals had paid their debts to the state by death, such ritual desecration implies that the dead are still deeply involved in earthly politics. In the libels of the 1640s and 1650s those put to death by the state are revived either to condemn the corrupt powers which took their lives or to make a posthumous confession of their guilt. Unlike Bradshaw or Cromwell, Strafford had been executed. However, his scaffold confession in 1641 was widely regarded as a proud refusal to fulfil the generic expectations of piety and penitence.[11] Rather than reconciling himself to Parliament, Strafford had complained of the people's bloodlust and prophesied a rising tide of violence. Several pamphlets resurrect the Earl to resolve this unfinished business by making a full and obsequious first-person confession. In his visitation to Laud, the ghost of Strafford admits that 'to dye I truely had deserved', because of his allegiance with Laud 'to subvert / The fundamentall Lawes and Government, / Confirmed by the course of *Parliament*', and 'To pull down truth and set up superstition' (*The Deputies Ghost* n.p.). Another pamphlet lists Strafford's atrocities in Ireland, before forcing the ghost to confess that 'I was made an Instrument i' my life time to set these warres o'foot, for which my afflicted

Ghost (haunted with horror) can take no rest, so long as they continue; ther's not a man falls, nor a wound given, but I am sensible of it, I smart for't, so closely am I follow'd by Divine Justice' (*The Earl of Strafford's Ghost* 2). Strafford's ghost shows that divine justice is consonant with earthly justice, concluding obsequiously that 'I cannot but acknowledge my thankfulnesse to you for freeing your Countrey of the danger my longer life would have made it lyable to ... as soon as you tooke off my head, my minde was alter'd' (2). In place of Purgatory, a punitive domain where human activity could still affect the fortunes of the dead, such spectral trials offer a secular, political contiguity between earth and the afterlife. Hell is a place where earthly justice is perpetually re-enacted; heaven is a refuge for the unjustly accused. These characterizations cast light on the validity of earthly judgements, sanctifying or undermining the decisions of the law.

These libels revive political actors in order to satisfy not their own unfinished business, but the reader's. The excesses of hatred, guilt, shame or anger which have not been contained by the execution or death of a political figure spill over into the afterlife. Pamphlet ghosts demand expiation, remembrance and mollification, often through political resistance to their successors. However, in the libels it is not the ghosts which pursue and torment the living but vice versa. The author's imaginative mobility is embodied as spectral vagrancy; the author's sense of injustice is symbolized by hellfire; and the author's need to continue the conversation with those made safe by death is satisfied by fictional dialogues. Ghosts allow writers to proclaim their secret knowledge and penetrate private spaces, to display their subject's secret interiority and to ventriloquize famous political figures. The traffic in ghosts binds together different temporalities (past, present and future) and different spaces (hell and heaven, the prison cell and the palace chamber). And by playing on the Protestant characterization of ghosts as either demonic or delusional, both qualities are attributed to political figures.

Ghosts can bind together members of a community. In the libels, the appearance of the ghost maintains that relationship between the writer, the reader and the dead which the rituals of execution, dying and burial have severed, and seeks a new community of political scepticism or activism through the shared encounter with ghosts. However, ghosts are also divisive figures. They are pursued by earthly justice in an afterlife which is made to seem not only interested in human activities, but contingent on them. They demonstrate to readers the infusion not only of the world by spirit but also of the afterlife by temporal politics. They also refer to forms of consensus which mechanist theories and political upheaval were eroding: the belief that divine retribution is a consequences of decisions made in this life, that the soul is immortal, that history is providentially organized and that the eye and the imagination—though manipulable—can give access to truth.

In the eighteenth century, Anna Laetitia Aikin justified the pleasures of horror as an expansion of the imagination: ghost stories 'awaken the mind, and keep it on the stretch', allowing the imagination to 'dart forth' and 'explore with rapture the new world which is laid open to its view', where it 'rejoices in the expansion of its powers' (283). The pleasurable excitation of the imagination expands the mind, to consider new possibilities through wonder and surprise. It is not difficult to see why the Gothic narrative, viewed in these terms, was dangerous, a correlate (as the Marquis de Sade had argued) of revolution. The case was quite different in the seventeenth century. In the decades following the British civil wars, the discourse of ghosts was scientifically and politically conservative: it was *scepticism* towards ghosts that was potentially revolutionary. Writers such as More and Glanville remembered that the Epicureans had been released by their disbelief in ghosts and the afterlife from their fear of the state. But Hobbes, Spinoza and Epicurus weren't the only authors teaching the people to be sceptical. The experiences of the 1640s showed that the ventriloquization of public figures could release political violence and dissolve the ties between generations and within communities. For More, Glanville and others interested in restoring the peace through rationalism and the reassertion of human and divine hierarchies, superstition must have been more attractive than the anarchy of a populace with no fear of death.

Notes

1 On the Senecan ghost, see Moorman. On the influence of the *Mirror for Magistrates*, see Farnham.
2 On Descartes' scepticism about ghosts, see Fix (540).
3 On More's response to Descartes, see Hall; Webster; and Cottingham.
4 See Walsham; Valletta (chapter 4); Capp (chapter 2); and Hill, *Antichrist in Seventeenth-Century England*.
5 On the English Platonists' attitude towards hell, see Walker 104–78.
6 This process was not uncommon in libels; see Shuger 96–7.
7 See also Cogswell 277, 288–93.
8 On the variety of means by which libels were circulated, see Bellany 154.
9 In 1635 Laud also encouraged the interrogation of a ghost, to find out what it had to say about the death of an infamous bishop, John Atherton (Marshall 78).
10 Adam Smyth writes that 'one of the features of libels that seems to have most alarmed those responsible for the control of the press was precisely their mobility and placelessness' (81).

11 On the ritual of the execution, see my *English Funerary Elegy in the Seventeenth Century*, chapter 4.

Works cited

A Dialogue betwixt the Ghosts of Charls the I, Late King of England: and Oliver the late Usurping Protector. London, [9 June], 1659.

Aikin, Anna Laetitia. 'On the Pleasure Derived from Objects of Terror'. *Miscellaneous Pieces, in Prose*. London: J. Johnson, 1773. Reprinted in *Gothic Readings: The First Wave, 1764–1840*. Ed. Rictor Norton. London and New York: Leicester University Press, 2000. 281–3.

'A Jacobin Novelist'. 'Letter to the Editor'. *Monthly Magazine* 4.21 (1797): 102–4. Reprinted in *Gothic Readings: The First Wave, 1764–1840*. Ed. Rictor Norton. London and New York: Leicester University Press, 2000. 299–303.

A True Relation of an Apparition in the Likeness of a Bird with a White Brest, That Appeared Hovering over the Death-beds of Some of the Children. London, 1641.

Baxter, Richard. *The Certainty of the Worlds of Spirits, Fully Evinced by Unquestionable Histories of Apparitions and Witchcrafts*. London, 1691.

Bellany, Alastair. 'A Poem on the Archbishop's Hearse: Puritanism, Libel, and Sedition after the Hampton Court Conference'. *The Journal of British Studies* 34.2 (1995): 137–64.

Bradshaw's Ghost. [London], 1659.

Brady, Andrea. *English Funerary Elegy in the Seventeenth Century*. Basingstoke: Palgrave Macmillan, 2006.

Browne, Thomas. 'Pseudodoxia Epidemica'. *Selected Writings*. Ed. Geoffrey Keynes. London: Faber and Faber, 1968. Book I chapt. 10.

Canterburies Amazement: or The Ghost of the Yong Fellow Thomas Bensted, who was Drawne, Hangd, and Quartered by the Meanes of the Bishop of Canterburie. [London], 1641.

Capp, B. S. *The Fifth Monarchy Men: A Study in Seventeenth-century English Millenarianism*. London: Faber and Faber, 1972.

Clark, Stuart. *Vanities of the Eye: Vision in early modern European Culture*. Oxford: Oxford University Press, 2007.

Cogswell, Thomas. 'Underground Verse and the Transformation of Early Stuart Political Culture'. *Political Culture and Cultural Politics in early modern England*. Eds Susan D. Amussen and Mark A. Kishlansky. Manchester and New York: Manchester University Press, 1995. 277–300.

Coleridge, Samuel Taylor. 'Lewis's Romance of the Monk'. *Critical Review* 19 (1797): 194–200.

Conway, Anne. *The Conway Letters. The Correspondence of Anne, Viscountess Conway, Henry More, and Their Friends*. Ed. Marjorie Hope Nicolson. Rev. edn. Sarah Hutton. Oxford: Clarendon, 1992.

Cottingham, John. 'Force, Motion and Causality: More's Critique of Descartes'. *The Cambridge Platonists in Philosophical Context: Politics, Metaphysics and Religion.* Eds G. A. J. Rogers, J. M. Vienne, and Y. C. Zarka. Dordrecht, Boston and London: Kluwer, 1997. 159–72.

Crawford, Patricia. 'Charles Stuart, that Man of Blood'. *The Journal of British Studies* 16.2 (1977): 41–61.

Digby, Kenelm. *Two Treatises, in the One of Which, the Nature of Bodies, in the Other, The Nature of Mans Soule.* Paris, 1664.

Doody, Margaret. *The Daring Muse: Augustan Poetry Reconsidered.* Cambridge: Cambridge University Press, 1985.

Edwards, David, Pádraig Lenihan and Clodagh Tait, eds. *Age of Atrocity: Violence and Political Conflict in Early Modern Ireland.* Dublin: Four Courts Press, 2007.

Farnham, Willard. 'The Progeny of "A Mirror for Magistrates"'. *Modern Philology* 29.4 (1932): 395–410.

Fix, Andrew. 'Angels, Devils, and Evil Spirits in Seventeenth-Century Thought: Balthasar Bekker and the Collegiants.' *Journal of the History of Ideas* 50.4 (1989): 527–47.

Glanville, Joseph. *Sadducismus Triumphatus: or, Full and Plain Evidence Concerning Witches and Apparitions.* London, 1681.

—. *A Blow to Modern Sadducism.* London, 1668.

Greenblatt, Stephen. *Hamlet in Purgatory.* Princeton: Princeton University Press, 2001.

Hall, A. Rupert. *Henry More and the Scientific Revolution.* Cambridge: Cambridge University Press, 1990.

[Hammond, Henry]. *Of Superstition.* Oxford, 1645.

Hill, Christopher. *The World Turned Upside Down: Radical Ideas During the English Revolution.* Harmondsworth and New York: Penguin, 1975.

—. *Antichrist in Seventeenth-Century England.* London: Oxford University Press, 1971.

Hobbes, Thomas. *Leviathan.* Ed. C. B. Macpherson. London: Penguin, 1968.

Hutton, Sarah. *Anne Conway: A Woman Philosopher.* Cambridge: Cambridge University Press, 2004.

Laud, William. *The Works of the Most Reverend Father in God, William Laud, D.D. Sometime Lord Archbishop of Canterbury.* Eds William Scott and James Bliss. 7 vols. Oxford: John Henry Parker, 1847–60.

—. *Breviate of the Life of William Laud, Archbishop of Canterbury.* Ed. William Prynne. London, 1644.

Lavater, Lewis. *Of Ghostes and Spirites Walking by Nyght.* Ed. J. Dover Wilson and May Yardley. Oxford: Oxford University Press for the Shakespeare Association, 1929.

[Le Loyer, Pierre]. *A Treatise of Specters or Straunge Sights, Visions and Apparitions Appearing Sensibly unto Men.* London, 1605.

Marshall, Peter. *Mother Leakey and the Bishop: A Ghost Story.* Oxford: Oxford University Press, 2007.

Moorman, F. W. 'The Pre-Shakespearean Ghost'. *The Modern Language Review* 1.2 (1906): 85–95.

More, Henry. *Sadducismus Triumphatus: or, Full and Plain Evidence Concern-*

ing Witches and Apparitions. Letter to Joseph Glanville. London, 1681.

—. *An Antidote against Atheisme, or An Appeal to the Natural Faculties of the Minde of Man, Whether There Be Not a God*. London, 1653.

Sade, Marquis de. *The One Hundred and Twenty Days of Sodom and Other Writings*. Trans. Austryn Wainhouse and Richard Seaver. London: Arrow, 1966.

Shuger, Debora. 'Civility and Censorship in early modern England'. *Censorship and Silencing: Practices of Cultural Regulation*. Ed. Robert C. Post. Los Angeles: Getty Research Institute, 1998. 89–110.

Smyth, Adam. 'Recycling Satire in the Mid-Seventeenth Century'. *Huntington Library Quarterly* 69.1 (2006): 67–82.

The Captain's Ghost Appearing to the Count. London, 1682.

The Case is Altered. Or, Dreadful News from Hell. London, [6 August 1660].

The Deputies Ghost, or, An Apparition to the Lord of Canterbury in the Tower. [London], printed in the yeare of our prelates feare, 1641.

The Earl of Strafford's Ghost. London, [22 August] 1644.

The King Advancing, or Great Brittains Royal Standard, with His Majesties Gracious Speech to His Loyal Subjects. London, 1660.

Tom Nash his Ghost, to the Three Scurvy Fellowes of the Upstart Family of the Snufflers, Rufflers and Shuffler ... York and London, 1642.

Valletta, Frederick. *Witchcraft, Magic and Superstition in England, 1640–70*. Aldershot: Ashgate, 2000.

Walker, D. P. *The Decline of Hell: Seventeenth-Century Discussions of Eternal Torment*. London: Routledge and Paul, 1964.

Walsham, Alexandra. 'Sermons in the Sky: Apparitions in early modern Europe'. *History Today* 51.4 (2001): 56–63.

Webster, C. 'Henry More and Descartes: Some New Sources'. *The British Journal for the History of Science* 4.4 (1969): 359–77.

Wharton, Henry, ed. *The History of the Troubles and Tryal of* [...] *William Laud, Lord Arch-Bishop of Canterbury*. London: Richard Chiswell, 1695.

Part IV
Persistence of the Gothic

11

Monstrous to our human reason: minding the gap in *The Winter's Tale*[1]

Richard Wilson

Before her time

'There was a man ... Dwelt by a churchyard': the story the young prince starts to tell the queen in *The Winter's Tale* cries out to be continued in the scary way for which she asked: 'come on, and do your best / To fright me with your sprites. You're powerful at it'. 'Poetically man dwells' (cf. Heidegger 213–29); but 'A sad tale's best for winter' (2.1.26–9), Mamillius grimly insisted when Hermione dared him to be merry. So together with his precocious blue jokes about the venereal diseases of her maids, there is an incongruous prematurity about this disturbed child's eerie bedside story for its mother that seems connected to the uncanny causality that Old Father Time cruelly warns will engulf the audience, when he turns his glass to 'leave the growth untried' of the following sixteen years: 'So shall I do / To th'freshest things now reigning, and make stale / The glistering of this present as my tale / Now seems to it' (4.1.6–15). It is as if somebody walks over our own graves when these winter words about the mysterious man who dwelt so ominously beside a churchyard are snatched out of hearing, excluded from the play with a metatheatrical glance that sweeps us up in the snub meant for those Ladies whose symptoms suggest they are not long for this world: 'I will tell it softly, / Yon crickets shall not hear it'. For in a drama determined by 'whispering nothing' (1.2.286), this tantalizing deferred narrative has the suspended animation of what remains entailed in every ghost story, 'a limbo quality all of its own', left hanging as it is upon an aposiopoesis: 'an unfinished statement, a sudden breaking off in the midst of ...' (Royle 145).

'There was a man ... Dwelt by a churchyard ... ': like one of Schubert's *Winterreise* Lieder that so haunted Samuel Beckett, the sad tale told by the fey child in *The Winter's Tale* distils in a few words all the features that would distinguish the *unheimlich* Gothic genre from the *heimlich* fireside story, the garrulous type of merry 'old tale' of Mother Goose or Mother Hubbard, which, we soon learn, 'will have matter to rehearse though credit be asleep and not an ear open' (5.2.55). Thus, 'Come on then, and give't me in mine ear', sighs the doomed queen (2.1.34). As its critics point out, unlike the folktale the Gothic is obsessed by narrative encryption, by *cryptomimesis* as a labyrinthine form of burial and concealment. So within the genre Mamillius initiates 'the crypt and the ear are inextricably implicated' (Castricano 48).[2] 'The ear is uncanny' (*Ear* 33), considered Jacques Derrida, for the figure of the mother is always implicit in 'the ear of the other' (51). Whatever the boy whispers in his mother's ear, to 'fright' her with his 'sprites and goblins' (28), therefore begs to be decrypted as the latent subtext of this play, an unhomely Gothic horror hidden beneath the homely dwelling of a romance in which to be lucky 'requires nothing but secrecy' (3.3.114). As the editors of the recent *Shakespearean Gothic* admit, 'to uncover the secret relation' between Shakespeare and the Gothic 'provides something of a Gothic story in itself, a tale of two long-lost relatives reunited at last' (Desmet and Williams 2). But it is a disinterment of a darker hidden side of Shakespeare that seems to be demanded by the cryptonymy of this text that insists upon both the 'joy and terror' of such a reunion (4.1.1), and which Time himself states will have the apocalyptic violence of an exhumation:

> since it is in my power
> To overthrow law, and in one self-born hour
> To plant and o'erwhelm ...
>   let Time's news
> Be known when 'tis brought forth.
>
> (4.1.7–9; 26–7)

The entry of Time in *The Winter's Tale* has been described as so 'out of joint' (*Hamlet* 1.5.189) that it suggests that the two parts of the play divided by a 'wide gap' (7) of sixteen years could be staged '*concurrently*, in the style of Tom Stoppard's *Arcadia*', with the past in the future, and 'no more behind / But such a day tomorrow as today' (1.2.64–5) (Gaston 78). With such unhinging of the unities of time, place and action, Time's assertion of his right to both 'plant and o'erwhelm' whatever is to be buried, the threat to desecrate 'The rich proud cost of outworn buried age' (Sonnet 64) that is the morbid preoccupation of Shakespeare's sonnets, where 'neither brass, nor stone, nor earth' but the Grim Reaper 'o'ersways their power' (Sonnet 65), must make the case of any man who pitches his dwelling beside such an aporia a grave one. We have visited too many Shakespearean cemeteries and ossuaries, and seen too many skulls emerge out of the earth, not to be alarmed at how 'Stones have been known to move' (*Macbeth* 3.4.122), 'canonized bones' tend to 'burst their cerements', and the sepulchre in which the body has been 'quietly enurned' is apt to 'ope his ponderous and marble jaws' to 'cast [it] up again' (*Hamlet* 1.4.28–32).

With Shakespeare, it is always necessary to mind the gap. As Derrida commented in *Specters of Marx*, with this dramatist who seems not to know whether he is coming or going, not only is it important to remember where the bodies are buried, 'but to make sure they stay there' (9). The haunted necrophile householder in Mamillius' fright story might then be said to be the harbinger of one of the key Gothic tropes foretold in *The Winter's Tale*, which is the house as crypt, the broken home as a tomb, and the crossing of the boundary that is meant to demarcate the future from the past, and the dwelling from 'The undiscovered country from whose bourn', we prefer to think, 'No traveller returns' (*Hamlet* 3.1.81) (cf. Wigley 174). For however it was supposed to be continued, the inauspicious nursery story told by this prepubescent male about a house built like a gateway on the yawning edge of a graveyard does fit *uncannily* Julia Kristeva's analysis in *Powers of Horror* of all such liminal spaces. Frontiers and partitions act as signifiers of the vital psychic barrier that protects the identity of the subject 'who will always be marked by the uncertainty of borders' from being subsumed by the 'wide gap' of the maternal 'void':

> This is precisely where we encounter the rituals of defilement ... which, based on the feeling of abjection and all converging on the maternal, attempt to symbolize the threat of being swamped ... The function of these religious rituals is to ward off the subject's fear of his very own identity sinking irretrievably into the mother. (64)

In *The Winter's Tale* it is said the pedlar can 'fit his customers' with prophylactic 'gloves' of 'all sizes', yet there is always 'some stretched-mouthed rascal who would ... mean mischief and break a foul gap in the matter' (4.4.190–5) by puncturing the precautionary sheath. Thus the Ladies' provocations about Hermione's pregnancy which frame her son's creepy storytelling provide a textbook cue for Gothic horror as an abjection of the 'foul gap' in the monstrous *mater*: 'The Queen your mother rounds apace ... She is spread of late / Into a goodly bulk' (2.1.17–21). The play's unease about the disruption of uncanny prematurity is therefore substantiated when the queen gives birth to a 'lusty' girl 'something before her time' (2.2.28–30), for the crucial element of the Gothic aesthetic is said to be 'disgust' (cf. Carroll 158). Thus feminist criticism offers an entire phenomenology of menstrual blood, milk, vomit, 'shit, etc.' to account for the genre's revulsion at 'changes of the wat'ry star' (1.2.1) which also explains why Mamillius is such a rapt listener to his father's misogynistic rant that there is 'No barricado for a belly ... It will let in and out the enemy / With bag and baggage'

(1.2.198–207) (cf. Creed 13). So when Leontes disrupts the boy's story-time with a hue and cry over his wife's alleged lover Polixenes, the king's panic, 'How came the posterns / So easily open?' (2.1.54), literalizes the borderlessness that is already the focus for the infant's revulsion from the defiling proximity of the home and tomb.

The Winter's Tale dramatizes the case of a husband like the man in the story, 'so grieving / That he shuts up himself' (4.1.18–19). Shakespeare images an uncanny topography for this nightmare of incarceration that therefore dimly prefigures the paranoid fortified architecture of moated walls, iron bars, and secret passages in the haunted Gothic house, when he has Leontes rave that the 'issue' will hiss him to the grave if his 'pond' is 'sluiced' and 'fished by his neighbour', for 'men have gates, and those gates opened, / As mine, against their will' (1.2.188–99). No wonder, then, Hermione tells Leontes his is 'a language I understand not. / My life stands in the level of your dreams' (3.2.77–8). In Jacobean England the 'foul gap' of the mother's physical confinement after delivery would be sealed over by her reincorporation into the social body at the Anglican purification ceremony of churching. But when Mamillius 'languish[es]' to death (2.3.17), and Hermione falls unconscious in post-partum shock, *The Winter's Tale* instead looks forward to the claustrophobic hidden enclosures of Gothic terror, when it projects a far more literally confining containment of contaminating female 'issue' in the cryptomimetic fantasy of incorporation by entombment:

> Prithee bring me
> To the dead bodies of my queen and son.
> One grave shall be for both. Upon them shall
> The causes of their death appear, unto
> Our shame perpetual. Once a day I'll visit
> The chapel where they lie, and tears shed there
> Shall be my recreation.
>
> (3.2.232–8)

When Leontes begins the work of mourning by envisioning the crypt where he will have his wife and heir interred, *The Winter's Tale* reverts to the one Shakespearean space above all that would supply Gothic writers such as Horace Walpole and Ann Radcliffe with a *mise-en-scène*. As *Shakespearean Gothic* shows, it was episodes like the monstrous Richard III seducing Lady Anne over the coffin of her husband, Claudio lighting torches in the vault of Hero, Hamlet leaping into the pit dug for Ophelia, and Othello smothering Desdemona until she is 'Still as the grave' (*Othello* 5.2.103) that shaped the eighteenth-century notion of the Bard as himself a voice from out of the tomb:

> Viewed this way [Shakespeare] is not a foil for the Gothic but an inspiring source ... whose troubling components are isolated and sharpened in Gothic retelling ... through a 'perversion' of Shakespeare, it brings the [play's] own 'perversities' to light. (Shapira 147–8)

To estrange *The Winter's Tale* by retelling it as a proto-Gothic text thus involves returning to the dead child's chiller about the 'gross and foolish' man who sets up home beside the gaping tomb with Paulina's intuition that these are 'Thoughts too high for one so tender' (3.2.194–5).

'Dwelt by a churchyard': Mamillius' tale has the formula of a Gothic vault or mirror, a story within the story, we infer, ushering in his father's cryptomania. For as a courtier objects, after so many years of having 'performed / A saint-like sorrow', it is Leontes' similarly excessive mourning that is asking for trouble: 'No fault could you make / Which you have not redeemed, indeed, paid down / More penitence than done trespass' (5.1.1–4). *The Winter's Tale* is a play much concerned with minding the gap of the place of burial, with the desire of the subject 'to fill his grave in quiet, yea, / To die upon the bed [his] father died, / To lie close by his honest bones', rather than 'Where no priest shovels in dust' (4.4.442–6): but not too close to this aperture, and *at the right time*. Sensible Cleomenes is therefore anticipating Freud's thesis in 'Mourning and Melancholia' that the work mourning performs consists of a painful yet possible withdrawal from the lost loved one by means of an interiorizing idealization which can be figured as a devouring (cf. Freud 244). But Paulina thinks she knows better, and foreshadows both Gothic fiction and Derridean deconstruction when she counters that 'Ten thousand years together, naked, fasting' (3.2.209) would not complete the mourning process, when it is precisely the *impossibility* of such an affective withdrawal that constitutes the subject, for if it is the spatial marker of disgust, the crypt is also 'the very figure of desire' (Wigley 176):

> If one by one you wedded all the world
> Or from the all that are took something good
> To make a perfect woman, she you killed
> Would be unparalleled.
>
> (5.1.13–16)

To murder her I married

Leontes acknowledges the strange logic of cryptomimesis when he asserts that the tears he looks forward to weeping in his daily dwelling over the family vault will be his *recreation*. With its transgenerational worry over what Anne Williams in *Art of Darkness: A Poetics of Gothic* terms

'the quintessential Gothic issue' (239), legitimate descent and rightful
inheritance, its gossipy whispers about homosexuality, syphilis and the
ageing female body, its intrusion of a savage animal, a storm, a foundling, a casket, a statue that bleeds and a purloined letter, not to mention
masked royalty and clueless peasants, *The Winter's Tale* rehearses a
veritable compendium of props and processes associated with Gothic
novels. But it is in situating the crypt at the heart of the house that this
text comes closest to a Gothic obsession with the phantasmal economy
of desire. For when Leontes gives orders to attend Hermione's deathbed
and 'tenderly apply to her / Some remedies for life' (3.2.150–1), he is
in fact obeying the uncanny aesthetics of revenance that govern the
fantasy of incorporation. As Derrida writes, 'one buries or burns what
is *already dead* so that life, the living feminine, will be reborn and
regenerated from these ashes' (*Ear* 26). In *King Lear* the father's frantic
calls to 'Look on her, look, her lips' (5.3.308), therefore abreact what
had earlier seemed to him a fulfilled desire to restore Cordelia to life:
'You are a spirit, I know. When did you die?' (4.7.49). Nicholas Royle
describes the literally unsettling irruption of this 'eerily posthumous'
(155) proceeding, figured in Lear's cry, 'You do me wrong to take me
out o'the grave' (4.7.45). And in *The Winter's Tale* we similarly experience as much horror as desire, 'both joy and terror', in Time's words,
at the disturbing aposiopoetic crypt effect, like that of the child's hauntingly interrupted story, which suspends the departed in the posthumous
yet premature twilight world of the living dead:

> I say she's dead. I'll swear't. If word nor oath
> Prevail not, go and see. If you can bring
> Tincture or lustre in her lip, her eye,
> Heat outwardly or breath within, I'll serve you
> As I would do the gods.
>
> (3.2.201–5)

Paulina's challenge asks us to project an offstage mortuary resuscitation
scene, like that when Lear cries to 'men of stones' to lend a 'looking
glass' in belief that if his daughter's 'breath will mist or stain the stone, /
Why then she lives' (*Lear* 5.3.256–62). Yet her unflinching command to
'Look down' into the lacuna of the gaping crypt, 'And see what death is
doing' (146–7) simultaneously insists on the stealthy imminence of the
bodily decay which Georges Bataille describes in *Eroticism: Death and
Sensuality* as the 'nauseous, rank and heaving matter, frightful to look
upon, a ferment of life, teeming with worms, grubs and eggs [which]
is at the bottom of the decisive reactions we call repugnance, nausea,
and disgust' (56). Such will indeed be the repellent condition in which
the figure of this 'undead' woman does shortly appear to return from

the morgue, in a classic instance of female abjection at the turning-point of the play. There, in a bizarre dream sequence that literalizes the loathsome void with the suspenseful structure of a horror film, an old courtier recounts how the ghost of Hermione has appeared to him in a nightmare, initially gliding towards his cabin like an immaculate bride, 'In pure white robes / Like very sanctity', and bowing its head modestly, only to raise its face in a sudden paroxysm of 'fury', and expose its ghastliness to the dreamer as the mother of 'the issue / Of King Polixenes', when 'gasping to begin some speech, her eyes / Became two spouts' (3.3.21–5; 42–3).

Editors point out that Antigonus' dream narration is the only occasion when Shakespeare systematically confuses his audience about the death of a character, and this blurring of borders seems bound up with the undecidability of a monstrous suspicion it plants: that Hermione is truly an adulteress. The shock of this hissing Medusa-like 'creature' in fact recalls that of the 'fiend' with 'two full moons' for eyes which waves its 'whelked' horns 'like the enraged sea' in the *vagina dentata* Edgar concocts to scare his blind father out of suicide in *King Lear* (4.6.70). Both of these hauntings occur on a seashore, the ultimate '*bor de me*' (Derrida, 'Living-On' 256) of the monstrous. Gloucester recoils from the verge of the void he imagines to be Dover Cliff. But 'Affrighted much' on the coast of Bohemia, Antigonus decides 'Dreams are toys, / Yet for this once, yea superstitiously, / I will be squared by this', after the vampiric spectre has pronounced that for letting his 'heart bleed' for her baby Perdita, he will forfeit his life. 'I never saw a vessel of like sorrow', the old man reflects, as 'with shrieks, / She melted into air' (3.3.38–51); and indeed this apparition is a perfect example of the tendency noted by Slavoj Žižek for the purgatorial 'undead' to linger on the borderline of life and death as melancholy sufferers, pursuing their victims with 'a kind of infinite sadness' (22–3). What follows by contrast, however, is surely the most complete if callous instance in literature of the healthy withdrawal of emotional attachment from the dead by process of psychic devouring, when Antigonus instantly crosses the 'wide gap' of the Stygian chasm, to '*Exit, pursued by a bear*' (SD 57):

CLOWN I'll go see if the bear be gone from the gentleman, and how much he hath eaten. They are never curst but when they are hungry. If there be any left of him, I'll bury it.
OLD SHEPHERD That's a good deed. If thou may'st discern by that which is left of him what he is, fetch me to th'sight of him.
CLOWN Marry will I; and you shall help to put him i'th'ground.
OLD SHEPHERD 'Tis a lucky day boy, and we'll do good deeds on't
(3.3.116–22)

If the Shepherds who take it on themselves to bury the leftovers of the 'poor gentleman' (93) figure in *The Winter's Tale* as luckily canny opposites of that uncanny man who dwelt by a churchyard, that is doubtless because, in Derridean terms, there is too little *remainder* of Antigonus after the famished bear has dined off him for much to be desired. Though he had three daughters, who like Lear he would rather see sterilized than 'honour-flawed' like 'the woman's flesh' of his dream (2.1.140–9), it seems not enough is entailed by the death of Paulina's husband to haunt the play. As his widow vows, even the chance that the baby he rescued might have been found alive 'Is all as monstrous to our human reason / As my Antigonus to break his grave / And come again to me, who, on my life, / Did perish with the infant' (5.1.41–4). It is of course comforting for Paulina to picture her loved one's remains resting in peace in some corner of a foreign field, rather than devoured and defecated by a wild beast. Yet in the end she has to be told how 'He was torn to pieces with a bear' (5.2.57). So her constant swearing upon her own life to things she cannot know merely confirms what Kristeva writes about the abject as the border of the living being: 'If dung signifies the other side of the border, the place where I am not and that permits me to be', it is the location of 'the corpse, the most sickening of wastes' (3). For the fact that we are aware that the lost baby has after all been found irresistibly raises the latent possibility which haunts the happy ending of this family romance, and tears Paulina "twixt joy and sorrow' (5.2.67), the proposition so 'monstrous to our human reason' when whispered in the ear, that the dead might indeed break through the 'foul gap' of their disrupted sepulture, and be among those things repressed which 'come again':

> No more such wives, and therefore no wife. One worse,
> And better used, would make her sainted spirit
> Again possess her corpse, and on this stage
> Where we offenders mourn, appear soul-vexed,
> And begin, 'Why to me?'
>
> (5.1.55–9)

'O, these flaws and starts / Impostors of true fear, would well become / A woman's story at a winter's fire', sneers Lady Macbeth as her husband reels from the sight of Banquo's ghost. But Macbeth's grisly reply, that 'If charnel-houses and our graves must send / Those that we bury back, our monuments / Shall be the maws of kites' (*Macbeth* 3.4.62–81), is given knowing the return of the repressed is not only what is feared but what will *feed*: as the 'temple-haunting martlet' is lured to 'breed and haunt' (1.6.4–9) in Macbeth's haunted Gothic castle of Glamis. Likewise, *The Winter's Tale* is haunted by the uncanny hospitality of haunting, as personified by the revenant who makes a home beside the catacombs. Dating from the time of the Jacobean witch trials, this text knows enough about the abjection of the monstrous feminine to understand that 'It is an heretic that makes the fire, / Not she which burns in't' (2.3.115). Leontes himself analyses the perverse reproductive logic of such *hauntology* in lines about spectrality that recall the fatal attraction of Marlowe's Faustus to the all-consuming succubus of Helen: 'Affection ... Thou dost make possible things not so held, / Communicat'st with dreams ... With what's unreal thou coactive art, / And fellow'st nothing' (1.2.140–4). 'Your actions are my "dreams"', he thus reproaches his wife; and 'The bug which you would fright me with I seek' (3.2.90), Hermione as spookily responds: 'Cry "Fie" upon my grave' (52).[3] Thus it is through the 'notion of an active contractual relationship' (Castricano 69) with the hungry dead, who become, in Michel de Certeau's words, objective figures of 'an exchange amongst the living' (qtd in Schor 3), that *The Winter's Tale* shares in the Gothic excitement at the *unheimlich* cohabitation of Eros and Thanatos, desire and death. Paulina endorses, in any case, the widower's Bluebeard-like determination that if he were to wed again his victim's ghost would have such unappeasable power 'she would incense me / To murder her I married' (5.1.60–2), and thus compel him to become a true serial wife-killer:

> Were I the ghost that walked I'd bid you mark
> Her eye, and tell me for what dull part in't
> You chose her. Then I'd shriek that even your ears
> Should rift to hear me, and the words that followed
> Should be 'Remember mine'.
>
>   (5.1.63–7)

The vanishing

'Remember me': the cry from the 'wide gap' of the tomb is always a plea to be re-*membered*, recomposed into the visibility the dismembered cadaver possessed before it became 'lazar like' and 'abhorred in imagination' (*Hamlet* 1.5.73, 91; 5.1.173–85). As Maurice Blanchot remarked in *The Gaze of Orpheus*, such is, however, the cry of the one *we have no desire to see*: 'Lazarus in the tomb, and not Lazarus saved, the one who already smells bad, is Evil, Lazarus lost and not yet Lazarus brought back to life' (46–7). Leontes' commemoration of his wife's eyes as 'Stars, stars, / And all eyes else, dead coals' (5.1.67), so more alive than burned-out sockets in the living, therefore invokes the economy of seen and unseen, light and dark, that always structures the aesthetics of the return of the dead. The analogy with Orpheus descending the staircase to the underworld only to look disastrously into the eyes of Eurydice, or Theseus to rescue Persephone, thus seems truly cryptomimetic. For as Derrida observed in *Athens, Still Remains*, his meditation on photography and ancient graves, 'Does not Persephone reign' (45) over the *mise en abyme* of all such reflections on reflection: 'Persephone, wife of Hades, goddess of death and phantoms. But also of the image, of water and of tears, at once transparent and reflecting, mirror and pupil?' (49). Such phantasmatic reflections will haunt the restaging of the legend of Pygmalion at the end of the play, for Leontes persists in memorializing Hermione as the object of desire, not decomposed by what Paulina warns us death is doing, as 'even now', he fantasizes, 'I might have looked upon my queen's full eyes' (52–3). In legend Autolycus, the rogue who leads these lovers out of Hell, was the son of Hermes, we recall, the god of gates and ghosts.

In *The Winter's Tale* the lover is imagined 'like a corpse', yet 'not to be buried, / But quick and in mine arms' (4.4.131–2). By ghoulishly anticipating Leontes embracing one 'such / As, walked your first queen's ghost, it should take joy / To see you in her arms' (5.1.79–81), *The Winter's Tale* thereby asks us to visualize the definitive Gothic encounter, an erotic assignation to which Shakespeare keeps returning, as when Romeo glimpses Juliet's catatonic body in the tomb and exclaims: 'Death, that hath sucked the honey of thy breath, / Hath no power yet upon thy beauty' (*Romeo* 5.3.92). Plans to equip morgues with alarms, refrigerators that open from *inside*, or coffins with phones, after reports of unfortunates screaming to be let out, explain the perennial power of this scene, as do its innumerable cinematic rewrites, such as the chilling 1988 Dutch film directed by George Sluizer, *The Vanishing*. And the uncanny interim of Juliet's cataleptic trance 'in the borrowed likeness of shrunk death' (4.1.104) would in fact become a favourite of the eighteenth-century stage, which 'capitalized blatantly' on its 'necrophilic tinge' by inventing an operatic funeral cortège 'in which Juliet's inert body, surrounded by mourners, torchbearers and musicians, made its slow way to the vault in a long drawn-out procession' (Shapira 146–8). As Jonathan Sawday points out, within the cultural matrix of early modern theatre there was in fact something peculiarly apposite about David Garrick's presentation of *Romeo and Juliet* on alternate nights with Edward Ravenscroft's grotesque farce *The Anatomist*:

> It was the macabre presence on stage of a corpse that comes to life and protests against its own anatomization, which drew the audience ... Here an unlikely conjunction of dramatic texts becomes significant ... *Othello, The Winter's Tale, Pericles* and, above all, *Romeo and Juliet*, were plays

which featured the revivification of female figures, as though death was to be understood, in some measure, as a liminal state. (45)

When Paulina solemnly declares Hermione dead, yet then challenges Leontes to think her body moves, 'it breathed, and that those veins / Did verily bear blood' (5.3.63–4), Shakespeare has constructed a reversible plot logic that reflects 'the unstable truth of "death"' in early modern medical discourses about hysterical disorders, as feminist critics have emphasized (Peterson 169 and passim). But on Shakespeare's stage the woman's suspended catatonic body is also what it will become in Gothic fiction, 'an idealized spectacle of female beauty, the focus of a desire which manifests itself in necrophilous jealousy' (Sawday 46). 'O son, the night before thy wedding day / Hath death lain with thy wife', Capulet therefore announces (4.4.62). As *Romeo and Juliet* thereby suggests, and *The Winter's Tale* confirms, the 'madman's dream' of the beautiful insentient woman held captive as a living corpse by an all-powerful male in the 'foul gap' of some underground chamber of horrors, like Persephone imprisoned by Hades, was 'a canny exposure of an anxious erotic fantasy already contained' (Shapira 146) within the Shakespearean text:

> Why art thou yet so fair? Shall I believe
> That unsubstantial death is amorous,
> And that the lean abhorred monster keeps
> Thee here in dark to be his paramour?
>
> (*Romeo* 5.3.201–5)

'*We have put her living in the tomb!* Said I not that my senses were acute? I *now* tell you that I first heard her feeble movements in the hollow coffin many, many days ago': the 'hideous import' of premature burial that resonates in Roderick Usher's 'gibbering murmur' (64) in Edgar Allan Poe's archetypal Gothic tale 'The Fall of the House of Usher' casts lurid retrospective light on the compulsive repetition of the same fantasy in Shakespeare. Thus, if a secret subtext of *The Winter's Tale* is the charnel horror of the return from the grave, this story has a darker encrypted implication, made unavoidable by reference to the flowers 'frighted' Persephone let 'fall / From Dis's wagon' woven into wreaths to 'strew o'er and o'er' one posing 'like a corpse' (4.4.117–29). 'As for *maman's* death', reflected Roland Barthes in his *Mourning Diary*, 'the certainty of having to die *by the same logic* soothed me' (206). And, 'What can one desire of a coffin if not to have it for one's own, to put oneself inside', mused Derrida ('Cartouches' 191). But no theorist quite prepares us for the cryptomimetic syncopation of Perdita and Florizel *playing dead* at the feast in *The Winter's Tale*, one of the most *unheimlich* episodes in all Shakespeare, as they imagine suffocation by the 'freshest things' dropped by the girl entombed in hell. 'The year growing ancient' (79), these flowers are themselves long 'made stale'. So Freud's explanation of the 'lasciviousness' of such fantasies of what 'the close earth wombs' (478), as memories of life before birth when 'the child was prisoner to womb' (2.2.62), does nothing to lessen the untimeliness of this playing possum to 'leave the growth untried' and pre-empt what, in his essay on the uncanny, the psychoanalyst called 'the most uncanny thing of all' (244), the anachronism of being buried alive:

> ... that you might ever do
> Nothing but that, move still, still so,
> And own no other function.
>
> (4.4.141–3)

'Saints do not move, though grant for prayer's sake' (*Romeo* 1.5.102): as Derrida saw, Juliet initiates an entire dramaturgy of anachronistic *contretemps* when to indulge her lover she tempts fate playing the 'marble statue in pure gold' (5.3.298) she becomes in the end (cf. 'Aphorisms Countertime'). Through the strange chiasmic countertime of *The Winter's Tale* the statue made by Romeo and Juliet will therefore be reversed in the living sculpture of Hermione created to 'move still, still so' by Giulio Romano (5.2.88). Philippe Ariès dated this fascination with post-mortem reversibility precisely to the era of these plays, when determination of the hour of our death first started to be unsettled in both the baroque playhouse and anatomy theatre (cf. 396–406). So though Paulina assures us there is neither 'tincture' nor 'lustre in her lip, her eye', when Hermione's body is examined, Poe's scientism throws doubt on any such diagnostic confidence about the borderline between apparent death and the living dead, for 'Who shall say where the one ends, and where the other begins?' he reasons, when 'We know there are diseases in which occur total cessations of all the apparent functions of vitality, and in which these cessations are merely suspensions ... temporary pauses in the incomprehensible mechanism'. With its suggestion of an automaton, Poe's scenario in his tale 'The Premature Burial', where 'A certain period elapses, and some unseen mysterious principle sets in motion the magic pinions and the wizard wheels' (301), provides an uncomfortable gloss on the denouement of *The Winter's Tale*, in which Hermione emerges from just such catatonia. For it forces us to speculate how Shakespeare's heroine has spent the 'many, many days' during the strange dormancy of 'that wide gap' of her vanishing; and to register the 'hideous import' of some untimely awakening 'as in a vault', like that death before life Juliet poleptically foresees for herself in the 'ancient receptacle / Where for many hundreds of years the bones / Of all my buried ancestors are packed':

> How, if I wake before the time that Romeo
> Comes to redeem me? There's a fearful point ...
> Alack, alack, is it not like that I,
> So early waking – what with loathsome smells,
> And shrieks like mandrakes torn out of the earth,
> That living mortals, hearing them, run mad ...
> O, if I wake, shall I not be distraught ... ?
>
> (*Romeo* 4.3.30–47)

The 'horrible conceit of death and night' (36) in Juliet's prevision of her own tomb allows us to stare back into the miasmic underworld which in *The Winter's Tale* Hermione will be spared, and that the play will 'slide o'er' with all its folksy homeliness. It also suggests the deep subterranean affinity between Shakespearean and Gothic narrative, especially the stories of Poe, which are also framed by the figure of perverse Time, armed, in 'The Pit and the Pendulum', with a descending blade of steel. Thus, 'Publish it that she is dead indeed", schemes the Friar in *Much Ado About Nothing*, after Hero faints like Hermione, accused of sexual infidelity: 'Maintain a mourning ostentation, / And on your family's old monument / Hang mournful epitaphs' (4.1.203–6). Likewise, her end is 'confirmed by the rector of the place' when in *All's Well That Ends Well* Helen reportedly dies on pilgrimage to Compostella (4.3.55); and in *Pericles* Diana's temple is 'Where till your date expire you may abide', Thaisa is surprisingly told no sooner than Cerimon has diagnosed her symptoms as those of hysterical syncope and proves 'This queen will live ... She hath not been entranced / Above five hours' (13.90–2; 14.13).

The 'moated grange' in which the 'dejected Mariana' hides from the world in *Measure for Measure* (3.1.254) seems only a variant on 'the figure of mortified virtue encrypted in the condition of the coma' (Lupton 178), and male habitation over her seemingly dead body, which thus recurs in all Shakespeare's later comedies, and will see a catatonic Innogen laid 'stark' dead in *Cymbeline* beside a headless corpse (4.2.210). It is easy to see how Poe's fantasia of the catalepsy that entombs Madeline Usher with 'a mockery of a faint blush upon the bosom and the face, and that suspiciously lingering smile upon the lip which is so terrible in death', might therefore have been inspired by immersion in Shakespeare's plays as much as in scientific journals. The American writer – named by his actress mother after Edgar in *King Lear* – would share with the Warwickshire one 'a similar ambivalence concerning subjective and objective phenomena', fascination with 'representation's capacity to reverse the relationship of life and death' and capacity to realize the proximity of the *unheimlich* and the *heimlich* in what Fred Botting calls the 'Homely Gothic' (122). And, according to his biographers, Poe's hair-raising tale of the woman heard breaking open her coffin lid, grappling with 'the iron hinges of her prison' ('Usher' 60), and then scratching 'within the coppered archway of her vault' (65), had its traumatic Shakespearean origin in an actual childhood visit to Stratford-upon-Avon.

The haunted house

In the late summer of 1817 Edgar Allan Poe's family lodged in Cheltenham, while his adoptive mother took the spa waters, and it was from there Edgar is supposed to have visited the site of a house in Stratford that furnished the impressionable eight-year-old with nightmarish information for 'The Fall of the House of Usher'. Built beside a church, on a street then called Dead Lane, the imposing town house of the once wealthy Clopton family had acquired an evil reputation after the dreadful events of 1564, the year of Shakespeare's birth, when Stratford's chief Catholic dynasty had been nearly extinguished by a string of disasters which began when the deranged Margaret drowned herself for love, floating dementedly down the Avon, it is said, like Ophelia, as she 'chanted snatches of old tunes, / As one incapable of her own distress', before 'the poor wretch' was pulled 'to muddy death' (*Hamlet* 4.7.146–54). Critics believe the dispute in *Hamlet* about whether the suicide should be granted only her 'virgin rites, / Her maiden strewments, and the bringing home / Of bell and burial', or a requiem mass, was shaped by memories of the hurried obsequies over the 'fair and unpolluted flesh' of this pathetic adolescent (5.1.214–22). Even more haunting, however, was the unspeakable fate of her sister Charlotte, who a few months later was struck down in an epidemic of the plague. For fear of infection, her abbreviated last rites were also conducted in unseemly haste:

> She was buried quickly in the family vault of Stratford church, but a month or so later this was re-opened (for yet another interment). Her coffin was found to be open, and her body discovered upright, leaning against the wall. She had been prematurely buried, and in her agony had bitten into her own arm. (Palmer 78)

A tale to make 'Your bedded hair, like life in excrements, / Start up and stand on end' (3.4.112), the story of the girl waking to a 'life in excrements' inside the Clopton vault became legendary in Stratford, and surely coloured Juliet's dread of waking in the tomb 'Environèd with all these hideous fears, / And madly play[ing] with my forefathers' joints' (*Romeo* 4.3.48–50). So it is tempting to picture the young Poe, like a reincarnated Mamillius, spooking his mother with this Gothic horror during the winter of 1817. If the boy did so he presumably continued the story, recounting how, after the shock of his sister's premature burial, the heir to the house of Clopton fled to Italy, allowing the family home to fall into the clutches of a ruthless property dealer by the name of Bott, whose crimes included poisoning his daughter to acquire her husband's estate. The murderer hid the arsenic under the dining room floor, but the deed was hushed up, as the Clopton owners would have lost the place to the Crown if Bott were hanged. So it was that this house of whispered secrets and hidden horrors was occupied by the killer thirty years later, when it passed to another dealer, with the unlucky name of Underhill, who had not quite exchanged contracts to sell when in July 1597 he too fell victim to poison, slain by his son. Technically, the building did now belong to the Crown; but eventually the buyer was able to establish his title, and could then dwell, if he chose, by Stratford's Gild Chapel for the rest of his life. To Poe that outcome might well have seemed truly uncanny, for this latest owner of New Place, the house on Dead Lane said to have ushered 'The Fall of the House of Usher', was Shakespeare himself.

'There was a man … Dwelt by a churchyard': as his biographer observes, in purchasing Stratford's grandest house cut-price Shakespeare 'got in the strange bargain a father's murder of a daughter, and the murder of a father by a son … the raw, primitive theme of family murder' (Honan 238) that he worked into the play he gave a name like that of his own young son Hamnet, who died on the eve of the sale. He also acquired those Gothic tales of watery suicide and premature burial, and the accursed legacy of ancestral owners who had striven with their complex transactions to save the inheritance, and whose descendants would, in fact, in a few generations regain the estate. We do not know what New Place looked like, as a later owner, oppressed by its unlucky history, had it demolished in 1759. Ongoing excavations have yet to yield evidence from its extensive cellars and foundations; but if ever a house deserved to be called haunted, it was the one with the unlikely utopian name Shakespeare bought. It may be no surprise, then, that the busy London playwright chose not to take up residence in his Stratford home for some sixteen years: until the time of *The Winter's Tale*. What biographers do find strange and psychologically intriguing is that it was in this cavernous mansion with the calamitous past that for all those years Shakespeare left his wife Anne immured by herself.

'I thought she had some great matter there in hand, for she hath privately, twice or thrice a day, ever since the death of Hermione, visited that removed house' (5.2.94–5): his wife's lonely sequestration makes Leontes disturbingly analogous to his creator, at this time when Shakespeare 'dwelt by a churchyard'. So, whether or not this 'great *mater*' is another allusion to the 'mother', Paulina's transposition of 'The chapel where they lie' within the family vault into a sculpture 'gallery' kept 'Lonely, apart' (5.3.18) inside a 'removed house' would seem to involve a Piranesian architecture that fulfils the occulting functions of the crypt as what Derrida calls 'a place *comprehended* within another but rigorously separate from it, isolated from the general space by partitions, an enclosure, an enclave, a *safe*: sealed, and thus internal to itself, a secret interior within the public square, but outside it, external to the interior' ('Fors' xiv). Yet when she leads the royal party into this occluded space, the revelation that it slides back into a 'chapel' is sure to cue 'more amazement' (86). For 'The statue of our queen', with 'life as lively mocked as ever / Still sleep mocked death' (10–20), stands within the secret chamber as a double of all those 'waxwork figures, ingeniously constructed dolls and automata' ('Uncanny' 226) of the Gothic imagination from which Freud was as anxious to keep distance as Paulina is to avert suspicions of necromancy, lest 'you'll think – / Which I protest against – I am assisted / By wicked powers' (89–91). 'Do not shun her / Until you see her die again, for then / You kill her double' (5.3.105–6), Paulina therefore says, foreseeing repugnance at a living corpse. So, no wonder this 'thinglike character' seems 'strange, *daemonie*' (Lupton 178). For if the abjection and exclusion of the disgusting is constitutive of the Gothic aesthetic, the terms with which its Frankenstein-like controller summons the creature back from what she expressly terms its empty 'grave' seem intended to raise ghosts:

> Come,
> I'll fill your grave up. Stir. Nay, come away.
> Bequeath to death your numbness, for from him
> Dear life redeems you.
>
> (5.3.100–2)

The redemptive language of *The Winter's Tale* invokes the only joyous return from that graveyard where 'Stones have been known to move': the resurrection of Jesus Christ. Paulina's insistence that the actions of the strangely disconnected or 'undead' revenant who is rehabilitated in the countertime of Hermione's funerary monument 'shall be as holy as / You hear my spell is lawful' (104–5) thereby seems to enact the cryptomimetic strategy of Shakespearean theatre itself, as it represses a dark hypothesis 'more monstrous standing by': that the dead who 'burst their cerements' might 'on this stage / Where we offenders mourn, appear soul-vexed'. 'Graves at my command / Have waked their sleepers, oped, and let 'em forth / By my so potent art', confesses the man of theatre, Prospero; and Shakespeare's entire career has been interpreted as an apology for the 'rough magic' of such a Faustian disruption of temporal order (*The Tempest* 5.1.48–50). Thus, 'Impute it not a crime', pleads Time (4.1.4), that the play is the transcription of an event yet to take place which both buries and exhumes; and 'If we shadows have offended, / Think but this', the actors plead, 'That you have but slumbered' (*A Midsummer Night's Dream* Epi.1–3) during the 'wide gap' of their vanishing. 'Nay, present your hand' (5.3.107), Paulina therefore rebukes Leontes. But 'the best in this kind are but shadows' (*Dream* 5.1.208); and when the panels slid back and 'the enshrouded figure of the lady Madeline' rose before Roderick Usher in Poe's version, we shudder to recall, she fell on him 'with a low moaning cry', and 'bore him to the floor a corpse, and a victim to the terrors he had anticipated' ('Usher' 65). So in *The Winter's Tale*, when the statue begins to move 'As walked (the) first queen's ghost' (5.1.80), the gaping grave it leaves can, if considered, only prompt the question: What returns from this 'wide gap'? And the most Gothic of responses: that whatever the thing is, that has arisen out of this 'foul gap' … '*It's alive!*'

Notes

1 An earlier version of this chapter originally appeared in *Sillages critiques* 13 (2011): 1–15.
2 My reading of Shakespeare's Gothic affinity is indebted throughout to this brilliant interpretation of the Gothic elements in Derrida's philosophy.
3 For 'hauntology' as opposed to ontology, see Derrida, *Specters* 10.

Works cited

Ariès, Philippe. *The Hour of Our Death*. Trans. Helen Weaver. New York: Alfred Knopf, 1981.

Barthes, Roland. *Mourning Diary*. Trans. Richard Howard. London: Notting Hill Publications, 2011.

Bataille, Georges. *Eroticism: Death and Sensuality*. Trans. Mary Dalwood. San Francisco: City Lights Books, 1986.

Blanchot, Maurice. 'Literature and the Right to Death'. *The Gaze of Orpheus*. Trans. Lydia Davis. Barrytown, NY: Station Hill, 1981.

Botting, Fred. *Gothic*. London: Routledge, 1996.

Carroll, Noël. *The Philosophy of Horror, or Paradoxes of the Heart*. London: Routledge, 1990.

Castricano, Jodey. *Cryptomimesis: The Gothic and Jacques Derrida's Ghost Writing*. Montreal: McGill-Queen's University Press, 2001.

Creed, Barbara. *The Monstrous Feminine: Film, Feminism, Psychoanalysis*. London: Routledge, 1993.

Derrida, Jacques. *Athens, Still Remains: The Photographs of Jean-François*

Bonhomme. Trans. Pascale-Anne Brault and Michael Naas. New York: Fordham University Press, 2010.

—. 'Aphorisms Countertime'. *Acts of Literature*. Trans. Derek Attridge. London: Routledge, 1994. 414–33.

—. *Specters of Marx: The State of the Debt, the Work of Mourning, and the New International*. Trans. Peggy Kamuf. London: Routledge, 1994.

—. 'Living-On: Border Lines'. *A Derrida Reader: Between the Blinds*. Ed. Peggy Kamuf. New York: Columbia University Press, 1991. 254–68.

—. 'Cartouches'. *The Truth of Painting*. Trans. Geoffrey Bennington and Ian McLeod. Chicago: University of Chicago Press, 1987. 183–253.

—. '*Fors*: The Anglish Words of Nicholas Abraham and Maria Torok'. Trans. Barbara Johnson. *The Wolf Man's Magic Word: A Cryptomyny*. Eds Nicholas Abraham and Maria Rook. Minneapolis: Minnesota University Press, 1986. xi–xlviii.

—. *The Ear of the Other: Otobiography, Transference, Translation*. Trans. Peggy Kamuf. New York: Schocken, 1985.

Desmet, Christy and Anne Williams. 'Introduction'. *Shakespearean Gothic*. Eds Christy Desmet and Anne Williams. Cardiff: University of Wales Press, 2009. 1–13.

Freud, Sigmund. 'Mourning and Melancholia'. *The Complete Works of Sigmund Freud*. Trans. James Strachey. Vol. 14. London: Hogarth Press, 1957.

—. 'The Uncanny'. *The Complete Works of Sigmund Freud*. Trans. James Strachey. Vol. 17. London: Hogarth Press, 1957.

Gaston, Sean. '*Enter* Time'. *Starting With Derrida*. London: Continuum, 2007. 60–80.

Heidegger, Martin. 'Poetically Man Dwells'. *Poetry, Language, Thought*. Trans. Albert Hofstadter. New York: Harper & Row 1971. 213–29.

Honan, Park. *William Shakespeare: A Life*. Oxford: Oxford University Press, 1999.

Kristeva, Julia. *Powers of Horror: An Essay on Abjection*. Trans. Leon Roudiez. New York: Columbia University Press, 1982.

Lupton, Julia. *Thinking With Shakespeare: Essays on Politics and Life*. Chicago: Chicago University Press, 2011.

Palmer, Roy. *The Folklore of Warwickshire*. London: Batsford, 1976.

Peterson, Kaara. *Popular Medicine, Hysterical Disease, and Social Controversy in Shakespeare's England*. Farnham: Ashgate, 2010.

Poe, Edgar Allan. 'The Premature Burial'. *The Complete Tales of Edgar Allan Poe*. London: Cosimo, 2009.

—. 'The Fall of the House of Usher'. *Selected Tales*. Ed. David Van Leer. Oxford: Oxford University Press, 2003.

Royle, Nicholas. *The Uncanny*. Manchester: Manchester University Press, 2003.

Sawday, Jonathan. *The Body Emblazoned: Dissection and the human body in Renaissance Culture*. London: Routledge, 1995.

Schor, Esther. *Bearing the Dead: The British Culture of Mourning from the Enlightenment to Victoria*. Princeton: Princeton University Press, 1994.

Shakespeare, William. *A Winter's Tale. The Norton Shakespeare*. Eds Stephen

Greenblatt, Walter Cohen, Jean Howard, and Katharine Eisaman Maus. New York: Norton, 2007.

—. *Hamlet. The Norton Shakespeare*. Eds Stephen Greenblatt, Walter Cohen, Jean Howard, and Katharine Eisaman Maus. New York: Norton, 2007.

—. *King Lear. The Norton Shakespeare*. Eds Stephen Greenblatt, Walter Cohen, Jean Howard, and Katharine Eisaman Maus. New York: Norton, 2007.

—. *Macbeth. The Norton Shakespeare*. Eds Stephen Greenblatt, Walter Cohen, Jean Howard, and Katharine Eisaman Maus. New York: Norton, 2007.

—. *Othello. The Norton Shakespeare*. Eds Stephen Greenblatt, Walter Cohen, Jean Howard, and Katharine Eisaman Maus. New York: Norton, 2007.

—. *Romeo and Juliet. The Norton Shakespeare*. Eds Stephen Greenblatt, Walter Cohen, Jean Howard, and Katharine Eisaman Maus. New York: Norton, 2007.

—. *Sonnets. The Norton Shakespeare*. Eds Stephen Greenblatt, Walter Cohen, Jean Howard, and Katharine Eisaman Maus. New York: Norton, 2007.

Shapira, Yael. 'Into the Madman's Dream: The Gothic Abduction of *Romeo and Juliet*'. *Shakespearean Gothic*. Eds Christy Desmet and Anne Williams. Cardiff: University of Wales Press, 2009.

Wigley, Mark. *The Architecture of Deconstruction: Derrida's Haunt*. Cambridge, MA: MIT Press, 1993.

Williams, Anne. *Art of Darkness: A Poetics of Gothic*. Chicago: University of Chicago, 1995.

Žižek, Slavoj. *Looking Awry: An Introduction to Jacques Lacan through Popular Culture*. Cambridge, MA: MIT Press, 1993.

12

Shakespeare, Ossian and the problem of 'Scottish Gothic'

Dale Townshend

There Shakespeare's self, with every garland crowned,
In musing hour his Wayward Sisters found,
   And with their terrors dressed the magic scene.
From them he sung, when mid his bold design,
   Before the Scot afflicted and aghast,
The shadowy kings of Banquo's fated line,
   Through the dark cave in gleamy pageant passed
Proceed, nor quit the tales which, simply told,
   Could once so well my answering bosom pierce ...

   From William Collins, 'An Ode on the Popular Superstitions of the
Highlands of Scotland, considered as the Subject of Poetry' (1749–50)

How many children had Lady Macbeth? Over one hundred years before
L. C. Knights made his facetious riposte to A. C. Bradley and the critical
modes of character analysis of which Bradley was the major exponent,
Mary Julia Young had negotiated the same question, albeit only momentarily and to less critical intent, in *Donalda; Or, The Witches of Glenshiel*,
a two-volume Gothic romance published by J. F. Hughes in London in
1805. Set in Scotland during the reign of King Malcolm, Young's narrative takes off where *Macbeth* ends, setting out to supplement Shakespeare's Scottish tragedy with a fiction that outlines the travails of the
heroine Donalda. Throughout, in fact, the events dramatized in *Macbeth*
constitute the novel's sense of the recent historical past: as even the villain
at one point notes, '"I wore that armour first when Malcolm, aided by
the English troops, invaded Dunsinane, and brave Macduff avenged his
own, and his *true* sovereign's wrongs, by piercing the usurper's cruel
heart"' (I: 223). A Gothic rendition of Shakespeare's play *Donalda*
certainly is, for, in the true spirit of the mode, Young's narrative plots
the course of its heroine through such harrowing experiences as repeated
exposure to the supernatural; the prohibition of her choices in romantic
love; at least three enforced marital alliances with men not of her own
desiring; and the ubiquitous threat of incestuous union.

Raised in a stately castle by the nefarious couple Lord Roderic and Lady Margaret Broomdale, Young's equivalents to the figures of Macbeth and Lady Macbeth, Donalda is made poignantly aware of her abject status as a foundling at Castle Broomdale from the start. Shortly after the action has commenced, the orphaned heroine is visited by the eponymous witches of Glenshiel, 'three terrific looking females' who are 'crowned with thistles' and transported in a bower-like chariot drawn by six large bats. 'Their large red eyes,' Young's description continues, 'glared horribly through their straight black hair that hung over their faces like a veil; they were each wrapped in a tartan plaid, and held a long black wand' (I: 8). Young's 'weird sisters of Glenshiel' (I: 166) put their powers of prescience to work exclusively in the support, encouragement and protection of the heroine, invariably appearing before her when her suffering is most extreme, and soothing her disordered sensibilities with lengthy, cryptic accounts of her past, present and future, all delivered, in unison, in narcotic rhyme. Promised by the witches of Glenshiel the eventual disclosure of her true familial origins, Donalda's imagination is for a moment horrifically captured by the possibility that she is none other than the daughter of Macbeth, the bloody assassin of Shakespeare's Scottish play: 'Who can I be? Not Macbeth's child, I hope! Oh, not that regicide's! If I am, let me not know it, gracious Heaven, lest I should think of Fife, and curse my father!' (I: 275). If only through the horrid phantasmatic imaginings that furnish her heroine's consciousness, Young's Gothic Shakespeare fills in the gaps, the vagaries and the inconsistencies of Shakespeare's play as if to provide, in anticipation, an answer to L. C. Knights's provocative question of so many years later: Lady Macbeth had at least one child, and Donalda was her name.

Predictably, the fantasy of Donalda's ignominious parentage is not long entertained before it is ruptured by the revelation of her true familial origins, revelations afforded, in characteristic fashion, by the guiding presence of the three witches. She is as relieved to discover that she is not the offspring of the regicidal Macbeth as she is to be freed of the unwanted passionate advances of Roderic, the Marquis of Broomdale, her erstwhile protector and symbolic father: 'Donalda felt herself quite relieved by the Marquis ceasing to be the lover, and likewise at the certainty of her not being the child of Macbeth, of whose cruelties she had heard so much, that she held his name in abhorrence' (II: 84). Instead, it is finally revealed that, as the daughter of the Earl of Glenshiel and the Princess Malcoma, Donalda is the granddaughter of King Malcolm, her parents having been killed, via an allusion to the scene of sibling rivalry in *Hamlet*, by her father's sister and brother-in-law, Margaret and Roderic. To the unwitting heroine, then, falls the obligation to revenge, the same redoubtable task faced by Shakespeare's Danish Prince: as her keeper in the Castle of Glenshiel puts it, 'thou hast been an instrument of vengeance in the hand of the Almighty – Yes, my child, thou hast been the innocent avenger of thy murdered parents!' (II: 230). Eventually restored to her royal lineage and inheritance, Donalda, the Flower of Yarrow, becomes the Duchess of Glenshiel, and is joined in matrimony to her hero Duncan, the Duke of Lochaber. Together, the couple takes up residence at the Castle of Glenshiel, at once supplementing the absences left there by the deaths of Donalda's parents. King Malcolm and Queen Margaret preside over the felicitous turn of events at the narrative's close as a warm and benevolent presence. Their restorative functions fulfilled, the witches make an appearance if only to bid Donalda their farewell, bestowing upon the happy couple no curse but a wish for future happiness and the promise of ongoing protection:

> Malcolm, hail! Hail, virtuous Queen!
> Few so good on earth are seen.
> Both the lures of vice disdain;
> Long and happy you shall reign.
> Royal bride, and noble youth,
> Heaven will bless your matchless truth,
> If dire Ambition never finds
> Harbour in your virtuous minds.
> ...
> For you shall be, O! favour'd pair!
> Still the Weird Sisters' care.
>
> (II: 308–9)

In *Donalda*, the felicitous endings attendant upon fictional romance are finally set in place as replacements for, and antidotes to, the violence, bloodshed and regicide of Shakespeare's Scottish play.

If Young's reworkings of *Macbeth* read like radical departures from the Shakespearean script, there is another, arguably more important aspect of the text that remains faithful to its source: Marquis Roderic of Broomdale, the villain of the piece, perceives spectres in ways identical to that of Macbeth. On hearing, in accordance with the witches' earlier prophesy, that he has been made Thane of Cawdor, Shakespeare's villain pre-emptively articulates, in an aside, a tendency towards spectral projection that will characterize his experience in the play from this moment onwards:

> I am Thane of Cawdor:
> If good, why do I yield to that suggestion
> Whose horrid image doth unfix my hair,
> And make my seated heart knock at my ribs,

> Against the use of nature? Present fears
> Are less than horrible imaginings.
> My thought, whose murther yet is but fantastical,
> Shakes so my single state of man,
> That function is smother'd in surmise,
> And nothing is, but what is not.
>
> (1.3.133–42)

As Macbeth's vision of the dagger in Act 2 scene 1 demonstrates, it is guilt that fuels and drives the process of hallucination in the play, whether spectral, visual, auditory or otherwise; as one of the 'horrible imaginings' referred to earlier, the dagger which Macbeth sees before his eyes is, in effect, 'A dagger of the mind, a false creation, / proceeding from the heat-oppressed brain' (2.1.38–9). But it is spectral hallucination in *Macbeth* that is the product of outwardly projected psychic guilt par excellence, and in Act 3 scene 4, the ghost of Banquo, invisible to all but the guilty Macbeth himself, enters the banqueting room to sit in Macbeth's place. Young's villain in *Donalda* is susceptible to the same disturbing visions, as the ghost of his murdered sister-in-law, Margaret, is envisioned by her murderer as entering the banqueting hall at the Castle of Broomdale in order to take up its place at the table:

> The gay appearance of the hall reminded him of former times, when it resounded with convivial mirth, and happiness enlivened his soul, which now felt appalled at the silent, cheerless pomp that reigned around him; the chair of state no longer appeared vacant – his disturbed fancy adorned it with the lovely Margaret, such as she was upon her bridal day, blooming in youthful charms and arrayed in splendour; his dark eyes beamed with a momentary delight, but in an instant the captivating vision faded away, and the ghastly form which had clasped him in its icy arms in the night, assumed the place, holding in its pallid hand a cup, from which he thought a wreath of faded roses fell, and the word poison, in flaming characters, glared in his eyes! (I: 186–7)

Though the effects of Roderic's ghostly hallucinations might be to 'harrow up the soul' (I: 210) in the manner of the ghost in *Hamlet*, they are, in each instance, direct replayings of the spectral episodes in *Macbeth*, and unseen, as such, by any other than the guilt-ridden villain himself. At times, Roderic's horrid symptoms combine those of Macbeth and his wife: at times as somnambulistic as Lady Macbeth, he is continuously plagued by the same 'terrible dreams' (3.2.18) as his masculine Shakespearean antecedent; the daggers of Macbeth and the bloodied hands of his wife combine in *Donalda* in the form of a blood-stained dagger that discloses Roderic's culpability in the murder or Donalda's parents (II: 12–3). During one particularly tense moment in the narrative, the

Witches of Glenshiel, like their Shakespearean originals in Act 4 scene i, summon up before the mind of the villain a ghastly pageant of spectres who chant 'Repent, repent, repent!' (II: 53) in an attempt at bringing his culpability to justice. Here too, the possibility remains that they are little more than external manifestations of Roderic's own psychic state. Through a direct appropriation of Shakespeare's *Macbeth*, ghost-seeing in Young's *Donalda* is the phantasmatic projection of a conscience that is riddled with guilt.

If this coupling of the 'Gothic' aesthetic with Shakespeare's 'Scottish play' in Mary Julia Young's *Donalda* implies an easy relation between them, it is important to acknowledge that the terms 'Scottish' and 'Gothic' had been inscribed in a complex relationship of tension, opposition and mutual antagonism in historical and political discourse from at least the end of the seventeenth century onwards. Sir William Temple's staunchly Whiggish *An Introduction to the History of England* (1695) would set in place a particular account of Scotland and its relations to the Gothic that would endure throughout much historiography of the eighteenth century: faced with the continuous onslaught of violence and aggression that hailed from the savage territories north of Hadrian's wall, the 'poor *Britains*' made an urgent appeal to the Goths, the erstwhile opponents of Rome, for assistance against the Scottish threat. Accepting the invitation of Vortigern, the elected British king, to enter the country, the Saxons, under the command of the brothers Hengist and Horsa, 'came over in great Numbers, to the Assistance of the Britains, in the year 450' (47–8). In subsequent years, further Gothic reinforcements would enter Britain with the arrival of the Angles and Jutes. In Temple's influential account, Gothic valour is pitted against Caledonian cruelty; from the outset, the Goths in Britain mobilize an energy that is distinctly anti-Scottish in nature.

While it is true that, following the Act of Union in 1707, exponents of what we have come to regard as the political 'myth' of Gothic origins made several concerted attempts at minimizing the perceived tensions between things 'Scottish' and 'Gothic' such as those set in place in Temple's *History*, accounts of the fundamental irreconcilability between the two terms persisted throughout the century, and well into the last three decades that witnessed the rise and consolidation of the Gothic aesthetic in the wake of *The Castle of Otranto* (1764).[1] Scottish poet and dramatist James Thomson, for instance, would drive a firm conceptual wedge between the Goths and the Celts, England and Scotland in his Whiggish paean to Gothic origins in the poem *Liberty* (1734). Here, the arrival of Gothic Liberty in Britain is figured as the dawn that interrupts the Celtic light: 'Now turn your view, and mark from Celtic night / To present grandeur how my Britain rose' (624–5). As it was for William Temple and several other historiographers, Gothic Liberty for Thomson is the imported antidote to Celtic violence. It soon becomes apparent that 'Gothic' as it is used in Thomson's poem is a synonym for things 'English', and 'English' coterminous with a restricted sense of Britishness that excludes Scotland.[2] So inveterate had this historiographic tendency become that David Hume in his six-volume tome *The History of Great Britain* (1754–62) set out not only to substantially revise commonplace perceptions of Gothic antiquity but also to reassess the position of Scotland in relation to the pervasive political mythology of Gothic origins. Refusing to celebrate the presence of the Saxons in Britain as the triumph of Gothic liberty over the violence of Caledonian aggression, Hume figures the Saxons as a race of bloodthirsty marauders, a nation of 'idolatrous ravagers' (14) who carved a path of slaughter and butchery as they processed. Hume seems equally opposed to the Whiggish tendency to ascribe the presence of political Liberty in Britain to the incoming Gothic tribes: far from embodying the principles of universal equality, Anglo-Saxon government in his account was invariably biased in favour of the interests of landed property. If the Anglo-Saxon period was to be perceived as an age of unprecedented political liberty at all, this liberty contained the seeds of its own downfall: an excess of freedom, Hume argues, leads invariably back to the very cause of subjection itself.

Shakespeare, England's national 'Bard', was controversially enlisted in the task of retelling the English nation's Gothic origins with the staging of *Vortigern: An Historical tragedy, in Five Acts* at Drury Lane on Saturday 2 April 1796. Purportedly a 'lost' Shakespearean play serendipitously 'discovered' by the young London-based man of letters, W. H. Ireland, the play was soon revealed to be an act of modern counterfeiting. The controversies that ensued following the exposure of Ireland's sacrosanct forgery have been outlined at length by critics such as Paul Baines, Jeffrey Kahan and Robert Miles. As Gamer and Miles have recently argued, *Vortigern* constitutes one particular moment in the literary history of the late eighteenth century in which the term 'Gothic Shakespeare' seems most appropriate: the tragedy claims to recount the arrival of the Saxons or 'Goths' in England following the appeal to them made by Vortigern, King of the Britons. Gamer and Miles have also argued that, in the context of its production, performance and eventual printing during the 1790s, the play might fruitfully be read in relation to the Jacobite threat to Hanoverian politics in the period (see Gamer and Miles). When situated in relation to eighteenth-century historiography, though, what is equally resonant are the broader comments on Scotland's relationship to the Saxon or 'Gothic' spirit that the play details, its stance on antique historical relations which predate the Jacobite uprisings of 1715 and 1745 by over a thousand years. Ireland's historical vision is not unlike that of David Hume, for the King Vortigern, far from being the celebrated King of British antiquity, is an ambitious and tyrannous anti-hero who is only narrowly afforded tragic stature in the play's closing scenes. Rewarded with a form of sovereign power-sharing when Constantius, Roman leader in Britain, devolves half of his authority to him as reward for his valiant military service, Vortigern immediately articulates the ambitions of a Macbeth or a Brutus: 'what! Jointly wear the crown? No! I will all!' (1.1). Proceeding, like Macbeth, to eradicate the king, Vortigern is plagued by visions of spectres immediately following Constantius's demise:

> O! This preposterous and inhuman act,
> Doth stir up pity in the blackest hell.
> Heav'n's aspect did foretell some ill this night,
> For each dread shrieking minister of darkness,
> Did chatter forth his rude and dismal song,
> While bellowing thunder shook the troubled earth,
> And the livid, and flaky [flame-like] lightning,
> Widely burst ope each crack in Heav'n's high portal.
>
> (1.5)

As in *Macbeth*, ghosts are the projections of a guilty mind. Vortigern exploits the anti-Scottish sentiments of his people in order to frame the Scots as Constantius's murderers. However, when he appeals to the Roman Aurelius for assistance against the Scots, his anti-Scottishness is disclosed for what it is – a ruse designed to conceal his own culpability. As the Rome-bound messenger observes to Aurelius, the elder son of Constantius,

> Know, Vortigern did alway [*sic*] hate the Scots,
> And hath oft times during your father's reign,
> Fram'd laws, most burdensome unto that people,
> But keen tooth of hatred and revenge,
> With double fury now will shew itself;
> For every noble Scot then found in London,
> Hath suffer'd under this fell tiger's fangs,
> And this to direst rage, hath stirr'd their blood.
>
> (2.2)

Ignoring Vortigern's false plea for enforcement, Aurelius and his brother Uter depart for Scotland, and plan an attack on the Britons residing there. By this stage of the action, the play has already generated a number of anti-British sentiments, for not only is Vortigern revealed to be a power-hungry tyrant but he has also threatened to coerce his daughter into a politically expedient alliance, despite her love for Aurelius. In fact, Vortigern rapidly assumes decidedly Gothic villainous characteristics, particularly through the intimations of his incestuous attraction to his own daughter: in the Preface to the printed version of the play, the editor notes how the king's incestuous desire for Flavia had been omitted from the text, being 'thought too gross for the public ear' (6). Faced with the threat of a Roman/Scottish alliance, Vortigern makes his famous appeal to Saxon assistance: 'Then 'twere policy / That we should court the Saxons to our aid' (3.1). But whereas, in a number of formal histories of the period, this moment had been positively heralded as the arrival of the Enlightened Goth on British soil, the Saxon brothers Hengist and Horsus [*sic*] in *Vortigern* do not represent a salutary alternative to the cycle of Scottish violence so much as an extension of Vortigern's desperate villainy. In each scene of military clash between the Saxons and the Aurelius-led Scots in Act 4, support lies clearly with the latter. When Hengist presents his daughter Rowena to Vortigern, Vortigern's desire to annul his marriage to his queen Edmunda so as to marry Rowena reads as a version of Manfred's designs to divorce Hippolita for the sake of marriage to Isabella in Walpole's *The Castle of Otranto* (1764). Vortigern's disingenuous appeal to divine principles in order to justify his disregard for marital law is a chilling echo of Manfred's fabrication of an incestuous bond between himself and his wife: 'True, I am married, and my wife doth live, / Yet none methinks by law can here be bound / When the dread wrath of Heav'n doth show itself, / And on his wedded wife doth send down madness' (4.4). In this way, the anti-Scottishness mobilized by Vortigern and his Gothic counterparts exists on the same plane as Vortigern's bigamous and incestuous desire; the very presence of the Goths in England is figured as a last-ditch attempt on behalf of a villainous ruler to secure his arbitrary and illegitimate power. The point is underscored when Rowena subsequently commits suicide. As Aurelius observes, 'Then hath a wicked soul taken its flight / From the most lovely frame that e'er was form'd / To charm or to deceive' (5.1). As in Hume, the alliance between the Britons and the Goths represented by the problematic relationship between Vortigern and the deceivingly beautiful Rowena is sustained only by the superficial attractions of private, sentimental romance. Vortigern is little more than a tyrant, the Goths nothing more than his ineffectual supporters. When, in the final scene, Aurelius is crowned King of Britain, he, his Scottish supporters and Flavia his queen have vanquished the chaos and disorder of Vortigern and the Goths; Aurelius desists from assassinating the tragic hero only for the sake of his love for his daughter. If *Vortigern* reads as a particularly subversive retelling of received historical narratives, it is something of which the Fool, in his closing speech, is particularly aware (5.4). Like Hume, Ireland in *Vortigern* has taken considerable liberties not only with Holinshed but with received accounts of the relationship between Scotland and the Goths from the end of the seventeenth century onwards.

Indeed, the only constant that was sounded in historiography of the period is that Scotland's political and historical relationship to things 'Gothic' was a vexed and complicated issue. It was precisely into this dark historical vacuum that James Macpherson projected his own romance of Scottish antiquity, his vision of Celtic Scotland sketched out, via the apparent 'translations' of the third-century Celtic bard Ossian, between the publication of *Fragments of Ancient Poetry, Collected in the Highlands of Scotland, and translated from the Galic or Erse Language* in 1760, through *Fingal* (1761) and *Temora* (1763), and into *The Works of Ossian, The Son of Fingal* (1765).[3] Perhaps unsurprisingly, Macpherson's vision of a Celtic Scotland, advanced not only in the Ossian poems but in his historiographic endeavours in *An Introduction to the History of Great Britain and Ireland* (1771) too, soon became inscribed in a hotly contested debate over the ancient origins of the Scottish nation, and one in which the term 'Gothic' featured significantly. Prominent Scottish historian John Pinkerton had made a significant contribution to eighteenth-century accounts of the ancient Gothic people in *A Dissertation on the Origin and Progress of the Scythians or Goths ...* (1787). Though Pinkerton would subsequently publish a substantial two-volume tome entirely devoted to the matter of Scottish antiquity in *An Enquiry Into the History of Scotland, Preceding the Reign of Malcolm III ...* in 1789, his interest in the historical origins of his native Scotland is disclosed even in the Preface to his earlier work. The Picts of Caledonia, Pinkerton here defiantly argues, are of German or Scythian origins: 'Being occupied with a most laborious research into the history of Scotland, preceding the year 1056, the author found it incontrovertibly settled from Tacitus, Beda, and the whole ancient accounts, that the *Caledonii* or *Picti*, the ancient and still chief inhabitants of that country, came to it from German Scythia, or Scandinavia' (iii). Contrary to the claims of Macpherson, Scotland, for Pinkerton, was of Gothic rather than Celtic extraction, not least of all in the Highlands of the country, the very locale in which Macpherson had identified traces of the ancient Celtic culture and language in its purest, most unsullied of forms (67). Pinkerton's philological endeavour, of course, is driven by certain vested political interests, for to identify the traces of the Gothic language in

Scotland is simultaneously to 'discover' there, via the people that spoke it, the archaic remains of the political myth of the Enlightened Goth. While it is easy to dismiss Pinkerton as a rabid eccentric, the labours and the forgeries of whom went entirely unnoticed, the very existence of his reservations points to the fact that, for the late eighteenth century, Scotland's ancient Celtic origins were taken as anything but undisputed historical fact. Coming towards the end of a century-long historiographical tradition in which Scottish antiquity was in continuous dispute, Pinkerton's *Dissertation* and *Enquiry* throw into relief, and render legible, the tensions between a Gothic Scotland, on the one hand, and a Celtic Scotland, on the other. Though literary scholarship in recent years has frequently invoked a notion of 'Scottish Gothic' as a critical term descriptive of a certain strain in the national literary canon, the term anachronistically occludes awareness of the real disputes in which Scotland's political and historical relation to the ancient Gothic past was inscribed.

This is not to suggest, against the claim of critics such as Ian Duncan (see 'Walter Scott, James Hogg and Scottish Gothic') and Angela Wright, that there is not a distinctive strand of the grotesque, the uncanny and the supernatural in Scottish fiction of the late eighteenth and early nineteenth centuries. Indeed, even a cursory glance at the work of Walter Scott and James Hogg, as well as some of the best-known poems by Robert Burns, suggests the very opposite. In this regard, the work of Fiona Robertson, Ian Duncan and Michael Gamer has gone a long way towards reversing received critical accounts of Scott's apparent 'distaste' for Gothic romance by detailing his extensive engagement with the thematic, formal and authorial conventions of the mode, both across his fictional oeuvre and in aspects of his literary criticism.[4] But it is to temper the application of the term 'Gothic' to Scottish culture in the late eighteenth and early nineteenth centuries with a greater sensitivity to political history of the period, taking care to differentiate between the political and the aesthetic implications of the term as well as acknowledging the complex relationship between them. As Alfred E. Longueil has cautioned, 'Gothic' as a critical byword for the grotesque, the ghastly, the uncanny and the supernatural strain in fiction is a category that might only anachronistically be applied to writing prior to the late 1790s in Britain, and this following a self-conscious act of metaphorical substitution: initially a signifier of things 'medieval', it was only later that the term assumed its modern, aesthetic meanings. Perhaps even greater caution should be exercised in the application of the term to a particularly Scottish context: occluding its anxious circulation in the historiographic disputes over the nature of

Scotland's past, 'Gothic' occludes a century-long legacy of heated political debate, and, as I shall argue below, one also played out between
Shakespeare and Ossian, the nations' respective poets. Crucial, too, is
the acknowledgement of the difference between the 'Gothic' elements
employed by early nineteenth-century Scottish writers such as Scott and
Hogg, and the ways in which Scotland, in the fashion of the opening
example of Young's *Donalda*, was figured, via Shakespeare's *Macbeth*,
as an aesthetically 'Gothic' locale in so many 'Caledonian', 'Scottish'
or 'Highland' tales and romances of the period, most of them written
and published in London by writers not necessarily of Scottish nation-
ality. Lacking in any clear and uncontroversial relation to the pervasive myth of Gothic antiquity – a national myth of origin that asserted
England's basis in the Enlightenment principles of equality, democracy
and liberty – Scotland became, in numerous late eighteenth- and early
nineteenth-century romances, subject to 'Gothic' uptake and treatment
in other senses of that word, a place of darkness, violence, superstition
and bloodshed.

Scotland in some senses was 'Gothic', that is, not through any
uncontested relation to the noble Gothic past but through the other
eighteenth-century connotations of the word: unenlightened, medieval,
barbaric and ineluctably other. This, certainly, was the representational
outcome of Dr Samuel Johnson's response to the Ossian debacle of
the 1760s: setting off in 1773 on a tour of parts of Scotland with his
younger Scottish friend and admirer James Boswell, Johnson recorded
his impression of Scotland and his responses to Macpherson's version of
its Ossianic past in *A Journey to the Western Islands of Scotland* (1775).
From the outset, Johnson's impressions are structured according to a
deep and underlying set of differences between the foreign territory, this
'unknown and untravelled wilderness' (61) in which he finds himself,
and his native England, a fundamental distinction that registers itself
as the political difference between 'non-Gothic' and 'Gothic' culture
respectively. In addressing the emigration of Scots from the Highlands
to parts of North America in the wake of the Highland clearances,
for instance, Johnson is led to compare unfavourably the Scots' fleeing
of this bare and deforested landscape to the legendary 'swarming' of
the Goths from the 'woods of Germany': in marked distinction to the
paucity of the Scottish diaspora, 'The Gothick swarms have at least been
multiplied with equal liberality' (104). If the Goths in Johnson's *Journey*
are tacitly figured as the harbingers of light, reason, civilization and
democracy, Scotland, summarily excluded by Johnson from this privileged political category, is a place of medieval savagery and darkness, a
land plagued by the internecine violence of the clan system, primitivism

and illiteracy, the vestiges of feudalism enshrined in Lairdship, and the persistence of popular superstitions, both Catholic and secular. But it is precisely this exclusion of Scotland from the category of political Gothicism that facilitates and informs his representation of the Scottish landscape, its histories and its peoples as a 'Gothic' space in the aesthetic sense of that term. With nothing but horror and terror reflected in the blankness of the natural world, the imagination of the English observer has no alternative but to be prompted to the ghostly, unrestrained imaginings of romance: 'The phantoms which haunt a desert are want, and misery, and danger; the evils of dereliction rush upon the thoughts' (61); 'These castles', he later continues, 'afford another evidence that the fictions of romantick chivalry had for their basis the real manners of the feudal times, when every lord of a seignory lived in his hold lawless and unaccountable, with all the licentiousness and insolence of uncontested superiority and unprincipled power' (146). Replete with roaring cataracts and ruined castles and abbeys, it is hardly surprising that 'a country of such gloomy desolation' (144) eventually comes to attest for Johnson not to the authenticity of Ossianic oral Celticism but to the truthful representations of English medieval or 'Gothick' romance:

> The fictions of the Gothick romances were not so remote from credibility as they are now thought. In the full prevalence of the feudal institution, when violence desolated the world, and every baron lived in a fortress, forests and castles were regularly succeeded by each other, and the adventurer might very suddenly pass from the gloom of woods, or the ruggedness of moors, to seats of plenty, gaiety, and magnificence. Whatever is imaged in the wildest tale, if giants, dragons, and enchantment be excepted, would be felt by him, who, wandering in the mountains without a guide, or upon the sea without a pilot, should be carried amidst his terror and uncertainty, to the hospitality and elegance of Raasay or Dunvegan. (88)

In the context of Johnson's *A Journey to the Western Islands of Scotland*, as in Young's *Donalda*, the category of 'Scottish Gothic' is a politically problematic one founded upon a self-consciously English disdain for its northern neighbour. Excluded from the myth of political Gothicism, Scotland becomes 'Gothic' in the negative, horror- and terror-inducing implications of that term.

Sir Walter Scott would address his native Scotland's complex relations to the Gothic in both the political and aesthetic implications of that term in *The Antiquary* (1816). During an early episode in the narrative in which Jonathan Oldbuck, Sir Arthur Wardour and William Lovel are all present, the conversation veers inexorably towards the controversial topic of Scottish antiquity. In keeping with his Protestantism, his Whiggish politics and his indefatigable interest in the remains of the Anglo-Saxon past, Jonathan Oldbuck, the eponymous antiquary, advocates and represents a Gothic Scotland, his friend, the Catholic and notionally Jacobite Sir Arthur Wardour, a Celtic Scotland. While Oldbuck remains sceptical and forthrightly damning of the authenticity of Ossian throughout, Sir Arthur regards Pinkerton as having impugned 'the ancient and trust-worthy authorities, upon which, as upon venerable and moss-grown pillars, the credit of Scottish antiquities reposed' (225). In defence of his claims to a Gothic Scotland, Oldbuck marshals the work of John Pinkerton, Alexander Gordon and Thomas Innes; counteracting him by turn, Sir Arthur cites the alternative versions of Scottish antiquity told by George Chalmers, Robert Sibbald and Joseph Ritson. Though the conflict between a Gothic and a Celtic Scotland plays itself out even towards the narrative's end, it is ultimately the historical claims of Oldbuck, Pinkerton and their school that are defended in Scott's novel. Though he by no means escapes Scott's satirical gestures, Oldbuck is sympathetically treated throughout, and, while he maintains his Gothic historicist stance and Whiggish political position to the end, Wardour, his Jacobite convictions a spectral 'shadow of a shade' (63) from the outset, is ruined by debt and the machinations of the German villain Dousterswivel.

Still, the vision of an Enlightened, Protestant Gothic Scotland ultimately set in place in the figure of Lovel and his restored Glenallan dynasty at the end of *The Antiquary* has not been achieved without a struggle. Seemingly in acknowledgement of the political problems encountered in fictional representations of Scotland as a dark and benighted nation, Walter Scott's vision of a legitimate, politically enlightened 'Gothic' Scotland at the end of *The Antiquary* is contingent upon the careful exclusion of the Gothic as an aesthetic mode. Scott's narrative up to this point has negotiated at least three possible sites of terror. In the first of these, Lovel is required to spend a night in the Green Chamber at Monkbarns, an apartment in Oldbuck's house that is supposedly haunted by the ghost of Aldobrand Oldenbuck, Monkbarns's original proprietor. Momentarily relocating Radcliffe's Castle of Udolpho to Scotland, Oldbuck, in a moment of well-meaning nationalistic pride, claims that 'every mansion in this country of the slightest antiquity has its ghosts and its haunted chamber, and you must not suppose us worse off than our neighbours' (89). However, this suggestion of a haunted Scotland is shortly thereafter dismissed when, upon spending the night in the apartment, Lovel is plagued not by the actual ghost of its former owner but only by a series of weird and unsettling dreams: 'He sate [*sic*] up in bed, and endeavoured to clear his brain of the phantoms which had disturbed it during this weary night' (101). A version of the 'explained supernatural', the very technique for which Scott, apropos of Radcliffe, had expressed his reservations in his review of Maturin's *Fatal Revenge* in 1810, is used to dispel all claims to a 'Gothic Scotland': the spectres that apparently haunt the nation's ancient mansions have no real existence outside of the minds of those who imagine them. In an equally pointed dismissal of Gothic-fictional convention towards the middle of the narrative, Edie Ochiltree returns by night with the German swindler, Dousterswivel, to the ruined Abbey of St Ruth. Already, the scene of dark architectural ruin is rich with the imaginative potential of Gothic romance, and it is not long before the two men witness before them the mirage of a candle-lit funeral replete with an open grave, a shrouded corpse, a Catholic priest dispensing Holy water and a crowd of solemn mourners dressed in sombre black. The effect of it all is nothing short of spectral: 'The smoky light from so many flambeaus, by the red and indistinct atmosphere which it spread around, gave a hazy, dubious, and, as it were, phantom-like appearance to the outlines of this singular apparition' (253). As Scott's narrator is keen to point out, though, such 'Gothic' perceptions of the Abbey are not appropriate responses to authentic experience so much as the suspicious and neurotic projections of Dousterswivel's decidedly Germanic way of seeing things: his is a mind 'stirred with all the German superstitions of nixies, oak-kings, wer-wolves [*sic*], hobgoblins, black spirits and white, blue spirits and grey' (252). What is momentarily conjured up as a scene of 'Scottish Gothic' in *The Antiquary* is rapidly dismissed as Scott's narrator, in keeping with much contemporary critical opinion, redirects the Gothic aesthetic away from Scotland to its apparent national sources and resources in the German *Schauerroman*. Skilfully invoking the Gothic mode in his gulling of the German swindler, Edie the quick-witted Scotsman has used the horrors and terrors of Dousterswivel's native country against him; as Oldbuck later tellingly confesses, '"I would have given a guinea ... to have seen the scoundrelly German under the agonies of those terrors, which it is part of his own quackery to inspire into others; and trembling alternately for the fury of his patron, and the apparition of some hobgoblin"' (418). In the third moment of Gothic-fictional potential in *The Antiquary*, Scott turns to address a historical issue that is of much greater national urgency and significance, namely the legacy of Scotland's aristocratic, Catholic past. If the funeral of the Countess of Glenallan in the ruined precincts of St Ruth is a scene of German-inspired terror, the threat that her existence posed to Scott's version of the nation's sense of itself while she was alive is Gothic in the extreme. Cruelly manipulating the romantic choices of her son, the Lord Glenallan, through a mendacious fiction of incestuous love, she

is, as Scott's epigraph to Chapter XXXII points out, a version of the
Countess of Narbonne from Walpole's Gothic drama *The Mysterious
Mother: A Tragedy* (1768). But whereas the incestuous bonds originally
engaged in and later unwittingly fostered by Walpole's now-reformed
and reforming countess are all too horrifically true, those proclaimed
by Scott's unrepentant and religiously un-reformed countess are false:
the horrid miasma of Catholic suspicion and superstition, incest, guilt
and suicide cast up by her machinations during her lifetime is penetrated
and dispersed shortly after her death by the humble confessions of her
servant Elspeth. Though the 'prejudiced horror of a bigoted Catholic and
zealous aristocrat' (334) might persist in the Lord Glenallan, her son,
Lovel, as the dynasty's true and ultimate Protestant heir, bears no resemblance or connection to the nightmare that is the nation's 'Gothic' past.
As in Carol Margaret Davison's reading of *Waverley*, Scott here might
be appropriating Gothic convention not only to foreground the horrors
and terrors of history but also self-consciously to parody, and thereby
resist, English renditions of Scotland as a 'Gothic space' in the tour-
narratives of writers such as Defoe and Johnson (see Davison 191–200).
The point to be made, though, is that the construction of a politically
'Gothic' Scotland at the end of *The Antiquary* is based upon the pointed
dismantling of the 'Gothic' fictions of ghosts and an incestuous Catholic
elite that have governed the nation's earlier representations.

When taken in a purely aesthetic sense, the category of 'Scottish
Gothic' also risks eliding the pronounced formal and thematic differences between very discreet bodies of cultural output, for the conflicts
between the Celtic and the Gothic given form in eighteenth-century historiography played themselves out in a number of fictional contexts too.
Upon first impression, there is much in Macpherson's early *Fragments
of Ancient Poetry* that might appear to be 'Gothic', particularly if by
Gothic we mean, first and foremost, a literary mode that is preoccupied
with the supernatural, the spectral and the ghostly. As Ian Duncan in
this respect has argued, 'the Ossian poems initiated one of the principal
"Gothic" strains in Scottish literature: the possession of the living by the
dead' (71). When, in the first Fragment, the warrior Shilric goes away
to fight in the wars of Fingal, his lover, Vinvela, pines her life away to
an early grave: 'With grief for thee / I expired. Shilric, I am pale in the
tomb' (14). Macpherson seems to prefigure in these lines a version of
the same melancholic absorption and death occasioned by the loss of
the love-object that would be detailed in countless Gothic romances of
the 1790s. And yet, when Vinvela subsequently returns from the grave
as a spectre, the scene begins to stake out its differences from the Gothic
aesthetic, as the ghost comes to serve for Shilric more as a familiar and

pleasurable object of remembrance than a phantom of disturbing and terrifying proportions: 'She fleets, she fails away; as grey / mist before the wind! – and, wilt though / not stay, my love? Stay and behold / my tears? fair though appearest, my love! / fair thou wast, when alive!' (15). Gothic writing of the late eighteenth century is caught within what we, following Jacques Derrida in *The Specters of Marx*, might term a 'Spectral circle' (140): ghosts are invoked if only in order to be eventually exorcized as the unbearable objects of horror and terror.[5] The invocation of the spectre in Gothic is only the prelude to a lengthy process of exorcism in which it is finally expelled, vanquished or laid to rest, whether through the exposure of the truth behind so many counterfeit renditions of death or through the salutary and appropriate mourning of those who, remaining hitherto unmemorialized, have plagued the living with their terrifying returns.[6] However, Shilric's responses to the spectre of Vinvela in *Ancient Fragments* indicate the extent to which spectres in *Ancient Fragments* are the products of an ongoing and continuous process of mourning rather than the symptoms of any curtailed rites. Moreover, far from serving as the agents of horror and terror, ghosts in *Ancient Fragments* are fondly courted and invoked as the remnants of public, national nostalgia and personal romantic attachment:

> By the mossy fountain I will set; on / the top of the hill of winds, when / mid-day is silent around, converse, O / my love, with me! Come on the wings of the gale! On the blast of the mountain / come! Let me hear thy voice, as / thou passest, when mid-day is silent around. (15)

In Fragment III, similarly, the persona invokes the evanescent spectre of one Malcolm, the presence of which is welcomed more as the source of comfort and consolation than as a Gothic figure of terrific sublimity: 'But, oh! what voice is that? / Who notes on that meteor of fire! / Green are his airy limbs. / It is he! it is the ghost of Malcolm! – Rest, lovely soul, rest on the rock; and let me hear / thy voice – He is gone, like a dream of the night' (17). Though these scenes of invocation describe the first hemisphere of Derrida's spectral circle, they never complete the revolution, through an act of dramatic exorcism, in order to become particularly Gothic. Unlike Walpole's Manfred, who had fled the ghost of his grandfather as a terrible sign of ancestral disapproval, the spirits of deceased ancestors in *Ancient Fragments* are called upon by the personas as the guarantee of an ancient tradition of national military prowess: 'At times are seen here the ghosts of the deceased, / when the musing hunter alone stalks slowly over the heath. Appear in thy armour of light, thou ghost of the mighty Connal! Shine, near thy tomb, Crimora! like a moon-beam from a cloud' (23). Though ghosts might infuse its landscapes, Celtic Scotland is spectral rather than Gothic: most tellingly, these spirits refuse to absorb and perpetuate the aesthetic of sublime fear that had characterized Gothic writing from the outset. 'Speak ye ghosts of the dead!' pleads the persona in Fragment X, 'speak, and I will not be afraid' (48).

Much the same applies to the precarious mixture of Macpherson's own imaginative reconstructions and the aural remains of Gaelic poetry offered up in *Fingal* (1761) and *Temora* (1763). Here, too, the poems mark their formal and thematic difference from the nascent Gothic aesthetic, for, if there was one thing on which the opinion of Antiquarians, scholars and politicians concurred, it was that Gothic mobilized an anti-Roman spirit in aesthetics, politics and cultural life more generally. When Elizabeth Montagu passionately embraced Shakespeare as 'our Gothic Bard' in her *Essay on the Writings and Genius of Shakespear* [*sic*] in 1769, she sought, against the tide of neoclassicism, to recuperate Shakespeare precisely because of his violation of the Aristotelian unities of time, place and action. In *Fingal* and *Temora*, by contrast, Macpherson makes incessant appeal to the poems' affinities with classicism, if not as source or antecedent to his own Scottish epics, then at least as literary parallels. Accordingly, epic conventions are extensively employed in both poems. But it is in the figuring of the supernatural that Macpherson most clearly marks his difference from the Gothic: his footnote to the scene in which the Irish soldiers are haunted by the spirits of recently deceased military heroes in Book I of *Fingal* asserts that, far from being a crude, sensationalist device, the ghost, though undoubtedly poetic, derives historically from authentic Celtic anthropological belief. The famous appearance of the ghost of Crugal in *Fingal*, too, is substantially denuded of the ghastly, sensational details contained in its classical parallel, the appearance of Hector's ghost in the *Aeneid*. Unlike the spectres of the Gothic, many of whom look to the ghost of Hamlet's father as their avatar, the ghost of Crugal seeks not personal revenge so much as the cautioning of his people on a broader national basis. When the ghost of Evirallin appears before her beloved Ossian in Book IV of *Fingal*, she comes more in beauty than in fear, and utterly without the egocentric demands attendant upon the ghostly injunction for vengeance. The ghosts of Ossian are the collective fallen heroes of national battles, motivated by the need for national commemoration rather than the settling of a personal score. While the Gothic ghost is singular, identifiable as the restless spirit of a particular named individual, Celtic ghosts are plural and collective, nameless and faceless. Far from serving as ciphers of the unbearable persistence of the past, the ghosts of Ossian are the welcome participants in a mythical celebration of the Celtic nation's heroic past. Countering the claim that the Celts had originated in Ireland, as well as challenging the 'pretensions' to Ossian's poetic vision on ancient Ireland's behalf, Macpherson in 'A Dissertation', the preface to *Temora* printed in the second volume of *The Works of Ossian* in 1765, unflatteringly dismissed the labours of Irish antiquarians in terms that strongly recall the conventions of modern Gothic romance:

> Their allusions to the manners and customs of the fifteenth century, are so many, that it is matter of wonder to me, how any one could dream of their antiquity. They are entirely writ in that romantic taste, which prevailed two ages ago. – Giants, enchanted castles, dwarfs, palfreys, witches and magicians form the whole circle of the poet's invention. (Gaskill 217–18)

Macpherson's Ossianic objectives were at considerable remove from the literary turns taken by the Gothic imagination. Ghostly though it was, Macpherson's Celtic Scotland was wholly unsuited to any extended uptake by the Gothic aesthetic, as preoccupied as it too might have been with the rendition of supernatural activity.

As Katie Trumpener has argued, writers of Gothic fiction from 1764 onwards responded to, and defensively warded against, a Johnsonian sense of the empirically dubious nature of Ossianic poetry through the emphasis that their narratives brought to bear upon such 'authentic' historical sources as discovered letters, manuscripts and documents.[7] The tensions between Ossian and the Gothic are further attested to by the numerous Gothic fictions which, though set in ancient Scotland, and though often citing Ossian as source and inspiration, fail to discover in the poetry much that could serve their aesthetic needs. Indeed, these fictions entirely bypass Ossianic renditions of spectres, turning instead to Shakespeare's *Macbeth* as a more suitable template for the 'Gothic' figuring of supernatural activity in ancient Scottish settings. In 1804, for instance, T. J. Horsley Curties published *The Watch Tower; Or, The Sons of Ulthona*, a four-volume Gothic romance set variously in the Highlands and Western Islands of Scotland during 1303 and 1304. Though the title page of the first volume invokes Mamillius's lines from *The Winter's Tale* – 'a sad tale is best for winter, / I have one of sprites and goblins' – Curties's dedication to his patron, E. H. Elcock Brown, cites Ossian as his novel's primary inspiration: 'tracking (though at humble distance) the wildly beautiful, yet terrifically sublime imagery of Ossian, I have explored the mazy regions of romance, together with the dark uncertainty of ancient historic chronicles' (vii). And yet, in the fiction that follows, Ossianic influence is confined, rather literally, to the margins of the text, in the form of occasional epigraphs to the chapters, most of them taken from shorter poems anthologized in the *Poems of Ossian* such as 'Carthon', 'Dar-thula', 'Berrathon' and 'Calthon and Colmal'. Far from sustaining and building on its Ossianic influences, the bulk of *The Watch Tower* is given over to a continuous reworking of Shakespeare, plundering such plays as *Henry VIII, Henry VI, Part II, Cymbeline, Troilus and Cressida, Titus Andronicus, Richard II, Pericles* and *A Midsummer Night's Dream* for epigraphs, and *King Lear, Hamlet* and *Macbeth* for aspects of its plot. The political and historical conflict between Celt and Goth here plays itself out via Curties's system of intertextual allusion. The romance opens upon a decidedly Macbethian note when the ambitious villain Morcar and his men storm the Castle of Ulthona, situated on a remote imaginary island to the west of Scotland, in order to murder the entire race of Ulthona in residence there. Recalling Macbeth's bloody assassination of Duncan, 'the ensanguined butchers,' we are told, 'plunged deep in the bosoms of Ulthona's faithful race their gore-drenched poniards!' (I: 3), eventually murdering in his sleep the noble leader, the Earl of Ulthona himself. Like his Shakespearean original, the Macbethian villain Morcar is troubled by the spectral projections of a guilty conscience from this moment onwards. That some of his victims, including the two sons of the chief, Sigismorn and Adelbert, are not, as it turns out, dead, seems irrelevant, for his conscience, believing itself to be guilty, is capable of conjuring up horrid ghostly imaginings all the same: 'The shades of Sigismorn and his murdered consort', the narrative reads,

> roamed through the terrific edifice, and Morcar, though obdurate to every other fear, was keenly alive to all the mystic horrors of superstition, whose principle (grounded on a sickly conscience) had, at times, the power to disarm his boldest designs, and inflict upon his guilt the inward tortures of a self-accusing spirit. (I: 108)

Continuously conjuring up the ghosts of those whom he has murdered, the mind of the villain Morcar is as 'full of scorpions' as Macbeth's own. At other moments, his symptoms recall those of the somnambulistic Lady Macbeth, for his, too, is a mind 'diseased with "thick coming fancies"' (I: 108); 'Dreadful to Morcar was the hated hour of noiseless midnight', for 'fantastic shapes and omens direful then seemed to surround his perturbed couch; and in his dreams oft presented wild cries of death, and presages of strange unheard of torments, anticipating all that the imagination can depicture of those hereafter woes that wait on unrepented crimes' (I: 108). Shakespeare's *Macbeth* furnished T. J. Horsley Curties with a particular way of ghost-seeing in *The Watch Tower*, one in which the guilty mind of the villain conjures up spectres and projects them on to objects and people around him. The other mode of ghost-seeing in the text, though refusing to explain away the spectre as the figment of the guilty imagination, is equally Shakespearean. Unbeknown to the villain, the two sons of Ulthona, Sigismorn and Adelbert, have been secreted away in a recess by Morcar's wife; both sons are visited by the ghost of their father, a spectre who, as in *Hamlet*, requires of them the setting to rights of past injustices: 'redress the murdered' and 'avenge the guiltless', the father's ghost super-egoically commands of the eldest son (I: 195). Clad in helmet and visor, this is a ghost who has returned 'from the deep immensity of death's unfathomable region', that 'hidden country, more heavenly than purgatorial, 'which must not be revealed to mortal ken' (I: 258). Ossian fails to give up the ghost, and Curties turns to the two distinct modes of ghost-seeing offered up by Shakespeare in *Macbeth* and *Hamlet* respectively: the guilty perceive spectres through the lens of *Macbeth*, the innocent via *Hamlet* (see Townshend, 'Gothic Shakespeare').

As the opening example of Mary Julia Young's *Donalda* indicates, *The Watch Tower* is not the only example of a text that turns to Shakespeare for what it cannot find in Ossian. Early Gothic romances with Scottish settings, most of them published in London, habitually perceive their subject matter through the lens of *Macbeth*. Some other examples in the mode include Ann Radcliffe's *The Castles of Athlin and Dunbayne* (1789); John Palmer's *The Haunted Cavern: A Caledonian Tale* (1796); and Curties's own *The Scottish Legend, Or the Isle of Saint Clothair* (1802). In all of these texts, as in many others, the same patterns repeat themselves: Scottish people, landscapes and histories are intertextually rendered through the terms of Shakespeare's Scottish play. All of those prone to guilty spectral hallucination in Radcliffe's *The Castles of Athlin and Dunbayne* are rendered so in ways that are similar to those of Macbeth, not least Radcliffe's villain, Malcolm, himself: at his moment of death, he appears lying 'on his couch surrounded with the stillness and horrors of death', but, his guilt having been exposed, he is "anxious to relieve the agony of a guilty mind" (220). By contrast, when the wronged Osbert, the noble Earl of Athlin, confronts the supernatural in the narrative, the scene becomes a direct replaying of *Hamlet* (161). Ultimately, the differences between the ghosts of Ossian and those of Shakespeare – a fundamental difference in which the very singularity of the Gothic aesthetic is at stake – might be summed up as follows: while Macpherson's ghosts constitute a significant part of a broader anthropological endeavour, Shakespearean spectrality, like the Gothic's own, remained a matter of dramatic entertainment. This is not to suggest that the ghosts in both Shakespeare and the Gothic were completely devoid of any broader cultural, anthropological imperative, or to claim that

Macpherson was in no way concerned with the aesthetic impact of his ghosts upon his readers. In relation to Shakespeare, at the very least, the work of Stephen Greenblatt in *Hamlet in Purgatory* suggests the very opposite to be the case: the ghost in Shakespeare's play is bound up in the complex theological disputes around mourning and the afterlife that preoccupied English culture in the wake of the Protestant Reformation. However, as even Greenblatt is led to concede, Shakespeare's plays never reproduce a consistent theological and political position on ghosts because, ultimately, it is dramatic entertainment that matters more. The same might be said of the Gothic: though originally a figure of theological dispute, the ghost, as E. J. Clery has argued, enters the 'machine' of popular Gothic fiction in *Otranto* as, first and foremost, a mechanism of theatrical entertainment. Two authorative accounts of Scottish spectrality published in the early decades of the nineteenth century, by contrast, suggest something different: Anne Grant's *Essay on the Superstitions on the Highlanders of Scotland* (1811) and Walter Scott's *Letters on Demonology and Witchcraft* (1830) demonstrate that what was ostensibly at stake in Scotland's relationship with spectrality was the matter of cultural anthropology, an interest in exploring the nation's ghostly heritage, documenting it, and conserving its rich superstitions. Scott's Enlightened critique of supernaturalism in the *Letters*, in fact, had used Shakespeare's three notable renditions of supernatural activity in *Macbeth*, *Hamlet* and *Julius Caesar* to foreclose upon the ghost's very existence. The dramatic suspension of ghostly disbelief opened up by Shakespeare, and thoroughly exploited by the Gothic, is closed down in Scott's rationalist account of the ghost's imaginative and organic origins, aetiologies which, in the course of the *Letters*, eventually push in the modern direction of the quasi-scientific, the material and the anthropological.

Perhaps Gothic Scotland, then, its landscape and its histories, its peoples and its ghosts, is a fiction that is woven on the loom of Shakespeare's Scottish play. The extract from William Collins's 'Ode on the Popular Superstitions of the Highlands of Scotland, considered as the Subject of Poetry' (1749–50) cited as the epigraph to this chapter would suggest as much: 'There Shakespeare's self, with every garland crowned, / In musing hour his Wayward Sisters found, / And with their terrors dressed the magic scene' (XI). *Macbeth* frequently served as the lens through which 'Gothic' Scotland was perceived and represented, not least of all in Samuel Johnson's *A Journey to the Western Islands of Scotland*:

> We went forwards the same day to Fores [*sic*], the town to which Macbeth was travelling, when he met the weird sisters in his way. This to an

Englishman is classic ground. Our imaginations were heated, and our thoughts recalled to their old amusements. (49)

Reading the region through English eyes, Johnson continues to list the Shakespearean associations throughout, including the road 'on which Macbeth heard the fatal prediction'; Calder castle 'from which Macbeth drew his second title'; and the 'castle of Macbeth' at Inverness (50–1). The uncomfortable colonizing effects of Johnson's appropriation of *Macbeth* did not go unnoticed by contemporary readers. In her corrective riposte to Johnson's negative impressions, Mary Ann Hanway's *A Journey to the Highlands of Scotland. With Occasional Remarks on Dr Johnson's Tour: By A Lady* (1776) took pains to assert the limits and inaccuracies of this particularly Shakespearean line of vision. Travelling, too, near Forres, where 'Shakespeare hath placed the first interview of Macbeth, and the wayward sisters' (127), Hanway expresses the following reservations:

> I have traversed over the spot thus solemnized by the monarch of the British drama, purely for the intellectual pleasure of treading on classic ground; but since the Witch Act has been repealed, I believe the very idea of enchantment and preter-natural appearances, is almost extinct, even in this, once superstitious country; at least I can assure your Lordship, I met, in *my* rambles across this charmed soil, no fine promises from either male or female conjurors. (127–8)

The Johnsonian fantasy of a 'Gothic Scotland' is ruptured in the same gesture that Hanway figures Shakespeare as a broadly 'British' dramatist, a category that includes both England and Scotland. But from the perspective of writers such as Collins, Johnson, Young and Curties, Scottish Gothic appears to be precisely the opposite: the phantasmatic projection of English writers constructed through the intertext of 'our Gothic Bard', for, when Elizabeth Montagu coined the appellation in 1769, she appropriated Shakespeare as more narrowly 'English' than inclusively 'British'. As Robert Crawford has argued, Shakespeare the dramatist, though constructed as the national writer from the beginning of the eighteenth century, became the national poet or 'Bard' only during the 1760s, that is, after, and in direct response to, the canonization of Ossian the Bard, and later Burns, in Scotland (see Crawford). Gothic Shakespeare arises directly in response to the threat of Scottish cultural nationalism, in much the same way that, as Trumpener has pointed out, the phenomenon of Ossianic 'Bardic Nationalism' had arisen earlier out of a need for the Celtic fringes to assert their cultural and national specificity within a context of increased internal English colonization. Early Gothic fictions register this conflict between Ossian and Shakespeare, the Celtic and the Gothic incessantly, giving form at the level of fiction to a conflict that had played itself out within broader contemporary antiquarian and historiographical debates. And if, as David Baker, Neil Rhodes and Christopher Highley have argued, *Macbeth*, within its original Jacobean context, perpetuates and supports the same political ideologies enshrined in James I's Union of the Crowns of England and Scotland (see Baker, Rhodes and Highley), the play in an eighteenth-century context is appropriated in Gothic writing as a means of asserting Scotland's otherness, its marked difference from England, its resistance to the politics of British Unionism. A Macbethian place of witches, ghosts and regicide, Scotland becomes as Gothic as Radcliffe's Italy or Lewis's Spain, literally 'another country' of darkness and distance, one that is opened up to the representational modes of Gothic fiction precisely because of its spatial, historical and political exclusion from ideological construct that was the noble Gothic past.

Notes

1 See, for instance, Viscount Henry St John Bolingbroke's *Remarks on the History of England*; Lord Kames's *Essays Upon Several Subjects Concerning British Antiquities*; and William Robertson's influential *The History of Scotland*.

2 Similar exclusions of Scotland from the category of political Gothicism were effected in *Northern Antiquities*, Bishop Thomas Percy's 1770 English translation of Paul Henri Mallet, and Charles de Secondat, the baron de Montesquieu's *The Spirit of the Laws* (1748).

3 For an account of the historiographic assumptions underpinning Macpherson's Ossian poems, see his *An Introduction to the History of Great Britain and Ireland*.

4 See Robertson's argument in *Legitimate Histories*; Duncan's reading of Scott's engagement with the Gothic in *Modern Romance and Transformations of the Novel*; and the chapter on Scott and the Gothic in Gamer's *Romanticism and the Gothic*.

5 See my argument in 'Gothic and the Ghost of *Hamlet*'.

6 See Lacan's reading of the ghost in *Hamlet* in 'Desire and the Interpretation of Desire in *Hamlet*'.

7 See, in particular, Trumpener's argument in the chapter of *Bardic Nationalism* entitled '"The End of an Auld Sang": Oral Tradition and Literary History' (67–127).

Works cited

Baines, Paul. *The House of Forgery in Eighteenth-Century Britain*. Aldershot: Ashgate, 1999.

Baker, David J. '"Stands Scotland where it did?" Shakespeare on the March.' *Shakespeare and Scotland*. Eds Willy Maley and Andrew Murphy. Manchester and New York: Manchester University Press, 2004. 20–36.

Bolingbroke, Henry St John. *Remarks on the History of England*. London, 1743.

Clery, E. J. *The Rise of Supernatural Fiction, 1762–1800*. Cambridge: Cambridge University Press, 1995.

Collins, William. *The Poetical Works of William Collins*. London: Bell and Daldy, 1859.

Crawford, Robert. 'The Bard: Ossian, Burns, and the Shaping of Shakespeare.' *Shakespeare and Scotland*. Eds Willy Maley and Andrew Murphy. Manchester and New York: Manchester University Press, 2004. 124–40.

Curties, T. J. Horsley. *The Watch Tower; Or, The Sons of Ulthona: An Historic Romance. In Five Volumes* ... Brentford: P. Norbury, 1804.

Davison, Carol Margaret. *Gothic Literature 1764–1824*. Cardiff: University of Wales Press, 2009.

Derrida, Jacques. *Specters of Marx: The State of Debt, the Work of Mourning, and the New International*. Trans. Peggy Kamuf. New York and London: Routledge, 1994.

De Secondat, Charles-Louis [Montesquieu]. *The Spirit of the Laws*. Trans. Thomas Nugent. 2 vols. London: George Bell & Sons, 1750.

Duncan, Ian. 'Walter Scott, James Hogg and Scottish Gothic.' *A Companion to the Gothic*. Ed. David Punter. Oxford: Blackwell, 2001. 70–80.

—. *Modern Romance and Transformations of the Novel: The Gothic, Scott, Dickens*. Cambridge: Cambridge University Press, 1992.

Gamer, Michael. *Romanticism and the Gothic: Genre, Reception, and Canon Formation*. Cambridge: Cambridge University Press, 2000.

Gamer, Michael and Robert Miles. 'Gothic Shakespeare on the Romantic Stage.' *Gothic Shakespeares*. Ed. John Drakakis and Dale Townshend. Abingdon: Routledge, 2008. 131–52.

Gaskill, Howard, ed. *The Poems of Ossian and Related Works*. Intro. Fiona Stafford. Edinburgh: Edinburgh University Press, 1996.

Greenblatt, Stephen. *Hamlet in Purgatory*. Princeton, NJ: Princeton University Press, 2001.

Hanway, Mary Ann. *A Journey to the Highlands of Scotland. With Occasional Remarks on Dr Johnson's Tour: By A Lady*. London: Printed for Fielding and Walker, 1776.

Highley, Christopher. 'The Place of Scots in the Scottish Play: *Macbeth* and the Politics of Language.' *Shakespeare and Scotland*. Eds Willy Maley and Andrew Murphy. Manchester and New York: Manchester University Press, 2004. 53–66.

Hume, David. *The History of England, From the Invasion of Julius Caesar to the Accession of Henry VII*. 2 Vols. London: Printed for A. Millar, 1762.

Ireland, W. H. *Vortigern: An Historical Tragedy, in Five Acts; Represented at the Theatre Royal, Drury Lane, on Saturday April 2, 1796.* London: J. Barker, 1799.

Johnson, Samuel and James Boswell. *A Journey to the Western Islands of Scotland* and *The Journal of a Tour to the Hebrides.* 1775; 1786. Ed. Peter Levi. London: Penguin Books, 1984.

Kahan, Jeffrey. *Reforging Shakespeare: The Story of a Theatrical Scandal.* London: Associated University Presses, 1998.

Kames, Henry Home. *Essays Upon Several Subjects Concerning British Antiquities.* London, 1747.

Lacan, Jacques. 'Desire and the Interpretation of Desire in *Hamlet*.' *Yale French Studies* 55/56 (1977): 11–52.

Longueil, Alfred E. 'The Word "Gothic" in eighteenth-century Criticism'. *Modern Language Notes* 38.8 (1923): 453–60.

Macpherson, James. *An Introduction to the History of Great Britain and Ireland.* Dublin, 1771.

—. *Fragments of Ancient Poetry, Collected in the Highlands of Scotland, and Translated from the Galic of Erse Language.* 2nd edn. Edinburgh, Printed for G. Hamilton and J. Balfour, 1760.

Mallet, Paul Henri. *Northern Antiquities.* Trans. Thomas Percy. London, 1847.

Miles, Robert. 'Forging a Romantic Identity: Herbert Croft's Love and Madness and W. H. Ireland's Shakespeare M.S.' *Eighteenth-Century Fiction* 17.4 (2005): 599–627.

Montagu, Elizabeth Robinson. *An Essay on the Writings and Genius of Shakespear [sic], Compared with the Greek and French Dramatic Poets ...* London: Printed for J. Dodsley, 1769.

Moore, Dafydd. 'James Macpherson and "Celtic Whiggism"'. *Eighteenth-Century Life* 30.1 (2006): 1–24.

Pinkerton, John. *A Dissertation on the Origin and Progress of the Scythians or Goths. Being an Introduction to the Ancient and Modern History of Europe.* London, 1787.

Rhodes, Neil. 'Wrapped in the Strong Arms of the Union: Shakespeare and King James.' *Shakespeare and Scotland.* Eds Willy Maley and Andrew Murphy. Manchester and New York: Manchester University Press, 2004. 37–52.

Robertson, Fiona. *Legitimate Histories: Scott, Gothic, and the Authorities of Fiction.* Oxford: Clarendon Press, 1994.

Robertson, William. *The History of Scotland.* 1759.

Scott, Sir Walter. *The Antiquary* (1816). Ed. Nicola J. Watson. Oxford: Oxford University Press, 2002. Oxford World's Classics.

Shakespeare, William. *Macbeth.* Ed. Kenneth Muir. London: Routledge, 1991. The Arden Shakespeare.

—. *Hamlet.* Ed. Harold Jenkins. London: Routledge, 1989. The Arden Shakespeare.

—. *Julius Caesar.* Ed. T. S. Dorsch. London: Routledge, 1988. The Arden Shakespeare.

Temple, William. *An Introduction to the History of England.* London: Printed for Richard Simpson and Ralph Simpson, 1695.

Thomson, James. *The Works of James Thomson. With his Last Corrections and Improvements. In Four Volumes*. London: Printed for A. Millar, 1762.

Townshend, Dale. 'Gothic Shakespeare.' *A New Companion to the Gothic*. Ed. David Punter. Oxford: Blackwell, 2012. 38–63.

—. 'Gothic and the Ghost of *Hamlet*.' *Gothic Shakespeares*. Eds John Drakakis and Dale Townshend. Abingdon: Routledge, 2008. 60–97.

Trumpener, Katie. *Bardic Nationalism: The Romantic Novel and the British Empire*. Princeton, NJ: Princeton University Press, 1997.

Wright, Angela. 'Scottish Gothic.' *The Routledge Companion to Gothic*. Eds Catherine Spooner and Emma McEvoy. Abingdon: Routledge, 2007. 73–82.

Young, Mary Julia. *Donalda; Or, The Witches of Glenshiel. A Caledonian Legend. In Two Volumes*. London: J. F. Hughes, 1805.

13

The rage of Caliban: Dorian Gray and the Gothic body

Andreas Höfele

The nineteenth century dislike of Realism is the rage of Caliban seeing his own face in a glass.

The nineteenth century dislike of Romanticism is the rage of Caliban not seeing his own face in a glass.

Wilde's famous aphorism forms part of the 'Preface to *Dorian Gray*' first published in *The Fortnightly Review* of 1 March 1891. One month in advance of the book publication of his novel, the Preface was meant to teach 'the wretched journalists ... to mend their wicked ways' (Wilde, *The Letters* 290), to deflate in advance the moral censure of his book which Wilde knew was in the offing and which in the event the Preface did little to prevent.[1] Braiding the two dominant strands of nineteenth-century literature, the aphorism invites discussion in the context of Wilde's aesthetics. This is the context in which Wilde himself most obviously positions it, along with the other articles of his artistic creed that make up the Preface, concluding with the assertion that 'All art is quite useless'.

At the same time, the aphorism also ties into the narrative of Wilde's novel because, as Virginia and Alden Vaughan point out: 'When Dorian Gray looks at his portrait, he sees the Caliban in his own nature' (113). In what follows I want to pursue a line of enquiry opened up by this remark. Caliban occupies a strategic place in the novel's Gothic imaginary. 'Shakespeare's changeling' (Vaughan and Vaughan 7) lurks in the innermost recesses of Wilde's melodrama of anthropological anxiety.[2] He embodies the monstrous legacy of a Renaissance which *The Picture of Dorian Gray* construes as both irrepressibly Gothic and ominously modern.

In the Folio cast list, Caliban features as 'a savage and deformed slave' (*The Tempest* 140).[3] His first appearance is accompanied by a volley of abuse from Prospero:

> Thou poisonous slave, got by the devil himself
> Upon thy wicked dam; come forth!
>
> (*Tempest* 1.2.320–1)

Dorian Gray, on the other hand, whose 'gracious and comely form' the painter Basil Hallward has 'so skilfully mirrored in his art' (Wilde, *Dorian Gray* 1), is introduced as a 'young Adonis', 'a Narcissus' (3), though he too will soon be, as it were, 'got by the devil'. The difference between the two characters – beast and beauty – could not be more extreme, nor would anything less extreme do for Wilde's plot. If the 'glass' of the painter's art is to eventually reveal a monster, the starting point of this deformation must be an angel, not only 'wonderfully handsome', but also wonderfully innocent, endowed with 'youth's passionate purity ... unspotted from the world' (15).

There is parallel, however, as well as contrast. Caliban, we learn, though apparently born 'spotted' (or at least 'freckled'; *Tempest* 1.2.283), once, too, existed in a condition of original innocence. When Prospero and Miranda arrive on the island he becomes part of the family,[4] and the initial phase of their living together appears in retrospect as a state of paradisiacal harmony:

> CALIBAN (to Prospero)
> When thou cam'st first
> Thou strok'st me and made much of me; wouldst give me
> Water with berries in't, and teach me how
> To name the bigger light and how the less
> That burn by day and night. And then I loved thee
> And showed thee all the qualities of the isle:
> The fresh springs, brine pits, barren place and fertile.
>
> (*Tempest* 1.2.333–9)

Detailing an Eden without labour, the passage looks forward to Gonzalo's Golden Age idyll, culled from Montaigne's 'Des Cannibales', where 'nature should bring forth / Of its own kind all foison, all abundance, / To feed my innocent people' (2.1.163–5).[5] The paradise evoked by Caliban's reminiscence draws not only on this New World adaptation of classical myth but also, and arguably more crucially, on Genesis. The bigger light and the smaller, the separation of day and night and the primordial act of naming all allude to the biblical account, with Prospero assuming the role of a quasi-Old Testament father-god and Caliban and Miranda cast as warped typological analogues of Adam and Eve. Turning Caliban, 'a thing most brutish' not 'know[ing] [his] own meaning', into a fully human being equipped with language and self-knowledge is an act of creation, albeit one that fails.

Caliban's Adamic innocence lasts only for as long as his acquisition of knowledge stops short of sexual knowledge. His attempted rape of Miranda/Eve is the original sin that plunges him from Eden to a postlapsarian condition of toil and trouble where food is eaten 'in the sweat of his face' and Prospero is a wrathful 'god of power' (1.2.10) who strikes, no longer strokes, his unruly subject.

Intimations of Genesis unmistakably also haunt the opening chapters of *The Picture of Dorian Gray*. The studio of the painter Basil Hallward is described as not so much the studio itself as the garden just outside the open door, a *hortus conclusus* of lavishly overabundant vegetation in an unseen, barely audible urban environment: 'The dim roar of London was like the bourdon note of a distant organ' (1). In fact, the city sounds like the sea surrounding Prospero's island, which is invariably 'roaring'[6] and in one instance has the tone of an organ added to its tempestuous maritime soundscape.[7] In this Edenic seclusion, Basil Hallward as loving creator, Lord Henry Wotton as tempter and Dorian as the unspotted innocent re-enact the Fall in an all-male *fin de siècle* ambience.

Like Satan in the Garden, Lord Henry – suitably introduced in a reclining position, exhaling serpentine 'whorls from his heavy opium-tainted cigarette' (2)[8] – also offers seduction in the form of knowledge. Falling under his spell, like Adam and Eve after eating of the forbidden fruit, Dorian has his eyes opened. Lord Henry's words 'reveal him to himself' (21), so that when he looks at the finished portrait it is 'as if he had recognized himself for the first time' (24).

The picture is incomplete without the words that make it a revelation to the beholder. Lord Henry the tempter, the destroyer of unself-conscious innocence, is thus a Mephistophelian co-creator. He takes on the part of 'the critic as artist' (Wilde, *The Critic* 1009–59), for Wilde the key role in contemporary aesthetics and the only one that holds any promise of authentic creativity at a time when every style, all original creation seems to have been exhausted.[9] Its crowning achievement is exemplified by Walter Pater. Leonardo's *Mona Lisa* may be great, but its spellbinding power is made infinitely greater by Pater. Through his writing

> the picture becomes more wonderful to us than it really is, and reveals to us a secret of which, in truth, it knows nothing, and the music of his mystical prose is as sweet in our ears as was that flute-player's music that lent to the lips of La Gioconda those subtle and poisonous curves. (Wilde, *The Critic* 1029)

Lord Henry's 'languid voice' (21) has the same kind of evocative power, and so do his hands. At the end of a passage summing up Dorian's first impression of his new teacher, they are easily the most striking feature of the description: 'His cool, white, flower-like hands, even, had a curious charm. They moved, as he spoke, like music, and seemed to have a language of their own' (21). If Lord Henry's words, as we read a few pages earlier, have 'touched some secret chord' in Dorian 'that had never been touched before' (18), then this 'touch' becomes (almost) physical in the erotic synaesthesia of Lord Henry's restless musical hands. How can Dorian know these hands are 'cool' without having felt them on his skin? Wilde teases the reader into recognizing 'the love that dare not speak its name' without its actually 'speaking'. Lord Henry's handling, his manipulation, of Dorian is both seduction and creation. Highlighting Lord Henry's hands draws on the ancient tradition of associating the hand, 'the instrument of instruments' as Aristotle calls it (423a), with human creativity, with art in the broader sense that prevailed well into the Renaissance, as well as in our narrower modern sense that began to emerge in the same period.[10] The artist's handiwork is to make form out of mere matter. And it is as 'maker' that he becomes most like, as Sidney put it, his 'heavenly Maker' (Sidney 217).

Both the ur-scene on the island where Prospero sets out to re-form the 'deformed' Caliban and the ur-scene in Wilde's metropolitan garden idyll are versions of the Creation. Dorian's train of thought reads like a pastiche of Genesis as he outlines a trajectory from chaos to form under the tutelage of Lord Henry's irresistible logos:

> Music had stirred him like that. Music had troubled him many times. But music was not articulate. It was not a new world, but rather another chaos, that it created in us. Words! Mere words! How terrible they were! How clear, and vivid, and cruel! One could not escape from them. And yet what a subtle magic there was in them! They seemed to be able to give a plastic form to formless things, and to have a music of their own as sweet as that of viol or of lute. Mere words! Was there anything so real as words? (19)

Over time, Caliban has become a catchword, a topos, a stereotype, and it is as such that Wilde employs the name in his aphorism. But what we actually find in *The Tempest* is arguably the most unfixed character in the entire Shakespearean canon, a figure made ever more indeterminable by the overdetermining of his characteristics.[11] 'What have we here, a man or a fish?' (2.2.24–5) asks Trinculo on his first encounter with Caliban. Learned commentators have been similarly puzzled. Morton Luce, in the introduction to his 1901 Arden edition of the play, declared that '[i]f all the suggestions as to Caliban's form and feature and endowments that are thrown out in the play are collected, it will be found that one half renders the other half impossible' (xxxv). And surely, if 'tortoise', 'fish', 'mooncalf', 'freckled whelp', 'cat' or simply 'beast Caliban' (*Tempest* 4.1.140) are all taken as literal descriptions, then indeed a veritable cocktail of species ensues, a chimera like those 'mountaineers / Dewlapped like bulls' or 'men / Whose heads stood in their breasts' that old Gonzalo speaks of (3.3.44–7). It is understandable that Luce, writing in the heyday of late Victorian stage illusionism, would scan Shakespeare's text for descriptors that could be plausibly and 'literally' visualized in the performing of the part. But no turn-of-the-century Caliban can hold a candle to the eighteenth-century illustrator Daniel Chodowiecki's flight of fancy. Literalizing Prospero's 'Come, thou tortoise, when?' (1.2.317), Chodowiecki turns Caliban into a monster tortoise that looks like the first draft of John Tenniel's rendering of the Mock Turtle in *Alice's Adventures in Wonderland*. The urge to decide Trinculo's question 'what we have here' has produced a pictorial history of 'humanimal' freaks[12] and, as its antidote, the Caliban of postcolonial criticism: an oppressed person of colour whose allegedly bestial nature is nothing but racist slander.

Take away the demonized animality and Caliban emerges as the subaltern (Homi Bhabha) whose humanity asserts itself despite, or precisely because of, being constantly denied. But plausible though it may be, this reading, too, seeks to impose closure on a figure that Shakespeare's text constructs as irreducibly open. This openness, Julia Lupton argues, is best conveyed by the term 'creature', *creatura*, whose Latin suffix *-ura* indicates a permanent state of becoming, of ongoing creation. 'Creature' captures the 'indeterminacy at the heart of Caliban' (Lupton 2), his 'oddly faceless and featureless being' (8). Suspended in a condition of emergence, '[c]reature … measures the difference between the human and the inhuman while refusing to take up residence in either category' (5).

'Creature' is also one of the first epithets given to Dorian Gray. Looking at his portrait, Lord Henry surmises that '[h]e is some brainless, beautiful creature, who should be always here in winter when we have no flowers to look at' (3). Like Caliban, Dorian Gray is perceived as an object of wonder, though not, of course, with contempt, but with admiration, yet an object nonetheless, one that 'looks as if [it] was made out of ivory and rose leaves' (3). The first dialogue prompted by this object is about whether to exhibit it or not.[13] First responses to Caliban also tend to turn him into an exhibit – a *monstrum* in the sense of something to be shown. Trinculo has never seen anything like this 'strange beast' but immediately knows what it is good for:

> Were I in England now (as once I was) and had but this fish [i.e. Caliban]
> painted, not a holiday fool there but would give a piece of silver. There
> would this monster make a man; any strange beast there makes a man.
> When they will not give a doit to relieve a lame beggar, they will lay out
> ten to see a dead Indian. (*Tempest* 2.2.27–32)

No less promptly than Trinculo, Antonio maintains that Caliban, this 'plain fish', however doubtful his appearance, is 'no doubt marketable' (5.1.266).

In the case of Dorian, the symbiotic exchange between person and portrait produces two internally split halves of an uncanny blend. Dorian, exempt from natural decay, is not quite a living being, nor the portrait quite an inanimate thing. Rather, each partakes in the condition of the other. The unchangingly youthful Dorian exhibits himself to the world as a perfect surface, a fixed 'picture of youth'; the dead object mutates organically into a living monster, a Caliban not 'stied' in a rock,[14] but stowed in a closet.

Creature Caliban and creature Dorian – inscribed in the term is not only the dependence on a creator, but also the threat of a force that escapes this creator's control. The created being will simply not stay as it is meant to. 'Caliban', Julia Lupton writes, 'appears as a *thing* made of *earth*', his 'earthen core recalls the first fashioning of conscious life out of an inert yet infinitely malleable substance, as if the very plasticity of mud prompted the idea of conscious life in the Creator' (8). But the subject created from this infinitely malleable substance (like the *sujet* or subject of Basil's infinitely malleable paint) possesses the irrepressible force literally to outgrow the creator's original purpose. 'And, as with age his body uglier grows, / So his mind cankers' (*Tempest* 4.1.191–2). Prospero's civilizing project has come to an impasse, pitting the far from infinitely malleable creature bitterly against his creator-colonizer. Yet the project cannot simply be abandoned or disowned. If Caliban's nature resists nurture, this hints at the possibility of a more pervasive failing of the civilizing effort. Prospero's admission in Act 5 – '[T]his thing of darkness / I acknowledge mine' (5.1.275–6) – reveals that Caliban is not just a foil but a constant challenge to Prospero's own sense of self, a challenge to the very notion of humanness to which he lays claim and which his island rule is committed to enforce. Caliban's 'darkness' rubs off on Prospero.

For Walter Benjamin, in his *Origin of the German Tragic Drama*, '[t]he Creature represents the flip side of the political theology of absolute sovereignty' (Lupton 5). The sovereign may be godlike in 'the creative-destructive potential of his decisive word' and 'his subjects are his creatures', but, Benjamin insists, 'the sovereign, unlike God, is himself a creature' (5–6). '[H]owever highly he is enthroned over subject and state', he writes, 'his status is confined to the world of creation; he is the lord of creatures, but he remains a creature' (Benjamin 85). Much in *The Tempest* bolsters the opposition between the master of the island and his subject: 'Sun and moon, Prospero and Caliban, Creator and Creature, king and subject' (Lupton 9). Caliban, Lupton writes, 'is Mere Creature, a creature separate (like Adam) from the Creator but (unlike Adam) not reflected back to the Creator as His image' (8).

This last claim, I would argue, takes the opposition one step too far. The creature Caliban *does* reflect back to his creator, and what Prospero sees reflected is himself as creature. If it were otherwise, if Caliban were as 'radically singular' as Lupton suggests, nothing more than 'a strange exception' (Lupton 20), why should he worry his sovereign 'creator' as much as he obviously does? The text hardly accounts for the intensity of Prospero's engagement with his creature. Not for a moment does Caliban's conspiracy pose a real threat. His political advantage exponentially increased by magic, Prospero has every conceivable instrument of power at his disposal. This should make him tower in unassailable superiority over his '[a]bhorred slave' (*Tempest* 1.2.352). But the fierce altercation that ensues on each of his encounters with the creature that is, or should be, 'all subject' as well as 'all the subjects that he has',[15] tells a different story. Caliban is and remains defiantly insubordinate, a constant thorn in the flesh of his master. Though 'rack[ed] … with old cramps' (1.2.370), he remains stubbornly unregenerate, answering the charge of attempted rape with an oddly gleeful regret for having failed:

> O ho, O ho! Would't had been done;
> Thou didst prevent me, I had peopled else
> This isle with Calibans.
>
> (1.2.352)

'O ho, O ho!' – with this, a language before the logos, Caliban launches a counter-history, an alternative pagan myth of violent beginning opposed to Prospero's narrative of an Eden lost through sexual transgression. Prospero keeps punishing the offender and by doing so keeps re-presenting, reiterating the offence. Being punished continuously, Caliban continues in readiness to transgress and transgress again. What ostensibly confirms Prospero's absolute rule – 'I must obey', says Caliban, 'his art is of such power' (1.2.373) – thus becomes a constant reminder of a rule that fails, a constant reminder also of a creation that fails and whose failure reflects on the creator.

The 'felt singularity' (Lupton 19) of a creature 'on whose nature / Nurture can never stick' (*Tempest* 4.1.188–9) does not prevent this nature from infiltrating or, rather, from always already inhabiting the human order Prospero seeks to create. Caliban persists as an irritant to the civility and humanness from which his freakish singularity forever excludes him. Caliban persists as a part of vexingly unfinished business even to the play's final tableau of general harmony. What Prospero finds in Caliban is the unreclaimed nature of the old Adam, a creatureliness not culturally disciplined into full humanity. His worry about 'the beast Caliban' (4.1.140) derives from the suspicion that his beastliness may be lurking, forever uncontrollable, under the brittle surface of normative civility, that the thing of darkness is not a thing out there but a thing within. Although Caliban is denied humanity, humanity somehow always seems to be at stake in him. Hence Prospero's inordinately agitated outburst over his failure to make a passable man of his 'brutish' ward: 'on whom my pains / Humanely taken – all, all lost, quite lost!' (4.1.189–90). Such agitation would hardly be warranted if Prospero had never expected more of the 'freckled whelp' than that he be trainable to fetch wood. The almost hysterically intense energy of abhorrence which the failed educator expends on the 'Hag-seed', the 'born devil', 'savage', 'Filth' thus becomes readable as a symptom of the deep bond between master and slave which neither is able to undo, and which every denial, however violent, only serves to confirm.

The Picture of Dorian Gray, too, tells the tale of an educational project gone wrong. Instead of tracing the hero's progress towards integral personhood, this Gothic *Bildungsroman* manqué shows him embarked on a course of irrevocable disintegration. In the end, the 'charms' of the novel's Prospero figure, Lord Henry, have thoroughly 'gathered to a head' at the same time as they 'are all o'erthrown'.[16] Dorian has assiduously followed his mentor's precept to 'be always searching for new sensations' (22) But in thus seeking to fulfil 'the highest of all duties, the duty that one owes to one's self' (17), he has destroyed that very self.

The paradox originates in Lord Henry's opening gambit:

'Have you really a very bad influence, Lord Henry? As bad as Basil says?'
    'There is no such thing as a good influence, Mr. Gray. All influence is immoral – immoral from the scientific point of view'.
    'Why?'
    'Because to influence a person is to give him one's own soul. He does not think his natural thoughts, or burn with his natural passions. His virtues are not real to him. His sins, if there are such things as sins, are borrowed. He becomes the echo of someone else's music, an actor of a part that has not been written for him. The aim of life is self-development. To realize one's nature perfectly – that is what each of us is here for'. (17)

Dorian's self-development is the product of someone else's influence. He becomes the echo of Lord Henry's music. His restless endeavours to perfect his nature result but in a perfect façade while his real nature 'cankers' in the portrait. Calling Dorian 'a wonderful creation' (20) and offering to reveal to him 'what you really are, ... what you really might be' (22), Lord Henry sets out to recreate him in his own image. Talking to Dorian, he reflects,

> was like playing upon an exquisite violin. He answered to every touch and thrill of the bow...There was something terribly enthralling in the exercise of influence ... To project one's soul into some gracious form, and let it tarry there for a moment; to hear one's own intellectual views echoed back to one with all the added music of passion and youth; to convey one's temperament into another as though it were a subtle fluid or a strange perfume ... (35)

Dorian's initiation is construed as a psycho-chemical experiment, a virtuoso performance on a perfectly attuned instrument and as an act of penetration. As Dorian succumbs, 'open-eyed and wondering' (23), Wilde has him gaze (somewhat obviously) at a bee 'creeping into the stained trumpet of a Tyrian convulvulus. The flower seemed to quiver, and then swayed gently to and fro' (23).

The eroticism of influence – the touch and thrill of parasitic desire – evokes two stock figures of the Gothic imagination: incubus and vampire. Confined to the half-life of a permanent observer, Lord Henry shows some resemblance to both these variants of the undead. But the vampirism of inhabiting the life of another ties into a larger anxiety of influence in late nineteenth-century culture, one that Wilde's work both instantiates and critiques.

The prospect Lord Henry holds out to his disciple under the label of '[a] new Hedonism' (22) draws on the notion of 'Renaissance Man' as expounded in Jacob Burckhardt's *The Renaissance in Italy* (1860), relayed to England by Walter Pater and absorbed by Pater's disciple, Oscar Wilde. Lord Henry's eulogy to the 'one man [who] were to live out his life fully and completely', the man who would thereby give the world 'such a fresh impulse of joy that we would forget all the maladies of medievalism' (17–18), distinctly echoes Burckhardt's famous celebration of the Renaissance Italians as 'the first-born among the sons of modern Europe' (Burckhardt 98). Just as Burckhardt's quattrocento Italians rejected the strictures of the medieval church, Lord Henry's 'new Hedonists' must reject 'that harsh, uncomely Puritanism' (130) which had come to dominate contemporary life and 'return to the Hellenic ideal' (18).

This new departure is thus a return, more precisely, the imitation of an earlier return, a renaissance as it were of the Renaissance; and the celebrated 'Renaissance Man' is a revenant, a mere imitation, 'the echo of someone else's music, an actor of a part that has not been written for him' (*Dorian Gray* 17). Lord Henry's ideal of self-realization launches his pupil into a lifestyle of omnivorous cultural vampirism or, to use Fredric Jameson's indictment of a much later culture that seems just as apposite here, 'libidinal historicism' (Jameson 18).[17] Chapter XI, which covers the eighteen years between Dorian's initiation and the final stages of his life, immerses the reader in an oppressively overstuffed *Wunderkammer* of rare and precious things, an echo chamber of late-nineteenth-century eclecticism, the storehouse of an age of exhaustion. What the *doppelgänger* motif of the living portrait brings into melodramatic focus, the inventory of Dorian's extravagances broadens out into a panorama of *fin de siècle* culture. Dorian's realization of his self boils down to a striking of imitative poses, a donning of costumes, an everlasting carnival.

For Max Nordau, whose international bestseller appeared a year after *Dorian Gray*, this carnival is the hallmark of degeneration (*Entartung*), the soulless *ersatz* culture of an age without distinctive art or style of its own:

> Let us follow in the train frequenting ... the receptions of the rich, and observe the figures of which it is composed.
>
> Amongst the women, one wears her hair combed smoothly back and down like Rafael's Madalena Doni in the Uffizi at Florence; another wears it drawn up high over the temples like Julia, daughter of Titus, or Plotina, wife of Trajan, in the busts in the Louvre; a third has hers cut short in front on the brow and long in the nape, waved and lightly puffed, after the fashion of the fifteenth Century, as may be seen in the pages and young knights of Gentile Bellini, Botticelli and Mantegna ... Here is one who covers her head with a huge heavy felt hat, an obvious Imitation, in its brim turned up at the back, and its trimming of large plush balls, of the sombrero of the Spanish bull-fighters, who were displaying their skill in Paris at the exhibition of 1889, and giving all kinds of *motifs* to modistes. There is another who has stuck on her hair the emerald-green or ruby-red biretta of the medieval travelling student.
>
> The men complete the picture ... One displays the short curls and the wavy double-pointed beard of Lucius Verus, another looks like the whiskered cat in a Japanese kakemono. His neighbour has the *barbiche* of Henry IV, another the fierce moustache of a lansquenet by F. Brun, or the chin-tuft of the city-watch in Rembrandt's 'Ronde de Nuit'. (Nordau 7–9)

For Nordau, as for Jameson, such historicist mimicry betrays a deplorable lack of substantive identity. What Nordau observes in this passage may indeed be described in Jameson's words (again referring to the postmodern condition, but applicable to the previous turn of the century as well) as 'the increasing unavailability of the personal style' which has 'engender[ed]' the well-nigh universal practice today of what may be called pastiche' (Jameson 16).

Friedrich Nietzsche saw a potentially liberating element in this cultural dead end:

> We are the first age to be educated *in puncto* of 'costumes,' I mean or morals, articles of faith, artistic tastes, and religions, and prepared as no age has ever been for a carnival in the grand style, for the most spiritually carnivalesque laughter and high spirits, for the transcendental heights of the highest inanity and Aristophanean world mockery. Perhaps it's that we still discover a realm of our *invention* here, a realm where we can still be original too, as parodists of world history of buffoons of God, or something like that, – perhaps it's that, when nothing else from today has a future, our *laughter* is the one thing that does! (Nietzsche, *Good and Evil* 114)

At least in his comic masterpiece, *The Importance of Being Earnest*, Wilde attained this realm with consummate success. Dorian, however, remains trapped, this side of the liberating laughter of parody, in his musty *musée imaginaire*, vampirically glutting himself on the spectral sensations of the past. 'How exquisite life had once been! How gorgeous in its pomp and decoration! Even to read of the luxury of the dead was wonderful' (Nietzsche, *Good and Evil* 137).[18]

The enumeration of exquisite things with which Chapter XI surfeits the reader is brought to a logical turning point when the principle of unlimited multiplication is directed from the world of things to the multiplication of personality, to the point at which the collector himself, as it were, becomes a collection. This turn is introduced with the observation – recycled from 'The Critic as Artist' – that insincerity 'is merely a method by which we can multiply our personalities' (Wilde, *Dorian Gray* 142–3). Dorian dismisses 'the shallow psychology of those who conceive the Ego in man as a thing simple, permanent, reliable, and of one essence' (143).

> To him, man was a being with myriad lives and myriad sensations,[19] a complex multiform creature that bore within itself strange legacies of thought and passion, and whose very flesh was tainted with the monstrous maladies of the dead. (143)

The dead means in the first place the line of his ancestors whose portraits Dorian scrutinizes, one by one, for symptoms of 'some strange poisonous germ crept from body to body till it had reached his own' (143). It seems no accident that this blood line begins in the reigns of Elizabeth and James I because, clearly, the Renaissance holds a privileged place among historical periods for Dorian. Besides blood relatives, he muses,

one had ancestors in literature ... nearer perhaps in type and tempera-
ment, ... and certainly with an influence of which one was more absolutely
conscious. There were times when it appeared to Dorian Gray that the
whole of history was merely the record of his own life ... (144)

The part of that 'whole history' that Dorian dwells on most tenaciously
and with which the chapter concludes is the Renaissance, not the bright
and happy age that Burckhardt painted, but a Gothicized version
of Walter Pater. It is the dark underbelly of humanism where man's
'noble reason', his 'infinite faculty' and his 'godlike apprehension'[20] are
reduced to devising cruelly ingenious murder, as in the case of 'Filippo,
Duke of Milan, who slew his wife, and painted her lips with a scarlet
poison that her lover might suck death from the dead thing he fondled'
(145).

From the things with which Dorian surrounds himself to the moods
and historical life forms he appropriates – absorbing them, but also
absorbed by them – the cumulative effect of this existence in a 'Palace
of Art' is curiously depressing, the multiplication of fascinating things
and selves just a form of evasion: a temporary 'escape ... from the fear
that seemed to him at times to be almost too great to be borne' (140).
Trapped in his golden cage, Dorian resembles 'my soul' in the twenty-
three–year-old Tennyson's 'Palace of Art', which 'make[s] merry and
carouse[s]' (Tennyson 3) in her 'lordly pleasure-house' (18) until 'Deep
dread and loathing of her solitude / Fell on her' (229–30), turning the
palace into a veritable chamber of horrors:

> But in dark corners of her palace stood
> Uncertain shapes, and unawares
> On white-eyed phantasms weeping tears of blood,
> And horrible nightmares,
>
> And hollow shades enclosing hearts of flame
> And, with dim fretted foreheads all,
> On corpses three-months-old at noon she came,
> That stood against the wall.
>
> (237–44)

For the young Tennyson's 'soul' there is a way out of this nightmare.
Throwing 'her royal robes away' (290), she moves to a humble 'cottage
in the vale' (291). This move has been persuasively interpreted as signalling a crucial move not only for Tennyson but also for the subsequent
direction of Victorian poetry of which Tennyson was to become the prime
representative.[21] It was to be a poetry that sought to make itself useful
to society; poetry of ethical value, committed, responsible, edifying –
precisely the kind of poetry Wilde's aestheticism totally opposed.

There is no such escape route out of Dorian's narcissistic nightmare. He no sooner thinks he has, for once, done something good than his corruption is compounded. Sparing the innocent Hetty Merton, Dorian sees himself embarked on a 'new life!' and avows that '[h]e would be good' (Wilde, *Dorian Gray* 221). But his hope that 'the signs of evil' in his portrait may have 'already gone away' (221) is cruelly disappointed. Only more 'loathsome' (221) than before, the picture now bears the mark of what for Wilde was the cardinal sin of contemporary society, the sin that summed up his age for him, hypocrisy: 'In hypocrisy he had worn the mask of goodness' (222). For Dorian Gray, then, there is no cottage in the vale where a term of humble social work might 'take away [the] sin' from his tainted soul.[22] Only a knife, the same knife 'that had stabbed Basil Hallward' (223), can restore his soul to his body, making him whole again as it lethally finalizes his division.

Dorian Gray's violent disintegration of self constitutes a prime example of what Kelly Hurley, in her study of the Gothic body in *fin de siècle* fiction, calls 'the abhuman':

> In place of a human body stable and integral ... , the fin de siècle Gothic offers the spectacle of a body metamorphic and undifferentiated; ... in place of a unitary and securely bounded human subjectivity, one that is both fragmented and permeable. Within this genre one may witness the relentless destruction of the 'human' and the unfolding in its stead of what I will call, to borrow an evocative term from supernaturalist author William Hope Hodgson, the 'abhuman'. The abhuman subject is a not-quite-human subject, characterized by its morphic variability, continually in danger of becoming not-itself, becoming other. (Hurley 3–4)[23]

The epistemic upheavals that gave rise to the proliferation of 'abhuman' figures in late nineteenth-century fiction are not difficult to make out: 'Evolutionism, criminal anthropology, degeneration theory, sexology, pre-Freudian psychology' (5). All of these figure conspicuously in Wilde's novel, and '[a]ll of these', Hurley writes, 'accomplished a radical destabilization of what had formerly been a fixed boundary between man and animal' (56).[24]

'Formerly' is potentially misleading here because it suggests that what was being destabilized in the later nineteenth century had previously *always* been fixed. Yet when Dorian Gray, looking at his portrait, 'sees the Caliban in his own nature' (Vaughan and Vaughan 113), he is also looking at the personification of an earlier destabilization of the human. This, after all, is what we have found Shakespeare's Caliban to be: the last in that long line of characters in whom the dramatist explores the culturally crucial, though highly problematic and permeable boundary between humans and (nonhuman) animals.[25]

The post-Darwinian discovery of the human–animal continuum is really an anagnorisis, a recognition or rediscovery of what was eclipsed by the foundational move of modern rationalism, Descartes's *cogito* and its concomitant segregating of men and beasts. Caliban predates the Cartesian rift that underwrites the dominant rationalist discourse of modernity. Dorian Gray and his fellow abhumans of the *fin de siècle* herald the emergence of a counter-discourse which revokes that rift. Nietzsche's anti-metaphysical project seeking '[t]o translate humanity back into nature' is the most radical paradigm of that revocation. Where Descartes needs the animal-as-machine in order to detach from it the 'cogital'[26] core of the human subject, Nietzsche applauds the scientific rigour of the machine idea but categorically rejects the detachment. 'Pure spirit', he taunts, 'is pure stupidity: if we deduct the nervous system and the senses, the "mortal frame", *we miscalculate* – that's all!' (Nietzsche, *Twilight* 137). Dorian Gray's thinking tends in a similar direction (Mann 691–2).[27] Men feel

> a natural instinct of terror about passions and sensations that seem stronger than themselves, and that they are conscious of sharing with the less highly organized forms of existence. But it appeared to Dorian Gray that the true nature of the senses had never been understood, and that they had remained savage and animal merely because the world had sought to starve them into submission. (130)[28]

Early modern discourses of the passions, as recent scholarship has shown, insisted on a thorough overlapping of man and the natural forces he shares 'with the less highly organized forms of existence'. The central insight of this scholarship, as Gail Kern Paster points out, is the extent to which the psychological was embedded in and even identified with the physiology of the humoral body in a cosmological framework of correspondences and analogies:

> The passions are like liquid states and forces of the natural world. But ... [i]n an important sense, the passions actually *were* liquid forces of nature, because, in this cosmology, the stuff of the outside world and the stuff of the body were composed of the same elemental materials. (*Humoring* 4)[29]

Lord Henry's advice strikes a similar note: 'Dorian, don't deceive yourself. Life is not governed by will or intention. Life is a question of nerves, fibres, and slowly built up cells in which thought hides itself and passion has its dreams' (Wilde, *Dorian Gray* 209).

In the Gothic fantasies of the *fin de siècle* the reassertion of such physical connectedness became a source of irrepressible *Angstlust*, a force of regression both horrifying and tempting, frightening and lustful. Stevenson's respectable Dr Jekyll cannot wait to regress to a state of being that is most succinctly captured in the double-exposed photograph showing the actor Richard Mansfield, who famously played the double role in the London stage adaptation of Stevenson's novella.

No less than such regression, its antithesis, the ideal of the 'Renaissance man' as propounded by Burckhardt is a fixture in the nineteenth-century cultural imagination. Caliban seems a far cry from this ideal, which in Wilde would evoke the male beauties of a Michelangelo. Yet Caliban's very indefiniteness aligns him with the key characteristics of 'man' in a work which Burckhardt celebrated as 'one of the noblest' manifestations of humanism in 'that great age' (Burckhardt 229). This is Giovanni Pico della Mirandola's 'Oration', usually referred to under the title 'On the Dignity of Man'. 'The nature of all other creatures', Pico's God declares, 'is defined and restricted within laws which We have laid down' (7). Man, by contrast, is impeded by no such restrictions. He alone is free to create himself, but also forced to do so because he is 'indeterminate', a 'Proteus' (6).

Pico's celebrated oration, Giorgio Agamben maintains, 'verifies the absence of a nature proper to Homo, holding him suspended between a celestial and a terrestrial nature, between animal and human – [a] being always less and more than himself' (29–30). Man's infinite plasticity launches a profound destabilization, one that is just as characteristic of the infinitely malleable earth creature Caliban as of Dorian Gray's mimicry of unlimited self-multiplication. 'Who then', asks Pico, 'will not look with awe upon this our chameleon?' (9). The plasticity of human character is inseparably linked with notions of fluctuating animality. Machiavelli famously counsels the prince to 'be a Fox, that he may beware of the snares, and a Lion that he may scare the wolves' (Machiavelli 322). Metamorphic and unstable, hovering on the permeable boundary between man and animal – the 'human nature' that emerges when we take a closer look at 'Renaissance Man' reveals a striking affinity with the Gothic 'abhuman'. Thus Wilde's beautiful youth rubs shoulders with Prospero's ugly 'thing of darkness'.

One indication of this affinity is a curious swap of epistemic affiliations. While Dorian Gray roots himself in Renaissance knowledge culture, Shakespeare's changeling is adopted into the image store of Victorian popular science. In the latter half of the nineteenth century, Caliban became the Shakespearean icon of Darwinism. He is identified as such in *Caliban: Shakespeare's Missing Link*, published by Daniel Wilson, a professor of history and English literature from Toronto, in 1873. The Bard's genius, Wilson avers, had already created for us the ideal of that imaginary intermediate being, between the true brute and man, which, if the new theory of descent from crudest animal organizms be true, was our predecessor and precursor in this world's humanity. (xi–xii)

The Darwinian missing link was Caliban's typical guise on the *fin de siècle* stage. The actor Frank Benson, preparing for the part in 1891, spent 'many hours watching monkeys and baboons in the zoo, in order to get the movements and postures in keeping with his "make-up"', which his wife described as 'half monkey, half coco-nut'. Benson then 'delighted in swarming up a tree on the stage and hanging from the branches head downwards while he gibbered at "Trinculo"' (Vaughan and Vaughan 185). And Herbert Beerbohm Tree's Caliban of 1904, famously portrayed by Charles Buchel (Karl August Büchel), 'crawl[ed] out' from his rock-sty 'with a fish in his mouth (Nilan 120)'.[30]

The Darwinian regression that became the standard image of the *fin de siècle* Caliban will hardly suit the abhuman progress of Dorian Gray, whose most relevant contemporary frame of reference is rather to be found in the criminology of Cesare Lombroso. While presenting itself as an uncompromisingly modern, scientific approach, Lombroso's doctrine is really steeped in the thinking of a much older, premodern knowledge tradition, and it is this tradition that provides perhaps the most fitting emblem for the morphic variability of Dorian Gray. Charles Le Brun's celebrated man–animal studies of 1668 offer a striking gallery of abhuman transformations. Epitomizing over a century of Renaissance physiognomy, they produce a disconcerting border-zone of human–animal indistinction. 'The human face divine' that Milton invokes in the famous passage from *Paradise Lost* on the loss of his eyesight seems to be invaded by 'flocks or herds' of animals.[31] Le Brun's physiognomy, the art of reading the human face, collapses the distinction between humans and other beasts. In this particular 'book of knowledge fair' (Milton), the most distinctly human of all of man's physical features needs to be translated into animality in order to be rendered legible. For all their late seventeenth-century rationalist clarity, Le Brun's demonstrations of human–animal likeness present a menagerie of troublingly indeterminate creatures. Every one of the chimerical specimens facing each other across the species divide is so thoroughly imbricated in its counterpart that it becomes well-nigh impossible to detach what is specifically human from its non-human other.

Wilde's Gothic tale confirms its Renaissance affinities in its central plot idea. The Faustian pact is implemented with recourse to the Renaissance 'art' or 'science' of physiognomy. As Dorian's soul 'cankers', his face – his 'true face', that is, the face in the picture – grows uglier:

'It is the face of my soul'.

'Christ! what a thing I must have worshipped! It has the eyes of a devil'.

...

Hallward turned again to the portrait, and gazed at it ... The surface seemed to be quite undisturbed, and as he had left it. It was from within, apparently, that the foulness and horror had come. Through some strange quickening of inner life the leprosies of sin were slowly eating the thing away. The rotting of a corpse in a watery grave was not so fearful. (157)

'There's no art / To find the mind's construction in the face', King Duncan says (*Macbeth* 1.4.11–12), but this is not Shakespeare's, let alone Wilde's last word in the matter. Much as *The Picture of Dorian Gray* draws on contemporary scientific trends, the rage of Dorian seeing his own face in a glass is stirred up from the legacy of a Gothicized Renaissance.

Notes

1 See the unsigned reviews in *Theatre* (1 June 1891) and *Atheneum* (27 June 1891) in Beckson, 81–2.
2 I borrow the term from Virginia Richter.
3 All *Tempest* quotations are from the Arden Shakespeare edition, edited by Vaughan and Vaughan.
4 'Family' certainly in the early modern sense of the word that comprises all members of a household including servants, but also something more than just a servant, a foster child rather.
5 That the name Caliban anagrammatically alludes to 'cannibal' is a commonplace.
6 'What cares these roarers for the name of king?' (*Tempest* 1.116–17). 'If by your art, my dearest father, you have / Put the wild waters in this roar ... (*Tempest* 1.2.1–2). 'To cry to th' sea that roared to us' (*Tempest* 1.2.149).
7 ALONSO Methought the billows spoke and told me of it; / The winds did sing it to me, and the thunder – / That deep and dreadful organpipe – pronounced / The name of Prosper. It did bass my trespass (*Tempest* 3.3.96–9).
8 Throughout the narrative, Lord Henry's preferred position is 'lying' (1) rather than sitting or standing.
9 I have discussed this in 'Oscar Wilde, or, The Prehistory of Postmodern Parody'.
10 Besides painting, Leonardo da Vinci's 'art' comprises engineering, mechanical inventions and anatomical experiments. But the beginnings of art in the modern, emphatic and more specific sense can be traced in Vasari's writing about the painters of the Italian quattrocento and cinquecento, Leonardo prominent among them.
11 I have developed the argument of this section more fully in *Stage, Stake, and Scaffold* 241–8.

12 The term derives from Michel Surya; see also Donna Haraway.

13 'You must certainly send it next year to the Grosvenor', Lord Henry suggests, while Basil insists that 'I really can't exhibit it. I have put too much of myself into it' (2).

14 See 1.2.343–5: 'and here you sty me / In this hard rock, whiles you do keep from me / The rest o'th'island'.

15 See 1.2.342–3: 'For I am all the subjects that you have, / Which first was mine own king'.

16 See *The Tempest* 5.1.1. Prospero: 'Now does my project gather to a head'. And Prospero's epilogue: 'Now my charms are all o'erthrown'. Lord Henry's last appearance in the novel shows a similarly despondent note to Prospero's epilogue. The hitherto unflappable dandy evinces real worry about getting old. Wilde, *Dorian Gray* 216.

17 I have discussed correspondences between Wilde's cultural moment and postmodernism in 'Oscar Wilde, or, The Prehistory of Postmodern Parody'.

18 The yearning for 'a world that had been refashioned anew … a world in which things would have fresh shapes and colours [and] in which the past would have little or no place' (131–2) is the escape fantasy of a civilization suffocated by its awareness of history. Cf. 'On the Use and Abuse of History [for Life]' 1–100.

19 Dorian Gray seems to anticipate Virginia Woolf's famous observation from 'Modern Fiction': 'Examine for a moment an ordinary mind on an ordinary day. The mind receives a myriad impressions – trivial, fantastic, evanescent or engraved with the sharpness of steel' (Woolf 149–50).

20 Cf. Hamlet's famous speech (2.2.305–10): 'What piece of work is a man! How noble in reason, how infinite in faculty, in form and moving how express and admirable, in action how like an angel, in apprehension how like a god – the beauty of the world, the paragon of animals! And yet to me what is this quintessence of dust?'

21 Still unsurpassed is the account of this poetical identity crisis given in Enzensberger.

22 See Tennyson 287–8: 'What is it that will take away my sin, And save me lest I die?'

23 William Hope Hodgson (1877–1918), a writer of fantasy fiction, uses the term 'Ab-Human' in *The Night Land* (1912) and in *Carnacki the Ghost-Finder* (1913).

24 *The Picture of Dorian Gray* hardly registers in Hurley's study except in connection with homosexuality and the Gothic city.

25 I am drawing here and in the following paragraph on my argument in *Stage, Stake, and Scaffold* 259–61.

26 Nietzsche, 'On the Use and Abuse of History', 94: 'I am permitted the empty *esse*, not the full green *vivere*. A primary feeling tells me that I am a thinking being but not a living one, that I am no "animal", but at most a "cogital". "Give me life, and I will soon make you a culture out of it" – will be the cry of every man in this new generation, and they will all know each other by this cry. But who will give them this life?'

27 Thomas Mann was one of the first to point to a more than superficial affinity between Nietzsche and Wilde.

28 Like Wilde, Nietzsche rejects what he sees as the fallacies of ascetic idealism (Platonic, Judaeo-Christian). And also like Wilde, he does not argue for an easy return to nature. Man cannot simply become animal, precisely because he is no simple animal, but the most complex, most problematic one. Nietzsche's ideal, like Wilde's, is a reunion of the physical with the spiritual.

29 See Paster *The Body*; James; Paster et al.

30 Quoting from Tree's prompt-book.

31 'Seasons return, but not to me returns / Day, or the sweet approach of even or morn, / Or sight of vernal bloom, or summer's rose, / Or flocks, or herds, or human face divine; / But cloud instead, and ever-during dark / Surrounds me, from the cheerful ways of men / Cut off, and for the book of knowledge fair / Presented with a universal blank / Of Nature's works to me expunged and rased' (Bk III, lines 41–9).

Works cited

Agamben, Giorgio. *The Open: Man and Animal.* Trans. Kevin Attell. Stanford: Stanford University Press, 2004.

Aristotle. *De Anima. Books II and III (with Passages from Book I).* Trans. and ed. D. W. Hamlyn. 2nd edn. Oxford: Clarendon Press, 1993.

Beckson, Karl E. *Oscar Wilde: The Critical Heritage.* London: Routledge & Kegan Paul, 1970.

Benjamin, Walter. *The Origin of the German Tragic Drama.* Trans. John Osborne. London: New Left Books, 1977.

Burckhardt, Jacob. *The Civilization of the Renaissance in Italy* (1860). Trans. S. G. C. Middlemore. Ed. Peter Murray. London: Penguin, 2004.

Enzensberger, Christian. *Viktorianische Lyrik: Tennyson und Swinburne in der Geschichte der Entfremdung.* Munich: Hanser, 1969.

Haraway, Donna. *When Species Meet.* Minneapolis and London: University of Minnesota Press, 2008.

Höfele, Andreas. *Stage, Stake, and Scaffold: Humans and Animals in Shakespeare's Theatre.* Oxford: Oxford University Press, 2011.

—. 'Oscar Wilde, or, The Prehistory of Postmodern Parody'. *European Journal of English Studies* 3.2 (1999): 138–66.

Hurley, Kelly. *The Gothic Body: Sexuality, Materialism, and Degeneration at the Fin de Siècle.* Cambridge: Cambridge University Press, 1996.

James, Susan. *Passion and Action: The Emotions in Seventeenth-Century Philosophy.* Cambridge: Cambridge University Press, 1997.

Jameson, Fredric. *Postmodernism, or The Cultural Logic of Late Capitalism.* London: Verso, 1991.

Lupton, Julia Reinhard. 'Creature Caliban'. *Shakespeare Quarterly* 51.1 (2000): 1–23.

Machiavelli, Niccolò. *The Prince*. Trans. Edward Dacres. 1640. *Niccolo Machiavelli, The Tudor Translations: Machiavelli Vol. 1*. London: David Nutt at the Sign of the Phoenix, Long Acre, 1905.

Mann, Thomas. 'Nietzschs Philosophie im Lichte unserer Erfahrung'. *Thomas Mann: Gesammelte Werke in dreizehn Bänden. Band IX. Reden und Aufsätze 1*. 2nd edn. Frankfurt am Main: Fischer, 1974. 675–712.

Milton, John. *Paradise Lost*. Ed. Alastair Fowler. 2nd edn. London: Pearson Longman, 2007.

Nietzsche, Friedrich, *Twilight of the Idols* and *The Antichrist*. Trans. R. J. Hollingdale. Ed. Michael Tanner. London: Penguin, 2003.

—. *Beyond Good and Evil: Prelude to a Philosophy of the Future*. Trans. Judith Norman. Ed. Rolf-Peter Horstmann and Judith Norman. Cambridge and New York: Cambridge University Press, 2002.

—. 'On the Use and Abuse of History [for Life]'. Trans. Adrian Collins. *The Complete Works of Friedrich Nietzsche: The First and Complete and Authorised English Translation. Volume 2: Thoughts Out of Season Part II*. New York: Russell and Russell, 1964.

Nilan, Mary M. '*The Tempest* at the Turn of the Century: Cross-Currents in Production'. *Shakespeare Survey* 25 (1972): 113–23.

Nordau, Max. *Degeneration*. 4th edn. New York: Appleton, 1895.

Paster, Gail Kern. *Humoring the Body: Emotions and the Shakespearean Stage*. Chicago and London: The University of Chicago Press, 2004.

—. *The Body Embarrassed: Drama and the Disciplines of Shame in early modern England*. Ithaca, NY: Cornell University Press, 1993.

Paster, Gail Kern, Katherine Rowe and Mary Floyd-Wilson, eds. *Reading the early modern Passions: Essays in the Cultural History of Emotions*. Philadelphia: University of Pennsylvania Press, 2004.

Pico della Mirandola, Giovanni. *Oration on the Dignity of Man*. Trans. A. Robert Caponigri. Washington, DC: Regnery, 1999.

Richter, Virginia. *Literature after Darwin: Human Beasts in Western Fiction, 1859–1939*. Basingstoke: Palgrave Macmillan, 2011.

Shakespeare, William. *Hamlet. The Complete Works*. Eds Stanley Wells and Gary Taylor. 2nd ed. Oxford: Clarendon Press, 2005. The Oxford Shakespeare.

—. *Macbeth. The Complete Works*. Eds Stanley Wells and Gary Taylor. 2nd ed. Oxford: Clarendon Press, 2005. The Oxford Shakespeare.

—. *The Tempest*. Eds Alden T. Vaughan and Virginia Mason Vaughan. Walton-on-Thames: Arden Shakespeare, 1999.

—. *The Tempest*. Ed. Morton Luce. London: Methuen, 1901. The Arden Shakespeare.

Sidney, Philip. 'The Defence of Poesy'. Ed. Katherine Duncan-Jones. *Sir Philip Sidney*. Oxford and New York: Oxford University Press, 1992. 212–50.

Surya, Michel. *Humanimalité: l'inéliminable animalité de l'homme*. Paris: Néant, 2001.

Tennyson, Alfred Lord. 'The Palace of Art'. *Tennyson: A Selected Edition*. Ed. Christopher Ricks. Harlow: Longman, 2007.

Vaughan, Alden T. and Virginia Mason Vaughan. *Shakespeare's Caliban: A Cultural History*. Cambridge: Cambridge University Press, 1991.

Wilde, Oscar. *The Picture of Dorian Gray*. Ed. Isobel Murray. London: Oxford University Press, 1974.

—. 'The Critic as Artist'. *Complete Works of Oscar Wilde*. Ed. Vyvyan Holland. London and Glasgow: Collins, 1969.

—. *The Letters*. London: Hart-Davis, 1962.

Wilson, Daniel. *Caliban: The Missing Link*. London: Macmillan, 1873.

Woolf, Virginia. *The Common Reader*. Ed. Andrew McNeillie. London: Hogarth, 1984.

Index